VISIONS *of*
LOVELINESS

VISIONS *of* LOVELINESS

great flower breeders

of the past

Judith M. Taylor

SWALLOW PRESS

Athens, Ohio

Swallow Press
An imprint of Ohio University Press, Athens, Ohio 45701
ohioswallow.com

To obtain permission to quote, reprint, or otherwise reproduce or distribute material
from Swallow Press / Ohio University Press publications, please contact our rights and
permissions department at (740) 593-1154 or (740) 593-4536 (fax).

Printed in the United States of America
Swallow Press / Ohio University Press books are printed on acid-free paper ♾ ™

24 23 22 21 20 19 18 17 16 15 14   5 4 3 2 1

Library of Congress Cataloging-in-Publication Data

Taylor, Judith M.
Visions of loveliness : great flower breeders of the past / Judith M. Taylor.
    pages cm
Other title: Great flower breeders of the past
Includes bibliographical references and index.
ISBN 978-0-8040-1156-3 (hc : alk. paper) — ISBN 978-0-8040-1157-0 (pb : alk. paper) —
ISBN 978-0-8040-4062-4 (pdf)
1. Flowers—Breeding—Europe—History. 2. Flowers—Breeding—United States—History.
3. Plant breeders—Europe—History. 4. Plant breeders—United States—History. I. Title.
II. Title: Great flower breeders of the past.
SB406.8.T38 2014
635.9—dc23
                                2014029551

TO MYRA AND BURT

Generous and loving

CONTENTS

Part 3. Plants by Genus

PREFACE

In 1970, the late Richard Gorer wrote in *The Development of Garden Flowers*, "It came as rather a shock to me, when I started work on this book, to find that no one had previously gone into the subject. Since so many of the flowers we grow in our gardens today are the result of growers interfering with nature, it seems surprising that no one has traced their descent." He went on to say that "this book is apparently the first word on the subject, but it assuredly will not be the last" (preface, p. 13).

Before setting out on my book, I made careful inquiries about work that might have brought his material up to date. There appeared to be none. It is now more than forty years since Gorer wrote his challenging words, and I have undertaken the foolhardy task of expanding our memory of the flowers' provenance. This book, too, will not be the last word on this fascinating subject.

VISIONS *of* LOVELINESS

Introduction

M Y PREVIOUS BOOK, *The Global Migrations of Ornamental Plants: How the World Got into Your Garden,* tells the riveting story of plant collectors who found plants in faraway places and sent them back to their own countries. The new plants had so many advantages over the indigenous ones that they rapidly overtook the latter, displacing them in commerce. From about 1870, modern American horticulture and the nursery business were transformed, but the transformation was built on at least a century of patient breeding and gradual incorporation of the new material as it trickled in. This book traces what happened to many of the plants after they reached their destinations.

We are the beneficiaries of centuries of work by remarkable flower breeders whose names are largely lost and forgotten. Starting with sometimes quite unpromising material, the exquisite vision in their heads led them to create new plants of surpassing beauty. Their heirs and successors continue to do the same thing.

Some of the stimulus lay in the unprecedented waves of new flowers arriving in Europe over the past four hundred years and latterly the United

States, slowly at first but accelerating rapidly by the middle of the nineteenth century. A very gingerly start to deliberate crossbreeding was made in spite of concern about interfering with nature and God's realm using known indigenous flowers in the early eighteenth century, but the huge outpouring of new varieties coincided with the arrival of new species. This avalanche swept away all remaining religious scruples against presuming to do the work of God.

Prehistoric people began taking essential seeds with them when they moved from one land to another, probably before recorded history. Farmers seeking more land in newly conquered territory and refugees fleeing persecution, wars, or disasters all took seeds of their staple foods with them. Ornamental plants were usually not taken intentionally, but as so many of such plants had ritual, medicinal, or culinary uses, they went along too. The ancient world has left a few records of these events. In the more recent past, one need look no further than the Puritan emigration to North America or Spanish settlement in Central or South America.

This utilitarian phase lasted well into early modern times. The discovery of the Americas gave rise to much increased exploration and, with this, the carriage of new and often very beautiful plants back to the home country in Europe. Before 1600, more than thirty American plants were grown in English gardens.

Frequent but seldom-recorded transfers of both types of plants were taking place throughout the much more advanced Far Eastern countries such as China and India at the same time. These countries had great accumulations of wealth, with gold, silver, jewels, and silk all stoking the greed of Western monarchs. Merchants and holy men traveled incessantly between the different Asian realms.

Learning about this rich and varied world excited not only rapacious Western rulers but also scholars, missionaries, and adventurers in large numbers. Patient gardeners in China, Japan, and Korea had slowly bred new varieties over the millennia, chiefly by selection but also possibly by active pollination. When the Westerners finally gained admission to China and Japan, they did not understand that the flowers they bought in the coastal nurseries were not necessarily pure species but the descendants of a long process of intentional breeding.

Less is known about plant transfers within South America and Africa in the same epochs. *Zea mays* (maize, also known as corn), for example, spread phenomenally quickly throughout Africa once it had been brought back from the New World by the Columbian expeditions. Within a few years, it became a staple.

The stories told in this book reflect the Western point of view. In spite of the long history of floriculture in many ancient lands, the aggressive mingling of commerce and aesthetics that makes up the modern international flower business is indeed peculiarly Western. People want to grow flowers because of their great beauty and, in some cases, meaning. During the past 150 years, farsighted nurserymen paid collectors to bring them new plants in enormously large numbers and then began modifying them to increase their allure for the public.

The scale of these operations and the systematic methods developed to accomplish their aims set them apart from what had gone on before. With modern techniques, the trend has been toward an ever-greater systematization and consolidation in a business based on beauty. The floriculture firms adapted and applied methods used by large manufacturers of other merchandise, employing largely anonymous flower breeders together with many other experts. Creating new types of plant is also done quite differently. With immense changes in molecular biology, the breeder no longer has to wait so long for the results of the macroscopic crosses of the past.[1]

In this movement forward, the names of many flower breeders whose work contributed to their success have been obscured. Some of them bred new flowers purely for the love of it—this is probably the majority of breeders. Working entirely empirically, both amateur and professional flower breeders managed to overcome some of the obstacles posed by genetic incompatibility, but their complete ignorance of what underlay the process limited how far they could go.

The paid professionals have also created many marvelous hybrids. They incorporated scientific advances very skillfully. One problem for a floriculture firm has been the high cost of developing a new plant and the difficulty of recouping the investment in it quickly enough. Evaluating new crosses takes up vast amounts of time and space needed for other, more lucrative plants that grow quickly and can be sold very profitably. In practice, this often means that amateurs are still important. They have the leisure to make numerous crosses and wait for the offspring to mature without the heavy commercial pressure of a corporation. They then sell their results to the professionals, who propagate them on a commercial scale, thereby avoiding a lot of "wasted time."

Large, slowly maturing plants like rhododendrons are an example of this useful coexistence. Even old family firms with a long tradition of breeding rhododendrons are finding it difficult to continue to develop new plants on their own. Amateurs still come up with important new orchid hybrids, too. For now, roses seem to be different; they are usually bred by a firm's own employees, perhaps because the market remains so strong.

In the Western world, the notion that plants could breed with each other like animals and produce a new variety was first clearly articulated by Rudolph Camerarius (1665–1721). He was an outstanding experimental botanist at the Tubingen Botanical Gardens and showed that when female monoecious plants such as mulberry and hepatica are isolated from the corresponding male plants they do not set seed. Earlier botanists such as John Ray and Nehemiah Grew had guessed that something like this was going on, but Camerarius proved it conclusively.[2] This discovery was exceedingly important for what would soon be possible.

In 1709, John Lawson, an Englishman, wrote in his *A New Voyage to Carolina*, "Bastard Spanish is an oak betwixt the Spanish and the red oak; the chief use is for fencing and clap boards. It bears good acorns." Whether Lawson knew that the tree was a naturally occurring hybrid between *Quercus falcata* and *Quercus rubra* is not clear, but his statement is suggestive. *Bastard* is an old word that can mean a plant hybrid as well as a child born out of wedlock. The word is still used in the botanical sense in modern German.

The idea of changing plants on purpose, to make completely new kinds, took a long time to emerge. One brake on enthusiasts' activities was the fear of divine retribution for interfering with God's work: only the Lord could create a new variety. This was quite different from the rough-and-ready selection process that went on for millennia. Farmers and gardeners did not hesitate to use naturally occurring sports or mutations to improve their crops.

In 1716, Cotton Mather recorded some of the earliest observations on spontaneous crossbreeding. A friend of his planted a field with rows of different colored corn, *Zea mays,* at some distance from each other. Mather noted that ears that previously had only yellow seeds now had red and blue seeds in them, clearly showing crossbreeding. Mather also recorded an amusing instance of plants being used punitively. To prevent theft, his friend planted some of the squash fields with rows of gourds. The resulting hybrids tasted very bitter, like the gourds. Thieves who raided the field were in for a nasty surprise.

Cotton Mather was a New England divine, yet he did not have any religious qualms about these experiments. The wind was the pollinator. They were not interfering with God's role. We shall see later that it was the deliberate pollination of another flower's stigma by a human being that frightened early hybridists.

The urge to tinker is overwhelming. Even flowers as glorious as orchids were not immune to fantasies about change. At first, the species plants were enough for even the most avid collectors, but that did not last long. The almost endless possibilities of modification created new excitement. The "what ifs" and the "if onlys" were just too enticing. This process accelerated as the nineteenth century progressed. From being a rare procedure, crossbreeding became almost standard, the immediate step upon receiving new species.

The eighteenth century may have been the age of enlightenment, but the nineteenth was the time of improvement. The Industrial Revolution had many flaws, but its benefits were immense and its energy inexorable. Everything that could be improved was subjected to this treatment. This restlessness applied to all aspects of daily life, from transport to textiles, domestic appurtenances, and the floral world.

Under often dour and reserved exteriors, a special breed of plantsman harbored wild dreams of color and form. Not all artistry is worn on the sleeve. Perhaps the most famous American plant manipulator was Luther Burbank. He is remembered and justly revered for the Burbank potato, but he also tackled ornamental forms throughout his life. Burbank developed numerous cultivars of orchard fruit, and one, the Santa Rosa plum, is still in commerce. The Shasta Daisy may be his best-known garden plant.

The art of crossing plants had begun before the scientific basis for success was understood. The 1830s and 1840s saw a tremendous increase in crossbreeding experiments. *Hybrid* was the Latin term for a half-breed such as the offspring of a tame sow and wild boar. It later passed into horticultural usage. At first, farmers and country dwellers called such plant crosses "mules," equating plant behavior with that of familiar animals.

One of the earliest intentional trials to be recorded in ornamental plants was when the English nurseryman Thomas Fairchild placed the pollen from *Dianthus caryophyllus,* the Wild Carnation, on the stigma of *Dianthus barbatus,* the Sweet William, in 1720. Fairchild (1667–1729) was an adherent of Nehemiah Grew, the scholar who recognized that pollen is the male fertilizing agent. Fairchild's experiment was successful but did not make much of an impression. In passing, it is interesting to note that both of Fairchild's experimental flowers were imports from the Norman era, not native to Great Britain.

The idea that men were working in God's province by changing the natural order of things in an active as compared to a passive fashion was very alarming. To atone, Fairchild bequeathed most of his fortune to his local church to found an annual lecture on religion and natural science. Lectures on this topic at the church were still being given into the 1970s.

All over Europe, and later in the United States, horticulturists would slowly tackle one genus after another. When the Abbé Gregor Johann Mendel published the results of crossing two forms of peas, yellow and green, with reproducible ratios in the succeeding generations, in 1866, the significance of his experiments was not picked up immediately. Only a very few scholars realized what it meant; for all intents and purposes, it was invisible.

Charles Darwin was dimly aware of the work but did not understand its significance. His heart was firmly set on "pangenesis," the constant gradual changing of species with evolution. In 1899, three scientists—Hugo de Vries, Carl Correns, and Erich von Tschermak-Seysenegg—came across Mendel's work and almost simultaneously recognized its importance. They promoted it very aggressively and effectively. Modern genetics are derived from Mendel's studies. Instead of purely intuitive, hit-or-miss crossings, the options could now be laid out in an orderly manner. The desired characteristic would appear after the F1 generation and could be planned for appropriately.

Every year, hundreds, maybe even thousands, of new plant cultivars appear on the market. Flowers and vegetables are constantly being "improved" or, at the very least, modified. In this book I only deal with flowers, or the ornamental plants.

The new varieties are trumpeted loudly in the glossy and enticing nursery catalogues, gorgeously decked out. They are introduced in a slightly more genteel manner at flower shows and horticultural society meetings. Garden writers report on them later in an even soberer fashion. Sometimes we find out who was responsible for breeding these wonders and how they came to do it, but often we do not. In the modern world of vertically integrated horticultural businesses, drawing attention to an individual is not in anyone's interest.

If one belongs to a specialty society, there is more chance of finding out who has done the crosses, because one is already on the inside. This opacity over who created the cultivars was not always so. At one time, titans stalked the earth and ordinary people knew about great plant breeders and their triumphs. Even so, a lot remains buried, and the aim of this book is to restore a human face to these now-forgotten flower breeders. Prominent flower breeders enjoyed considerable renown and prosperity during their lives. These people have now been reduced to fragile memories, sometimes with only the name of a street in a modern housing development to commemorate them. Resurrecting them heightens everyone's enjoyment of the flowers.

It also seeks to understand how some apparently ordinary person became besotted with a particular plant and spent much of his or her life improving it. From what I can tell, one would not have suspected Victor Lemoine of being a great artist if one happened to meet him in the street. He was said to be gruff and taciturn. I am sure he did not think of himself as an artist and would have vehemently scoffed at any such notion as absurd, but that is how he appears to me.

Who knew? Here are a few of the dramatis personae. In 1908, Miss Hemus of Upton-upon-Severn in Worcestershire won the Award of Merit for her sweet pea cultivar 'Evelyn Hemus' at the annual show of the Royal Horticultural Society in London. It was a fine achievement, very rare for a woman at the time. "Miss Hemus" sounds demure and very proper, like someone out of a Jane Austen novel. This was intriguing. I wanted to find out who she was, yet in trying to resurrect her life and learn more about her as a person, I came up against a brick wall. It was not until I enlisted the help of Simon Wilkinson, a devoted historian of Upton-upon-Severn, that some facts emerged.

His diligent research uncovered the story of six siblings—four girls and two boys, all apparently very strong-willed and with complex personalities. The prim title "Miss Hemus" gave no hint of what lay beneath. For the rest of their lives, because of resentment and misunderstanding about the credit for the prizes, some of the sisters did not speak to each other or mention their sisters' names to their children or grandchildren.

In 1911, Lord Northcliffe, the Rupert Murdoch of his day, offered an award of one thousand pounds for the best vase of new sweet peas bred and grown by an amateur. This was a very large sum of money at the time. The first prize was won by Mrs. D. Denholm Fraser (Nettie), the wife of a Presbyterian minister in Kelso, Scotland. The third prize was won by the Reverend D. Denholm Fraser.

One wonders what the atmosphere was like in that manse for a time. Did the children take sides? It makes one think of Trollope's masterful Mrs. Proudie, the bishop's wife in *Barchester Towers*. A year or two later, the Reverend Fraser issued a small book, *All About Sweet Peas,* capitalizing on the family's success. The minister excused his rather worldly behavior by indicating that his church needed a large sum of money for repairs. The fifty pounds of prize money came in very handy and was attributed to the will of God.

Some time after the family's victory, the Reverend Fraser endorsed Carter's Tested Seeds, informing the public in the most genteel manner possible that the seeds for his prizewinning sweet peas came from that company. It could be that some additional emoluments were associated with the endorsement. The Frasers appear to have been a canny pair. There is even, heaven forfend, the possibility that the Reverend Fraser bred all the sweet peas himself and used his wife's name as a ruse to increase his chances of winning.

Ernst Benary established his nursery and seed store in Erfurt, Germany, in 1843. That was a very unusual business for a Jew at the time. Within twenty years after Ernst founded the company, all his immediate family had converted to Christianity, while his brothers retained their old religion (and some were well known as rabbinical scholars). Benary's business grew rapidly. One customer was of particular interest: the firm supplied flower seeds to the abbot of the Augustinian monastery of Saint Thomas in Brno, Moravia, otherwise known as Gregor Mendel.

Only a few records of their dealings have survived. After Mendel died, the monks burned every scrap of his private papers. The only ones they spared pertained to his work as abbot and the abbey's business. Buying seeds for the garden was the abbey's business. For this reason, the Mendel Museum still has some invoices from Benary, one in 1856 supplying vegetable seed and another for flower seeds in 1874. The Benarys, who still run the business today, lost almost all of the tangible memories of their history as a result of World War II and the confiscation of their firm by the Communist government of East Germany.

Louis Van Houtte of Ghent never intended to become a flower breeder. He came from a middle-class family, and his mother thought he would go into banking. These plans all evaporated after his wife died very unexpectedly at a young age. His grief was overwhelming. To take his mind off it, he accepted an offer to go to Brazil for six months and explore for new plants outside Rio de Janeiro. Although he did not find the great Amazon water

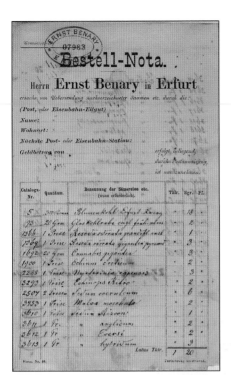

An invoice for seeds and bulbs sold to the Augustinian monastery of Saint Thomas in Brno by Ernst Benary's Bestell-Nota nursery in Erfurt, Germany, said to be from 1856.
Reproduced by permission of the Augustinian Abbey of Saint Thomas in Brno, Czech Republic

A list of seeds and bulbs ordered by Gregor Mendel in his own hand from Ernst Benary's Bestell-Nota nursery in Erfurt, Germany, 1878.
Reproduced by permission of the Augustinian Abbey of Saint Thomas in Brno, Czech Republic

lily, *Victoria amazonica* (Poepp.) J.C. Sowerby, he was the first person in Europe to succeed in getting it to bloom after he returned and opened the first of his nurseries.

Henry Eckford was a widower with seven children when he opened his own nursery in Wem, a small market town in Shropshire. Trained in the merciless Scottish apprenticeship system, he had worked for wealthy employers who wanted him to breed new varieties of Victorian staples such as verbena. His move coincided with the rise of the sweet pea from almost complete anonymity to center stage among plant breeders and enthusiastic acceptance by the public.

Sweet peas were the rage, and Eckford cleverly focused on them at just the right time. The pictures show us a benign-looking patriarch with a long white beard, but under that fluffy surface there was a shrewd business mind. Eckford made sure he sold his sweet pea seed to large seed houses and even across the Atlantic in the United States.

Isabella Preston was a single woman who had to follow her married sister to Canada from Liverpool in the early years of the twentieth century. Without parents or close relatives nearby, propriety prevented her from staying in England alone. She had no other choice. For thirty years, Miss Preston bred lilies of astounding loveliness. A few years after World War II, the American government invited a well-known Japanese admiral to visit the United States. They laid out an itinerary, but he asked, if it were all the same to them, could he go and visit Miss Preston in Canada? He was a dyed-in-the-wool lily fancier.

The old adage of chance favoring the prepared mind can be seen in the story of George Russell and the lupin. At the peak of his success in the mid-1930s, more than eighty thousand people traveled to Boningale in Yorkshire to see the fields of brilliantly colored, stalwart lupins quite unlike anything anyone else had ever bred. In June 1937, they paid sixpence a head for the privilege, and the resulting two thousand pounds were donated to a local institute for the blind.

Russell was a jobbing gardener, which means that he worked for more than one household; in 1911 he was said to have looked at a vase of lupins in one employer's kitchen and (silently) said to himself, "I can do better than that."

How and why was that? What went on in his head? A formidable combination of early training at two major nurseries and the experience of crossing his own plants presumably allowed him to assess the shape and form of the plant, see what was lacking, see what had to be done, and go forward and develop a more perfect spike. His efforts took over twenty-five years of his life, but he achieved lasting fame. No one will ever know what he actually thought. Nothing was recorded at the time.

How did he know what to do? We are back at the initial concept, that the one setting out to produce a perfect plant has to have the vision in his head, a "vision of loveliness."

Brother Charles Reckamp of the Society of the Divine Word missionary order in Illinois expressed his own vision of the ideal daylily quite clearly: "What I am after mostly is wide petals that are round and sepals that are not rolled back. I think it is unfortunate if the sepals or the petals roll back because the only way you'll see them is to go behind and look at the flower from the back! If the flower opens up as if it's facing you, smiling at you, you can see the entire petal and the entire sepal. And that's a quality I have been working for—fairly wide petals and wide sepals, if you can get them and segments that are rounded, not coming to a point. That's my favorite. That doesn't mean the others are no good but that's what I like."[3]

Even this extremely brief canter through the personal history of a few striking plant breeders shows that it is not all a dry recounting of pollen and stigmas, of cultivars and prizes, but a vibrant story of very human individuals living life however it came to them. The ultimate paradox still remains: outwardly they seem to have been like anyone else, but visions of loveliness were dancing in their heads.

Something about flowers triggered a deep response in people's minds. Any attempt to explain the behavior scientifically sounds banal and rather superficial. If a thing is very lovely we want more of it, or to put it another way, if some is good, more has to be better.

Consider roses. In the annual cycle of seasons, the original European roses lasted only a few weeks. People looked forward to their blooming and felt sad when the procession of flowers inevitably ceased. This cessation was not only disappointing in itself but also signaled the closing of summer and the consequent loss of pleasure and warmth. The moods coalesced.

When it turned out that this need not happen any longer and that roses could bloom all summer long and into autumn, certain types of person sprang into action. Presumably there was some sort of void in their lives and it was suddenly filled. *Obsession* may be too powerful a term. *Monomania* describes their behavior without giving it a pathological dimension.

A perfect example is the Sixth Duke of Devonshire. He was suddenly transfixed by a gorgeous orchid at a flower show in 1845 and spent the rest of his life devoted to these plants. William Cavendish was "the bachelor" duke, drifting about unhappily because he was deaf (and even maybe gay) and could not enjoy society. He had gone along unenthusiastically to open the show because that was what you had to do if you were a rich duke, but then he was smitten.

A golden *Oncidium* trapped his soul forever. Many wonderful things resulted from his embracing the plant world, apart from never having to face ennui again. One of them was his finding Joseph Paxton, who created the great glasshouses at Chatsworth and later built the Crystal Palace.

More sophisticated desires were driven by a person's aesthetic sense. A flower's shape may please the eye, but some people still saw possibilities for improvement. Hybrid tea roses have an elegant elongated bud. Nothing else for it but roses had to be bred for the shape of the bud, while fragrance almost disappeared. Rules for rose shows insist on the bud being of a certain style and shape if a competitor is to have any hope of winning a prize.

Sweet peas hummed along for about two hundred years until Henry Eckford decided to get rid of the hood and expand the size and shape of the petals. This opened a whole new future for the flower and laid the ground-work for competition rules. Once the breeder has internalized the rules, there is no one more hidebound in existence. Regardless of other matters, the rose or the sweet pea has to conform to these specifications year after year.

Color is another crucial driver. A desire for richer hues and a wider range of colors energizes many breeders. Most people think of delphiniums as blue. This is not enough for addicted delphinium fanciers, who want them to be pink and red. Then there are the impossible dreams. Some flowers seem never to come in certain colors (for example, blue roses, yellow petunias), and naturally those are the very colors to which someone devotes his or her entire life. It is now known that special genes control the production of the relevant pigment. Delphiniums are blue because of the delphinidin gene.

Making a rose blue by splicing the delphinidin gene into it doesn't count; it is not sportsman-like, akin to cheating.

Another challenge is that of a pure white clivia. Work is continuing on that one all the time. In their day, marigolds posed a similar problem. W. Atlee Burpee announced a prize of ten thousand dollars for the first person to breed a pure white marigold with seeds that would come true. That was in 1954. The prize was won by Mrs. Alice Vonk, a farmer's widow in Iowa, in 1975. These are challenges similar to those of climbing Mount Everest.

Another significant factor behind all this is pure competitiveness. Men needed to become "top dog" in all their activities. They had succeeded in business by elbowing everyone else aside. They could not suddenly park this behavior at the office and become tolerant and angelic at home. It is not by chance that the floral societies, starting with the Royal Horticultural Society, all fostered competition from the outset. Even professionally meek men like those of the clergy exhibited amazing ferocity when it came to their roses or sweet peas. Women who were involved also revealed some quite unladylike qualities in the heat of battle. Finally, there must have been some people who did feel a sense of power, maybe of divine possession, in this ability to manipulate the natural world so effectively.

In some ways, these aspects of the new movement were not all bad. Many improvements come about as a result of competition. Breeding a better type of apple or potato was valuable for feeding the public. People's pleasure in flowers fed other needs.

Documentary evidence of all this work remains in the form of the catalogues issued by each nursery firm. From year to year, new varieties appeared, offering a useful trail for the scholar to follow. While there are fallacies in depending on catalogues for the date when a new species was imported, they are more likely to be accurate when recording the introduction of a new cultivar. There are still a few caveats. If a nursery did not have its own experimental staff, it might buy new varieties from another house, with or without acknowledgment, and introduce them at a different time, but in general these data are reliable.

The catalogues have other charms, too. Nurseries spent a lot of money on artistic renderings of the flowers using woodcuts, steel engravings, hand-colored plates, and so forth. More recently, color photography has dominated the field. Catalogues are beautiful and, in many cases, true works of art.

Katharine White, legendary editor at the *New Yorker* magazine, paid them the ultimate compliment of taking them at face value as works of art and literature; in 1979, she wrote a charming critique, titled *Onward and Upward in the Garden*[4] in which she remonstrated with the nurserymen very seriously over their choice of words or illustrations.

If you stay with me through the pages that follow, you will be treated to a judicious mixture of science and gossip in almost equal parts, reviving the memory of people who have been unjustly forgotten. We start with a little science.

There is a tendency among Anglophones to stick to history within the English-speaking world. Doing this impoverishes our understanding of what has been accomplished. Where possible, I have attempted to cover a broader range of stories from other cultures. This has been easier in some situations than others.

In organizing the chapters, I had to make some very difficult choices. Some of the figures described here were such giants that they merit whole chapters to themselves. I elected to mention many others in the context of the plants they bred, like roses or azaleas. Finally, space would not allow me to cover every flower or shrub.

You will look in vain for the iris. Clarence Mahan did such an extraordinarily brilliant job in his book *Classic Irises and the Men and Women Who Created Them* that trying to repeat his achievement made no sense.[5] I also did not attempt to cover the tulip, for a similar reason: Anna Pavord claims that crown.[6]

PART ONE

HISTORY OF PLANT BREEDING

IN EUROPE AND AMERICA

1

The Compression of History

I N R E C O U N T I N G the development of modern horticulture and the resulting profusion of floral cultivars, one is struck first by the extraordinary stagnation and torpor surrounding farming and gardening through
the millennia and then the immense acceleration in the rate of change.
Discovery after discovery appeared in quick succession in the relatively recent past. The ratio is of more than ten thousand years to at most four hundred years.

Edible plants were domesticated—that is, made to grow where and when
humans decided to do it—before recorded time. This was a colossal discovery,
taking different form on different continents. Hunting and gathering began
to be superseded by sedentary agriculture and was eventually almost totally
replaced by it. Fields in which crops were sown in rows and reaped all at once
arose from haphazard temporary "plantations" within or near sites of human
habitation. Very few places are left in the world where native people can truly
gather their food in the wild. Flowers growing close to edible plants were the
precursors of modern ornamental plants; hence, tracing the trajectory of agricultural crops is relevant.

THE DEVELOPMENT OF
SCIENTIFIC BOTANY

Horticultural science arose in parallel with the other sciences, encompassing the contributions of individual observers, each investigating a question that puzzled him. Beginning in the late seventeenth century, the physiological processes that allowed a plant to grow, thrive, and reproduce itself began to be understood in Europe. By the time the Abbé Gregor Mendel started his work in the 1850s, most of the key pieces were in place. What still remained was finding out how a plant transmits its specific characteristics. This was what Mendel wanted to learn. It was very important at the time, when developing new varieties of plant was gathering steam. Floriculture had the potential to become a very big business, though Mendel was driven by a need to know for its own sake. This was the time at which the Dutch government recognized the way the industry was developing and sponsored a competition in 1831 to find the most useful information available.

A larger question loomed behind this one. Carolus Linnaeus had made it possible to classify and sort plants and animals with the binomial system. This system had many faults and has been modified several times, but the basic concept of giving each living thing both a generic and a specific name has survived. The question was, how did species form and separate from one another? Linnaeus tried to find out for himself by crossing different plants with each other. The results were inconclusive, but he chose to believe that he had in fact created new species. Charles Darwin's work eventually led to a better understanding of this process with the theory of evolution, described in *The Origin of Species,* though Darwin had no idea of how it was actually accomplished.

Hybridization frequently occurs naturally without human intervention, but for several centuries gardeners and scientists have intentionally pollinated selected plants to create new hybrids under controlled conditions. Formerly, they were working in the dark and had no idea of what was actually happening, but information slowly accumulated about the function and structure of pollen, leading eventually to an understanding of how it fertilized the ovary. Some of these huge strides were made with the aid of Anton Van Leuwenhoek's microscope.

Selection alone works by capitalizing on the spontaneous improvements in a standard crop. Plants within the crop either fertilize themselves or breed with the others in the field. In either case, new seedlings are formed. Any changes that are observed result from the normal process of cell division. The redistribution of genes during the formation of gametes affects the composition of the new plant or phenotype. In addition, spontaneous mutations called "sports" occur, either in the plant as a whole or in one segment of it, causing new features to emerge. Despite exhibiting considerable differences, the new form still fits the criteria for the crop in question. In flowers, it could be a red blossom on a camellia bush that normally has only white blooms or a blossom with double the number of petals.

It is true that plant breeders had managed very well without knowing exactly what was happening after they made their crosses, but they ran into problems in plant compatibility that were frustrating and prevented them from going forward. Intraspecific crosses worked pretty well, interspecific ones less so, but intergeneric crosses mostly failed. The great mass of new ornamental cultivars began appearing during the second half of the nineteenth century and continued well into the early twentieth century, long before any of the mechanics of how traits were transferred were known. Master plant breeders like Victor Lemoine and his son Emile who worked on what I call the "heroic scale" depended on skilled observation, unlimited imagination, very simple tools, good memories, and in most cases very precise records. It is hard to imagine how much more the Lemoines might have accomplished had they known the theory of genetics. Everything was done empirically, with the usual hit-or-miss results. Perhaps there might have been more "hits," but after the 150th cultivar of lilac what more could they do?

The great irony is that even after Mendel published his results in 1865, their significance was not understood for another thirty-five years. The first conference to present and evaluate his work was not held until 1900, but once the findings were made widely known, their impact was explosive and application began immediately.

The words *genes* and *genetics* as well as the brand-new vocabulary needed to describe experiments were coined by William Bateson, a Cambridge scientist. Other scientists repeated Mendel's experiments to be sure his findings were accurate. His results could be reproduced, though the very precise ratios he found were not so exact in other hands. In spite of that, the results were considered to be close enough not to cast doubt on his work.

Agronomists such as Rowland Biffen at Cambridge were looking for improved strains of wheat. Using Mendelian methods, Biffen rapidly moved ahead in his research. In 1905, his wife, the former Mary Hemus, entered a display of sweet peas at a Royal Horticultural Society competition in the Mendelian Genetics class and won the gold medal. Bateson was retained by John Innes to organize and run a research institute in his name to expand the application of genetics to improve edible crops. Nikolai Vavilov, the distinguished Russian botanist and geneticist, studied at the John Innes Horticultural Institution (later known as the John Innes Institute) in 1913–14 with Bateson and his colleagues.

Mendel's great insight was to combine field observation with a mathematical conclusion, giving his work a logical basis. He did have important predecessors whose contributions were not negligible. It is worth spending a little time looking at what they did before going on to examine Mendel's work in greater depth.

NEW MOVEMENT IN HORTICULTURE

Thomas Andrew Knight

Mendel was not the first person to use vegetable peas in breeding experiments. One of the men who preceded him, Thomas Andrew Knight (1759–1838), has largely been forgotten as a pioneer in horticultural science.[1] Knight responded to the search for improved British crops and animal husbandry that arose in the eighteenth century. In 1789 he started his series of experiments in plant physiology, including hybridizing, and published the results over the ensuing forty years. Mendel was aware of Knight's work and read his papers carefully.

Knight is important to this study because he bred numerous useful crosses of edible and ornamental plants and reigned as president of the Horticultural Society of London for twenty-seven years, from 1811 to 1838. The society received a royal patent from Prince Albert in 1861 and was allowed to be known as the Royal Horticulture Society. Knight was also a large landowner. He died in his carriage en route to a winter meeting at the society from his home in Herefordshire, a very long and cold journey.

Knight set the tone of the society right away. Prompted by Sir Joseph Banks, who corresponded with him voluminously, Knight laid out a prospectus for the society, a document that today might be called the mission

Thomas Andrew Knight was president of the Horticultural Society of London during its most formative years and made valuable contributions to the science of plant breeding.
Courtesy of Royal Horticultural Society

statement. He was not one of the seven founders but joined the following year, 1805, also at the insistence of Banks. Banks's genius lay in recognizing talent in quite unlikely places. He then pursued that person aggressively if necessary and wore down any resistance they might have felt.

Knight's father was a clergyman who came from a wealthy landowning family. The founder of the family fortunes, Richard Knight, was an ironmaster (owner of a foundry) who left a very large sum of money for the time.

Thomas was the second son. There were four children in the family, but his two sisters both died in their teens. His father, the Reverend Knight, died when he was five years old. The family was said to be in so much confusion that they neglected to see that the boy learned to read, an omission not repaired until he was nine. He was the sort of man who emerges from a strangely laissez-faire environment without being harmed by it, but it is hard to know how much of the story about his youth is true and how much is apocryphal.

In fact, it was his elder brother, Richard Payne Knight, who was left to his own devices. Thomas attended infant school in Ludlow and Dr. Crawford's prep school in Chiswick. In spite of the rocky foundations, both brothers ended up valuing scholarship very highly.

Thomas went on to Eton and then to Balliol College in Oxford. No science was taught at the ancient universities at that time, so Thomas read classics. He excelled at the university. His close friend Dr. Robert Baillie remembered that Knight learned very fast and had an almost photographic memory, though that term had not been invented yet. This left him plenty of time to wander around the countryside, ostensibly hunting but most probably simply looking and learning. He had already found the path he wanted to follow in that fallow childhood period.

Knight's brother Richard decided to transfer Downton Castle, the family estate in Herefordshire, to Thomas while still quite a young man. Thomas was very unpretentious. Before becoming so wealthy, he was not above building his own equipment and working with his hands, mildly shocking his more snobbish neighbors. Once he owned the whole estate, he had more than ten thousand acres on which to experiment.

Thomas Knight began his horticultural career by examining the diseases of old apple trees. His first paper was on the demise of old trees because of chronic infections; eventually an old apple tree will die no matter how many new young scions are grafted onto it. Knight advocated replanting orchards from seed. This was in 1795. Observing the extraordinary variety of plants that resulted from growing apple trees from seed may have been part of the motive for crossbreeding many other plants intentionally.

Thomas Knight then started the series of experiments that would occupy the rest of his life. Knight was interested in how plants functioned physiologically, just as the Reverend Stephen Hales had been. Hales had established empirically some basic facts about plants' metabolism and nutrition. This work was fundamental to the understanding of plant function. Like Darwin, he looked into how plant organs moved in situ. Why did roots go down into the earth and shoots go up into the air? Knight attached the tips of germinating seedlings to a vertically rotating disc and showed that the roots could be made to turn upward and the shoots downward under the influence of this force. One would need exquisite dexterity to perform such an experiment.

In his work on vegetables, he used green and yellow podded peas and some of the other varieties that were later available to Mendel. His work was rigorous and he made accurate observations, but he did not think of counting the numbers of variations that came from his crossings. Had he done so, he might have anticipated Mendel by thirty years. His papers show that he grasped the ideas of dominance, recessiveness, and heterosis (hybrid vigor). The results of his work overall increased the quality and quantity of crops and improved yield.

He wrote up the results of his experiments meticulously and published them in the journals of the Royal Society and the Horticultural Society of London.[2] For many years he refused to read other men's work, to avoid being influenced in his thinking, but eventually Banks pushed him into overcoming that scruple.

The ability to create new hybrids by deliberate pollination was fostered by the fact that Rudolph Camerarius had established sexuality in plants in 1691 experimentally and Nehemiah Grew had recognized that pollen was the male principle in flowers by the end of the seventeenth century. With clearly defined male and female parts, plants could be bred like animals.

When Thomas Fairchild first crossed a Wild Carnation, *Dianthus caryophyllus,* with a Sweet William, *D. barbatus,* in 1723 the resulting plant was known as "Fairchild's mule" for years.[3] He had done this with great trepidation because of the impiety of interfering with God's prerogative to create new forms of life.

Two German physicians, Josef Gottlieb Koelreuter and Karl Friedrich von Gärtner, subsequently took up the challenge and explored the deliberate hybridization of plants with care, trying to establish whether new species could be developed by breeding. Linnaeus's claim that such crosses would lead to new species was received skeptically. Careful observers found that after a few more generations some of these plants reverted to their previous forms.

Josef Gottlieb Koelreuter

After Fairchild, Josef Gottlieb Koelreuter (1733–1806) was the next person to cross separate species deliberately and observe the outcome. Linnaeus's claims interested him and led him to try his own experiments. Trained as a physician, he initially worked in St. Petersburg as keeper of the natural history collections of the Imperial Academy of Sciences for a short time. It was there where he began his research into the structure and function of pollen, pollination, and fertilization in plants—even though his titular duties were to take care of the fish. In 1761 he returned to Germany. He had no private income and had to take whatever jobs he could find, dragging his plants in pots wherever he ended up.

Koelreuter was also very anxious about the possible wrath of God. He carefully crossed *Nicotiana rusticana* with *N. paniculata* in 1760 and was startled when the resulting plants looked like *N. paniculata,* the pollen parent.[4] This was unexpected, and some of his colleagues did not believe him. At that time, scholars were divided into two camps regarding fertilization in plants: the "spermists" believed that the new plant was contained within the pollen granules when they were soaked in water, while the "ovists" denied pollen any role in fertilization. The general view at that time was that fertilization was carried out by an exchange of fluids. Koelreuter had to come up with some explanation of his findings within these strictures.

He was actually glad that the offspring turned out to be sterile, for this fitted with his view that crossing two species led to sterility. At least he had not altered nature's laws permanently. Some years later when he crossed *Dianthus,* a few of the hybrids were fertile, and this caused him some soul-searching. In spite of very active hostility by the staff of his aristocratic patron, the Margrave of Baden, presumably on religious grounds, Koelreuter managed to experiment with more than 130 species. The Margravin Caroline was very interested in his ideas and protected him. As soon as she died in 1786, he was dismissed. He is commemorated by the genus *Koelreuteria* (the Golden Rain Tree is *K. paniculata*).

One must not underestimate the power of religion and its hold over the population. Anyone working in the field of flower breeding had to contend with the religious zealots. Committed Christians believed that changing the color or structure of plants intentionally was intruding on God's prerogative of creation and thus highly impious. The "natural order" laid down in the Garden of Eden had to be preserved. Altering species fractured that order and led to confusion.

THE MUTABILITY OF SPECIES

In the New World, hints about the mutability of species were emerging based on a series of small informal observations. Colonists were always anxious about having enough food, so improving corn by making it grow more abundantly was a necessity. Corn was the most important crop for many years. Farmers and landholders did not consider that they were doing scientific work, but that was really what it was.

Soon after Cotton Mather's observations, Paul Dudley in Martha's Vineyard found that the mixing of colored grains in corn (*Zea mays*) could take place even when the different plants were separated by a ditch. In other words, whatever was occurring had to be transmitted in the air. The roots were not connected.

The governor of Pennsylvania, James Logan, published a short treatise on pollinating corn in 1735.[5] He corroborated the idea that pollination was a sexual function. Other than this important contribution, Logan is remembered as a mentor to Benjamin Franklin and John Bartram. He taught the latter Latin so Bartram could become the king's botanist in America. Logan was born in Ireland but was teaching in an English school when William Penn asked him to go to America as his secretary.

A later example of how a practical working farmer could improve his crops of fruit and vegetables, Joseph Cooper, began planting vigorous spontaneous hybrids on his New Jersey property in 1799.

When the United States began its expansion westward, wheat was among the major crops. Settlers encountered soil and climate very different from what they knew. Just as with corn, the seed they planted was the usual haphazard mixture of many kinds. Harsh reality quickly taught them how to choose the seed that would do best on a frozen prairie. In 1858, John H. Klippart in Ohio recorded the fact that within a few successive seasons the entire character of the crop would change to the plants that survived the best.[6] Klippart knew nothing about Darwin or Wallace, but he was describing the survival of the fittest.

Karl Friedrich von Gärtner

Karl Friedrich von Gärtner (1773–1850) was another pioneer. He too had studied medicine, like Koelreuter and Linnaeus before him. Unlike Koelreuter, he had a wealthy father who was a distinguished botanist, and thus he had solid resources for a life of study. He could afford to employ a staff of gardeners to help him with his experiments. Gärtner, *père,* had met Koelreuter, and the young Karl read Linnaeus's and Koelreuter's writings. He was fascinated by the question of whether crossbreeding plants led to new species and decided to see for himself.

He lived and worked in a very quiet backwater of the Black Forest and did not hear of scientific trends and movements until long after they had been current.

In 1837, he submitted the sole entry in the contest sponsored by the Dutch Academy of Sciences on hybrids and hybridization. He was seven years late, but as no one else had even bothered to submit anything at all, the examiners paid a lot of attention to his work and gave him the prize. Winning this prize had considerable impact. The recipient was promoted widely and became quite famous in his way, in addition to receiving money.

The academy wanted to shift public opinion and explore how plants could be improved by deliberate crossing. In particular, the academy was interested in the commercial prospects of plant crossing. Their challenge in 1830 was "What does experience teach regarding the production of new species and varieties through the artificial fertilization of flowers of the one by the pollen of the other and what economic and ornamental plants can be produced and multiplied in this way?"[7] Developing new and vigorous plants for commerce would benefit the already-significant Dutch horticultural industry markedly.

Gärtner had studied more than 700 species and had performed more than 10,000 crosses in a controlled manner. He came up with 250 hybrid plants and published the results in a book that influenced Darwin powerfully: *Experiments and Observations Concerning Hybridization in the Plant Kingdom*.[8] The importance of his work lay in its thoroughness and the fact that he had left nothing to chance. He very satisfactorily accounted for all the possibilities that might have led to his findings, including repeating many of his predecessors' experiments to confirm their results. He concluded that hybridization did not lead to the appearance of new species and that only crosses between members of the same species lead to fertile hybrids.

Darwin thought that there was more valuable material in this book than in "all the others put together." Gärtner had shown that hybridization could work to create new plant entities but not how it worked. His results confirmed his notion that species were fixed and immutable. A short form of the book was initially published in Dutch to satisfy the requirements of the prize committee, but in 1849 a more complete version was reissued in German.[9]

Both Koelreuter's and Gärtner's results showed that the first generation of hybrids, F1 in modern terminology, seemed fairly uniform but that the subsequent generations after that, F2, revealed all the diversity of the grandparents.

PROSPERITY RESULTING FROM PLANT HYBRIDIZATION

Belgian and Dutch horticulture were the most advanced and up-to-date in the world at that time. Enterprising nurserymen acted on the possibilities inherent in the new environment and began to do so on a gigantic scale, responding to the shifting social environment. Industrial advances led to a huge new class of wealthy people anxious to show that they had arrived socially. They built greenhouses and conservatories and filled them with plants. The Dutch Academy of Sciences was prescient: the vastly expanded number of handsome cultivars did indeed lead to horticultural prosperity.

The Dutch seedsmen were clustered in various parts of the country where soil and climate had proved to be excellent for different crops. Flowers did best in the region around Aalsmeer. Trees and shrubs were mainly grown in or near Boskop. These districts remain the centers of plant production to this day.

One of the earliest Dutch seed firms was Sluis & Groot (Nanne Sluis and Nanne Groot).[10] Nanne Groot began to sell selected vegetable seeds in the first decade of the nineteenth century. His grandson created a much larger firm by merging with his in-laws, the Sluis family, forming the business in 1867. A later descendant, Simon Groot, has expanded the family business to include East Asia. His East-West Seed company works in Thailand, developing and distributing the most productive strains of commonly used vegetables in the Thai diet.

Others who did much the same thing included Louis Van Houtte, who set up a huge business in Ghent in the early 1830s. His greenhouses covered many acres, though everything has since been swept away by modern development in that city. Enthusiastic townsmen erected a statue of Van Houtte in 1872. It is still there.

Victor Lemoine, from Lorraine in eastern France, spent a few months with Van Houtte and returned to start his own nursery in Nancy.[11] He crossed almost everything he could lay his hands on, starting with portulacas and ending with lilacs. Lemoine issued a torrent of new ornamental varieties year after year. His output was so vast that the secretary of the horticultural society in Nancy, which Lemoine himself had founded, complained about it.

Lemoine never dealt in vegetable or agricultural seeds. From the start, he gambled that the skillful development of flowers and shrubs alone would sustain a business. His attitude was unusual, but he had seen Van Houtte succeed with that policy and believed he could do it too. Many of the other nurseries that offered a rich variety of ornamental plants also sold vegetable seeds, and a few still sold agricultural supplies.

These are only a few of the more noticeable businesses benefiting from hybridization becoming commonplace because of Gärtner's groundbreaking work.

ADVANCES IN BIOLOGICAL THOUGHT

Perhaps the most famous of the experimentalists was the Abbé Gregor Mendel (1822–1884) of the Augustinian monastery of Saint Thomas at Brno in Moravia. The work he published in 1866, which went essentially unnoticed until 1900, changed the face of modern biology.

The middle of the nineteenth century was the period in which modern biological thinking emerged. At that stage, the physical sciences were quite well established. Botany had been the first scientific discipline to be a separate department at a university. Magdalen College at Oxford had appointed Robert Morison to a chair in botany in 1669, but botany remained descriptive and not experimental, while other sciences moved forward.

William Whewell of Kings College, Cambridge, had already coined the word *scientist*. Gottfried Reinhold came up with the word *biologie* to describe the study of living things in 1802. It was first used in English by James Field Stanfield in 1813.

Giving names to these endeavors, calling them "science" and "biology," was an important function in itself, separating and delineating them from an amorphous natural history. Important advances in biological thought soon began to appear.

One was the publication of *The Origin of Species* in 1859 by Charles Darwin, with its implications for evolution.[12] His work excluded the need for supernatural or religious forces. As a result, Darwin (1809–1882) faced immense hostility in the God-fearing English society of the time. Those arguments waxed and waned throughout the years and remain controversial among some segments of modern American society, although the scientific fraternity and the larger public have accepted the theory.

Another advance was the concept that nature could be reduced to chemistry and physics. There was no need to invoke a special "life force," or vitalism, in understanding biological processes. The synthesis of urea from two inorganic chemicals by Friedrich Wöhler (1800–1882) in 1828 had been the first concrete evidence for that idea. This observation argued against the theory of vitalism: life was just a special case of a mechanistic process. It took almost twenty years before skeptics accepted his work.

The observation that all living beings were composed of individual cells was firmly established at about that time. Robert Brown in England and Theodor Schwann and Jan Purkinje in Germany laid this down unequivocally.

Still another advance was understanding how inheritance worked. Koelreuter and Gärtner had shown that intentional hybridizing could succeed macroscopically. Mendel showed how to do it predictably. Only when cytology and other advances in basic science such as improved microscopy emerged could scientists understand what was taking place at the cellular level. Molecular biology then allowed scientists to work at the intracellular level. The recognition that the nucleus of the cell was made up of DNA in the form of chromosomes and that the bands seen on the chromosomes were the genes took a good deal of the guesswork out of breeding new plants.

Previously mysterious and insurmountable barriers between species and genera were seen to be due to an incompatibility of the chromosomes. A basic tenet was that there had to be an even number of chromosomes for a plant to be fertile. If there were an odd number like three or five, such a plant was sterile and would not produce seed or crossbreed.

When James Watson and Francis Crick published a description of the double helix splitting longitudinally to create the gametes and the latter then recombining to create new forms in 1953, biology entered a new era.[13] It became possible to go beyond classical Mendelian genetics and interfere at any level to introduce new desired characteristics into the reproductive process at will. These techniques became useful for all aspects of reproduction, not only horticultural. (The interested reader is referred to books such as George

Acquaah's *Principles of Plant Genetics and Breeding* to learn more about these topics.)[14] Several competent experimenters had looked at heredity in a qualitative way, making very useful observations, but the use of both mathematics and the physical sciences to examine biological phenomena was what proved revolutionary.

Mendel had had training in elementary statistics and also in natural science. Melding these together was his genius. This was what differentiated Mendel's work from other well-conducted experiments. He found ratios of inheritance that indicated some basic principle was at work. Plant crossings built on these ratios had a very good chance of succeeding. The old days of hit or miss had gone.

Gregor Mendel

Johann Gregor Mendel (1822–1884) was born into an extremely poor family.[15] (The friars at the monastery required him to take on a new name, and he reversed the order of his given names on ordination.) His early teachers recognized his gifts and arranged for him to continue his studies when a lack of resources almost forced him to drop out.

Achieving an education at all was a triumph for the son of a very poor farmer. His younger sister sacrificed much of her dowry to enable him to carry on studying after their father died. He never forgot her generosity and in return supported her sons for many years.

The success of such small farms depended almost entirely on the efforts of the men in the family. No one could afford to pay for help. Johann Gregor was the only son in that family and was expected to devote himself to farming. He refused to do it.

Mendel was driven by ambition, not for worldly goods but in things of the intellect. He also knew that if he gave way to the family demands, he could never move ahead. Part of the price he paid for the education was a heavy burden of guilt as he continued to study after his father was crippled by a serious accident.

In spite of his distress, he received an excellent education in science and the classics. If he had come from a middle-class background, this should have fitted him for a fine career. Because of his grinding poverty, the only feasible choice for him was to take holy orders. He entered the Augustinian monastery of Saint Thomas in Brno, Moravia.

Abbé Gregor Mendel established the basis of modern genetics with his experiments in crossing vegetable peas. *Courtesy of the National Library of Medicine*

Saint Thomas's was the obvious place for a young man in Mendel's circumstances, but an additional advantage from its location was that he would also benefit from the ferment in animal husbandry, sheep breeding in particular, in the region. It set the tone, promoting questions and new ideas.

Brno was the center of the wool and textile industry. There were also thriving orchards, with all the potential for improvement that offered. Sophisticated and enlightened landowners were anxious to improve yields and gain economic advantages. They too benefitted from the rich intellectual atmosphere at the monastery. The Enlightenment was in full swing in the Czech lands.

Sheep breeding had been moving ahead in England for the previous 150 years. Centuries of breeding horses for strength, endurance, and speed lay in the background. The accumulated wisdom led to certain basic tenets: start with healthy animals and take proper care of them; animals from another country could survive if tended appropriately; and the tendency for the latter's race to deteriorate could be prevented by breeding programs based on desired characteristics, and that this was in the hands of the breeder.[16] No one knew what was inherited or how it happened. Everything was still empirical.

At that time, the finest wool to be had was from the Merino sheep in Spain. The fibers were far smaller and less coarse than those of other sheep. European breeders made great strides by using Merino sheep for their experiments.[17] In Brno, the secretary of the regional agricultural society, Christian André, stayed on top of advances in the wool industry as well as in the orchard and vineyard industries. He made sure his society reaped the benefit. Czech landowners imported the crossbred sheep as well as modern spinning jennies and looms. Some of these men belonged to the popular natural history society of Brno and listened eagerly to the discussions. Mendel was not working in a vacuum.

During his college studies, he came under the influence of some very skeptical and competent scholars and rapidly mastered what they had to teach him. This was while he subsisted on an exiguous income and often went hungry. At the university in Vienna, Professor Fritz Unger talked about the plant-breeding experiments that were going on in the Netherlands and England. He introduced Mendel to Koelreuter's and Gärtner's work. Mendel retained all this information and used it to illuminate his work.

At the monastery, Abbot Napp presided over a remarkable set of men. Friar Klacel was an active revolutionary, seeking Slav independence from the Austrians. Tomas Bratranek was a philosopher and Goethe scholar, while Friar Krizhovsky was a renowned musician.

Once Mendel was a friar at Saint Thomas's, things still did not go smoothly. For various reasons he failed to obtain a formal teaching certificate, but in spite of that the abbot made very good use of him. Mendel was sent to teach science and classics as a substitute in a local school (*Realschule*) in the neighboring town of Znojomo and turned out to be a very good teacher.

The variation between individuals had always interested him, and he decided to study how they could be transmitted in some detail. Using his small amount of free time, he set out to study the inheritance of different features in mice. Mendel kept separate cages of wild mice with dark coats and cages of albino mice in his cell and bred them carefully. Unaware of a pending episcopal visit, he was counting the number of offspring with dark or light coats as they were born when the bishop came to do an inspection.

Bishop Anton Ernst Schaffgotsch was a rigid and authoritarian prelate who distrusted the monastery's brilliant and extremely astute abbot, Cyrill Franz Napp. The friars were strong on natural science and independent thinking but a little suspect on ecclesiastical rote. If it had been up to Schaffgotsch, the monastery would have been firmly shut down. Napp had other ideas, and he ran rings around the bishop.

Among the sources of Bishop Anton's displeasure, the fact of Mendel watching even very small mammals copulate loomed large. He reprimanded the abbey officials in 1854 for this unseemliness, forgetting that many monks came from farms where animal breeding was a frequent event.

Mendel then decided to switch to peas, *Pisum sativum.* This time the authorities gave permission. Somehow plants were less controversial in their minds, but as Mendel is said to have put it very slyly, "My lord bishop forgot that plants also have sex."

Napp was so convinced that what Mendel wanted to do was important that he paid for a greenhouse to be built in the monastery's garden. Napp was not a mathematician, but he did understand that large numbers of experimental subjects were needed to get any sort of result. Mendel had to have enough room to grow all his experimental plants in a protected environment.

The results of Mendel's experiments were published in Brno in 1866 and lay more or less unnoticed for more than thirty years.[18] This received view is a popular story much beloved of science journalists. Recent careful research indicates that this silence was not total.[19] There were, in fact, at least eleven references to Mendel's work, but Robert Olby and others believe that the leading scientists did not wish to think about the implications of his findings: their minds were made up, and mere facts were insufficient to change them. The pivotal events of 1900 took place because science had moved on, making Mendel's work suddenly relevant.

Mendel's biographers tell a rather poignant tale of not only passive neglect but even active malice by the recipients of the reprints that he had mailed so eagerly. In most cases, the leaves were not even cut. One of his teachers who did read the paper and who should have supported his goals, Carl Naegeli, dismissed the results very contemptuously and chided Mendel completely inappropriately.

For years it has been assumed that because Naegeli had been his teacher and he had great respect for all those who had taught him, Mendel endeavored to do what Naegeli wanted, that is, to crossbreed *Hieracium*, hawkweed. When he did it, the results were quite inconclusive. Hawkweed did not have the genetic stability and clearly demarcated traits needed for his type of observational work, but there was no way he could have known that at the time. Alas, here is another myth that has to be exploded. By carefully reading

Mendel's correspondence, Jim Endersby has shown that Mendel started to do this work on his own before he heard from Naegeli.[20]

Throughout his career, Mendel had tried to breed a lot of other plants without the defined results that peas gave him. He began his ultimate work in 1856 and published a paper in 1865. This paper is available in translation and is very illuminating.

When he presented it in two sessions to the Brno Society for Natural History, the work was politely received, but the surviving comments show that the audience, though well educated and sophisticated for the time, simply did not realize what he had achieved. No one else had done anything quite like it. They looked at it as an experiment in crossing peas and made nothing else of it. Many of the members already knew about hybrid plants reverting to the parental phenotype and did not think he had added anything to their knowledge.

For our purposes, the section on methods is the most instructive; it explains how and why he chose vegetable peas over other types of plants. One reason is that they have the advantage of large flowers, making them relatively easier to pollinate artificially. He could pull out the stamens and dust the stigma with foreign pollen. Each plant has both male and female organs, so they can fertilize themselves when not disturbed. Another advantage was that peas grow rapidly. The results appear quickly.

Mendel took a few years to reach this conclusion, breeding different plants to see which ones provided a reliable endpoint. In starting out, Mendel was careful to keep some plants as controls, another new concept.

He chose to work with seven clearly delineated traits: flower position, flower color, plant height, pea shape, pea color, pod shape, and pod color. The experimental characteristics tested were these: axial flowers/terminal flowers, purple/white flowers, tall/short plants, round/wrinkled seeds, yellow/green seeds, constricted/inflated pods, and yellow/green pods. He rigorously prepared separate pure breeding lines of peas with the traits he wished to study for two years before starting his actual experiments. This was one reason he wanted the enclosed greenhouse; he reduced the chance that bees might accidentally pollinate his experimental flowers by keeping his plants indoors.

In the first experimental year, Mendel carefully placed pollen from the chosen male source on the stigma of the plant chosen to be the female recipient. The experimental flowers were protected by little cloth covers. (One wonders who made the hundreds and hundreds of these little covers, since Mendel was not likely to have spent his time sewing. Maybe he paid young women or girls in the village school to do this important job.)

As the plants matured, he collected the seed, labeled it, and saved it for the following year. The hybrids formed in this generation are known as F1. They look uniform and give no hint of what is to come. He had no need to do any more pollination after that. In the succeeding years, he planted the experimental seed and examined the offspring.

The results are now famous. He established the existence of dominant and recessive traits, various traits caused by factors (now called genes) that segregate independently in a planned way and remained uninfluenced and unchanged throughout generations, even when not expressed.

Crossing the F1 offspring produced the well-known ratio of one homozygous dominant, two heterozygotes, and one homozygous recessive, or a 3:1 ratio. Even though he probably bred about thirty thousand pea plants, modern scientists are a little wary of his very neat conclusions.[21] His experiments have been repeated enough times for his ratios to be found but perhaps not quite so exactly. Mendel bred the peas both ways, reversing the male and female roles in equal numbers. The results held when he bred for more than one trait at a time.

The two universal laws of heredity, the law of segregation and the law of independent assortment, were adduced long after Mendel's death. The first law states that paired factors (genes) segregate randomly during the formation of the gametes. Each gamete can receive one or the other form. This is very important. Mendel showed that traits do not blend with one another along a sliding scale but remain separate from one generation to the next.

The second law indicates that when two or more pairs of traits are considered simultaneously, the factors (genes) for each pair of traits are distributed independently to the gametes. Some scholars believe that Mendel himself did not fully realize what he had accomplished. He was seeking the smallest element of the trait in question, such as "yellowness" in the yellow peas, calling it an *Anlage*, a word best translated as "rudiment." What was it that made a yellow pea yellow or a green pea green?

His choice of *P. sativum* turns out to have been inspired. After the experiments with *Hieracium* species failed, he felt discouraged and accepted the position of abbot. He was then immersed in administration and had no more time to himself. When he died, his colleagues burned almost all his papers, including the notebooks with his experimental results.

Re-creating Mendel's life and work is further hampered by the fate of the monastery during successive political upheavals. The worst period was under the Communist government of Czechoslovakia. In the past few years, concerned scientists have begun to collect money to restore the monastery and maintain it as a place of pilgrimage for scholars and students. The green-house is long gone, but the "footprint" of where it stood in the garden can still be seen.

As discussed earlier, he obtained some of the seeds for his work from Ernst Benary of Erfurt. One of Benary's catalogues from 1886 has a frontis-piece of various green and yellow peas. Margot Benary, married to one of Ernst Benary's great-grandsons, said she was told that the firm had indeed supplied some of Mendel's seeds.[22]

Another possibility is that the nursery at which Benary did his appren-ticeship, Haage & Schmidt, also in Erfurt, supplied some of the seeds. Haage & Schmidt had been founded in 1823 and specialized in vegetable seeds in the early period. Later the firm would become renowned for their succulent plants. A third source could have been Vilmorin-Andrieux in Paris, already old and well established by then.

One scientist who did mention Mendel's work in the next thirty-five years was Wilhelm O. Focke, in a monograph on heredity in 1881.[23] If this had not happened, the paper might never have come to light. For instance, Charles Darwin's younger colleague George Romanes is said to have cited Mendel in an article simply because Focke had included him.

There is no evidence that Romanes or Darwin ever read the paper. Even if they had, they might not have recognized the fact that this was the mecha-nism underlying the theory of natural selection. Their minds were set on the nebulous notion of "pangenesis." The converse was not true. The library of the Saint Augustine monastery still has Mendel's copy of Darwin's *Origin of Species* in German, carefully annotated.

The almost total silence ended abruptly in 1900. Two highly regarded sci-entists found the reference in Focke more or less simultaneously and actually read Mendel's paper: Carl Correns (1864–1933) in Berlin and Hugo de Vries (1848–1935) in Amsterdam both recognized its importance.

The third man usually credited with the rediscovery, Erich von Tschermak-Seysenegg (1871–1962), is now believed to have missed its point and is no longer a central figure in the story. He was an experimental agronomist and went on to breed several useful cereal cultivars. By an odd coincidence, von Tschermak was the grandson of Eduard Fenzl, one of Mendel's teachers.

Hugo de Vries had been working on a theory of mutations to explain heredity and came close to understanding much of what Mendel illuminated. He had done numerous plant crossings and independently found the 3:1 ratio too. Only a very powerful conscience prevented him from displaying an extremely bad temper about being trumped.

Correns too had an indirect connection with Mendel; he had been a student of Naegeli, Mendel's teacher. Correns had been crossing many species of plants and came up with similar results to Mendel's without knowing it. He looked for confirmation in the literature and found Mendel's paper.

There was an international conference on heredity at the Royal Horticultural Society in London in 1902. De Vries published his work in *Comptes Rendus* in 1900, citing Mendel's paper as a precursor. At almost exactly the same time, Correns did it in the German literature and von Tschermak in Vienna.

This apparently amazing coalescence of scientific ideas had most famously occurred previously when Alfred Russel Wallace submitted his paper on natural selection to the Royal Society in 1858. When seen from the vantage point of a century or more, it is hardly surprising to us any more. There is almost an inevitability to the strands of thought moving in the same direction.

William Bateson (1861–1926), a biologist at Cambridge, and later director of the John Innes Horticultural Institution in Northamptonshire, immediately recognized that the work explained some of his own experimental findings on inherited characteristics.[24] He gave a paper on Mendel at the conference.

Bateson became the apostle of Mendelian theory, frequently doing battle with the biometricians such as Karl Pearson. They were examining the phenotypic response, whereas Mendel's work was at the level of the genotype.

One of Bateson's signal contributions was to coin the term *genetics* in 1906. He also came up with some of the other valuable terms, such as *allelomorph*. Mendel's paper was published in English with a preface by Bateson in 1902. By 1930 much of the heat had gone out of the fight. R. A. Fisher's synthesis of biometrics with Mendelian inheritance led to modern evolutionary biology. Since then, the whole now-familiar train of chemical and molecular events has unfolded.

There are two other curious resonances surrounding this epoch. One was that Bateson and Vavilov worked together for a time. Vavilov was given a travel grant by his college, the Moscow Agricultural Institute, to study in England under Bateson at the John Innes Horticultural Institution in 1913. In return, Bateson visited Vavilov in Russia in 1925. The other was that Hugo de Vries trained the future brilliant collector of Chinese plants Frank Meyer.

For those who accepted Darwin's theory of evolution, it did not seem possible that one hybrid generation after another would keep breeding in the same ratios, with the same characteristics emerging time after time. They assumed that there was a continuous shifting of species, or "pangenesis," leading gradually to the new types. Even until about 1935 this idea held sway. During this period, the chromosome, the gene, and nucleic acid (essential vehicles for genetic modification) had all been isolated and identified.

The statistician Ronald A. Fisher showed how Mendelism could work to change species, and eventually the leading biologist of his day, Ernst Mayr, accepted the new process. Bateson correctly spotted the connection right at the beginning without fully understanding how it would work. He fought a very uphill battle and paid a high price for his constancy.

At a human level, Mendel was affable and companionable but a bulldog on important issues. In his last years, his tenacious fight against monastery taxes took on a highly paranoid flavor and embarrassed his colleagues. In spite of the presumed austerity in a religious house, the monastery's housekeeper enjoyed spoiling him with his favorite dishes, with the result that he became extremely corpulent. This could have been why he died comparatively young, at sixty-one.

De Vries was very gruff, rather a different type of personality. Frank Meyer found him overbearing. Correns and Tschermak were socially adept. Bateson was a harsh taskmaster, combative and exacting. Some of his assistants were idealistic young scholars from the newly established women's colleges in Cambridge. Edith Rebecca ("Becky") Saunders, lecturer in botany at Newnham College, was one of them.

He was utterly insensitive to her as a person and treated her as an indentured servant. It was to his credit that he accepted the fact that women could be trusted to do accurate scientific work and put her name on the paper they wrote together, but that is as far as he went.

Because Bateson was not in the mainstream of Cambridge thought, he had no access to research funds. He had to make do with whatever he could find, using his own house much of the time. His children were often unceremoniously pushed out of their rooms to make way for chicken brooders or other experiments. One of his sons was Gregory Bateson, the anthropologist and at one time the husband of Margaret Mead.

William Bateson was ultimately rewarded for his prescience. The philanthropist John Innes, who died in 1904, left funds in his will for the foundation of an independent horticultural institute to study plant breeding, and Bateson became the first director in 1910. The institute remains a leader in the field.

COMBINING THEORY WITH EMPIRICISM

The Dutch led the way in European agriculture with the use of root vegetables as animal feed. This allowed them to keep adult cattle alive through the winter. Until this became possible, most farmers slaughtered their adult cattle in the autumn. Charles Townshend (1674–1738) was an active politician but also very interested in agricultural matters. He retired to his estate in Raynham and imported turnips at some time in the 1730s. This gave rise to his nickname of "Turnip" Townshend.

Improved crops and the concomitant improvement in their herds were not a dry academic matter for large landowners. Many of them depended on farming for income. With improved yields, their income increased, and that was all they cared about. Feeding the expanding population was of almost no interest to them.

Looking back, the choice of peas as one focus of experiment was quite significant. After grain, pulses (an old generic term for the seeds of leguminous plants) were the principal source of food for the masses. Peas had been grown from the earliest times. The seeds were routinely dried and the results cooked into what was called "pease porridge." Not until the fifteenth century did anyone think of eating fresh peas straight from the garden. When it was first introduced, this innovation created a sensation.

If one could improve the yield of seeds, increase the plants' range, or expand tolerance of weather changes, more money could be made. Extremes of temperature in the temperate zones were one of the worst problems. Breeding the plants for cold and heat tolerance was very helpful in extending the season. If the plants could be made resistant to disease, that would be an enormous help.

Thomas Laxton

Darwin himself also experimented with vegetable peas. He crossed enough peas to make statistical deductions, but he too failed to think of that possibility. Darwin briefly corresponded about this work with Thomas Laxton in 1866 when the latter sent him several packages of his own crossbred peas. They exchanged two letters that year and another one in 1876.[25]

Darwin was careful to open each box he received on a separate table to avoid the peas getting mixed up, as he states in the following letter to Laxton:

> *Down. | Bromley Kent.*
> *Oct 31.*
> Dear Sir.
>
> The Box arrived safe this evening I have not yet opened it—I will never open 2 parcels at the same time or if I ever do it shall be on *separate* tables, so you may rely on the seeds not getting mixed.—I am most grateful for the confidence you place in me by allowing me to look at your collection, which fairly astonishes me from the amount of labour which must have been bestowed on so many crosses. I will consider your generous offer of keeping certain peas; but I certainly shall want very few & possibly none, for it is not at present the character of the full grown offspring, only certain points in germination which interest me. But I shall be able to judge best after examining the Peas.

He was scrupulous about Laxton's work, in the end keeping only one seed from some groups even though the latter had offered to let him keep them all.

Darwin noticed in one group that the hybrid was smooth like the paternal parent, not wrinkled like the maternal one. He wrote again:

> But I observe in lot 1 (except one pea) & in a lesser degree in 2, & in 3. 5. 6. & 8 that the crossed peas are smooth like the paternal stock, & not wrinkled & cubical like the mother pea—Can this loss of wrinkling be due to mere

variation, or to the effect of some peculiar culture, or is it the direct result of the pollen of the father? I should be grateful for an answer on this head—I know I am rather unreasonable, but I should be very much obliged if you would write a single word in answer to 3 queries on the enclosed paper.

He was seeking evidence of pangenesis, whereas we would consider this to be the expression of the dominant gene.

Thomas Laxton (1830–1890) is largely remembered for developing valuable varieties of vegetable peas, some of which are still grown today. He is important in the context of this chapter because he took his work one step further than other skillful plant breeders and actually outdid Darwin without realizing it.

Laxton was born in the village of Tinwell in Rutlandshire but grew up in Stamford, Lincolnshire, where he practiced as a solicitor. The family lived near Burghley House, the source of a very fine apple, *Malus* 'Lord Burghley'. Thomas went to London to read law, lodging in Hoxton, the home of several important nurseries of that time.

When he returned to practice as a solicitor in St. Mary's Hill, Stamford, he also took up breeding apples very seriously. In 1858, he introduced *M.* 'Stamford Pippin'. Gardening was his principal avocation. Both he and his father were known for their interest in gardening.[26] Thomas Laxton Sr. belonged to the Stamford Floral and Horticultural Society. Later his son won prizes at the shows. In 1871, Thomas Laxton won a first prize for his double pelargoniums. He was also elected an officer of the society. From records in the local newspaper, the *Stamford Mercury,* it appears that the grandfather, John Laxton, was a seedsman.

Because he sold his hybrid apples, he was deemed to be a commercial nurseryman at a time when this was inconsistent with the practice of the law. He was struck off the rolls in 1878, a severe punishment, and lost his license to practice law. That may be why he moved to Tavistock Street in Bedford. In the 1881 census, he appears as a "seeds grower." He and his wife had five children by then. Laxton left a major legacy in eleven kinds of fruit and vegetables. He is remembered as the developer of a fine race of strawberries as well as apples and the peas. Most experts believe that his *Malus* 'Allington Pippin' was the best apple he ever bred.

Thomas Laxton knew of Knight's work but moved ahead of him in drawing conclusions from his experimental crosses. H. R. Fletcher notes that Laxton recognized and recorded dominance in peas in a paper published in

1866, a one-page abstract. In 1872, Laxton published another paper with records of the ratios of inherited traits in crossbred peas.[27]

This quite astonishing work was not recognized either in 1866 or in 1872 for what it was. Even once Mendel's results were publicized, there was still no similar response to Laxton's results. It was not only that his report was in a relatively obscure publication.

Laxton was content with his conclusions and did not connect them to the basic questions of life. That required the broader intellectual vision of prominent biologists. Then, when the scientific world woke to what Mendel had done, they evidently did not feel the need to look for other corroborating work. The scientists themselves set about verifying it and proving to their own satisfaction that the ratios could be reproduced.

Laxton also observed that the artificially pollinated pea flower was almost immune to chance pollination by insects. He allowed his experimental plants to grow quite close together, for he knew that they were unlikely to be contaminated. He believed that the pea ovary would not react to a second dose of pollen once it was covered by a first one:

> We do not find it necessary to protect each individual bloom from insects if the pollen is applied in the early stages, as the pistil is already well protected from outside interference by the pollen grains applied. The pea, being what is termed a self-fertiliser, is almost, if not perfectly, immune from insect interference. Hence the practicability of growing side by side various types of peas, and securing a true stock on re-sowing. The late Mr. Laxton was one of the first experimentalists to prove this, and to point the fact out to Darwin.[28]

Laxton also introduced many fine varieties of strawberries, potatoes, roses, and other ornamental plants, including some sweet peas. Two of his sons carried on his work. William was the elder, but Edward seems to have had the greater talent for breeding the varieties. One of the Laxton rose varieties was named *Rosa* 'Charles Darwin'. Laxton's output of roses was small, but they were good enough to be included in Henry Ellwanger's valuable little book.

The Laxton brothers introduced excellent apples, pears, and plums. The family orchards in Bedford remained productive until the mid-twentieth century. The usual economic forces of change coupled with a probable infection of the soil, which can result from many succeeding generations of the same variety being planted on the same spot over and over again, combined to sap the nursery's survival. The land was sold for development. Today only a street name indicates where this thriving business once stood.

In 1906, William Laxton read a paper at a genetics conference.[29] The account of his family's work is very sobering, but quite likely he was recording most plant breeders' experience. It is instructive to see just how hard and frustrating the work could be.

> Having made the crosses and got our seedlings up, we expect to find some bearing the desired characters in an improved form, but in actual practice we are often greatly disappointed, and feel inclined to throw them all away.
>
> We have, however, been taught by Mendel to be patient, and not to expect too much in the first generation; if Mendel has only done this he has done more good than one at first realises, for he has saved from destruction many latent improvements of future generations, and encouraged the cross-breeder to proceed with his work instead of abandoning it in disappointment and disgust. But we must not expect too much from Mendelism.
>
> Great as are the benefits arising from the knowledge of Mendel's law, we find that we cannot arrive at any desired result without much labour and patience, and still something must be left to chance in the *combining* of many desirable characters in *one* plant, and great quantities of crosses will have to be made before we attain the end.

ANCIENT CHINESE ADVANCES

To counter the impression that the only valuable work was happening in Europe, one must consider the advances made in China over more than a thousand years. In keeping with their philosophy of harmony, the Chinese plant breeders did not interfere crudely with the breeding process by artificial pollination but worked diligently with nature and where its processes led them. Their work was based on skilful selection and the exploitation of sports, much as earlier Europeans had done.

For several reasons, Western scholars did not know about the Chinese results. The most important was ignorance of the Chinese language, but equally as important was the notion that the Chinese were a backward people not worthy of serious consideration. How wrong that was. In addition to their groundbreaking work with rice, vegetables, and fruit, the Chinese had a thousand-year history of ornamental plant selection. They worked with both native and imported plants and developed sophisticated horticultural techniques such as grafting as they went along.

The country abounds in endemic species. It has more than ninety species of roses. Early gardeners experimented with such flowers as camellias, chrysanthemums, peonies, roses, and azaleas and happily adopted the magnolia after it came from India in about 800 BCE. They recorded their work, but until Western scholars could interpret the records, the latter knew little about this.

Joseph Needham outlines early Chinese botanical studies in volume 6 of his Science and Civilisation in China series.[30] Chinese horticulturists did not have any philosophical concern about the legitimacy of modifying plants to their own wishes: nature was there to be exploited. There does not seem to be any evidence that the ancient Chinese gardeners deliberately placed external pollen on the mother plant's style, a point at which the Western breeders moved rapidly ahead. This maneuver was not done in China until the modern era.

After this brief look at the science available to early plant breeders, it is useful to take another brief look at the extraordinary changes going on in the plant world at that time.

2

The Onrush of New Plants

LTHOUGH THIS topic is explored at length in *The Global Migrations of Ornamental Plants: How the World Got into Your Garden,* it is worth a brief review for those who have not read that work. By the mid-nineteenth century, exciting new ornamental plants were steadily reaching Europe from the Americas and the western parts of Asia, as well as Africa and Australasia. This process had started slowly in late medieval times. The Americas were not yet discovered. All plant movement began to accelerate just before the seventeenth century. Finding the Americas helped speed it up. Once the Far East opened to Western trade in the 1840s, the trickle of exotic plants to Western Europe rapidly became a torrent. The United States also began to receive the new imports directly toward the latter half of the century. This enormous collection of new plants formed the substrate for the hybridizers to go into high gear.

Let me set the scene. At first, the collectors were primarily from Europe, and their discoveries traveled to the home country before being exported again to America. This was something of an irony. Hundreds of plants had gone from the Western Hemisphere to Europe as exotics, and now in its turn the Western Hemisphere became a recipient of plants from other parts of the world. Later in the century, a few American collectors sent their material solely to the United States and not to Europe.

Americans who collected plants while traveling in places like Japan, such as Charles Sprague Sargent (1841–1927) from the Arnold Arboretum and Dr. George Rogers Hall (1820–1899) from Rhode Island, come to mind, as well as Joseph Rock (1884–1962), yet even as they were doing this, collectors from Great Britain remained in the ascendant. Some of the most striking finds were made in the first half of the twentieth century by men like Ernest H. Wilson (1876–1930), Frank Kingdon Ward (1885–1958), and George Forrest (1873–1932), all from the United Kingdom. Looking back over this from a modern vantage point confirms the truth of Noel Coward's humorous line that "mad dogs and Englishmen go out in the midday sun."

By 1949, most of this activity had ground to a halt. World War II had made such travel almost completely impossible. Frank Ludlow (1886–1972) and George Sherriff (1898–1967) were perhaps the last to make the treks to Tibet and northern Burma in 1949 as private citizens.

One of the important points to be kept in mind is that there was money to be made in this business. Science stood to benefit, but the profit motive was very powerful. The immense amount of discretionary income in the British upper classes before the First World War made it economically feasible for an individual nursery to dispatch one or more employees to Asia or South America, knowing that the plants they sent back could be sold at a splendid profit.

The classic example was the Veitch nursery.[1] Veitch saw that there was a second step that could be taken, developing and "improving" the raw material he received from his collectors. That was a bold move, requiring a lot of capital to support several years of bench work without any prospect of immediate sales.

Orchids epitomized the Victorian obsession with tropical flowers as symbols of wealth and status. Once the Duke of Devonshire gave them his imprimatur, battle was joined. John Pierpont Morgan's comment about owning a yacht, "If you have to inquire what it costs you cannot afford it," had applied to orchids long before he made it.

James Veitch (1815–1869, referred to as "James Junior"), one of John Veitch's grandsons and newly in charge of the firm, realized he could increase his business by taking advantage of the craze for these orchids and other rare highly decorative plants. He did not undertake this lightly. Before coming to a decision, he consulted with the most eminent botanist of the era, Sir William Hooker (1785–1865), director of the Royal Botanic Gardens at Kew, and took Hooker's advice.

It seemed to be a risky venture for a single business to support a collector, with all that was entailed. Most of his contemporaries thought he was overreaching. They were envious of him anyway and quietly hoping he would fail. James was ambitious and complex and had antagonized quite a few people in his haste to succeed. He was something of a visionary and a little impulsive but not really rash or hotheaded. In fact, he was very close with money.

This caused all the men he sent out to have real difficulties coping in the faraway foreign countries. He never gave them enough funds for the job to be done. In spite of all the problems, he not only made a small fortune but garnered many prizes and walked off with the cream of the carriage trade.

James Veitch received his wealthy patrons most obsequiously at the Royal Exotic Nursery in Chelsea, ensuring that they came again and again to buy his incomparable orchids. He knew how things were done. White gloves, hushed tones, immaculate starched collars, much bowing and scraping, and immediate satisfaction of the fickle clientele's every whim became second nature in that nursery. He received the more august customers himself to underscore their importance; otherwise, it would be "Our Mr. Robinson will take care of you, madam." The competitors who had derided him had to eat their words and chew their fingernails in frustration.

Right on the heels of the orchid craze came the passion for begonias. These semitropical flowers were also thought to need hothouses and at first were limited to the wealthy. *Begonia* is a very large genus with about 1,500 species. Starting in about 1820, a few species began trickling into Europe, but their true potential did not emerge until later in the century.

Nurserymen had the task of filling the conservatories of the *nouveaux riches* as well as those of the established families with beautiful flowers. They also supplied plants whose foliage was the center of attraction, but these were less likely to need hybridizing.

One of the mainstays of the foliage plants was the fern. Ferns had, and continue to have, their own following. In a convenient confluence of traits, the rex begonia combined the charm of modest flowers with outsized and impressive foliage—the ideal indoor plants. Long before the tuberous and other begonias evolved enough to become fashionable and highly desirable, there was a steady trade in the rex.

James Veitch was not alone in following this course, but his became the most prominent of the various nurseries involved. The textile merchant A. K. Bulley in Liverpool sent George Forrest to China, thus ensuring himself a place in history. The Irish physician Augustine Henry (1857–1930) supplied Kew with staggering collections of plants from his sojourn in China while working as a doctor for British Customs on the Yangtse River. Bulley came across Henry while corresponding with him about the cotton excise and promoted his plant collecting.

A few other European countries, not just Great Britain, had botanical and horticultural collectors in the East.[2] French missionaries spread to remote parts of China as part of their missions to convert the native people. Many, such as Père Armand David (1826–1900) and Père Pierre d'Incarville (1706–1757), were distinguished scientists and naturalists, but they always subordinated their scientific work to their religious imperatives. Collecting for them meant increasing scientific knowledge.

They had little or no interest in finding commercially valuable plants. Most of this exploitation was left to the British. The specimens the missionaries sent back at such cost languished in the basements of the Jardin des Plantes and other institutions for years before the scientists even began to examine them. By the time they had classified most of the specimens, the British had overtaken them and introduced the best ones into commerce, but even so there was plenty for firms like Vilmorin et Cie in Paris to choose.

The impetus for the French missionaries had faded before 1900, but there were still some devoted German and Austrian collectors like Heinrich Handel-Mazzetti (1882–1940), trapped in China during World War I. Horticulture was a major industry in Belgium and the Netherlands throughout the nineteenth and early twentieth centuries, but very few of those men explored for plants in foreign countries any more. The Belgian Jean Linden (1817–1898), once a fearless collector of orchids in Central and South America, was now a sedate nurseryman.

The days when Russian botanists treated China as part of their own backyard had gone forever. Grigori Nicholaevich Potanin (1835–1920), Alexander von Bunge (1803–1890), and Carl Maximowicz (1827–1891) had all made superlative discoveries in China, working out of the ancient Russian embassy in Beijing.

The Russian Revolution and the world wars put paid to all such exploration. Whatever collecting went on later was on a very small scale, nothing like the monumental expeditions of the previous era with dozens of porters and bearers.

The politics were insuperable. Only large organizations and ad hoc consortia or syndicates were subsequently able to afford the expense of sending a group of collectors to a country that now put all sorts of obstacles in their path. Finally the 1973 international treaty Convention on International Trade in Endangered Species (CITES) established the rights of an individual country to the fruits of its own natural resources, further limiting the scope of foreign collections.

Floras all over the world thereafter became jumbled up, with native and exotic plants more or less on a par. Commercially the exotic plants now outnumber the natives, particularly once the huge number of hybrids is taken into account.

DISTRIBUTION OF
THE IMPORTED PLANTS

Where did everything go? The heart of this book is what happened to the plants once they reached their destinations. At the end of the eighteenth century, England was the principal repository of new and exotic plants, though France still had plant explorers in the Pacific and Caribbean regions.

New plants fanned out in various ways. The closest places for Great Britain were across the English Channel or the North Sea, but the exchange of plants with France was sporadic for a time due to political troubles. After the seemingly bloodless invasion of England in 1688 by Prince William of Orange and his wife, Queen Mary, daughter of James II, England and the Netherlands were closely linked in all types of trade, including horticulture.

In the 1790s the problem with France was its Revolution, followed shortly afterward by the Napoleonic wars. This slowed down, if it did not completely halt, plant importing and exchanges. In the Low Countries, equivalent political discontent interrupted commerce. During normal periods the Netherlands was a source of bulbs because of Clusius's work. Carolus Clusius (Comte Charles de l'Ecluse, 1526–1609) was a founding botanist at the time the science started to emerge from herbalism. Among his most important contributions was the wide dissemination of the tulip after it came from Western Asia.

At that time the Netherlands encompassed both Holland and Belgium under Austrian rule. Belgium did not become a separate country until 1830. Queen Victoria's uncle Leopold was appointed to be its king. A local floral market in Ghent had begun very early in the eighteenth century, preparing the way for what was to come. It offered potted plants closely associated with the region and many types of bulb. The Belgians had formed the habit of importing their exotic plants from England. In 1774 an enterprising Belgian florist, Judocus Huytens, chartered a ship and imported rhododendrons, azaleas, and fuchsias from London, laying the foundations of major markets in Ghent.[3] After a shaky start, Belgium became a leader in horticulture and hybridization.

Currently Belgium is considered to be a small country, but its influence in the development of modern horticulture was quite disproportionate. Plants such as the pelargonium, which were almost the signature of Ghent, originally came from England but underwent amazing alteration and development in the Belgian nurseries. *Azalea indica* (now *Rhododendron indicum* L.) is another plant firmly associated with Ghent and Belgium.

One critical step was the establishment of a botanical garden in Ghent with a strong scholarly basis. The appearance of a figure like Louis Van Houtte in Ghent can thus be seen not to be purely due to chance. In addition to the botanical garden, Ghent also offered an agricultural and botanical association. This further strengthened the industry.

Napoleon blockaded Continental ports in 1806 in an attempt to bring English commerce to its knees. Belgium had freed itself from the Austrians only to be taken over by the French. By 1815 the French yoke was lifted, and the floral business in cities like Ghent revived very rapidly. There were 120 nurseries and florists in Ghent in 1837. At first only the rich could afford the new plants, but as nurseries grew ever larger, producing more plants, the prices came down, allowing midlevel professional people to buy them too.

The exotic imported plants were distributed in different ways, but the nurseries and organizations that sponsored the collecting trips took most of the booty. Botanical gardens wanted various species to round out their scientific collections, though a dried herbarium specimen was just as useful to them as a living plant. Wealthy people grew the new arrivals on their estates. Some of the aristocracy were avid plant collectors, and several had strong scientific interests. Many amateurs dabbled in plant breeding.

Large numbers of the new exotic plants were shared with commercial nurseries that had skillful and knowledgeable operators. In the first half of the nineteenth century, expeditions like that of Lewis and Clark were sponsored by the young U.S. government, sent to find out what was growing in their own territories. The huge quantity of material brought back by later expeditions overwhelmed the tiny laboratory facilities available in Washington, D.C., and much of it was sent on to well-known nurserymen like Bernard M'Mahon in Philadelphia.

On the Continent, the middle class was small but ambitious, anxious to move into aristocratic circles. This was the time of the Second Empire in France. Building a large showy house with a large showy garden and a conservatory for good measure was a first step on the ladder to social success. Here were additional customers for the nurseries' new and improved wares. Others were also in the offing.

Constant repression and the dislocations of the Industrial Revolution were leading to rebellion among the lower classes. Political and social change was coming. Something had to be done to stave off another round of revolutions. The 1848 uprisings in Berlin and Paris were a stark reminder of what simmered under the surface. Poverty and hunger were the lot of most urban workers. Even though famine afflicted Ireland the worst, the other western European countries also suffered from the potato blight, exacerbating an already fragile situation.

Land use was a huge grievance. A disproportionate amount of land was locked up in the hands of a very few. The idea of free public parks emerged, of land set aside directly for the people by right and not just by the unreliable noblesse oblige of the upper classes. Municipalities often bought the land to create parks of this sort or received blocks of land as gifts in perpetuity. Until then, almost all property apart from the commons in ancient towns had belonged to royalty or the nobility, and there was no access to open space without permission.

One exception had been the cemeteries, the property of the church. Families visited them for many reasons even once the funeral was over. As epidemics continued to erupt throughout the nineteenth century, enlightened physicians became concerned that diseases still lurked in the cemeteries and were being spread by mourners after the burials.

Men like Dr. Jacob Bigelow led a movement to clean up the cemeteries by building wide paths and planting many trees and shrubs to purify the air. The theory did not stand up to modern scrutiny, but the unintended effects of the landscaping were splendid.

With all these changes, the market for new ornamental plants expanded very rapidly. Nurseries abounded. Gardening was a recognized trade or career, governed by apprenticeship. Very often sons followed their fathers into gardening on the large estates or into the family nursery business. It was time to show what could be done to gild the lily and improve on the grandeur of nature by breeding new versions.

EXOTIC PLANTS NOW COMMONPLACE

There had been an enormous amount of trial and error, mostly error, in taking advantage of the new plants as they arrived in Europe. For example, Peter Collinson, a London linen draper and devout member of the Society of Friends, led a syndicate importing and distributing the collections of the Bartrams from Philadelphia in the early eighteenth century.

One of the recipients wrote to him mournfully after receiving his share of the plants: "Pray tell me how to care for these plants. My gardener is a very ignorant fellow."[4] Of course, Collinson had no more idea of what to do than the man in the moon. That gardener was not alone in his ignorance.

The outlook was not totally bleak. Some head gardeners of great estates were very skillful men who had served apprenticeships and understood their work well.[5] Joseph Paxton was a supreme example of such men. Silas Cole, the Earl Spencer's head gardener, was another.

The losses en route due to conditions on the decks of the ships were astronomical, and only a small percentage of the material sent by people like John Bartram arrived in good condition. These losses in their turn were compounded by the failure to recognize the significance of climate and soil in the new country. The invention of the Wardian case in the early 1840s helped a great deal, markedly increasing the chances of survival. This enclosed wooden case with glass sides held moisture in and kept injurious agents out.

Keeping the new plants alive in alien new territory was hit or miss for many years. If the plants came from the tropics, the immediate response was to plug them into a "stove," a building with many windows heated in various ways but usually by a large stove. Never mind that quite a few came from higher altitudes and needed a cooler environment. The general philosophy was that one size fits all.

Orchids illustrate these dilemmas. Orchids were kept warm by the pots being placed in beds of steaming manure fresh from a cow or a horse. The ambient temperature in the hothouses was also very high. This system worked very well for pineapples. Both the masters and the gardeners thought this was the only thing to do, and they were very disconcerted when orchids died by the dozens.

One of Joseph Paxton's great contributions to horticulture was recognizing that some orchids needed a more temperate environment. He opened the transoms of the great hothouse he had built for the Duke of Devonshire, and lo and behold, those orchids did very well.

In spite of all these "two steps back for every one step forward" mishaps, the critical mass of imported plants continued to build and eventually became stable and reliable. With that, the impulse to improve and vary the new species rapidly grew and became irresistible. A huge breakthrough occurred when the unobtrusive little Chinese rose *R. chinensis* var. *spontanea* (Rehd. & Wils.) T.T. Yu & Ku was used to create the first Western repeating roses.[6]

In the more recent past, hybridizers have tended to concentrate on one or two species at most. They have narrowed their ambitions down from the heroic scope of the past. It must have been utterly exciting to have dozens, even hundreds of new species to work with, none of them yet exploited to any extent. The horizon seemed limitless, but as that material was developed, it became necessary to choose. Newly discovered species continued to swell the ranks of other genera, making it feasible to stick to one kind, like sweet peas, begonias, lilacs, and so forth. The more one learns about a species the more its fascination increases.

PART TWO

IMPORTANT FLOWER

BREEDERS

3

Flower Breeders in Europe

ERNST BENARY

THE FIRM OF Ernst Benary Samenzucht sells a very large amount of flower and vegetable seed, more than 50 percent of the total output of the German horticultural industry, according to the company's website. The founder of the company, Ernst Benary (1819–1893), was a Jew born in the city of Kassel. The position of the Jews in the German territories had changed radically after their emancipation in 1806. Before the emancipation, with a few exceptions, Jews had been subject to severe social and political disabilities. The majority had been confined to menial occupations or money lending and were not allowed to farm or own land. These disabilities were lifted after Napoleon's edict.

The Benary family had been one of the very few prosperous ones throughout those difficult times, with successful bankers on both sides. Benary was the eighth of nine children and the youngest son. Unfortunately, the Benarys lost all their money because they were forced to make loans to the ruling prince in Hessen.

Ernst Benary founded a seed company that is still in existence today.
Reproduced by permission of Rudolf Benary/Matthias Redlefsen

Ernst Benary's certificate of apprenticeship from Haage & Schmidt of Erfurt.
Reproduced by permission of Rudolf Benary/Matthias Redlefsen

By the time Ernst should have been ready for a career, his father had died and his brothers had no money to educate him. Ernst had shown some interest in plants and natural history. They decided to apprentice him to Friedrich Haage, a well-known nurseryman in Erfurt. Erfurt is in Thuringia, part of the former East Germany, and has been a horticultural center since the early nineteenth century.

Christian religious communities had set things in motion, planting vineyards and growing *Isatis tinctoria,* the plant from which woad is extracted, early in the ninth century. At the end of the Thirty Years' War, the monks were disestablished but agriculture and horticulture continued to flourish. A German landowner, Christian Reichart (1685–1775), set the standard in the eighteenth century. He developed his own land and using this as a template wrote a six-volume set of agricultural and horticultural textbooks.

Haage was among the first German nurserymen to introduce and breed cacti. The firm of Kakteen-Haage is still extant after many vicissitudes and still owned by the same family. Horticulture was an unexpected occupation for a Jew of the period. It is significant that Haage accepted Benary. He must have been a very serious young man, though the family teased him, calling him their "Thuringian farmer boy."

As noted elsewhere, plant breeding on a commercial scale was developing on the Continent in the 1830s, just at the time Ernst was choosing a career. He traveled to England, France, and possibly Belgium while becoming a horticulturist, presumably to polish his skills.

Belgium was a major center of the floral industry in the nineteenth century. Louis Van Houtte was starting his meteoric rise in Ghent in the early 1830s. He taught not only Ernst Benary but also Victor Lemoine, another titan in the plant-breeding world.

After Benary married the daughter of a successful merchant, he was able to open his own business in Erfurt in 1843. In 1847 Ernst Benary Samenzucht issued its first catalogues, in French and English as well as German. In spite of the forced impoverishment, the Benary family as a whole maintained its high level of culture. Ernst Benary had one brother who was a scholar in Oriental languages and another who was a noted physician. His children converted to Christianity and eventually lost contact with the Jewish community.

Ernst Benary Samenzucht initially stocked vegetable seeds. That was an important segment of the market and less susceptible to fluctuation, but Benary soon began to hybridize ornamental plants. In 1859, he released *Lychnis × haageana*, the result of crossing *L. sieboldii × L. fulgens*.[1]

Lobelia erinus 'Crystal Palace Compacta', another of his early cultivars, remained available until very recently. As his sons grew and took on more of the business, they continued the tradition of hybridizing and in turn passed that on to their children. The firm is now run by Klaudia Benary Redlefsen, a direct descendant in the sixth generation. The firm is still issuing new cultivars of begonia as well as many other plants.

In 1909 Benary introduced the F1 hybrid *Begonia × gracilis* 'Primadonna'. (For a list of the genera that the Benary firm modified, see appendix.)

There is a faint possibility that the firm supplied the Moravian friar Gregor Mendel with the pea seeds he needed for his experiments. A Benary invoice for flower seeds from 1878 is in the Mendel museum at the Saint Augustine monastery, the Mendelianum. Conceivably, Mendel had dealt with the firm before that. The notion lingered in the family for several generations.

Margot Benary, a writer who was married to one of Ernst's great-grandsons, Wilhelm, wrote a brief family memoir in 1960.[2] She indicated that her husband's grandfather, also named Ernst, had told her that this was the case. He also told her that his grandfather Ernst and his wife, Bella, the mother of six children, worked very hard and lived very frugally. They had to establish themselves and build up a clientele. After long, hard days at the nursery, they sat in the kitchen making up packets of seed and doing the thousand and one little odd jobs that were needed.

Ernst knew that reliability and quality were the basic ingredients of success but that to rise above the average he needed something to make people take notice. This ambition was what drove him to develop striking hybrids. Once the family began working on begonias, they were very careful about the seed. Begonia seed is as fine as dust and easily lost and dispersed. Margot Benary was told that the new seed was always kept in a safe. Only the most favored customers were allowed to have even a pinch of the new seed, although the cultivar appeared in their catalogue.

She tells a delightful story that may be apocryphal but conveys the mood and flavor of the period. In the early years of the twentieth century, a wealthy Englishman, a "Milord" as she says, traveled to Erfurt with his head gardener, his valet, and his secretary. All he wanted to do was to see the latest cultivar of begonia. After looking at it briefly, he placed an order and left for England the same day. He was not interested in seeing any of the wonderful sights in their region.

Two candidates for this story come to mind. The most likely was Sir George Sitwell, father of the three famous Sitwell siblings and a most eccentric man. He was, however, an inspired and noted gardener at his properties in England and Italy. Slightly less likely though no less eccentric was A. B. Mitford, Lord Redesdale, grandfather of the famous Mitford sisters. He was an authority on bamboo but was also very serious about his garden. Of course, if this episode actually occurred it could have been any one of many people.

Benary worked on African violets very early. The firm won prizes year after year at the major garden shows. This renown brought them important customers. Perhaps the peak of Benary's social ambition was met when Kaiserin Augusta visited them. He realized that the kaiserin would be hot and tired after a long journey and earned immense gratitude by setting aside the drawing room for her and her attendants and serving them refreshments quietly. Benary did not let any of this go to his head. He remained pleasantly modest and down-to-earth.

As the Benary firm grew and expanded, it eventually controlled twenty hothouses, miles of open fields, and six thousand forcing frames, all over an area of about fifty hectares. Fourteen farms in different parts of Germany grew seed for Benary, and about a hundred other "multipliers" were under contract in various countries, depending on their climate and suitability for particular plants.

The Benary firm was very enlightened in its concern for the employees. Long before sickness funds and disability compensation were widely available, Benary provided them in house.

Benary's grandson Ernst was quite a friend of George Ball's in Chicago. George Ball's family name had been Balzhimer, and they were of German descent. George Ball may have been fluent in German. Benary visited Ball in Chicago several times. As Ball's business prospered, he made regular trips to Europe quite late into the 1930s, including visits to Germany. World War II made visits impossible, but he and Benary picked up the friendship again after the war ended.

Sweet peas, *Lathyrus odoratus,* serve as an example of changes in the sale of flower seed. Benary listed thirty-seven types of sweet pea seed in the 1893

Long before it was standard practice, the Benary firm gave its employees many benefits, such as a holiday camp, pictured here.
Reproduced by permission of Rudolf Benary/Matthias Redlefsen

catalogue. (This catalogue was reissued in 1993, to celebrate the sesquicentennial of the firm.) At that time, Eckford's seeds were prominent among Benary stock, offered as a mixture. In the 2005–7 catalogue, twenty-four *Lathyrus* cultivars were listed, all part of three series: Mammoth, Royal, and Elegance.

All these series are American in origin and quite closely connected. Benary does not breed its own sweet peas. Mammoth was introduced by Denholms of Lompoc in California as a successor to its Early Multiflora Gigantea Series in 1960. In 1982, they introduced Elegance. The Royal Series derived from the 'Cuthbertson', a spring-flowering variety developed by Frank Cuthbertson for the Ferry Morse Seed Company in California. These series represent high durability, stability, and reliability and can be confidently put out for sale without hesitation. This is crucial in today's competitive markets.

The firm of Benary underwent enormous difficulties during both world wars. In World War I, most of their men were drafted and they had to switch to growing vegetable seed to feed the population. Restoring their stock and rebuilding their business was hard, but they had some champion hybrids of begonia and petunia that were very important to this process.

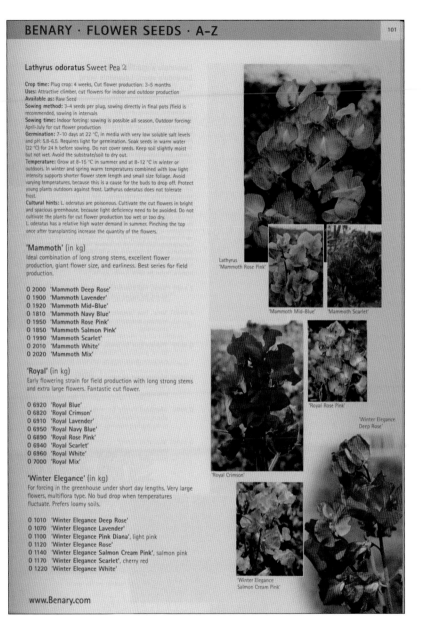

Lathyrus odoratus Sweet Pea 2|

Crop time: Plug crop: 4 weeks, Cut flower production: 3–5 months
Uses: Attractive climber, cut flowers for indoor and outdoor production
Available as: Raw Seed
Sowing method: 3–4 seeds per plug, sowing directly in final pots /field is recommended, sowing in intervals
Sowing time: Indoor forcing: sowing is possible all season, Outdoor forcing: April–July for cut flower production
Germination: 7–10 days at 22 °C, in media with very low soluble salt levels and pH: 5.8–6.5. Requires light for germination. Soak seeds in warm water (22 °C) for 24 h before sowing. Do not cover seeds. Keep soil slightly moist but not wet. Avoid the substrate/soil to dry out.
Temperature: Grow at 8–15 °C in summer and at 8–12 °C in winter or outdoors. In winter and spring warm temperatures combined with low light intensity supports shorter flower stem length and small size foliage. Avoid varying temperatures, because this is a cause for the buds to drop off. Protect young plants outdoors against frost. Lathyrus oderatus does not tolerate frost.
Cultural hints: L. oderatus are poisonous. Cultivate the cut flowers in bright and spacious greenhouse, because light deficiency need to be avoided. Do not cultivate the plants for cut flower production too wet or too dry.
L. oderatus has a relative high water demand in summer. Pinching the top once after transplanting increase the quantity of the flowers.

'Mammoth' (in kg)
Ideal combination of long strong stems, excellent flower production, giant flower size, and earliness. Best series for field production.

0 2000 'Mammoth Deep Rose'
0 1900 'Mammoth Lavender'
0 1920 'Mammoth Mid–Blue'
0 1810 'Mammoth Navy Blue'
0 1950 'Mammoth Rose Pink'
0 1850 'Mammoth Salmon Pink'
0 1990 'Mammoth Scarlet'
0 2010 'Mammoth White'
0 2020 'Mammoth Mix'

'Royal' (in kg)
Early flowering strain for field production with long strong stems and extra large flowers. Fantastic cut flower.

0 6920 'Royal Blue'
0 6820 'Royal Crimson'
0 6910 'Royal Lavender'
0 6950 'Royal Navy Blue'
0 6890 'Royal Rose Pink'
0 6940 'Royal Scarlet'
0 6960 'Royal White'
0 7000 'Royal Mix'

'Winter Elegance' (in kg)
For forcing in the greenhouse under short day lengths. Very large flowers, multiflora type. No bud drop when temperatures fluctuate. Prefers loamy soils.

0 1010 'Winter Elegance Deep Rose'
0 1070 'Winter Elegance Lavender'
0 1100 'Winter Elegance Pink Diana', light pink
0 1120 'Winter Elegance Rose'
0 1140 'Winter Elegance Salmon Cream Pink', salmon pink
0 1170 'Winter Elegance Scarlet', cherry red
0 1220 'Winter Elegance White'

Lathyrus
'Mammoth Rose Pink'

'Mammoth Mid-Blue'   'Mammoth Scarlet'

'Royal Rose Pink'

'Winter Elegance
Deep Rose'

'Royal Crimson'

'Winter Elegance
Salmon Cream Pink'

www.Benary.com

Sweet peas in the Benary catalogue. Benary originally offered Eckford sweet peas. In this picture from 2006, three modern series are shown: Mammoth, Royal, and Winter Elegance.

Reproduced by permission of Rudolf Benary/Matthias Redlefsen

World War II caused them more of the same problems, only worse. Even after such a long period of time, they were still considered to be Jewish. Their senior employees and many good townspeople strove to protect them from the worst Nazi harassment.

Supplying the German forces with vegetables allowed them to stay in business. They kept their heads down and managed to meet the quotas of potatoes and cabbage. Allied raids destroyed many of their offices. The fragile greenhouses repeatedly lost much of their glass, and of course glass was almost impossible to replace.

All the men went into the German armed forces, including Heinz Benary, Heinrich's only son. He had been groomed to take over the business in due time. Heinz never came back. When the time came for the firm to celebrate its centennial in 1943, mourning and tragedy were very close to the surface, and it was not a very happy occasion.

For a short time at the end of the war, the Americans controlled the territory, but in less than three months they moved west, abandoning Thuringia to the Russians. Once that happened, the Benarys knew things would only get worse. They needed to act quickly.

In 1946, Friedrich Benary, the great-grandson of the founder, went to Hannover Münden in West Germany to rebuild their concern. He had to do it without the capital or backing they once had: the original firm was in the new Soviet sector, and he was not permitted to transfer money.

A typewritten Benary catalogue from 1949, written in English, was miraculously saved and shows how hard it was to get going again. In 1950, the catalogue reflected some improvement in their circumstances. It was set in type and on a better-quality paper. The 1950 catalogue was closer to what had been it had been like before the war, but there was still no color.

Finally it became clear that they had to abandon everything they had built up in Erfurt in what was now the separate country of East Germany and all flee to Hannover Münden. They did this in 1951.

The East German authorities, the DDR, confiscated their business in 1952 after a clearly political trial on trumped-up charges, accusing them of defalcations with the company's charitable funds. That was a complete lie. The business was restored to them in 1991, after the reunification of Germany, but they chose to remain in the west.

The founder's grandson, Ernst Benary, Friedrich's father, bore the brunt of all the upheaval and distress. He was honored by the University of

The Benary catalogue, 1949. A stark reminder of the effects of World War II on a thriving business.
Reproduced by permission of Rudolf Benary/Matthias Redlefsen

ERNST BENARY
SEED GROWER SINCE 1843 IN ERFURT
HANN.MUENDEN, GERMANY, BRIT.ZONE

NOVEMBER
1950

Wholesale Price List for Seedsmen
containing
Special Flower Seeds for Winter Sowing and Novelties

CABLE ADDRESS BENARY HANNMUENDEN
PHONE HANN. MUENDEN 347

The Benary catalogue, 1950. Signs of recovery after the Benarys moved to West Germany.
Reproduced by permission of Rudolf Benary/Matthias Redlefsen

Hannover for his contributions to horticultural science and received the All-America Selections Award in 1968.

In spite of all the tragedy, he lived to see the success of the new business and died at the age of ninety-four. Considering how many men died in both major wars, it is amazing that almost all the Benary sons lived and were able to pick up the reins of the business. Their vital role as growers of food saved them, although the Nazis were often not logical in their destructive impulses.

BLACKMORE AND LANGDON, OR A BRIEF TREATISE ON THE DELPHINIUM

Blackmore and Langdon are best known for their delphiniums and begonias. At the end of the nineteenth century, when J. D. Blackmore and C. F. Langdon joined forces, the begonia was still a luxury item (for the story of the begonia, see chapter 6), while *Delphinium*—or to use its folk name, larkspur—was an old favorite and found in many cottage gardens. It was tall and blue and gave an air of grandeur to even the humblest of premises. The inhabitant might be poor and in rags, but if he had a martial stand of delphiniums, he could hold his head up with the best of them.

Serious crossing of the dominant species, *Delphinium elatum, D. formosum,* and *D. tatsiense,* began in the early 1840s, in France. *Delphinium grandiflorum* was imported into Europe in the late nineteenth century.

Victor Lemoine of Nancy introduced a hybrid *Delphinium* in 1852. Working directly from two species, he called this *D. ornatum.* It was the first semidouble-flowered cultivar. A double flower has a greater number of petals than the single form, at least twice as many. They are derived from stamens. In a semidouble flower, the additional whorl of petals is incomplete. The majority of modern hybrids are descended from one or another variety of *D. elatum.* Lemoine's cultivar is the "signature" delphinium, the one people visualize when talking about these plants. Their flowers form spikes. Other varieties have racemes and are often called "belladonniform," characteristically with branching flowering stems rather than single spires of flowers. In the present era, the plant known as *D. elatum* is a complex mixture.

There are several hundred wild *Delphinium* species, with about a quarter of them endemic to the western United States. About 60 percent are found throughout Asia. Approximately 10 percent of the species are found in Europe. Delphiniums from Europe were taken to England very early in the eighteenth century and rapidly became part of the standard flora. The European delphinium is perennial, but in North America the plant has to be treated as an annual.

The Lemoines introduced numerous hybrid delphiniums right up until 1933. Almost all of them were double or semidouble flowered, but the color palette shifted over the years, from very bright blues to lavender, mauve or rose/lilac, deep indigo, and purple. It is not clear why this happened.

In 1906 Lemoine produced *Delphinium* 'Statuaire Rudé', a pastel bicolor form that was the ancestor of many modern varieties. Blackmore and Langdon exhibited it, and the plant won an Award of Merit at the Royal Horticultural Society show that year.

In England, James Kelway (1815–1899) specialized in gladioli, delphiniums, pyrethrums, and peonies at his nursery in Langport, Somerset. He introduced the first delphiniums in England in 1859. His son, William, spent many years breeding new varieties of delphinium, and the Kelway catalogue carried both Lemoine's and their own cultivars. Of 170 cultivars listed in the 1889 Kelway catalogue, 137 were their own hybrids. For a time, Kelways was the largest of all the English commercial nurseries. The firm suffered serious reverses in the 1970s but has been reconstituted recently. The Kelways and the Lemoines found that even though there are many species, only a few lend themselves to useful crossbreeding, no doubt because of genetic incompatibility.

The firm of Blackmore and Langdon, which began in the West Country with a shop in Bath, remains in family hands. James Langdon's grandson Brian Langdon was the third generation to run the business, and the fourth generation is now involved.

James D. Blackmore (1856–1921) opened his own nursery in 1900. The following year, Charles F. Langdon (1868–1947), the Reverend E. Lascelles's gardener in Newton St Loe near Bath, joined him. The rector collected delphiniums and put Langdon in charge of his treasures. Lascelles had many Kelway varieties, and Langdon was fascinated by the range of color. Their first catalogue listed delphiniums.

Clearly such an important decision as leaving full-time employment and going into business for oneself has many factors, but it is interesting that one reason that has come down is the love of color. George Russell was also moved by beauty and form when he began his work with lupins.

Langdon set to work very quickly. He gave a box of his seedlings to another Bath nurseryman, A. A. Walters. In a nice gesture, one of the cultivars was named *Delphinium* 'Reverend E. Lascelles'. Walters showed it at the Royal Horticultural Society and won an Award of Merit. The flower was a rich purple-violet, and the white eye was unusually large. It stood about twenty inches, slightly shorter than the standard, but the intriguing color and flower form led to its becoming enormously popular for years.

It still appeared in the Blackmore catalogue in 1939. Later on, some members of the Delphinium Society resurrected it for a show in 1975. All who saw it were very impressed by its contrasting colors.

Blackmore and Langdon's catalogue for 1907 listed fewer than ten cultivars: one from Kelway and two of their own. They used cultivars from various sources for breeding and did not resort to actual species until 1960, when they wanted to breed a red flower. Then they turned to *D. cardinale*. French, Belgian, and Dutch nurseries supplied many of the cultivars they needed.

Lemoine's *Delphinium* 'Statuaire Rudé' provided them with parentage for two outstanding cultivars in 1919: 'Sir Douglas Haig' and 'Millicent Blackmore'. They could have been created in 1910, but the war interfered with all such activity. These varieties also prospered in the years afterward.

Brian Langdon, a university-educated horticulturist, writes that most of the English cultivars that followed them contained genes from one or the other of these two.[3] The firm created a sensation at the Chelsea Flower Show in 1914 with an exhibit of delphiniums in pots.

More new cultivars emerged in the 1930s from California. Frank Reinelt created the Pacific strain of delphinium at the same time he was breeding his extraordinary tuberous begonias. The Pacific delphinium was slightly shorter than the English forms, though it also derived from *D. elatum*. Reinelt gave his cultivars names based on the Arthurian legends. He used native species such as *D. cardinale* to infuse bright color into the hybrids.

Reinelt wanted to produce delphiniums that would grow true from seed, each variety with its own clear color. For years, Blackmore and Langdon carried the Pacific strain of delphinium as well as Reinelt's begonias. In turn, Reinelt carried their cultivars.

Unlike many other major breeders, Blackmore and Langdon began to keep very careful records of their crosses after 1922. Reinelt also kept records. His daughter, Aphra, now Mrs. Katzev, managed to save one of his notebooks, small enough to fit into a back pocket but filled with tiny legible handwriting. The nuns in Moravia had done their work well. Mrs. Katzev did not know what happened to the rest of the books. They were not found in the University of California at Santa Cruz archives despite an extensive search.

The Lemoines did not keep records, nor did the Kelways. Luther Burbank's failure to keep records weakens the impact of his work, as no one could ever reproduce it. The reason Blackmore and Langdon wanted to keep track of what they had done was that tall delphinium plants frequently lacked staying power, or what they called a strong "constitution." Breeding a superior flower with striking color and form onto a soft, floppy plant was bad for business.

The public expected a perennial plant to stay productive for several years. If the framework for their gorgeous flower fell over in a high wind or rotted in the wet English winters, they were disappointed and angry. This concern led to Blackmore and Langdon's subordinating the range of color and form to overall performance. For a time, Blackmore and Langdon's lines hovered around mauve and blue, but they never ceased trying to breed a pure blue flower with a strong constitution. That happened in 1939. *Delphinium* 'C. F. Langdon' was released in 1948, a year after Charles Langdon died.

The records were maintained as long as breeding continued. Every year they raised between five thousand and ten thousand seedlings. Each year they won numerous awards at the important shows.

After World War II, they picked up the work and methodically bred known lines to combine the best qualities in each. Novel colors were still very important commercially, as well as being attractive. They introduced a mulberry-rose flower, *Delphinium* 'Strawberry Fair'; a white flower, *D.* 'Icecap'; and a cream one, *D.* 'Butterball'.

The changes in English life after World War II meant that fewer people could afford, or even find, a gardener. Very tall delphiniums needed staking and a lot of mollycoddling. No one wanted to do all this work. Shorter plants were the answer. Two new kinds emerged spontaneously as sports.

In 1952 Blackmore and Langdon spotted a seedling based on their *Delphinium* 'C. F. Langdon' that had a good dark color and stood only three and a half feet tall. Another firm, Bishops, also found a short delphinium, later named *D.* 'Betty Baseley', among their fields of seedlings, purely by chance.

At the end of the 1970s, Blackmore and Langdon stopped hybridizing new delphiniums. They felt they had met most of their objectives by then.

Their catalogues were adorned with numerous photographs of gloriously blue double-flowered plants.

KARL FOERSTER

Between about 1920 and 1970, Karl Foerster (1874–1970) introduced a remarkable series of delphinium in Germany, starting with *Delphinium* 'Berghimmel'. Foerster was born in Berlin but after serving in World War I moved his perennial nursery to Potsdam. His father was the director of the Royal Gardens, and Karl served two apprenticeships, one in Germany and the other in Italy.

In the Nazi era, he was supposed to grow plants only of impeccable German origin, but he resisted this directive. He is also said to have employed Jews in his nursery, at great risk to his own life. As if all this were not difficult enough, the advent of Soviet rule after World War II made things even worse in some ways, though he no longer feared so acutely for his life. Very few gardeners in the West knew about his work or could obtain his plants until the end of that era.

Foerster allowed his cultivars to be formed by pollination. The witty Irish garden writer Helen Dillon commented that each morning he would march through his trial grounds, followed by a terrified garden boy, and smash any plant with inferior flowers into oblivion.[4]

Mrs. Dillon grows some of his cultivars, such as *Delphinium* 'Perlmutterbaum' and *D.* 'Berghimmel', with great satisfaction. She also wrote warmly about an old Blackmore and Langdon cultivar that persisted in her garden for more than thirty years. Foerster cultivars are tough and reliably perennial and do not need all the attention the great tall varieties demand. To use Blackmore and Langdon's expression, they have a strong "constitution."

The former editor of *Horticulture* magazine and current executive director at Timber Press, Thomas Fischer, brought Foerster's work to our attention in 1998.[5]

Much current breeding is carried on either by the employees of vertically integrated corporations or by amateurs.[6] The indefatigable David Bassett documents progress carefully, noting the Centurion Series based on F1 hybrids of British named cultivars. He produces his own Dowdeswell Millennium

Series. The process of perfecting the delphinium will never cease as long as he draws breath.

CARTER'S TESTED SEEDS: A MEDITATION UPON THE SWEET PEA

Carter's Tested Seeds was a very large and respected enterprise that only recently ceased operating. It began almost two hundred years ago. The firm of James Carter, Dunnett and Beale had premises at 238 High Holborn, a street in London near Saint Paul's Cathedral. Dunnett and Beale first appeared in a London directory in 1804. Carter opened a shop in Drury Lane in 1834, initially as the agent for a German firm, Ramann and Mohring. In about 1838, Carter bought Dunnett and Beale's business and changed the company's name. A catalogue from 1842 is that solely of James Carter and Co.

The floral world was astonished when the scarlet sweet pea, *Lathyrus* 'Invincible Scarlet', won a prize in 1865. The Royal Horticultural Society gave it a First Class Certificate that summer. No sweet pea had ever won a prize before. The new cultivar has always been attributed to James Carter and Co., but I would like to clarify what actually happened.

James Carter did breed sweet peas. In 1837, he listed a few new varieties. The catalogue from 1845 shows that he sold mixed colors, black, 'Painted Lady', purple, scarlet, striped, and white varieties. These were all spontaneous variations of the original species *Lathyrus odoratus,* imported in 1699. There were also the Tangier pea, the new striped pea, and two varieties of winged pea, *Lathyrus tetragonolobus.* (For the history of the sweet pea, see chapter 6.)

He did not, however, breed *L.* 'Scarlet Invincible', because he died in 1855. In addition, none of his sons survived to adulthood, so there was no one called James Carter at the seed house in 1865. Steven Brown of Sudbury bred the flower and handed it to the James Carter firm to distribute.[7] This is the reason Carter has been considered the winner all these years.

James Carter was born in 1797. A possible antecedent to James Carter may have been William Carter, a seedsman of West Smithfield in London, but the connection, if any, is not clear. William Carter's business was listed in

1811. (At that time, Smithfield was a large wholesale meat market.) William Carter died in 1819. He had a daughter, Ann, and a nephew, William.

The award led to a frenzy of enthusiasm among both the public and the professionals. For the next fifty years, the sweet pea was the most popular flower in the British Isles, other English-speaking countries, and some of the countries on the Continent. A reasonable correlation between the product and the price prevented sweet peas from becoming a "bubble" like the tulip in the 1660s, but some psychological aspects of the madness were evident.

In one instance, a young bride used only sweet peas for all the floral requirements of her wedding. She carried a bouquet of white sweet peas, the bridesmaids had pink ones, and the tables were decorated solely with vases of other colored sweet peas. There is no record of how the cake was iced, but doubtless it had facsimile sweet peas in sugar, just as some cakes have roses piped onto them.

Even a quick glance through nursery catalogues of the period, from Germany to New Zealand, indicates this devotion to the sweet pea. Any large, well-run nursery could offer more than one variety of most plants, but time after time, the sweet pea offerings run into two or three pages. Only roses were available as abundantly. From a business standpoint, such excessive choice was self-defeating. It led to very few purchases being made of any one variety.

The excitement is the more unusual when one thinks about the appearance of sweet peas in the garden. The great majority of them have to be grown on a trellis or support. They contribute only minimal artistic value to the landscape as a whole. Seen at a distance, they resemble a vineyard rather than a pleasure garden.

In spite of that, the color and perfume of the flowers were so overwhelming that people were devoted to them. Catering to that devotion permitted some firms to grow very rich and successful. Carter's was among them, but as the fad waned, they took up other valuable plants and weathered the downturn effectively. Business was business.

The First World War was such a turning point. Sweet peas continued to be grown and sold, but in nowhere near the same numbers after 1916. Other plants, such as roses, which were always important, came to the fore. Sweet peas still had a presence as late as 1954; Carter's offered two pages of sweet pea cultivars in that catalogue. In the present era, it is possible to buy quite a few varieties of sweet peas, and there are firms that specialize in heritage seeds.

Carter's issued truly handsome catalogues throughout its operation. They were in large format with a rich blue stock for the cover, quite often imprinted with gold letters. Carter's, which had a royal patent, proudly displayed the royal coat of arms on its catalogues. Facsimile images of the firm's gold medals were also placed on the cover.

Each page was illustrated with steel engravings, until color photography became standard. Nurseries took up color very early because of its magnetic effect on the public. Colored pictures of sweet peas are seen in the 1908 catalogue.

Carter's sold begonias as soon as they became available, in 1879 offering seven varieties. Some of these were bred in their own nursery, but they also sold Veitch cultivars and others. Unlike the sweet peas, begonias never lost their popularity.

The company has come into the modern era simply as Carter's Tested Seeds. From about 1860, Dunnett had growing grounds in Essex, at Jupes and Hill Farms. This was a great boon during a time of agricultural depression in the 1890s. By 1902, 1,500 acres were in production. Flower seeds provided a lucrative alternative to standard crops for impoverished farmers.

The firm took on additional premises—Crystal Palace Nursery in Sydenham, a suburban area where presumably seed was grown and hybridization took place in the late 1850s. Carter and his family never lived there.

It is not clear just who did the later work at the nursery. Someone entered sweet pea hybrids in the name of James Carter and Co. in national and international competitions. The 1860 catalogue listed more than half a dozen types of sweet pea. In 1869, Carter's won awards for new pelargoniums at Hamburg. They won prizes and medals in Vienna and informed the public that they were "seedsmen to His Serene Highness Prince Metternich." Testimonials from the nobility were a crucial selling point for tradesmen who wished to succeed, and the royal imprimatur was essential.

The 1897 catalogue coincided with Queen Victoria's Diamond Jubilee. Carter's decorated the front cover of the catalogue with her picture and the dates 1837–1897. The year 1837 was a seminal date for the firm and sweet peas, as well as the queen's ascent to the throne. James Carter introduced the first striped sweet pea into commerce in 1837. For much of his life he experimented with sweet peas and may have laid the groundwork for *L.* 'Invincible Scarlet'.

One wonders why he did it and what he felt about *Lathyrus odoratus,* the sweet pea. Unlike the people who followed him and jumped onto the bandwagon, he was a pioneer. Before him, only the seedsman John Mason of Fleet Street had paid much attention to this obscure flower. Did James Carter grow sweet peas in his own garden and did his wife or daughters enjoy the perfume?

During the last quarter of the nineteenth century, Edward J. Beale (1835–1902) remained a senior partner in the firm. In the twentieth century, Dunnett and Beale resumed control of the company but still used the name "Carter's Tested Seeds." Harold Beale was one of the three Beale brothers, who with W. H. Dunnett took charge. Beale was a very distinguished man. In 1929, he was president of the National Sweet Pea Society. Harold Beale wrote that Carter's strict adherence to its philosophy of "Constitution, Vigour, Length of Stem and Quality of Flower" led to improved sweet peas. The society awarded him the Eckford Gold Medal in 1937, an extremely high honor.

The principal center of activity was the Carter property at Raynes Park, just west of London. During World War II, he and another member of the staff, Mr. Ness, helped to keep the firm going in spite of the Germans bombing their greenhouse. The list of the firm's novelties by year indicates that James Carter and Co. consistently won prizes for sweet peas until 1937. From then to 1946, there were no new cultivars. The war prevented such work.

Carter's Tested Seeds no longer exists. It has been incorporated into Suttons.

HAAGE & SCHMIDT

Friedrich Adolphe Haage (1796–1866) opened a small seed store in 1822. He settled in Erfurt, a town that rapidly became a center of similar businesses. It is in Thuringia, part of East Germany (the DDR) after World War II. The climate and soil were highly conducive to commercial horticulture. By the end of the nineteenth century, dozens of successful nurseries were well established there.

The great upheavals of the twentieth century had a terrible impact on these peaceful operations, but once the government of East Germany fell in 1989 and Germany was reunified, some of them managed to get going again.

Friedrich A. Haage, founder of Haage & Schmidt.

Reproduced by permission of Ulrich Haage

Kakteen-Haage is currently owned by Ulrich Haage, a direct descendant of Friedrich Haage.

The family's experiences in World War II and its aftermath resembled those of Benary but differed in that Ulrich's grandfather, Walther Haage, was better able to cope with East German rule. The East German government finally expropriated Kakteen-Haage in 1972 after years of intimidation and harassment. It was a time of immense privation. There was almost no fuel for the human population, and very little thought was given to the needs of exotic plants.

The business became VEG Saatzucht Zierpflanzen–Brigade Kakteenzucht, and Walther's son, Hans-Friedrich Haage, was the "brigade leader." By a curious irony, one of the highly placed Russian officials in charge of Erfurt was Professor Baranov of the Leningrad Botanical Garden, who was very sympathetic to a struggling nursery. He arranged to have coal delivered to the Haages, and this enabled them to keep their tender succulents alive until times improved. In 1996, the firm was restored to its rightful owners.

THOMAS LAXTON

Thomas Laxton was born in Tinwell in Rutlandshire but grew up and lived most of his life in Stamford, Lincolnshire. Laxton practiced as a solicitor, but his avocation was horticulture, particularly the breeding of improved forms of both flowers and vegetables. (For more information about Thomas Laxton, see chapter 1.)

VICTOR LEMOINE

No one has left a finer legacy of glorious garden plants than Victor Lemoine. Evidence of his work is still everywhere in the modern nursery and garden center, yet very few people have heard of him. Driven almost entirely by inward vision, he tackled one genus after another. He was blessed with an extremely tenacious memory and a very clear idea of what might be possible.

Pierre Louis Victor Lemoine (1823–1911) came from a family of skillful gardeners, accustomed to working on a very large scale.[8] His father and grandfather had both been in charge of large estate gardens. They moved to Delme in Lorraine before he was born. The village was not far from a well-regarded school for boys. It says something about the family's prosperity that he could attend the school for the full duration of the terms; they did not have to take him out at an early age to do his share of the work.

Victor also became a gardener but with considerably more education than his forebears. Instead of serving the standard apprenticeship close to home, he attached himself to three important horticulturists of the time.

France had a powerful tradition of horticulture. For example, Louis XIV's gardener, Jean-Baptiste de la Quintinie, was a significant figure at court, in control of huge plantations, where he grew food and ornamental plants. The king had to have fresh melon and peaches for breakfast every day of the year, winter or summer. Coping with such exacting requirements took a very special sort of skill.

By spending time learning from the masters, Lemoine prepared himself very seriously. He worked in the nurseries and earned his keep that way. He first went to E. A. Baumann in Bolwiller, a village in Soultz-Haut-Rhin, probably in 1840 when he was seventeen. Very little is known about Lemoine's activities at this stage, not even how long he stayed there. E. A. Baumann was not just a master gardener but also a botanist to whom Lemoine later dedicated many of his hybrids. In 1838, Baumann issued a catalogue with more than five hundred varieties of rose.

Les Frères Baumann was an important nursery long before Lemoine went there. In 1810, Augustin Pyrame de Candolle undertook a grand tour of France and Belgium to evaluate both the natural resources and the state of agriculture in those countries for his government at the request of the Swiss minister of the interior, Monsieur J. B. Champagny.[9] After he passed through Strasbourg, he was taken to meet the Baumanns, Joseph Bernard and Augustin, in Bolwiller. Their father, François Joseph, had started the nursery with a few employees. By the time de Candolle reached them, they employed one hundred men. Augustin Baumann was in charge of the orchards and agricultural side of the firm. Joseph dealt with the ornamental plants.

De Candolle saw several types of *Robinia pseudoacacia,* one with blue flowers, and many other exotic plants from South Africa and North America. He was impressed by Baumann's careful methods to ensure germination. Baumann explained to de Candolle how to encourage a hydrangea to have blue flowers. The brothers may have been in a quiet country area, but they were superb professionals.

It is possible that Lemoine learned the technique of hand-fertilizing plants to obtain new varieties from Baumann, who was one of the earliest nurserymen to do deliberate hybridizing or plant breeding, not just selection of attractive variations in existing plants. Baumann issued new camellias and roses, among many other flowers.

Lemoine next went to Van Houtte in Gand (more commonly known to English speakers as Ghent), Belgium. Van Houtte was another one of the specialists who received plants from explorers all over the world. When he was older, Lemoine thought that this had been the most formative of all his experiences.

Van Houtte was a skilled horticulturist, an artist, and a scholar. He published *Flore des Serres et des Jardins de l'Europe* (Greenhouse and garden flowers in Europe) at regular intervals in fascicles, describing and naming the new exotic material as it arrived.[10] He had himself traveled in Brazil on a planthunting expedition for the king of Belgium.

Finally, Lemoine spent another unknown amount of time in Esquermes near Lille, with the firm of D'Auguste Miellez. Once again he left almost no record of why he went or how long he stayed.

Auguste Miellez (1809–1860) was also a very important person in the horticulture field. He bred many excellent peonies, for example, and clearly understood what was involved. Quite possibly he influenced Lemoine when it came to breeding peonies. His father, Louis-Xavier Miellez, was heavily involved with rose breeding, particularly gallicas.

After Lemoine finished the apprentice period, he immediately made it clear that he was going to do new and different things. In 1849 he bought a small piece of land in Nancy, forty miles away from the family business, and opened his own nursery in the Rue de l'Hospice. He obtained the money from his father.

Nancy was a good choice. The textile industry was expanding rapidly, and the town was prosperous. The merchant class supported thirteen horticulturists and four nurseries, as well as forty market gardens for produce. In spite of his impressive credentials, it took Lemoine a little longer than one would expect to become established.

Lemoine was a taciturn man, not given to recording very much about himself. The reason for the slow start may have been because of his broad ambition. Possibly he did not want to grow the obvious things that the public buys. He began almost immediately to select and crossbreed certain flowers. Those readers who remember the story of Dr. "Franceschi" (Emanuele Fenzi) in Santa Barbara will recall that he too was so devoted to science and rare varieties that he never made very much money.[11] In Lemoine's case, this state of affairs did not last very long.

By 1852 he was selling the first documented double flower he had produced, a double purslane, possibly *Portulaca grandiflora,* originally from Brazil. The purslane was the reason there was a brief mention of Lemoine's name in *Revue Horticole.* This was the first time his name appeared in a horticultural publication.

By 1854, there was a double potentilla, 'Gloire de Nancy'. The actual species with which he worked is not recorded. Within a few years, he began to prosper; by 1855, he had bought a much larger piece of land opposite the railroad station. There he was able to indulge his passion for selecting and hybridizing on a grand scale but also had room to provide the standard stock everyone wanted.

Lemoine married a woman from his home village, Marie Louise Gomieu (1834–1905), and they had three children within four years. The youngest was his son, Emile (1862–1942), who inherited many of the same qualities and talents that made Lemoine so remarkable. Emile's two elder sisters never married and had no children, but he married one of his Gomieu cousins. Their son, Henri, was also an important plant breeder and horticulturist.

One must not overlook the significant contribution made by Lemoine's wife, Marie Louise. She was a countrywoman, familiar with gardens and growing things, but her husband also taught her the precise techniques needed to crossbreed flowers. She did it extremely effectively. The tools they used were very simple and easily available to anyone: a watercolor paintbrush, fine pincers, a needle, and small scissors.

The family owned the firm until Henri closed it in 1968. Born in 1897, he lived on until 1982. The Lemoines had weathered the great tragedies of the Franco-Prussian War (1870–1871), the First World War (1914–1918), and the Second World War (1939–1945) but were defeated by the post–World War II peace. Precisely what happened is unclear, but in part their fading fortunes may have come about because they did not adapt to the new circumstances.

One anecdote has come down from that period. When a distinguished German horticulturist, Gerd Krüssmann, asked to see the nursery after the war, the Lemoines refused to admit him.

Their catalogues had never made any concessions to charm or popular taste, but after 1946 they became even more spartan. The dull white paper with its plain black print was replaced by thin "utility" (austerity) paper, the only kind permitted by the French government during the agonizing phase of reconstruction. This was also the only type of paper allowed in England at the time. Curiously, the postwar catalogues were written in English. The huge range of varieties was drastically pruned, and the whole pamphlet consisted of only two or three pages. This serves as a clear indication that the firm was probably no longer viable.

Victor Lemoine remained extremely active until the 1890s but then started to slow down. The work was continued by his son, Emile. During the Franco-Prussian War, when food was almost nonexistent and the news consistently bad, the Lemoines consoled themselves by going into the nursery and breeding a new race of lilac. It was a release from distress. Later plant varieties were issued under the name Lemoine, but in fact the work was largely Emile's by then.

Lemoine was a very civic-minded man, serving for more than eighteen years as a municipal councilor. He supported the planting of trees in the streets and managed the affairs of the town's parks.

Besides the stream of new varieties with which he enriched so many gardens, he left another legacy. Lemoine, together with François Félix Crousse (1840–1925), started the Nancy Horticultural Society (Société Central d'Horticulture de Nancy), based on the model from Paris, Societé National d'Horticulture de France (SCHN). Founding an institution of this sort has immense importance in the development of a branch of science or industry. The European countries, including Great Britain, were small enough and homogeneous enough to benefit from centralized societies.

The United States was too large and sprawling to give rise to similar organizations in the earlier years. The closest equivalent was the Massachusetts Horticultural Society, founded by C. M. Hovey in 1834. There was no American Horticultural Society until 1911.

The SCHN was a very serious organization, holding annual flower shows with prizes and awards and keeping meticulous records of each event and meeting. The secretary was another nurseryman, Ernest Gallé, a most forthright and earnest individual. He did not hesitate to express himself forcibly when he disagreed with Lemoine, or anyone else, for that matter.

As the stream of hybrids and modified flowers gushed out of Lemoine's premises, Gallé questioned the constant need to make all these changes. He thought that many of the predecessors had been glorious and worthwhile and had barely been digested by the industry before being displaced again and again. This was actually a good point.

At this stage, one enters the realm of superlatives. Discovering Lemoine's monumental achievements sparked the creation of this book. Two hundred and fourteen cultivars of lilac are attributed to the Lemoines. Almost all of them were commercially viable. As noted previously, Lemoine started to breed lilacs in 1870.

He had had a rather unassuming lilac bush in his garden for several years, with bluish double flowers, *Syringa vulgaris* L. 'Azurea Plena'. Another Belgian nurseryman, Libert-Darimont of Liège, had introduced the plant back in 1843. Breeding from this plant had been in the back of Lemoine's mind for a while, and that was why he had bought it.

The story of that first year of crossbreeding is illuminating. The ovaries in lilac flowers are often hard to find. It required the fine eyesight and steady hand of Mme. Lemoine to put the *S. oblata* pollen on the *S. vulgaris* ovary correctly. The next year they recovered seven seeds. When they planted these seeds, they began to get more specimens with which to work. Gradually they built up a series of crosses until the pool was big enough.

Turkish *S. vulgaris* and the Chinese *S. oblata* Lindl., collected by Robert Fortune in 1856 for the Horticultural Society, were the commonest but not the sole lilacs available at the time. The late Thomas Brown compiled an extremely useful list of lilacs available before 1900.[12] Examining a few pre-1870 French and Belgian catalogues shows that there were numerous other lilacs in commerce. Baltet Frères claimed to have fifty varieties. Auguste van Geert said he had "many" but gave no specifics.

In Germany, Ernst Benary and Haage & Schmidt also offered several varieties of lilac. None of these must have been too exciting, because in a short time Lemoine dominated the field. The Lemoine cultivars were the first to have showier double flowers and a wider range of colors.

After further breeding, the whole race of "French Hybrids" was created and formed the foundation of the modern lilac with giant double flowers. From 1878 to 1900, sixty-seven lilac cultivars were introduced by the house of Lemoine.

Another sixty-four varieties were released between 1900, when Victor Lemoine was seventy-eight, and 1911, the year he died. Emile and later his son, Henri, released sixty-two cultivars between 1912 and 1933. It is hard to know which of them bred any particular plant. The transition was seamless.

From lilac one can go to almost any other frequently grown garden plant and find the hand of Victor Lemoine. The transformation of the straggly little pelargonium into the giant scarlet geraniums so beloved of municipal parks departments began in 1866. Lemoine released the first double scarlet zonal plants that year, *Pelargonium* 'Gloire de Nancy'. A couple of years later he released *P.* 'Mme Lemoine', a double cherry-pink flower, and *P.* 'Le Vesuve', a double red flower. The Pelargonium Society of England awarded him a prize in 1877.

Although the lilac fanciers hug Lemoine to their bosom, the tuberous begonia put his name on the world stage. Lemoine did not initiate the begonia

Syringa 'Edith Cavell', a lilac cultivar by the Lemoine family.
Reproduced by permission of Freek Vrugtman (Peart and Walton, photographers)

frenzy. Starting in 1867, Veitch in England introduced six species of tuberous begonia. The French nurseryman Felix Crousse led the way in volume of tuberous begonias; he grew at least ten thousand plants a year in his fields.

When William Lobb seemed to disappear in North America (see chapter 5), James Veitch recruited another young gardener, Richard Pearce, in his place. Pearce (1836–1868) was far more personable than the Lobbs. He wrote long informative letters from the field and was even seen to smile occasionally.

Pearce found the exciting begonia *B. boliviensis* A.DC. in Bolivia, in 1864. The next year he sent home *B. pearcei* Hook. from Bolivia, important because of its yellow flowers. This was followed by *B. veitchii* Hook.f. Two more species were found by other collectors, but the final ancestor, *B. davisii* Veitch ex Hook.f., was sent to Veitch by their Mr. Davis in 1876.

James Veitch died while Pearce was out in the field. The younger Veitch wrote to Pearce and promised to honor his late father's agreement. This was very generous of Veitch but despite that, still smiling and bowing, Pearce came back and defrauded young Veitch by trading behind his back with Sir William Hooker at Kew in such a way that there was nothing young James could do about it except to discharge Pearce and stamp his feet impotently.[13] Pearce simply moved to the nursery across the street in Chelsea and began collecting for that firm. He died at the age of thirty-two while traveling in South America.

It is unlikely that Lemoine knew about these unpleasantnesses. He just happily bred the different strains of begonia. With a few hundred here and a few hundred there, pretty soon the numbers begin to add up. Lemoine took up gladiolus in the 1880s, adding *G. purpureo-auratus* to the strain. It is said that he bred almost four hundred gladiolus cultivars over the course of his career. One benefit of Lemoine's breeding gladiolus was the introduction of the warm brown tint that extended the range of colors.

Victor Lemoine started out with a vision of how he wanted certain species to look. He had the technical skill, the powers of observation, and the memory, persistence, and patience to carry it all to fruition. Even more amazing was the way he communicated this fervor to his son and grandson. A great many of the varieties attributed to Victor were actually the work of Emile, but that is not important. Next time you are in a nursery or looking out over your garden, think of Lemoine and his hybrids.

GEORGE RUSSELL

In 1911, when he was fifty-four years old, George Russell (1857–1951) was a jobbing gardener barely making ends meet. While working in one of his clients' gardens he saw a vase of lupins on his employer's kitchen table. For some inexplicable reason, he immediately recognized that the flowers' form needed improvement and that he was the one who was going to do it. Even polished and articulate people have difficulty in explaining how such moments arise, and Russell was neither polished nor articulate.

He was born in a small Yorkshire village, Stillington, the son of a cobbler. Although life was very spartan, his father was sufficiently well off to enjoy two newspapers each day and took his son to the village flower show in season. This instilled a love of plants and flowers into him very early. Becoming a gardener was a logical choice.

George received as much education as was possible in the circumstances. The National Education Act was not enacted until 1870, and compulsory primary education had not yet begun.

He started to work for Backhouse, a distinguished nursery in York. This firm was noted for its tropical plants, alpine plants, fruit trees, and many types of hardy plants. Backhouse regularly issued very impressive catalogues. It was a good place for an apprentice and journeyman gardener.

From there he moved to Lincoln and worked for the Pennells, another solid and successful nursery. All this training and experience were important to him. Once he married, he moved back to York and lived with his wife and son. Then Mrs. Russell developed a serious illness. In order to look after her, he left the nursery and became a jobbing gardener. This allowed him more flexibility with his hours and possibly a little more money.

Unfortunately, she died and he was left a widower. No one has been able to find out what happened to George Russell's son.[14] Archivists in the City of York have tried to trace him without success.

Russell continued to work for several employers, and it was in a Mrs. Micklethwaite's kitchen in 1911 that his epiphany was said to occur. The lupins available to the public at the time were probably the California perennial, *Lupinus polyphyllus*. The plants grow to be very tall and rather lax, with colors ranging from violet and blue in the wild to pink and white in commerce.

George Russell with some of his lupins, 1937. Russell transformed the garden lupin. Few now remember his name.

Reproduced by permission of Pat Edwards (artist unknown)

Pat Edwards, the woman who led the fight to revive the lupins long after Russell's death, wrote in her brief biography of Russell that Baker's Nurseries in Wolverhampton listed their "Old Fashioned Lupin" in white and pink for sixpence each in 1909.[15] She believes that these could have been the flowers on Mrs. Micklethwaite's table.

Chance favoring the prepared mind is an overworked cliché, but no other expression can explain what happened next so well. This was no wide-eyed amateur suddenly seeing the flowers anew. In his spare time, Russell worked on his allotment like so many other men, growing vegetables but also crossing *Aquilegia* (columbines) as a hobby.

The fact that it was the lupin that caught his eye is less significant than that he was ready to take on a challenge. There is a difference in degree but not in kind between his obsession and that of the Duke of Devonshire with orchids. In those days, to be fifty-four was to be considered quite old. Russell was probably a lonely man but did not seem to be depressed. He never re-married. His neighbor Mrs. Heard took care of his housekeeping, and he repaid her by taking her ailing son, Arthur, always subsequently known as "Sonny," under his wing. Russell called him Sonny, as so often is the case with little boys, and the name stuck.

Russell set out to create his ideal lupin: a consistently perennial plant, compact and free of disease. It should be available in all possible colors, and each spike should be so packed with florets that the stem was completely oc-cluded from sight. In order for that to happen, the floret had to be enlarged with a large fat bell, or keel, and the posterior petals, or standards, should stand straight up. If they folded forward or backward, they diminished the effect. Forward folding created a "hood." If the plant itself were sturdy and compact, there would be no need for staking. Deadheading should allow the plant to go on flowering and prevent it from setting seed.

Careful readers will see some resonance with the sweet pea, another le-guminous plant with a keel and standards. The standards on the sweet pea formed the hood. Henry Eckford bred that out in his Grandifloras.

Russell had to have had the vision in his head, the "vision of loveliness." Everything he did, every step he took, came from within himself in a steady progression of sure-footed moves. He does not seem to have had mentors or discussions with like-minded people.

Afterward, Russell's vision was transmitted by "Sonny" Heard, his in-formal apprentice and apostle. Sonny had listened carefully over the years and could repeat everything exactly as he heard it to Mrs. Edwards and other people who wanted to restore the line long after Russell's death. Heard's career reflects a path similar to that of the great American botanist John

Torrey in New York. Amos Eaton, a leading botanist of the time, was put in jail, probably for debt, and Torrey was the son of the jailer. Eaton instructed the eager boy by the hour. Chance placed the two in proximity.

There was a considerable choice of lupin species, and there were some early hybrids in England at the time. James Kelway had crossed *L. polyphyllus* with a tree lupin, *L. arboreus*. The tree lupin has short spikes on a shrubby plant. The fragrant flowers may be blue or yellow. This could well have been a good place to start.

William Robinson listed about a dozen other species of lupins in his 1903 book *The English Flower Garden*.[16] Many were so similar that he thought they were not worth separating, but he noted that "the smaller annual lupins are very pretty." Their value for Russell lay in the fact that they offered a great array of colors.

In 1909 Backhouse also sold packages of lupin seed for threepence, a very modest sum even in those days and comparable to perhaps a quarter in the United States now. For that price, the purchaser received seeds of *L. albococcineus nanus* (crimson and white, from the Levant), *L. cruikshanksii* (dark blue and white, from the Peruvian Andes), *L. hartwegii* (royal blue, from Mexico), *L. hybridus atrococcineus* (scarlet with white tips), *L. mutabilis roseus* (rose/apricot, from South America), *L. nanus* (blue and white, short, from California), and *L. sulphureus* (old gold/bronze). In short, Russell had almost every color he needed except for yellow. His solution for that was to use an annual lupin, *L. luteus*. This plant came from southern Europe and had been in England for four hundred years.

A few of these three-penny packages started him off. He also may have written to nurseries in other countries for additional strains. The number of seedlings resulting from all these plants being pollinated by the bees grew very fast, and he soon needed to request a second allotment. In England, residents of a community were entitled to the use of strips of the town's land, or an "allotment," for their personal recreation. This system goes back to medieval times. After the railroads were laid down in the nineteenth century, the otherwise useless strips of land on each side of the railbed were commonly used as allotments.

Russell refused to entertain any payment for his work. He never wanted to sell his plants, despite being offered very high prices. His pride was very strong. By the mid-1930s, even though he was over eighty, Russell continued to purify the strains and cast his merciless eye over the seedlings with as much rigor as ever.

Finally one very persuasive nurseryman, James Baker of Codsall, penetrated the protective shield and arranged to buy the entire line on the condition that "Sonny" Heard should go with the plants as manager and curator of the collection. Russell undertook to pass his remaining goals and methods on to Heard in return for being able to do what he did best without any financial worries for the rest of his life. Baker's argument that keeping the lupins to himself was selfishness stung Russell, and he capitulated easily.

World War II and Russell's death in 1951 led to the decline of the lupins. Baker died, and the nursery was run by men with fixed ideas and no imagination. For many years the lupins were neglected and, worse than that, became infected with the cucumber mosaic virus. Michael Edwards tried working there for a time but could not overcome this inertia.

Instead, Michael and Pat Edwards bought nearby Ashworth Nurseries in the late 1950s. Twenty years later they bought what was left of Bakers, by then a division of Bee's. They found a very sorry situation. The Edwards attempted to restore the line, a heartbreakingly slow business. It was compounded by Michael Edwards's untimely death in 1986.

Mrs. Edwards consulted Arthur Heard and under his guidance learned how Russell had achieved his results. Now the collection is listed as a heritage site under the National Council for the Conservation of Plants and Gardens for the lupin. One key to the collection's success is the constant vigilance for genetic drift and renewal of the varieties by removing anything less than perfect.

Heard passed Russell's methods along to Mrs. Edwards completely unalloyed. She sometimes found herself pleading for one or another attractive plant, but he was inexorable, just as Russell had been—"Out with it!"

In 2004, Arthur Heard's daughter, Mrs. Barlow, lent the City of York a scrapbook her father had created, with the history of the Russell lupin laid out in letters, newspaper clippings, and other memorabilia. It was used as the basis of an exhibition and was very well received by the public.[17] A very ancient city, York had not previously recognized the striking achievements of one of its native sons.

Mrs. Edwards's biography of George Russell contains many brilliantly colored photographs of the flowers at their peak.

SUTTONS SEEDS

The firm of Sutton, seedsmen of Reading, also basked in the reflected glory of royal patronage. In the 1890s, their catalogues showed facsimiles of letters from Buckingham Palace, always very effective with the British public. Like so many of the other companies examined here, Suttons remained in family hands for several generations. Photographs of the three brothers, Martin J., Arthur H., and Leonard Sutton (Martin Hope Sutton's sons), with their cousin Herbert appeared proudly inside the covers of the catalogues.

Sweet peas were one aspect of their success, but the business had been founded on the more mundane and indispensable seeds for wheat and agricultural crops by their grandfather John Sutton in 1806 and consolidated by their father, Martin Sutton, through the 1830s. Martin Hope Sutton (1815–1901) had very scholarly leanings and a great love of botany as a boy but had to subordinate his own desires to the urgent needs of his father's business.

Once conditions improved, he expanded the firm's range to include flowers and began to show his skill and originality. He opened the first testing ground in the country and joined the Royal Horticultural Society in 1834.

The seed business was controlled very tightly by cartels in London, and outsiders were prevented from participating. Martin very cleverly went around them, developing his own networks of growers and suppliers in the West Country. He never depended on the corrupt London exchanges to succeed.

Some measure of recognition came in 1846 and 1847. The Irish potato blight, *Phytophtora infestans,* led to the devastating famine. The government of Sir Robert Peel, and later Lord John Russell, called upon Sutton to provide the seeds of vegetables that would grow quickly and overcome the loss of the potato. Many more orders for such vegetables continued to pour in after the crisis passed.

One of the results of the cartels was that seeds were commonly adulterated, and very little could be done to change that. Martin Hope Sutton was a very upright man, an Evangelical Christian, and abhorred this cheating. The day always began with prayers. He made his staff discard all unsold seed at the end of the season and sell only fresh seed each year. (In the United States, Dexter Ferry adhered to the same standards and built an enviable reputation as a result.) Eventually Sutton led a campaign for laws to rid the industry of seed adulteration.

Sutton was also one of the first seedsmen to start improving the flowers and vegetables he sold, initially by selection. In 1840 he opened the first seed testing laboratory to check for purity and germination capacity. He gradually took over the firm from his father and by 1870 could say with some assurance that he had the largest and most successful seed company in the British Isles and even in Europe.

The catalogues reflect this superiority. The pages of the early years are adorned with very large engravings of sumptuous vegetables and contain many choices of novelty in all the major flower groups. Suttons also used colored pictures as soon as they could. In fact, they started the trend of sending catalogues by mail rather than exhibiting at the shows as a means of publicity. The cost of preparing the exhibits was far more than the value they could derive.

Every sort of flower tumbles off the pages: annuals, perennial shrubs, climbers. In 1897 they offered two pages of sweet peas and two pages of wallflowers. One could buy penstemons, phlox, primulas, and polyanthus, and that was just in the "Ps."

One can read between the lines and see that Martin Hope was a driven, rather difficult man. His brother Alfred could not tolerate the demands Martin made of him, even though Martin made the same demands of himself. As was true of so many Victorians, he had vaguely defined ill health, which manifested itself in odd ways, but he lived to a good age. Interestingly, many of these illnesses resulted in his getting something he did not like changed. Being an invalid was sometimes a position of strength in those pre-Freudian days. (Think of Florence Nightingale changing the face of nursing from her invalid couch.)

Flower breeding was done in-house by the staff he built up over the years of expansion. His son, Arthur, made a pilgrimage to Germany in 1887 to visit the Benary firm in Erfurt and obtain new plant material. When Sutton released new cultivars, they all had the prefix "Sutton." In 1907 there were more than four hundred varieties of sweet pea in the Sutton trials. As late as 1970, one still had a vast choice in sweet peas.

Most of the Sutton varieties were Spencers and had the term "Frilled" as a prefix: 'Frilled White', 'Frilled Sky Blue', and 'Frilled Cream' are some examples. They liked blue: 'Oxford Stripe', 'Cambridge Stripe', 'Imperial Blue Spencer', and 'Spencer White Striped Blue' are a few. (Oxford University teams wear dark blue uniforms, while Cambridge teams wear light blue. This is the meaning of these names.) Suttons did not introduce sweet pea varieties by the dozen or the hundred, but the ones they did introduce were very successful.

Even at the height of the sweet pea craze, Suttons, together with other serious houses, also offered many begonias. Learning to improve their skill with begonias was probably the reason Arthur went to Erfurt.

Both world wars affected Suttons very seriously. After World War II, labor was extremely short. They were reduced to seeking women employees, a radical move for this very traditional and male-dominated company. The 1941 catalogue and the 1946 catalogue tell of men killed and close friends lost. An acute shortage of paper prevented them from producing the usual large sheets; the pages were half size. The family is no longer directly involved in Suttons, but the company remains vigorous at over two hundred years of age.

LOUIS VAN HOUTTE

Victor Lemoine worked for Van Houtte soon after the latter had opened his establishment, though whether this was an apprenticeship or paid employment is unclear. He did not stay there very long, but it is certain that he learned a great deal simply by watching what was happening. Van Houtte eventually expanded on an enormous scale, something Lemoine's more frugal soul could not accept. Even when the Lemoine nursery was at its largest, he never had the acres of greenhouses and ponds his mentor built.

As a young man, Louis Van Houtte (1810–1876) worked in the Ministry of Finance in Brussels.[18] He spent all his free time studying plants, both at the botanical garden and at private estates. He was friendly with wealthy men like Parmentier, Parthon de Von, and D'Enghien, as well as local gardeners. His father had been a military engineer, and his mother expected him to follow a sedate and respectable career as a civil servant.

In November 1832, Van Houtte founded *The Belgian Horticulturist,* a monthly magazine. At roughly the same time, he opened a shop in Brussels to sell seeds and gardening equipment. He continued his study of plants and was especially interested in the tropical plants that had begun to pour into Europe.

Louis Van Houtte pioneered the development of nurseries on a very large scale. He taught Victor Lemoine.
Reproduced by permission of Luc D'Haeze

A year later, his wife died after they had been married for only a very short time. He was devastated and accepted an offer from Parthon de Von to go to Brazil and collect orchids and cactus. The king of the Belgians wanted orchids, and the botanical garden said it would take any new seeds. Van Houtte handed the magazine over to the well-known botanist Charles Morren and closed the shop.

On January 5, 1834, he sailed for Rio de Janeiro. The weather was so bad that he did not reach Rio until May 1834. The ship had stopped for a short time at Mayo, one of the Cape Verde Islands. While there, he explored the island and collected a few specimens.

Once at Rio, he visited the Tijuca mountains, climbed Corcovado, and explored Jurujuba on the other side of the bay. He went by himself and could not carry all the plants he found. When he went to the Organ Mountains, he hired a black porter, Domingo, to assist him. Later Domingo saved his life during one of the journeys, though it is unclear what happened.

Van Houtte stayed in the region for four months, as a guest of Mr. March, an English settler. The March hacienda was at a fairly high altitude. Van Houtte referred to this period of travel and exploration only once, in *Flore des Serres* in 1847. He commented on the geology, flora, and fauna in broad terms, without detail. Van Houtte had met another plant explorer, George Gardner, and noted in *Flore des Serres* that some of what he recollected had been part of Mr. Gardner's memories.

After returning to Rio de Janeiro, he left again for Minas Geraes, staying there for seven months. He was inspired by the continuously changing landscape, traveling from Villa-Rica to Ouro-Preto, from the land of palm trees to pine forests (*Araucaria brasiliensis*), at three thousand feet in elevation. Subsequently, Van Houtte visited Mato Grosso, De Goyaz, São Paulo, and Parana, sometimes botanizing with the English plant collector John Tweedie, whom he had met in Banda Orientale.

He spent a total of two years in Brazil and even though he seldom referred to the experience, it had made an indelible impression. In 1875, a year before his death, he concluded a study of *Araucaria brasiliensis* with the words "Adieu, Brazil, land of sweet reminiscences."

Van Houtte returned to Belgium at the end of 1836, with many botanical specimens. His achievements were so important that he was appointed the director of the Brussels Botanical Garden. He founded the Belgian Royal Horticultural Society, modeled on the one in London.

When he decided to open his own nursery at Gendbrugge les Gand near Ghent (Gand in Dutch), he took Adolf Papeleu as his partner.[19] They remained in business together until 1845. Papeleu came from a wealthy family and may have brought some financial backing with him. He had also been a plant explorer, in Central America, but his health failed and he had to return to Belgium. After the rupture, Papeleu moved to another town and branched out into arboriculture. That business ended in 1874.

Van Houtte founded his magazine *Flore des Serres et des Jardins de l'Europe* in 1845 and published a new volume annually until his death in 1876. The books were designed and created at his nursery in Ghent. This publication was very well received and enjoyed a vast circulation. Several excellent Belgian lithographers, including Severeyns, Stroobant, and De Pannemaker, worked for Van Houtte. They were able to print colored images from stone.

Ray Desmond has shown that van Houtte was not too scrupulous about where he contained copy and illustrations for *Flore des Serres*.[20] The whole of the first few issues consisted of articles lifted bodily from the English and French journals of the day. The most egregious case was when Van Houtte "hijacked" and printed an image of *Musa ensete* prepared for an 1861 issue of the London *Botanical Magazine,* without attribution and a year before it even appeared in England.

Van Houtte was a very important citizen of Ghent and served as mayor for almost twenty years.[21] He eventually married again and had a son, Louis Jr., and two daughters. The French rose breeder Jean-Claude Ducher named one of his cultivars for Louis's daughter Marie Van Houtte in 1871. It is a tea rose with delicate pink and white coloring. In 1910, the centennial of Van Houtte's birth, the city fathers of Ghent put on a splendid event, complete with poetry and recitations.

In the hothouses, Van Houtte grew palm trees, orchids, and ferns. He knew that ferns were destined to be valuable commercially. Pineapple was another valuable crop he could sell.

A newspaper report of a royal visit to the nurseries in 1840 noted that "the place was so vast that one needed a map." This comment must be taken with a pinch of salt: it was quite early in his career, and there had not been enough time to have expanded so fast.

Once Louis Van Houtte was in business, he depended on other plant collectors to send him specimens. At one time the great orchid collector Josef von Warscewicz worked for him, but von Warscewicz later preferred to deal with George Ure Skinner, an English orchid specialist. Van Houtte was quite annoyed by this.

He waited for a few years before going into hybridization seriously. This means that Lemoine would not have seen crossbreeding on a large scale when he was in Ghent in 1833. In 1843, Van Houtte began to work with calceolarias. He added petunias in 1846 and then azaleas in 1849. At the same time he received alstroemeria seed from the French consul in Chile, and he began to experiment with it. In 1865 he was the first European to receive seed of Peruvian alstroemeria. The Chilean hybrids never became very popular.

Those who have not heard of Louis Van Houtte for any other reason may still know that he was the first person on the Continent to get the giant water lily, *Victoria regia* (now *V. amazonica*), to flower. He built a special

LOUIS VAN HOUTTE'S COLLECTIONS AT HIS NURSERIES IN GHENT

(from Le Texnier, Louis van Houtte, 1911, translated by Judith M. Taylor)

V AN HOUTTE initially started only with camellias, geraniums, and azaleas but expanded rapidly. Within five years he had a huge establishment, presumably helped by credit from his banking friends.

In 1840 he added many azaleas as well as rhododendrons and dahlias from England. By 1843, he needed three greenhouses. In 1844, this number rose to four greenhouses. (Soon after Joseph Hooker's collections of Himalayan rhododendrons arrived in England, they spread rapidly throughout Europe. By 1868, van Houtte offered 138 varieties of rhododendrons and 277 kinds of azaleas.)

The seed business expanded fast. In 1843, he sold 1,400 varieties of seed of ornamental plants and 400 types of vegetable seed. There were ornamental alliums, hyacinths, and so forth.

His open-air stock included phlox, potentillas, lobelias, peonies, carnations, verbenas, and delphiniums, many pansies (from England), strawberries, as well as deciduous and evergreen trees and shrubs. There were 900 varieties of conifers and 1,700 varieties of roses.

The unheated greenhouses held calceolarias, fuchsias, verbenas, cinerarias, petunias, and also orange and lemon trees. There were numerous cacti, about 225 varieties. Van Houtte also introduced Cape heather from England (175 varieties).

Louis Van Houtte built extensive nurseries, where one of his employees was the first person in Europe to get this water lily, *Victoria amazonica,* to flower.
Reproduced by permission of Luc D'Haeze

hothouse for it and put a talented young assistant, Edouard Ortgies, in charge. Ortgies also hybridized more aquatic plants. The water lily flowered for the first time in 1847. The seed came from the Duke of Devonshire at Chatsworth, where it had already flowered. Van Houtte took this as a challenge.

Van Houtte was always very interested in aquatic plants. James Bidwill had found a handsome blue water lily, *Nymphaea gigantea,* in northwestern Australia. When Van Houtte introduced this plant at the Universal Exposition in 1855, he won his fourteenth gold medal.

He employed another remarkable assistant, Benedict Roezl, in his propagation department. Roezl later lost his left arm in an industrial accident in Cuba, but this did not end his career. Afterward when he collected orchids in the South American hinterlands, the natives were terrified by the sight of his hook and hastened to do everything he wanted.[22] The principal hybridizer was François de Taye. Van Houtte believed that the prizes the firm won in Brussels, London, and Ghent were due to de Taye's efforts.

Roezl helped Van Houtte hybridize begonias starting by crossing *Begonia xanthina* × *B. rubro-venia* Hook. (now *B. hatacoa* var. *hatacoa*). When they received *B. rex*, they crossed it with *B. reichehemi* (obsolete nomenclature) in 1859. The following year, two other assistants bred *B. rex* with *B. xanthina* and *B. griffithii*. The offspring were very successful commercially.

Van Houtte worked with *Barbacenia* Vand., a small, slightly unobtrusive plant that had come from Brazil in 1788, introducing a hybrid in 1856. His staff crossed other plants, too, such as weigela and deutzia, both of which Lemoine used for hybridization. In the 1870s, Van Houtte's nursery turned to tuberous begonias, using the species brought from South America by Veitch's men.

Van Houtte spent a lot of time on the azalea and eventually brought out more than nine hundred cultivars. In the end he suppressed many of them because they were not acceptable. Van Houtte's work on the camellia remains important. He was active during the height of interest in the camellia. H. Harold Hume comments that this peaked by about 1860 and became dormant for many years before recurring in the twentieth century.[23]

As if all this were not enough, Van Houtte hybridized roses very successfully. He kept his eye on business, and roses always brought good prices. To make sure the firm succeeded, he created separate facilities and put separate staff in charge. Well-known rose breeders of the period considered him to be a serious contender.

The other enterprise that enshrines Van Houtte's name is his school of horticulture. He had enormous vision and knew that by attracting ambitious young people he would increase the scope and range of his work. The school began officially in 1849, shortly after Lemoine had left.

Those who knew Van Houtte closely considered his personality to be rather crude. He used colorful or perhaps one should say "off-color" language freely but was open and frank in his dealings with other men. His energy and application were prodigious. The records show that he was at the nursery first thing in the morning and did not leave until about 10 p.m.

In spite of all this extraordinary activity, we do not really associate any one plant with Van Houtte in the same way we associate lilac with Lemoine. His contributions lay in the dissemination of ideas and developing good commercial practices. It is perhaps interesting that he was born in the same year as the great composers Chopin and Schumann. There is a statue of Van Houtte in the town of Ghent, but almost nothing else remains to mark his existence. After his death, his widow and children carried on until 1889. The business then became a corporation.

World War I caused everyone great difficulties. Belgium hung on the edge of famine because of the German blockade. In 1920 the business was transferred to another important nurseryman, Charles Pynaert. Finally the city of Ghent bought what was left of the old Van Houtte premises in 1951 and turned them into a public park.

VILMORIN-ANDRIEUX

The seed house Vilmorin-Andrieux has been at the same address in Paris for more than two hundred years. Philippe-Victoire Vilmorin (1746–1804) founded the firm in 1775 after marrying the daughter of Pierre Andrieux, a seedsman and botanist in the quai de la Mégisserie. Andrieux's wife, Claude Geoffroy, was the expert. Together they became the suppliers of seed to Louis XV, a huge advantage in those days. What happened at court set the standard for everyone else. Philippe-Victoire was a physician with a keen interest in plants. The firm prospered for six generations, but about thirty-five years ago it was sold to a large conglomerate and is now part of Groupe Limagrain.

At the outset, Vilmorin-Andrieux concentrated on agricultural seed. Philippe-Victoire's sons and grandsons developed important strains of sugar beets and carrots. These were very astute business decisions and allowed Philippe-André (1776–1862) to move his family into an elegant château at Verrières, a former hunting lodge of Louis XIV's, in 1815. They and their descendants transformed the park, designed by André Le Nôtre, into an outstanding arboretum. This move could have been eased by the flight of its former aristocratic owners during the revolution. Vilmorin must have played his cards very cleverly to avoid being executed, in light of his association with the royal house.

Louis Vilmorin (1816–1860) did the work on the sugar beet at Verrières. His son Henry was an authority of the genetics of wheat. Henry understood plant genetics very early and contributed to the advance of that science. The Vilmorins maintained a key collection of potatoes. The company added ornamental plants very early and became known for its roses, introducing new varieties for many years. One or another of the Vilmorin brothers was always in demand as a judge or a speaker at floral society events. They often won prizes at chrysanthemum shows.

In the twentieth century, the sons continued to manage the firm, while Louise, the only girl, rebelled, becoming an avant-garde poet and novelist. She married and moved to the United States. In the complex shifts among large commercial horticultural enterprises over two hundred years, Vilmorin-Andrieux is one of the few companies that remained in business into the recent past. Its founders would not recognize it, but adapting to change and moving forward are the qualities of successful firms.

Flower Breeders in the United States

THE CHOICE OF a relatively modest number of people for this chapter is by no means intended to slight the veritable array of distinguished flower breeders in the United States. Many of them are discussed in the chapters on individual flowers. The flower breeders introduced in this chapter all had additional exceptional characteristics.

GEORGE BALL

George Ball (1874–1949) founded a remarkable dynasty. He combined great skill as a horticulturist with business acumen, a pairing not often seen. His legacy is the vertically integrated BallFloraPlant (Seed) Company, owned and run by his granddaughter, Anna Ball. Her brother, George, now owns the Burpee Seed Company.

George Ball Sr. started with a florist's shop in Chicago and began to breed new varieties of flowers to sell to his customers. In 1923 he introduced several new varieties of sweet pea.

Eventually he switched entirely to the wholesale business, finding it much more satisfactory than retail. He bought more land and expanded until he acquired a large property in West Chicago, where the firm's headquarters remain.

George Ball was a very methodical man. He kept a daily diary, which has recently been published by his family. It reveals his concerns, his plans and wishes, and how he got things done. The diary is a very valuable document.

Keeping on top of trends and developments in horticulture meant that he had to travel very widely. Every year he would go either to Europe or to the Far East. In this way, he cemented warm friendships and made new ones. The Benary family had very similar interests, and both George and his wife, Anna, visited them in Erfurt. Sometimes the Benarys would go to the United States.

World War II interrupted this relationship, but it did not fray. Once the war was over, they resumed their visits until George Ball's death. Ball also visited California, where much of the firm's seed was grown.

LUTHER BURBANK

If you ask members of the public whether they have heard of any flower breeders, chances are they will mention Luther Burbank. He has an indelible reputation. "The Wizard of Santa Rosa" captured the public imagination in the early 1900s, and the attraction has never dimmed.

Luther Burbank (1849–1926) was the eldest child of Samuel Burbank and his third wife, Olive Ross, a relative of the Burpees. He had twelve older half siblings from the first two Mesdames Burbank and two younger full siblings. Burbank was born on a farm in Lancaster, Massachusetts, in Worcester County. He did not seem to be a particularly promising child. One of his much older half sisters was the schoolteacher in their small town, but he paid very little attention to formal lessons. The exceedingly shy young Burbank was usually to be found roaming the fields and countryside around their farm rather than doing his homework indoors. Still, it is clear he learned enough to read widely later on.

The constant observation of nature and farming taught him a great deal, and in his late teens he used his share of his father's bequest to buy a small piece of land. He revealed the astuteness of his mind when he focused on growing potatoes, which at that time brought in a very good return. Burbank thought he could improve the tuber and its yield by doing some crossbreeding.

His empirical approach was bolstered by independent learning from books. Burbank was fortunate that the librarian at the Lancaster Pubic Library was open-minded and stocked the controversial works of Charles Darwin. *The Variations of Animals and Plants under Domestication* appeared in the United States in 1869, just as Burbank was forming his plans.[1] It explained the value of backbreeding and other methods to obtain pure lines.

Burbank made a number of crosses using the potato variety 'Early Rose' and noticed an unusual seed ball on one of the offspring. When he planted these seeds the resulting tubers were exceptionally large. This was truly a major find and changed one aspect of commercial agriculture for good. Burbank always said he was committed to improving food both quantitatively and qualitatively. This was his opening shot, before he was twenty-one years old. Over the next few years he propagated his new cultivar and grew bumper crops of the improved potato.

The image we have of an unsophisticated hayseed on his remote farm is partially dispelled by the fact that in 1875 he sold the rights to his cultivar outright to a local farmer for $150 and moved to California. It is clear he had been observing and thinking about the national scene. He knew enough about California to understand he could improve his lot by moving there. The naïveté showed in his business arrangement. A cannier man would have made a more favorable deal than an outright sale of the rights. In subsequent years he paid closer attention to the business side of new crops. At first he worked for a nursery in Petaluma, but in 1877 he opened his own business.

The influence of his mother was very important. Shortly after Luther left Massachusetts, Olive Burbank moved to Santa Rosa and lived with her son for the rest of her life, jettisoning her other children. She had been a very strict stepmother to the older Burbank children and she ruled every aspect of Luther's life. He appears to have acquiesced in this and in fact probably felt it gave him cover in unpleasant situations. She wore the "black hat" in delivering harsh verdicts, and he could insouciantly wear the white hat.

Burbank always said that Santa Rosa was a fragment of heaven down on earth. Whatever he put in the ground flourished. He was particularly interested in orchard fruits and nuts. His output of new forms of fruits and nuts was extraordinary. Perhaps the best known is the Santa Rosa plum, based on a new type of plum tree recently imported from Japan.

He paid a great deal of attention to flowers. The culmination of this was the development of the ubiquitous Shasta daisy (*Leucanthemum × superbum*, 'Becky'). Burbank improved many bulbous plants such as *Amaryllis, Hippeastrum, Crinum,* and *Lilium.* Lilies were some of his favorites. They were one of the reasons he was drawn to California.

One of the sources for the wild species he needed for his breeding program was Carl Purdy of Ukiah, north of Santa Rosa. Purdy was a prominent nurseryman and plant collector, an outstanding horticulturist, and one of the few people who could keep Burnbank's ego in check. He collected wild California lilies to sell for a profit, and while not understanding the long-term effects of his decimating the natural species for his personal gain, was still clear eyed when it came to Burbank's activities.

David Griffiths, who created the "Bellingham Hybrids" twenty years later, claimed he was inspired by Burbank.[2] One of the reasons none of Burbank's lilies survived was lack of resistance to pests. The Bellinghams did better.

Not everything worked out well. The spineless cactus appeared to be such a good idea when he bred it. It was supposed to let cattle thrive in the arid Southwest where grass was not abundant. The cactus did its part by growing well, but it did not nourish the cattle and many of them began to die.

In *The Garden of Invention,* Jane Smith lays out the background of many of Burbank's finds and examines how he marketed them skillfully.[3] In spite of the veneer of shyness, he was a clever and effective self-promoter, regularly corresponding with the important political figures of the day. Theodore Roosevelt paid him a visit in his special train. Henry Ford came to see for himself how Burbank did it. Albert Einstein said he was a savior of mankind.

Burbank's reputation has waxed and waned over the century since he died. From the dizzy peaks of the 1920s when he could do no wrong, his contributions have been assessed and reassessed. The principal complaint against him, which cannot be ignored, is that he kept no notes and thus his work cannot be duplicated. No one can say for sure what he actually did. In many cases he used artificial pollination, but in others he used his gimlet eye in selecting promising new seedlings from open pollination. He was brilliantly ruthless in making his choices and destroyed all material he did not use in enormous bonfires at the end of the season.

Burbank's lack of education was one reason he did not understand the value of keeping records. The other was his intense secrecy based on an almost paranoid fear of being copied or forestalled. All his employees had to empty their pockets every evening when they went home.

Right now Burbank is on an upswing. Scientists agree he did not use scientific method but still believe he made a gigantic contribution. In a recent article, Neal Anderson and Robert Olsen argue that his methods of financing new cultivars and the germplasm he left behind are the basis of all subsequent flower breeding.[4] They estimate that he worked with ninety-one genera of flowers and introduced about one thousand new cultivars into the market. Almost none of these are still in commerce apart from the Shasta daisies.

Seemingly larger than life, Luther Burbank did not do well with strangers. This did not stop him from marrying a very worldly and attractive woman he met on a train and, of course, living to rue the day. His second wife, Elizabeth, was much younger than he was and an altogether more suitable mate even if only because she understood how to coexist with his formidable mother. Olive Burbank was legendary, running her son's life down to the smallest daily detail.

W. ATLEE BURPEE

The story of how Burpee reached the position he did is of some interest. W. Atlee Burpee (1858–1915) was a most astute businessman. At the end of the 1890s, one of his traveling buyers saw the enormous agricultural and horticultural ferment in California and informed his employer. The firm mostly grew agricultural seed to feed animals.

Burpee showed his mettle very young. As a teenager he dealt in fine poultry, breeding exotic fowl and corresponding with many adults twice his age all over the country. It started as an avocation. Breeding fancy chickens was very fashionable in the 1870s. His family in Philadelphia was respectable and even distinguished. Papa Burpee expected his son go to college and enter one of the learned professions, not to become a poultry merchant. Fortunately, W. Atlee's mother had a soft spot for her wayward son and lent him enough money to set up in business.

As the chickens were dispersed across the United States, the purchasers often wrote to young Atlee asking what feed he used so that they too could coax the fowl into fine condition. He began supplying the grain and after a fairly short time realized he was making more money from the feed than from selling the chickens. From this, it was not a big step to growing his own feed and later other food and vegetable seed.

Burpee had apparently been thinking for some time about adding California to his holdings. He put together several parcels of desirable land on the Central Coast, in Lompoc and the surrounding valley. He sent his family to live in a simple house on the property and learn all they could. When he died in 1915, his son, David, was ready to take over.

The Burpees noticed that ornamental plants were very lucrative and moved into that field. Sweet peas were one of the first vehicles (see chapter 6). David had great gifts in marketing. P. T. Barnum's precepts about the gullibility of the public impressed him deeply, and he took them to heart. After the sweet pea phase died down in the 1920s, he decided that the marigold should be the next popular flower. By sheer force of will David Burpee brought that about.

A competition fed the public's fancy, and the prospect of a fat prize excited a lot of attention. He offered ten thousand dollars for a perfectly white marigold. His money was safe for many years: not until 1975 did a farmer's wife in Iowa, Mrs. Alice Vonk, send him the winning plant. In the interim, he received lots of ivory and cream cultivars, which were not without charm.

He believed the crowning achievement would be to have the marigold named the national flower of the United States. To accomplish that he enlisted the help of Senator Everett Dirksen of Illinois in 1959, the minority leader of the Senate at the time. It is not clear why he chose Dirksen, though the senator was known to be a passionate gardener. Maybe it was because both were Republicans. Even Burpee's son Jonathan cannot say how it came about.

For years Burpee lobbied the senator, who at first was leery of getting involved. Burpee sent innumerable packets of marigold seed to many politicians and used every lever he could think of. The Illinois delegation wanted the corn tassel to be the national flower of the United States, and Dirksen could hardly pit himself against them. Eventually the senator came to believe very strongly in the virtues of the marigold and took the matter forward as far as he could. In the end it did not succeed and the senator died in 1969.

His widow wrote a memoir about her husband and called it *The Honorable Mr. Marigold.*[5] In 1986 President Reagan signed legislation making the rose the U.S. national flower.

David Burpee died in 1980 and the firm was sold. It passed through several corporations and now belongs to George Ball, grandson of the founder of the Ball company. In 2014 Senator Mark Kirk of Illinois planned to introduce a bill into Congress naming the marigold the emblem of the House and Senate, thereby trying to complete Burpee and Dirksen's work. Senator Kirk sits in the "Dirksen" seat. One of the supporting documents for this bill is the author's article "The Marigold in California."[6]

ELLWANGER AND BARRY

Ellwanger and Barry was the preeminent nursery in the United States in the nineteenth century. George Ellwanger settled in Rochester, New York, and laid down important standards for the nursery business. Many emigrants in California started orchards and gardens after the gold rush and ordered their plants from Ellwanger and Barry. The enormous distance led to uncertainties. It could take as much as six months for the saplings to reach California. The journey was very long and taxing for growing plants, and many plants died for different reasons, chiefly neglect.

One customer who had bad luck with her order was Eliza Farnham. This very strong and resourceful woman traveled to Santa Cruz in 1850 to occupy land left to her by her late husband, a lawyer who had hoped to move his family to the new territory.[7] She decided it was suited for orchard fruit and ordered her trees from Ellwanger and Barry. The journey took six months, and almost all her trees were dead when they arrived. Mrs. Farnham threw herself upon the mercy of her neighbors and was allowed to take cuttings from nearby orchards.

In spite of these problems, orchards in the western states prospered. After a while, the young trees survived because Ellwanger and Barry learned how to protect them for the long voyage. There were other nurseries involved, but Ellwanger and Barry held the lead for decades.

Rochester was an epicenter of horticulture and nurseries because of its location, which provided physical and climatic advantages. The East Coast was maturing, and energetic younger people were moving westward. Western New York was a land of opportunity, and "Clinton's Ditch" (the Erie Canal) contributed to that.

Ellwanger and Barry's nursery became the largest in the whole country and dominated the field until about 1900. The sheer number of acres, greenhouses, orchard fruit trees, berry canes, and grapevines, as well as seedlings germinated, rose cuttings rooted, and seasonal and permanent employees, was almost astronomical. Even today, with the advantages of computer controls, managing an enterprise of this size would be hard.

Its decline was ironically because of competition from the western states it had supplied so liberally. Patrick Barry's son took charge and did not spot what was happening. The firm failed to look for new markets. From 1900 to 1918, only two years were profitable. Nothing new was planted after 1912, when the younger Barry also died. By 1918 it had gone out of business. The huge property was subdivided for building lots, and there is nothing tangible left.

Ellwanger's most striking legacy is Highland Park, where John Dunbar later bred his lilacs. Ellwanger donated twenty acres of land for a park to the city of Rochester in 1888 as a gift and to showcase his nursery. Before his offer, Rochester had not even had a parks department. He stimulated this important function. The city fathers were very cool to the idea. They resurrected the old "What do the poor want with parks?" argument, but a leading physician in town who knew that the public was using the Mount Hope Cemetery as a place of recreation prodded City Hall into accepting the gift.

George Ellwanger

George Ellwanger (1816–1906) was born in Gross-Happach, Wurttemberg, Germany. His family had once owned profitable vineyards, but the long Napoleonic wars and a series of bad seasons left them in very poor circumstances. He needed to leave Wurttemberg just to earn a living, let alone have a career. In preparation for his bold move, George apprenticed himself for four years to a large nursery in Stuttgart. He planned to emigrate to America. It was essential to have a useful trade.

He arrived in the United States in 1835 and first traveled to Ohio because he had some relatives there. He traversed New York state by canal and saw Rochester briefly as they stopped to unload freight. The surroundings impressed him, and he recognized that horticulture, particularly orchards, would succeed in that region. An effective canal system carrying heavy goods to and from the lake emphasized this.

He was prescient. Rochester did indeed become a major center, both regional and national, although it was still embryonic when he got there. Many famous nurseries, such as that of James Vick, thrived in Rochester. There were so many that it was often called the "Flower City."

Another factor leading to its success was the onset of large-scale immigration from Europe. The Irish needed land even before the famine emptied the countryside, and the Germans also needed opportunity. This movement included skilled and semiskilled workers, not just the poverty-stricken peasants who came later in the "hungry forties." A flood of immigrants armed with Old World skills and culture arrived ready to work extremely hard in the New World. (A century later, in the 1930s, the flood of professional and artistic refugees from Nazi Germany brought equivalently unprecedented levels of culture to the United States.)

Ellwanger decided to move to Rochester. His English was still a bit weak, but his work was not totally dependent on knowing the language too well. (The career of the Moravian Frank Reinelt had a similar pragmatic foundation.)

At first Ellwanger worked for an established nursery, but in 1839 he opened his own business, Mount Hope Nursery. His skill and experience were the basis of a very successful partnership with Patrick Barry. Barry was more accomplished in horticulture than he was and a native speaker of English, but they formed a complementary team. Ellwanger often traveled to Europe and brought back new seeds and plants. He died in 1906. Ellwanger's son Henry (1850–1883) continued the work until his early death from typhoid. Henry became a noted authority on roses (see chapter 5).

Patrick Barry

Patrick Barry (1816–1890) was born in Ireland, near Belfast. Barry had had a more thorough academic education than Ellwanger. He managed to stay in school until he was eighteen, which was rather unusual for a poor boy at that time. He taught for a while, but in 1836 he too emigrated. He worked for a nursery at Flushing, on Long Island, learning the trade. By 1840 he was ready and joined Ellwanger in Rochester.

Barry wrote extensively. He edited *The Genesee Farmer* from 1844 to 1852 and *The Horticulturalist* from 1852 to 1854 and also wrote *Treatise on the Fruit Garden* and *Catalogue of the American Pomological Society*.[8]

He made enormous efforts to have fruit farming recognized as a serious endeavor, insisting on prizes being awarded at the state fair. The nursery introduced the idea of dwarf fruit trees, showing that a large tree used up so much energy producing woody branches and twigs that little was left for the fruit.

CLAUDE HOPE

The name of Claude Hope (1907–2000) is almost synonymous with the impatiens.[9] The approximately six hundred species of this large genus are found in tropical and semitropical regions, including Africa, India, and Southeast Asia.[10] Relatively few of them have been exploited horticulturally. Partly this is due to the workings of chance, that is, which particular species was available in Europe. One species, *Impatiens balsamina* L., was known in Europe quite early. Linnaeus named it in 1753. It was a very popular garden plant in the nineteenth century but slowly slipped out of favor.

Nothing much happened in the impatiens world for a long time, but the next species to come to everyone's attention, *Impatiens walleriana* Hook.f., lent itself to immense and gratifying modification. Sir Joseph Hooker wrote a definitive monograph on the impatiens in 1859, but very little practical work took place. The name "walleriana" commemorated the botanist Horace Waller, who traveled with David Livingstone in Africa, collecting plants as he went.

Once its potential was recognized, the results were so attractive that there was very little need to look for other species. It does have one drawback: it is not an easy plant with which to work. One of the principal challenges is the way the seedpod shatters on contact. This is, of course, the source of the name, "impatiens." Remarkably, in spite of this feature, numerous naturally occurring hybrids are found in the wild.[11]

The flowers are lovely, the plant thrives in the shade, it comes in dozens of colors, and it has a long blooming season and is easy to plant and grow, not being at all fussy about its culture, that is, almost foolproof. There are reasons something becomes a cliché. What had started out as a somewhat

Claude Hope made immense contributions to the development of impatiens and its worldwide popularity.
Reproduced by permission of Ball Horticultural

unlikely flower is now the mainstay of public and private gardens all over the world. Perfection actually becomes boring after a time.

Impatiens hawkeri was found in Papua New Guinea and provided the next golden opportunity for inspired crossings and a whole new range of glorious plants. The first commercial cultivars were released in 1970 and created a sensation. A Lieutenant Hawker of the Royal Navy was an English naval officer who found the plant in Papua New Guinea in 1884. *Impatiens hawkeri* 'Tango' came out in 1989.

Two firms revolutionized *I. walleriana* Hook.f. Breeders at the Ball Seed Company, Bob Reiman and William Marchant, worked on *I. walleriana* in the 1940s. Reiman introduced the first modern cultivar in 1956. They tamed its legginess and made it bushier, the key to modern success, and then handed their material on to Claude Hope.

Claude Hope's firm, the PanAmerican Seed Company, released the Elfin Series and the Super Elfin Series in 1968. Hope bred an additional eight colors in his series. The Elfins and Super Elfins led to the vast expansion of impatiens being used throughout the world. Curiously, although anecdotal evidence suggests that impatiens is one of the three leading floriculture crops in the United States, the U.S. Department of Agriculture did not collect accurate statistics on it until 1994.

In the 1970s, Toru Arisumi employed very complex methods to cross *I. walleriana* with *I. auricoma,* including colchicine to modify the chromosome count. New colors emerged—the softer apricots and corals that are so appealing.[12] Dr. Arisumi died in 2002.

Hope was a plant geneticist trained in the Texas and Michigan university systems. During World War II, he was ordered to serve in Costa Rica, evaluating the experimental *Cinchona ledgeriana* (Howard) Bern. Moens ex Trimen on plantations. The cinchona bark was desperately needed to supply quinine for troops fighting in malarial areas. Hope may have known about Richard Evans Schultes's wartime work to secure an adequate supply of wild rubber in South America. For the army to employ an officer in the sphere for which he had been trained was said to be quite unusual; all too often the recruit's talents and strengths were wasted in an inappropriate department.

While in Costa Rica, Hope came across a wild impatiens, a rather straggling and quite humble plant. This plant was not a native of Costa Rica but an import that had naturalized. It had been introduced into England in 1896 from Tanzania by Dr. John Kirk and then was scattered around the world. At that time, it was also known as *I. sultanii* and *I. holstii.*

Hope's previous training and experience allowed him to recognize the plant's potential. After the war ended, he founded the PanAmerican Seed Company with Charles Weddle and W. D. Holley. They established the Linda Vista Ranch in Costa Rica as a farm for floriculture.

At first, Hope and Weddle devoted themselves to breeding commercially valuable hybrids, attractive tropical plants with great garden value such as petunia and snapdragon. They released a yellow multiflora petunia. Hope is said to have created the first hybrid petunia, the red 'Comanche'. At this point, it is necessary to review some of the background to the petunia story. There are hybrids and then there are hybrids.

Mrs. Theodosia Burr Shepherd was crossing petunias in the 1890s in Ventura, California. She even taught one of her neighbors, a Mrs. Gould, to do it, as she was too busy herself. The flower she was modifying was *Petunia hybrida grandiflora*, something of a nonsense name by modern standards. Another name for *Petunia hybrida* was *P. multiflora*.

There are twelve species of petunia, all from South America. To show how the hybrids have taken over, the American Horticultural Society's *A to Z Encyclopedia of Garden Plants* does not list a single individual species, only the hybrid races.[13]

All the initial breeding was done with *Petunia nyctaginiflora* Juss. (syn. *P. axillaris*), with white flowers, and *P. integrifolia* (Hook.) Schinz & Fell (syn. *P. violacea*), with purple flowers. *P. axillaris* reached England in 1823. *P integrifolia* got there in 1831. Because of the genetic makeup of these flowers, the diploid hybrids are fertile. The plants can be crossbred and propagated by seed. That explains Mrs. Gould's success.

In her epoch, the only petunias available were either grandiflora, with a few fairly open flowers on compact plants with large leaves or multiflora, with several smaller flowers on a larger plant with small leaves. These petunias were not suited to bedding out. They were only grown as potted plants.

Petunia grandiflora was itself a mutation of a multiflora plant, found in 1881. In 1888 another important mutation appeared, *P.* 'Superbissima'. That was the variety Mrs. Shepherd exploited so successfully, using skillful selection and vegetative propagation of the clones. She called one of her cultivars 'California Giant'. It was popular until about 1930.

Weddle and Hope's cultivars were developed differently. By the time they came to do this work, Benary had released the first inbred multiflora types grown from seed, during the 1930s. Weddle introduced *P.* 'Ballerina', an F1 hybrid grandiflora, in 1952. Petunias could by that time stand up to the rigors of bedding out. They also turned out to be very tolerant of drought. This quality propelled them into the commercial foreground. Everyone got busy looking for even better cultivars. The great success of this complex breeding led to multiflora and grandiflora characteristics merging, but paradoxically much of the flower's charm for the public was also lost. Compact plants all had nice large flowers, but they were no longer so drought or pest tolerant and free of disease.

In the past twenty years, new varieties have been released, using wild germplasm and going back to older cultivars for specific qualities. For example, the BallFloraPlant Company has patented Wave petunias, based on a naturally occurring flower with wavy petals, bred in Japan. Flowers like this have recaptured the public's favor.

Hope never returned to live in the United States. His efforts formed the basis of modern mass production of bedding plants. Linda Vista was among the five companies selling the most impatiens hybrids worldwide. Sluis and Groot in the Netherlands was another, as well as Goldsmith Seeds in Gilroy, California, and Bodger Seeds in Lompoc, California. (See chapter 6 for more about Bodger.) All these firms developed and sold viable F1 hybrids. The original line of Super Elfins has been refined and improved, with many newer versions now available.

Many flower breeders enjoyed visiting and working with Hope at the ranch. They have fond memories of his kindness and generosity. The prominent orchid breeder Leon Glicenstein worked there in the 1960s. Leon worked in Indianapolis for many years, with particular emphasis on the masdevallia, but has now retired.

Friends and employees all referred to Hope as "El Capitan" as a term of respect. It reflected the seriousness and discipline instilled in him by a farming family struggling to survive in an arid part of Texas, the town of Sweetwater. (The very name is ironic. The one thing they lacked was water.) He was the ninth of twelve children, and farm chores shaped the pattern of his life. Before he could go to school in the morning, he had to milk the cows and feed the pigs.

Farm work is never ending, and he had to do all the same chores again in the afternoon. Then he had to do his homework. There was very little time for play. This all went on until he left for college. He attended the Texas Technological College, majoring in horticulture. After college he worked for the Department of Agriculture in Arizona for a few years but then enrolled at Michigan State University for graduate studies. One of his teachers was Liberty Hyde Bailey (1858–1954), an early proponent of horticultural taxonomy and one of the cofounders of American Society for Horticultural Science. Bailey's encyclopedias and dictionaries have informed generations of horticulturists, an essential source for any work in this field. Bailey's daughter, Zoe, took over her father's work after he died.

Claude Hope recognized that many of his Costa Rican workers had very deprived backgrounds, and he made every effort to improve that. Linda Vista was an enlightened workplace, and he fostered a caring environment. They set up a pension fund and health benefits just as at a U.S. firm. Some of the awards he won were for this aspect of his work.

In his brief biography of Hope, Ricardo Arias Martinez, an employee at the ranch, wrote and emphasized something not seen in other sources. Hope needed extra assistance in certain field operations and thought that women would do a much better job than men because of their lighter touch and greater dexterity. Nowadays this attitude would be excoriated as sexist thinking, but in the circumstances it had very good results. It was unheard-of for women to work for money outside their homes in that patriarchal society, but Hope persisted, and quite soon the families realized the enormous benefit of extra income. Earning some money allowed the women to be more independent and to exercise some control over their lives.

Ball Seed Company eventually merged with the PanAmerican Seed Company. Employees of the Ball Seed Company were able to spend months at a time in Costa Rica with Hope, combining study with actual production. At present, the ranch is an integral part of Ball, used for extensive production of F1 hybrids of semitropical plants. The Linda Vista Ranch also introduced new varieties of kalanchoe, lisianthus, and coleus through the years. Hope won many prizes and awards for his introductions.

FRANK REINELT

Frank Reinelt (1900–1979) was born on Christmas Day in the village of Kunicky in the eastern part of Czechoslovakia but moved to the nearby town of Mystek-Frydek as a very small child. His father was a miller, and both his parents valued education. There were relatives who were engineers and teachers. To make ends meet, his mother grew flowers to sell in the market. He recalled helping her in the fields.

By the age of fourteen, he began to work at a nursery in the town. It was near a cemetery, and he rescued chrysanthemums that had been left there by

Frank Reinelt transformed the tuberous begonia and made striking contributions to the delphinium. *Reproduced by permission of Aphra Reinelt Katzev*

mourners. He made amateurish attempts to breed plants with larger flowers from them. His master derided him, but when he succeeded with one of the flowers the master did not hesitate to put it on sale as his own work.

Frank joined the Austrian army as a drummer boy in about 1915 but never said very much about his experiences. His children believe that he had a very difficult time.

The family had thought he should be apprenticed to a machinist, but one of his older cousins who had already left for the United States recommended he become a gardener. In her opinion, gardening was the work of the future. If he emigrated to America, this occupation would give him more opportunity. Even if his knowledge of English were weak, he could still work. The family correspondence is in Czech.

He attended the Pomological Institute in Brno, Moravia, after the First World War ended. This school was founded in 1886. There was a strong tradition of enlightened agriculture in the town and its surrounding countryside. The Czech government encouraged an academic approach to agriculture and horticulture. Nine such colleges were opened between 1870 and 1902.

According to Frank Reinelt, that tradition had become ossified by 1915, and he found the place stifling and no place to learn anything. The director used the students as indentured labor, digging potatoes for his own family. The Abbé Gregor Mendel, founder of modern genetics, had done his experiments in the garden of the Saint Thomas Abbey in Brno but had died in 1884, before the school was founded.

The institute is still in existence at the same address but is now called the Secondary Vocational School of Horticulture. A brief review of its website reveals that the curriculum has come a very long way since 1919.[14]

Reinelt served apprenticeships in both Bohemia and Romania and then worked as a gardener for Queen Marie of Romania at her summer palace on the Black Sea. The queen, a granddaughter of Queen Victoria, had built Tenha Nuva (Serene Nest) to escape the rigors of her life in Romanian politics and the machinations of her dreadful son, Prince Carol. Frank Reinelt's daughter says that he could speak Polish, Russian, Romanian, German, and English.

Frank left Romania in 1926, immigrating to the United States. One of the reasons he wanted to go to America was to visit Luther Burbank, confirming the fact that he was already very interested in plant breeding, but Burbank died while Frank was at sea.

The U.S. Census for 1930 lists Frank as a gardener living in Santa Clara County. For a short time he had stayed with his farming cousins in Santa Rosa, but he soon moved on to a job at the Marvin estate in Palo Alto. He became a citizen in 1931. Every week or two he wrote home to his mother. The relatives in the Czech Republic have all these letters, and his daughter is currently translating them into English.

In 1936 he married his wife, Elaine Gorton, a native of Oakland and descended from an old established California family. They met through a mutual interest in gardens. Mrs. Reinelt died in 1997.

His daughter told me that he liked to go down to Capitola at the weekends to swim in the sea. Frank Reinelt met the Vetterle brothers while they were struggling with the French and Belgian begonia seed. They knew that he had already begun to breed begonias successfully at the Marvin estate while working in Palo Alto.

According to Frank Reinelt Jr., his father knew how to deal with the exceedingly fine and difficult begonia seed better than anyone else. His employer, Mr. Marvin, was a slightly eccentric but wealthy and open-handed lawyer. He did not hesitate to buy the seed plants and whatever else Frank needed. All this was happening during the Great Depression.

They found begonias in Germany, maybe from Benary or Haage & Schmidt in Erfurt, both centers of begonia breeding, yet begonias were not the only plants Frank bred for Mr. Marvin. He also worked with irises, phlox, gerbera daisies, and delphiniums.

Reinelt had not realized that a nurseryman could make a living by selling begonia hybrids until he met Henry Hyde at a flower show. Hyde's nursery was in Watsonville, about twenty miles south of Capitola. Another similar firm was the Brown Bulb Ranch in Capitola. The Browns pioneered growing begonias on an enormous scale.

Not only did Reinelt increase his understanding of what was possible, but he also bought many relatively inexpensive begonias from these men to improve his own work. At the same time, he began to think about what he might do and thus was primed when he came across the Vetterle brothers. There was an almost immediate recognition of the benefit in joining together.

The Vetterles put up a substantial sum of money to start a partnership with Reinelt, and they gave him access to their growing grounds in return for the extensive new business they foresaw. As a stopgap, the new firm initially made sure of improving its cash flow by selling more cut flowers, but they did not have to continue doing that for long, because the begonia business was successful right from the start.

Reinelt shared in the profits of the business but not the ownership of the buildings. Reinelt's department was in the front section of the showroom, and the Vetterles used the back half. Later he added polyanthus and delphinium and marketed them under the name Pacific Strains.

Begonias were still somewhat rare and very fashionable. There was money to be made, but Frank Reinelt was a tireless, even driven, plant breeder who did it for the challenge and the beauty.

He transformed the tuberous begonia. The double form took on myriad shapes: rose form, camellia form, ruffled form, marigold form, picotee, double ruffled picotee, and more besides. The hanging-basket varieties, derived from the species once known as *Begonia lloydii*, were also modified profoundly. In all cases, the range of colors was expanded, from the palest whites to the richest and most glamorous reds. Each flower could be up to ten inches across.

In the 1964 catalogue, Reinelt looked back over his years of experimentation. It was the thirtieth anniversary of the firm of Vetterle and Reinelt. Among other things, the begonias used in hanging baskets had originally been straggling little plants. Because an English breeder named John Lloyd had worked on them for some time, they became known as *B. lloydii* hort but in fact were *B. × tuberhybrida*, pendula type. They are also known as *B. × pendula* hort.

Frank Reinelt completely remade them, culminating in *Begonia* 'Pink Shower', with flowers like rosebuds. This task had taken twenty years. During World War II, the entire stock was lost and he had to start again from the beginning.

Reinelt reflected on the picotee variety in that same catalogue. It had taken him ten years to transform the "insignificant" *Begonia marmorata* into the exquisite picotee form. The ruffled form had taken about one hundred years to reach the present state of complexity. It began with four small flowers from the Andes, and Reinelt had completed the process.

Frank Reinelt also transformed races of primula and delphinium. The delphinium was a great challenge. Obtaining the clear sky-blue color took him many years. He wrote about his frustrations with delphinium in the *Journal of the California Horticultural Society* in 1947.[15]

In his "spare time" he crossed daffodils, though not for commercial exploitation. His closest friend was Sydney Bancroft Mitchell, the dean of library science at the University of California at Berkeley and a noted breeder of iris. Mitchell also wrote a number of books about gardening in California.

Both of Reinelt's children recall many visits and expeditions with "Uncle Sydney" and "Aunt Buddie." Frank Reinelt did not work commercially on iris, but he was friendly with the Mitchells' neighbor, Carl Salbach, a professional iris breeder.

I asked his children whether their father ever mentioned Victor Lemoine, the nineteenth-century French hybridizer whose work ultimately led to the modern garden center as we know it. They told me that he talked about Lemoine very often and indeed felt as if he were a reincarnation of Lemoine. He said that every hundred years a little boy would be born who would carry on Lemoine's work and that he was that little boy.

Blackmore and Langdon in England were leading breeders and producers of begonias in the 1930s and after. Once Vetterle and Reinelt went into high gear, Blackmore and Langdon bought the preponderance of their output. Brian Langdon describes this in his excellent book about begonias.[16] He is the grandson of the original Langdon and continues the family business.

Reinelt planted thousands of seedlings a year. He selected a hundred of his crosses to be followed up and then chose only a fraction of this set for future development. This unerring capacity to choose correctly and a certain ruthlessness are the hallmarks of great hybridizers.

Quite unintentionally, Reinelt became a star. His son noted that Frank Sr. was not interested in awards, publicity, or other baubles, only in putting his visions of floral beauty into concrete form. When his wife chided him for not having a hobby and relaxing in the evenings, he agreed with her. He took up the hobby of breeding a specialized series of tuberous begonias at home!

The children were expected to be useful from a very early age. Aphra told me that she was paid for weeding as a little girl. As she grew older, she did increasingly complex tasks. She and her brother helped to pack the cut flowers for the market. When she met her future husband while a student at Stanford, she took him home to meet the family, and he was promptly pressed into service. There was never any time to go away on a conventional vacation. An enterprise on the scale of Vetterle and Reinelt required almost constant attention most of the year.

The Hollywood film stars and major and minor royalty who bought his hybrids year after year came from what would nowadays be called the "A list." Alfred Hitchcock was one of them, the Duke of Windsor another. Edward Steichen the photographer stayed at their home many times. Steichen's brother-in-law Carl Sandburg came only once but Frank Jr. recalls him as staying up all night drinking. The "Georgia Peach," Ty Cobb, also wrote to them. Frank Jr. now regrets throwing the letter out, but he did not care for Ty Cobb's arrogant assumptions at the time.

Frank Reinelt received several of the most significant horticultural awards in the world. In 1956, the Massachusetts Horticultural Society gave him its Thomas Roland Medal. The other person honored at that event was Eugene ("Papa") Boerner, the creator of the Floribunda rose series.

In 1962, Reinelt received the Veitch Memorial Medal from the Royal Horticultural Society in London. It has been given to a non-British person only a few times since its inception. Victor Lemoine was one of its recipients. Although the date of the award is 1962, it was reported on in the "Report of

U NDER THE heading "The Veitch Memorial Medal—awarded to those who have helped in the advancement and improvement of the science and practice of horticulture," it states, "To Mr. F. Reinelt—Gold Medal for his work in connection with the breeding of delphiniums, begonias and polyanthus." It goes on to quote the president of the society, Lord Aberconway: "Mr Reinelt started his gardening career some fifty years ago in the service of the Royal house of Roumania. He then emigrated to California, where as a partner in his hybridizing firm he has become world famous for the Pacific strain of delphiniums, begonias and polyanthus. He is a man of great activity and enthusiasm, and a friend tells me his plans will certainly occupy the second fifty years of his life. Unfortunately he is too busy to come all the way for his medal, so we must post it to him."

proceedings of the one hundred and fifty-ninth annual meeting of the Fellows of the Society, held in the Society's Old Hall, Vincent Square, Westminster, on Tuesday, February 19, 1963, at 3 p.m.," which appears in the *Journal of the Royal Horticultural Society.*[17]

Frank and Elaine Reinelt did not go to England to receive the award, and he returned to his native land only once. Poor health was the cause of his retirement. His wife wrote that he began planning what he would do quite methodically, looking into varieties of succulents that would thrive in Nevada. He died on December 3, 1979. C. Burr wrote a brief obituary of him in the summer issue of *Pacific Horticulture* in 1980.[18]

PART THREE

PLANTS BY GENUS

5

Shrubs

AZALEA AND RHODODENDRON

You have to be motivated, in the mind's eye, by sheer delight of
the beauty you are expecting to create.

—David Goheen Leach

HYBRIDIZING RHODODENDRONS is not for sissies. It requires
not only industrial levels of patience and fortitude but also
enough open space to accommodate the dozens or even hundreds of seedlings generated by the crossings to grow to matu-
rity. Somewhere along the way, the grower also has to make a living. In spite
of these obstacles, many wonderful people devote their lives to the rhododendron and azalea. We are enriched by their accomplishments.

All shrubs, including roses, and indeed all plants have the same onerous
requirements. Creating new cultivars of anything from the smallest crocus
to the largest tree makes equivalent demands, but the large size of the mature rhododendron shrub is an additional complication. Patience, a cool

head, and a clear understanding of the goals are essential in any plant breeding program.

There seem to be two main drivers in this endeavor. One is the intense satisfaction the breeder gains by conquering the impossible, both in the aesthetic sense and in self-vindication. Satisfying curiosity is a part of this feeling.

The other driver is commercial success, a perfectly worthy goal. The old adage "If you build it they will come" can be applied here: "If you breed it they will come." Even someone like the wealthy Lionel de Rothschild, who had no need to sell the results of his efforts, had to make some provision for outsiders to obtain seeds. He occasionally issued a single typewritten sheet listing what was available.

Nursery owners needed the boost that a new and preferably unique cultivar gave them. In a very competitive business, the person with the most drive and energy usually succeeded. Bringing out new versions of familiar plants that promised better performance took enormous effort but paid off.

EVOLUTION OF THE RHODODENDRON

Rhododendron, which is in the family Ericaceae, is among the oldest flowering shrubs known, based on fossil evidence. The majority of rhododendron species are found north of the equator. There are only a very few tropical species, known as the vireyas. They are distinguished by having fine hairs on the leaves and flowers. Australia has a single native species, *R. lochiae*.

One of the fascinating things about the genus *Rhododendron* is its distribution over both the Eurasian and North American land masses. The richest source of species seems to be the triangle between Burma, Yunnan (in China), and Tibet. The distribution across disjunct continental regions suggests that the genus's appearance predates the breakup of the old super-continent, Pangaea.

For a long time the azalea and rhododendron have been united in one genus, but for the gardener they still remain distinct. Linnaeus thought they were two separate species, but as early as 1834 George Don pointed out that that was not correct. The azalea is part of two of the eight subgenera of rhododendron: the *Pentanthera* (deciduous) and *Azaleastrum* (evergreen).

The term *evergreen* does not mean the same thing in azalea as it does in cryptogams. Cryptogams have the same set of leaves all the time. The azalea puts out two sets of leaves each year and so appears not to lose its leaves in the same way as a deciduous plant. The two principal sources of azalea for garden purposes are North America and Japan. In North America, sixteen of the twenty-six native rhododendron species are azaleas.

Linnaeus was muddled about where some of the plants given to him to classify came from, and he named the first azalea he received *Azalea indica* (now *R. indicum*), thinking that it came from India, just as he did with the first Chinese rose. We should not feel too superior. It was very difficult for him way up in Uppsala to know about the actual travels of the plants that reached him.

In the United States, the majority of the native rhododendron species are concentrated in the Pacific Northwest and the Mid- and Southern Atlantic regions, with azalea being more common in the latter. At first, European plant collectors were active in the eastern states.

IMPORTING RHODODENDRONS INTO THE BRITISH ISLES

Rhododendron collections started to be assembled piecemeal throughout the British Isles in the eighteenth and early nineteenth centuries, coming from various sources but setting up a rich pool of material useful for later breeders. Because many species hailed from quite high altitude in the Himalayas, the original plants were fairly hardy. Crossbreeding led to a loss of this quality, and it had to be bred back into future generations.

John Tradescant the elder grew the first rhododendron known to be cultivated in an English garden, *Rhododendron hirsutum*, in Lambeth.[1] It was listed in his son's catalogue circa 1656. The plant came from the central and eastern Alps. Gorer comments that in many cases deciphering which plants Tradescant meant from the names he used is difficult, but evidently this one is not in doubt.

Almost one hundred years later, *Rhododendron ferrugineum* was being cultivated in Britain. The common name *alpenrose* seems to have been used indiscriminately for both *R. hirsutum* and *R. ferrugineum*. This species is a native of the western Alps and the Pyrenees.

English explorers brought *Rhododendron ponticum* into the country from Gibraltar in 1763. It has an extensive range, being found throughout southern Europe into Russia and the Black Sea region. Its name, *R. ponticum*, indicates its origin in the Pontus Mountains. This plant established itself very effectively, almost to the level of being a pest. A few years later, the Russian plants reached the British Isles.

At the end of the eighteenth century, stories about *Rhododendron arboreum* came from India, but no documented record exists of it being in the British Isles before 1817. Its treelike dimensions were a disadvantage, but the gorgeous red color of the flowers made up for it. Up until then there were only a few more-pastel colors.

Nathaniel Wallich (1786–1854), superintendent of the Royal Botanic Garden at Calcutta, sent the seeds to Sir Joseph Banks, director of the Royal Botanic Gardens at Kew in 1817. He had packed them in brown sugar to keep them from rotting. This was an important advance.

Wallich was a Jew born in Copenhagen. He served as a naval surgeon in the Danish colony at Serampore in India. The colony was ceded to Britain after the Napoleonic wars, and his botanical abilities were quickly recognized. One of his contributions was to recognize how tea could be grown in India.

The very tender tropical vireya species began to appear in England at about the same time. *Rhododendron javanicum* came from Malaysia in 1823, *R. jasminiflorum* in 1850. It was not long before Veitch started to cross them and issued a cultivar called *R.* 'Princess Royal', named for Queen Victoria's eldest daughter. This hybrid was then crossed with *R. jasminiflorum,* giving rise to *R.* 'Princess Alexandra'. Five other species came into England in that same epoch. The best estimate is that there are almost three hundred species in the wild, of which only about forty were known in the West until recently.[2]

Crossing the vireya is not a simple matter. Most of the best work has been done in Australia, where the climate is more conducive to breeding the plants. One of the best-known hybridizers of vireya is Brian Clancy of Bentleigh in Australia.

In addition to the continental imports and the Indian discoveries, an American rhododendron was arriving almost simultaneously. Bishop Henry Compton in London, a gardening cleric who actually enjoyed being out of favor at Charles II's court, as it gave him more time for his plants, heard about a "swamp honeysuckle" from Virginia in 1691, probably *Rhododendron visco-*

sum. The bishop supported missionaries in America, and one of his proté-gés, John Banister, sent him a drawing. Some experts believe it could actually have been *R. atlanticum,* which looks very similar. Seeds are not known to have been in England before 1734.

By the early and mid-nineteenth century, great numbers of rhododen-dron were reaching the British Isles as a result of Nathaniel Wallich's and Joseph Hooker's expeditions into Nepal and other Himalayan countries. Hooker collected forty-three species, of which thirty-six still remain distinct.

Robert Fortune, who went to China in 1843 (soon after it was opened to the West) under the auspices of the Horticultural Society in London, sent back an elegant plant that John Lindley, the secretary of the society and a foremost taxonomist of the day, named *R. fortunei.* Fortune's collecting was wide and extensive. *R. fortunei* has been a parent in more than eighty cultivars, confer-ring hardiness, beautiful color, fragrance, and a fine dark-green foliage.

Later in the century and continuing into the next, rhododendrons con-tinued to be found in Asia and were sent to Europe and the United States in unprecedented numbers. Ernest Wilson, George Forrest, and Frank Kingdon Ward led in these collections. Eventually these exotic species were all widely distributed, with huge possibilities for crossbreeding.

Joseph Rock, an Austrian scientist and scholar who became an Ameri-can, also sent back many rhododendrons, but a lot of them were duplicates. Wilson traveled to Japan, Korea, and Taiwan (still called Formosa in his day), collecting rhododendrons and previously unknown deciduous azaleas.

Certain key species conferred valuable benefits, principally colors and levels of hardiness not previously available. The following is only a brief and superficial list: *Rhododendron catawbiense* and *R. maximum* were very cold hardy, *R. brachycarpum* even more so. *R. edgeworthii, R. griffithianum,* and *R. fortunei* conferred fragrance. *R. hirsutum* can tolerate soil with a limestone base. *R. sinogrande* has enormous leaves, perhaps the largest of any species. *R. keiskei* is yellow. *R. yakushimanum* has undergone many name changes, but its chief features are compactness and hardiness.

Breeding winter hardiness into the plants was more than a trivial whim; it was essential if more people were going to enjoy the handsome imports. Ernest Wilson was frequently disappointed by foreign species failing to adapt but observed that some hybrids with North American parentage such as *R. catawbiense* did well at the Arnold Arboretum near Boston, Massachusetts.

These varieties stayed vigorous and alive for quite a few winters. Wilson named these his Iron Clad Group. His original selection has now been updated with more-modern cultivars.

The British public started to plant rhododendron in their gardens close to the beginning of the nineteenth century. A gradual increase in the prosperity of the middle class created these possibilities. They were able to buy European and American shrubs at a number of leading nurseries: Veitch, Loddiges, Waterer, Thompson, Lea & Kennedy, Russell, and Standish & Noble.

RHODODENDRON HYBRIDIZATION
BEGINS IN ENGLAND

Hybridizing began spontaneously and unexpectedly at William Thompson's nursery. He reported a spontaneous cross that took place between an azalea, *Rhododendron calendulaceum*, and *R. ponticum*. Thompson called this is an azaleodendron. He must have disseminated it, because the Royal Botanic Garden at Edinburgh listed *R. subdeciduum* 'Thompson's Hybrid' in its 1819 catalogue. Thompson had been Lord James Gambier's gardener at Iver in Buckinghamshire and was principally known as the developer of the modern pansy.

The Reverend William Herbert of Spofforth in Yorkshire, and later Dean of Manchester, was an early proponent of intentional crossbreeding. He and like-minded plantsmen crossed *Rhododendron catawbiense* and *R. maximum* from North America with *R. ponticum* and *R. caucasicum* from Europe. After *R. arboreum* arrived, they added that to their palette.

In 1833, Dean Herbert crossed *Rhododendron arboreum* with *R. caucasicum* to produce *R.* 'Jacksonii' ('Venustum'). 'Jacksonii' was a low-growing shrub despite the *arboreum* genes and flowered earlier in the year. All this inspired the dean's elder brother, the Earl of Carnarvon, to start his own breeding experiments in Berkshire.

Several nurserymen became active in breeding rhododendron for hardiness halfway through the nineteenth century. This was the period of the "hardy hybrids." Standish & Noble of Sunningdale and the Waterers of Bagshot issued many cultivars, grafted onto *R. ponticum* stock. This turned out to be unfortunate: the scions were weak and failed frequently, leaving large clumps of the much less attractive, but exceedingly hardy, *ponticum* bushes scattered around.

Modern breeders also used *ponticum* as rootstock. One story is told about Halfdan Lem, the great Washington state hybridist (see later discussion). He had prepared a large number of special hybrids at the request of one of his customers but was not able to supervise their planting. The client's gardeners simply showed up at his nursery with a truck and took them away. Some years later, Mr. Lem visited Southern California and called in at the estate. To his horror, almost all the plants were pure *ponticum*. The grafts had not been successful.

He apologized abjectly and offered to stay as long as it took to replace everything. The client did not take him up on it. As far as the client was concerned, he had a garden full of handsome rhododendrons, and he was perfectly happy.

The modern era of rhododendron breeding came in with the wide-scale distribution of Asian species, particularly *Rhododendron griffithianum*, *R. thomsonii*, and *R. fortunei*. By 1917, J. G. Millais, a son of the famous artist, could list 454 hybrids in his two-volume book.[3] More than half of these, 292 cultivars, were bred by the Waterer family. Clearly these were important figures in the story.

Michael Waterer

The founder of the Waterer nursery was Michael Waterer (1770–1842), who inherited John Taylor's nursery in Knap Hill, Woking, Surrey, in 1825 (or possibly 1829) from an aunt.[4] He bred the hybrid *Rhododendron* 'Nobleanum', crossing *R. arboreum* with *R. caucasicum*. *R.* 'Nobleanum' blooms in December, in time for Christmas.

His brother, John, later moved into the nursery and worked it with three of his sons, Frederick, Michael, and John. They had a branch in Bagshot. Because they concentrated on American rhododendrons, the nursery was known as the American Nursery of Bagshot, Surrey.

The Knap Hill Nursery in Woking had almost half of its acreage devoted to growing these shrubs by 1879. They frequently won prizes at shows. Anthony Waterer (1822–1896) worked with deciduous azalea, crossing Belgian hybrids and several other species. He used species from both the eastern and the western states of North America, as well as plants from China and Asia Minor.

Gomer Waterer, one of Anthony's sons, developed the cultivar *Rhododendron* 'Mrs E. C. Stirling' and also worked extensively on *R.* 'Pink Pearl', first bred by his father. *R.* 'Pink Pearl' was a winner, first of an Award of Merit in 1897 and then a First Class Certificate in 1900. Queen Alexandra admired *R.* 'Pink Pearl' very much, and its popularity has endured. It finally became a symbol of all that is wrong with the public's taste, through no fault of its own.

Waterer's nursery still specializes in rhododendron. Their cultivars can almost be considered immortal, used as the basis for many skillful crossings by new generations of breeders. Dig a little beneath all sorts of series and one will find Knap Hill genetic material lurking in almost every cultivar.

Lionel de Rothschild

At one time the landed gentry led the way in rhododendron breeding. In England, Lionel de Rothschild reigned supreme at his Exbury estate in Hampshire. There were many other able rhododendron breeders in the British Isles, but few of them were as rich as Rothschild.

C. E. Lucas Phillips, a noted rhododendron expert, and Peter Barber, who managed Exbury Gardens, have left a very valuable (and revealing) description of Rothschild himself and his methods of plant crossing in *The Rothschild Rhododendrons.*[5]

Lionel de Rothschild (1882–1942) was a thrill seeker and speed fiend as a young man. His immense wealth allowed him to buy and race very expensive vehicles of different types, including speedboats.

He acquired a small estate in Hampshire when he married Marie Louise Beer, a descendant of the opera composer Giacomo Meyerbeer, in 1912. They were very happy there, but it was not big enough for what he wanted to do. Once the First World War was over, he bought the Exbury estate from his neighbor Harry Forster in 1919. This marked a turning point for him. His competitive spirit was channeled into a more constructive pursuit. As a young man at his parents' house, he had begun to grow rhododendrons and now wanted to do it on a large scale.

Exbury was badly overgrown but had some notable cypress trees in the woods. Lord Redesdale, ancestor of the Mitford family and an authority on bamboo, had recorded their presence. Rothschild employed several hundred men to clean up the property and prepare the grounds to suit his plans. He was determined to save the cypress trees. It was not long before dappled glades glimmered between the trees in the Home Wood, ready to take his seedlings. While all this work was going on, the historic *Cupressus sempervirens* trees were saved. They had been grown from a seed in a wreath at the Duke of Wellington's funeral in 1852.

Every weekend during the appropriate season, Rothschild drove his two-seater Rolls Royce from London down to Hampshire to work on his azaleas. Do not imagine that he put on an old tweed jacket and muddy Wellies and sallied forth with a hoe. "Work" meant lining up his forces and marshalling the staff for his purposes. Rothschild had thought long and hard about the genealogy of his treasures in the preceding days and issued very detailed instructions about which plants he wanted crossed. It was not too difficult when there were twelve or thirteen gardeners and undergardeners at one's disposal.

On Monday mornings he departed, confident in the knowledge that everything would be done as he had planned. This is one way to breed rhododendrons and azaleas. The results were superlative, but World War II put an end to it. The very social fabric that was based on serried classes of workers had evaporated, to say nothing of the actual loss of men in fighting. Elderly men working as jobbing gardeners after the war were the only ones left. Rothschild's son, Edmund, faced a lot of difficulties in keeping Exbury going, but the Exbury azaleas remain very important.

Here are just a few of the Rothschild cultivars: *Rhododendron* 'Albatross', 'Avalanche', 'Brocade', 'Carmen', 'Chelsea', 'Eldorado', 'Fortune', and 'Galactic', in simple alphabetical order. He named one cultivar *R.* 'Charlotte de Rothschild' for one of his aunts. Hybrids from the Knap Hill nursery provided him with a jumping-off place to get started on azaleas, but he also worked with the hardy hybrid rhododendron race.

Most observers agree that rhododendron breeding was primarily a British and European phenomenon at first, passing to the United States later. The idea of crossbreeding the American endemics arose after it had been done in Britain. The Royal Horticultural Society is the international registration

authority for rhododendron hybrids. Both azalea and rhododendron cultivars number in the thousands.

BREEDERS IN CORNWALL AND
THE WEST COUNTRY

J. C. Williams

Many other talented breeders worked in Cornwall, sometimes called the
"English Riviera" and considered a more clement region of the chilly, damp
British Isles, though anyone who was there in March 2007 might dispute that
claim. J. C. Williams (1861–1939), of Caerhays Castle, the Lord Lieutenant of
Cornwall, contributed to some of the syndicates assembled by the Royal Bo-
tanic Garden of Edinburgh to send collectors to Burma, Assam, and Tibet.

As a result, he received his share of Ernest Wilson's plants directly. He
quickly began developing a series of hybrids named for familiar birds, like *R.*
'Blue Tit', 'Yellow Hammer', and so forth. *R.* 'Blue Tit' was a popular dwarf
plant, the result of crossing *R. augustinii* with *R. impeditum* in 1933.

His great-nephew Charles Williams now owns Caerhays but also operates
a distinguished specialty nursery close by in Redruth, Cornwall. Many of Wilson's original plants are still extant in Caerhays' glorious woodland grounds.

Cornish landowners were the backbone of the new Rhododendron Society, founded in 1915 with eighteen members. The society kept careful records of crossbreeding between the newer Himalayan species and the
previous ones from America and China.

John Luscombe

John Luscombe (1848–1937) of Lower Coombe Royal in Devon had a powerful interest in horticulture and was noted for his citrus trees. He was an enthusiastic gardener who corresponded with Sir William Hooker at Kew and
received seeds of the first Sikkim rhododendrons, brought from India by Sir
William's son, Joseph.

John Luscombe was one of the first hybridizers of rhododendrons, and he
raised hybrids such as *Rhododendron* 'Luscombei' (a cross between *R. fortunei*

and *R. thomsonii*), 'Coombe Royal', and 'Luscombes Scarlet'. *R. fortunei*, introduced in 1859, first flowered in this garden in 1866 and was illustrated in *Curtis's Botanical Magazine* in that year.

James Henry Mangles

James Henry Mangles (1832–1884) issued important cultivars based on *Rhododendron griffithianum*. Mangles was one of three children of Captain James Mangles of the Royal Navy. His brother and sister both inherited his work, but before his death he had sent some specimens to Sir Edmund Loder. Mangles wrote about twenty articles on rhododendron for the *Gardener's Chronicle* between 1879 and 1882.

After Mangles died, Sir Edmund Loder assumed his mantle. Loder's *Rhododendron* 'Loder's White' has been famous for a long time. The lineage of this cultivar is *R. catawbiense* 'Album Elegans' × *R. griffithianum*, pollinated by *R.* 'White Pearl' (*R. griffithianum* × *R. maximum*).

Loder bought Leonardslee in Sussex from his wife's parents, the Hubbards, and turned it into a remarkable property. One of his first steps was to visit India in 1876 and see rhododendron in the wild. He was already deeply interested in natural history, and this only strengthened his wish to devote his time to improving plants for everyone's enjoyment. Loder named one of his cultivars for the great Australian singer Dame Nellie Melba.

E. H. M. Cox

The Cox family in Glendoick, Perthshire, has made enormous contributions to rhododendron collecting and breeding. E. H. M. Cox went to Burma with Reginald Farrer in 1919 and later wrote a very useful and readable book about the history of plant hunting in China.[6] Cox wrote that one of the reasons George Forrest sent back so many species of rhododendron was that J. C. Williams independently gave him a bonus for each one.

Euan Hillhouse Methven Cox (1893–1977) was the son of a Scottish jute manufacturer and was very well educated.[7] For a time he worked at the Foreign Office in London, where he was John Buchan's secretary. After he had been in London for eight years, his father needed him to come home and run the family business. He never went back to China to collect plants but did travel widely and write extensively. His passion for plants passed down to his children.

Cox's son, Peter, also collected plants and wrote several books about rhododendrons.[8] Peter's son, Kenneth, now runs the nursery. The firm has introduced numerous dwarf hybrids, named for game birds. It also imported species of rhododendron that Joseph Rock sent back to the United States but had never previously reached Britain.

In 2001, Kenneth Cox retraced F. Kingdon Ward's steps in Tibet and re-issued the latter's *Riddle of the Tsangpo Gorges* after filling in the blank places Ward could not reach.[9] This was not only a fine collecting expedition but also a geographical tour de force.

RHODODENDRON HYBRIDIZING
IN THE UNITED STATES

American breeders did not have Rothschild's resources. The leaders tended to live in quiet country areas where they could afford a large tract of land and not have to worry about making it earn its keep. A key feature of rhododendron hybridizing in the United States is the basic division into the eastern and western segments of the country. Almost nothing was done in the midsection of the country until quite recently because of the harsh climate. Rhododendrons and azaleas were native to large sections of the East and West Coasts but are not found far inland. Prospective breeders in the colder inland parts, such as the Midwest, have benefited from work done in Scandinavia and other countries.

Anyone wanting to plant rhododendron in their gardens in the early years of the twentieth century on either coast had a narrow choice of the native plants or a very few imported hybrids. The native species are very attractive, and this limitation was not a serious deprivation, but the potential gardener had to put up with the existing size, color, and seasonal behavior of these plants. No matter how lovely it is, pale pink becomes boring after a while.

When the foreign azaleas began to enter the United States, the principal importers were nurserymen from the northeastern states. They simply assumed that these azaleas would not survive the rigors of a northern American winter. Perhaps the most creative of this group was Louis Boehmer, a Massachusetts man who opened a nursery in Yokohama, going directly to the source.

This was during the Meiji restoration and the huge wave of enthusiasm in Europe and America for all things Japanese.

The early hybridists were so successful that an era in which there was almost no choice in color, hardiness, or size has been happily forgotten. Doing his work too well dooms the pioneer to oblivion. My idea is to rescue them from that undeserved fate. There were about half-dozen luminaries who proved it was possible to grow a wide range of rhododendron in the northern Atlantic states. Here are the stories of a few of them.

One of the things they had in common was the devoted efforts of a champion or small group of champions who maintained the collections and memory of the originator. In each case, once the driving force was removed, the legacy foundered until someone recognized its value and struggled to maintain it. Members of the American Rhododendron Society played a huge role in preserving and protecting the heritage of extraordinary individuals.

Eastern United States

Charles Owen Dexter

Charles Owen Dexter (1862–1943) was already a serious rhododendron breeder when he retired as president of the Beacon Manufacturing Company in New Bedford and bought more than seventy acres of land in Sandwich, Massachusetts. His wife felt that this interest sustained him through retirement and probably kept him alive for many more years than he might have expected. Charles Dexter was descended from the Alden family, which came to America in the *Mayflower*.[10]

The climate in that part of the cape was much milder than in the rest of Massachusetts. It benefited from a segment of the Gulf Stream coming very close in shore.

Dexter made extensive use of *Rhododendron fortunei*, and many of his cultivars were very fragrant. When Paul Bosley and his wife, nursery owners from Mentor, Ohio, first visited him in the early 1930s, they found the fragrance quite surprising. They were not used to it. Dexter gave them a lot of cuttings to take home with them. Paul Bosley grafted the cuttings and put them out in his grounds but ultimately none of them survived very long in northern Ohio.

Charles Owen Dexter devoted his retirement to breeding new races of American rhododendron.
Reproduced by permission of Heritage Museums & Gardens, Sandwich, Massachusetts (photographer unknown)

Dexter also gave Bosley a carload of various mixed rhododendrons that were just coming into bloom. One variety had some *Rhododendron catawbiense* in it, and he hoped that variety would be hardier. The following winter, 1933–34, was the coldest on record in Ohio at that time, and thirty-five out of the fifty plants they received from Dexter died. Bosley's son, Richard, recorded the fact that some thirty years later, about ten distinctive varieties were still viable.

Dexter was not very methodical about keeping records. In addition, there is occasional doubt about which variety he was using. Heman Howard writes, "[T]he actual source of his parent plant or pollen was not known for sure, even by him."[11] Some of his parent plants may also have been hybrids themselves. He started out with native rhododendrons from North Carolina but also bought exotic Asian ones from a nursery in Barnstaple, ten miles away. Some of the latter had in turn come from the Robert Veitch nursery in Exeter, cousins of the larger London firm of Veitch and Sons.

In addition to *Rhododendron fortunei* and *R. catawbiense,* he also used *R. griffithianum, R. haematodes, R. discolor,* and *R. decorum* in his crosses. Ernest Wilson often gave Dexter new species when he returned from his collecting trips. In any one year, Charles Owen Dexter planted out between five thousand and ten thousand new seedlings.

Richard Bosley indicates that Charles Owen Dexter was a kindhearted and generous man. This generosity sadly led to a lot of confusion about the nature of many of his crosses, as he gave away huge numbers of unnamed and unmarked seedlings.

Some years ago, when the property was being restored, it took experts a long time to retrace his steps, but they are now able to say with confidence that they have recovered specimens and tracked down what he did for almost all of his hybrids. He seldom named his cultivars but used a numbering system at times.

It has been left to the present generation to supply names. Dr. John Wister and his colleagues worked extremely hard to create a viable series incorporating the Dexter lines. Wister himself bred many cultivars using a Dexter numbered variety as a parent. This new work increased the survival rate for somewhat tender plants adapted to the cape's milder climate.

As a result, there is a distinct series of Dexter hybrids available across the country. Some of the Dexter varieties are *Rhododendron* 'Scintillation' (a great favorite), 'Giant Red', 'Champagne', 'COD' (with Everitt), 'Dexter/ Bosley 1020', and 'Cherry Red'. The Sandwich estate is now a not-for-profit foundation, Heritage Plantation, and open to the public.

Joseph Gable

Joseph Gable (1886–1972) had a nursery in central Pennsylvania.[12] His family had owned orchards and farmed for several generations. Their property included otherwise "useless" woodland that became his laboratory. The Gables traced their arrival in Pennsylvania to a Hessian mercenary who settled in America after the war of independence. Although they were always country folk, they believed in education.

Gable's father was a schoolteacher, and he tried to get his son an even better education, but Joseph had other ideas. After his military service in World War I, he returned to Stewartstown, married, and began farming.

The Gables had strong views about temperance. His father and grandfather were opposed to alcohol, and the story is told that his grandfather gave money to the men at a barn raising rather than supply the usual keg of whisky.

Joseph's interest in rhododendron and azalea developed in parallel with his strenuous life as a mixed farmer. As far as is known, the passion began with his curiosity about the wild azaleas growing near his farm. Gable wrote to Charles S. Sargent and Ernest H. Wilson at the Arnold Arboretum looking for help in identifying these plants. They turned out to be *Rhododendron nudiflorum*.

Sargent and Wilson were impressed by his persistence and curiosity. They recommended that he get in touch with a transplanted Scot in British Columbia, George Fraser. Fraser (1854–1944) went through that indispensable Scottish gardening apprenticeship but decided he wanted his own land and emigrated in 1883, finally settling in Ucluelet, a tiny village on the coast of British Columbia. He built a nursery and began crossing numerous types of plant, trying to improve the yields of fruit trees and getting new forms of rhododendron to bloom.

Sargent heard about his work and commended it. Fraser enjoyed his correspondence with Gable and suggested that the latter write to E. J. P. Magor in Cornwall for more help and advice. For about twenty-five years, the three of them wrote back and forth, with ideas, pollen, and sometimes even plants. Gable told Guy Nearing that Magor was his guiding spirit and that he owed a great deal to him.

Only after about thirty years did the appeal of the shrubs push aside his basic livelihood, and he allowed himself to become a full-time nurseryman. At that point he is reported to have said, "I never really did enjoy being nurse-maid to a cow."

Gable pursued the grail of cold hardiness as well as variation in color and habit. Stewartstown is about forty miles north of Baltimore and prone to very cold winters. His nursery sold native rhododendrons and azaleas as well as other shrubs and trees, but he soon became particularly interested in rhododendrons that could survive the rugged climate.

Gable wanted to evaluate rare species and create his own hybrids, and he spent forty years doing this. He corresponded with all the experts, often obtaining seed and pollen for his work. His letters to Guy Nearing, a notable breeder of rhododendrons, show very clearly what he aimed to do and how difficult it was to achieve it.

As a working farmer with very limited resources, he built whatever he needed himself and put things together the best he could. One example was how he handled pollen when it arrived. He had nowhere to keep it for more than a day or two, so he would apply it to any prospective mother plant that might approximate what he intended to do.

This was where the wooded land came in. Gable planted the new crosses out there and left them to fend for themselves. He was only interested in the ones that survived this harsh environment. This was very much what Dr. Griffith Buck did with roses in Iowa. Buck had no financial backing for his work. His only recourse was to leave them outside to fend for themselves.

Some of Gable's azaleas can survive down to -5°F. Examples are *Rhododendron* 'David Gable', rosy pink; 'Forest Fire', blood red; 'Louise Gable', salmon pink; 'Purple Splendor', rich purple; 'Rosebud', bright pink; 'Rose Greeley', white; and 'Stewartstonian', deep red. One cultivar, the purplish 'Herbert', is hardy to -15°F.

In the end, he left a legacy of one hundred named hybrids. He evaluated another hundred species and at least ninety group crosses. Gable's series are not frequently sold, but they are very tough and suitable for much of the eastern United States.

Gable named hybrids for his daughter, Caroline, and his wife, Mary Belle. He used a system in which he combined the syllables of the parent plants' names. *Rhododendron* 'Cadis' indicates a cross between *R.* 'Caroline' and *R. discolor.* One of his groups, or "grexes," was called "Catfortcampy," indicating parentage from *R. catawbiense, R. fortunei,* and *R. campylocarpum.* Another example of this idiosyncratic naming was 'Catalgla', a portmanteau word put together from *R. catawbiense* and *R. album glass.* A great many of his crosses were highly fragrant.

His champion was Commander Richard Steele, a retired naval officer in the Royal Canadian Navy and veteran of both World War II and the Korean War, who became an outstanding hybridizer in his own right. Steele created a nursery in Nova Scotia, where the winters can be exceedingly cold. He corresponded actively with Gable, and the latter's work encouraged him to persist in making very cold-hardy hybrids. After Gable died, Commander Steele took as many of his hybrids back to his own property as he could. Steele probably has the signature collection of Gable hybrids.

Benjamin Y. Morrison

Benjamin Yoe Morrison (1891–1966) was a specialist in rhododendron and azalea at the U.S. Department of Agriculture (USDA) who bred the Glenn Dale series. He was a handsome and remarkable man with many other talents, including music, drawing, and painting.

Morrison graduated from Harvard in 1915 with a degree in landscape architecture. He won the Sheldon Fellowship, which enabled him to visit Asia. While there, he was struck by the azaleas in Japan. Morrison grew up in Atlanta and had seen beautiful large-flowered *Azalea indica* (now *Rhododendron indicum*) in the South. They were much too tender to survive farther north. The Japanese azaleas opened his eyes.

As a result of this trip, he chose horticulture rather than landscaping as a career. Morrison joined the USDA at the Glenn Dale Station of the Department of Plant Exploration and Introduction and eventually became the first director of the National Arboretum. Other azalea experts valued their correspondence with him. He retired to Pass Christian in Mississippi in 1951 and opened a nursery.

While in Maryland, he worked on azaleas at his home in Takoma Park, as well as at the USDA station. His vision was to create a hardy series of azalea

Benjamin Yoe Morrison among his azaleas, circa 1954.
Reproduced by permission of Hunt Botanical Institute

that do just as well in harsher climates. In the end, there were 454 cultivars in the Glenn Dale series. It is amusing that he named one of them *Rhododendron* 'Yeoman'. The series had a wide range of color with striped and patterned varieties among them. The icy clear whites may be some of the very best.

Weldon Delp

Weldon Delp (1920–1999) probably created more cultivars than anyone else. He began his nursery in 1947 after a variety of other types of work. He was educated as a chiropractor and served in the U.S. Army medical corps at the end of World War II. Delp opened his Crystallaire Nursery in Harrisburg, Pennsylvania, and closed it in 1993 only after teaching his daughter, Joyce, how to propagate his varieties.

To get an idea of his huge output, one can consider a list created by Paul James, "Top 50 Rhododendrons by Weldon Delp."[13] A list of 50 indicates the presence of many more where those came from. The counts vary, but he registered 389 cultivars before he stopped crossing in 1993. Paul James in Roanoke, Virginia, may have the greatest number of Delp's hybrids and was in a very good position to choose the best.

At last count, Mr. James had 391 varieties in his garden. Mr. James was born and brought up in Virginia. He owes much of his enthusiasm for plants to his wonderful grandparents, who took him for long walks in the country-side as a child, explaining everything they saw. Paul James holds the national reference collection of rhododendrons.

Delp's enormous and speedy production was controversial in some quarters. Serious rhododendron people questioned his prolific output, believing that he did not test each variety thoroughly before releasing it. He lived in west-central Pennsylvania and wanted to create plants that would be really hardy in that zone.

Some experts were suspicious of how quickly he was able to get new seedlings to bloom, keeping them in his greenhouse rather than allowing them to suffer the hardship of being outdoors. Delp encouraged seeds to germinate rapidly, using special methods of his own, another efficient shortcut that one gathers was not considered to be quite sporting. Fairly often, the plants themselves would not be sturdy in spite of having gorgeous flowers.

At present, only a very few of his varieties are sold commercially: In Jackson, New Jersey, *Rhododendron* 'Angel Powder', 'Delp's Dream', 'Gosh Darn', and 'Smoke Signal' are available. In Michigan, one can find 'Delp's Sunsheen', 'Gen. Schmidt', and 'Pink Pixie'.

Delp and his wife, Virginia ("Ginny"), were an unpretentious couple with a friendly, down-to-earth style, and the names of some of his cultivars reflect this. *Rhododendron* 'Gosh Darn' is a sample (*R.* 'Catalgla' × *R.* 'Mrs H. R. Yates' F2). There was nothing stuffy about him. They called one cultivar 'Bold and Breezy' (*R. brachycarpum* ssp. *tigerstedtii* × *R. eclecteum* Cox). Both of these are on Paul James's list.

Rhododendron brachycarpum ssp. *tigerstedtii* has an interesting history it-self. In 1935, seeds from Japanese and Korean rhododendrons were received at the Mustila Arboretum near Helsinki in Finland, a northern European country above the 60th degree latitude. It was hardly the sort of environment in which rhododendron would flourish, but they did survive.

At the time they had not been identified botanically, but in 1970 they were found to be *Rhododendron brachycarpum*. Peter Tigerstedt, professor of botany at Helsinki, named this subspecies in honor of his father, C. G. Tigerstedt, the man who had raised the plant successfully. This variety is considered to be the most cold hardy of all. It withstood temperatures below 0°F. The plant is a form of a rhododendron that is endemic to Japan but flourished in the mountains of northern Korea.

In 1973 Professor Tigerstedt began a plant breeding program based on *Rhododendron brachycarpum*. In all, 22,000 seedlings were planted at different sites, in conjunction with the Helsinki Parks Division. Other species included *R. smirnowii*, *R. metternichii*, and a few forms of *R. catawbiense*. It did not take long for the Finnish winter to decimate these seedlings.

By the end, only eighty plants survived. The best of them were carefully propagated, and within a few years nine cultivars were available commercially. Gardeners in Minnesota or Iowa find them valuable, as very few other varieties survive in their climate. Professor Tigerstedt named the new cultivars for legendary characters in Finnish history, made famous by Sibelius's *Kalevala Suite*. It made a lot of sense for Delp to use *Rhododendron brachycarpum* ssp. *tigerstedtii* in his breeding program.

When Delp was told that there was no way he could create a hybrid between a lepidote and an elepidote, he named the successful cross *Rhododendron* 'NoWay'. Another triumph was *R.* 'Ididit', an azaleodendron few others would have spent the time creating. Other charming names were 'Holy Toledo', 'Goody Goody Gumdrop', and 'Cherry Jam'.

This low-key style did not preclude Mrs. Delp from keeping very careful records of each cross, allowing future breeders to re-create what he did and give them a place to start. She created her database in 1985, recording all the characteristics needed to register a new hybrid formally.

The Dawes Arboretum in Newark, Ohio, offered to create a Delp section in its grounds, leading the Delp Study and Preservation Committee to collect as many together as they could, knowing that the varieties would be preserved and protected as a group.

Canadian breeders have evaluated Arctic species such as *Rhododendron lapponicum* for even better cold hardiness than the ones noted above.[14]

Western United States

With its huge reservoir of endemic species, it is hardly surprising that rhododendron breeding in the Pacific Northwest is very active. Growers continue to make enormous contributions to the field. Because the plants are native to the region, climate and soil are immediately under control. This group of devotees does not only stick to local species, but some of the difficulties of cultivation are less exigent for these breeders.

Halfdan Lem

Halfdan Lem (1886–1969) developed many new cultivars at his woodland property near Seattle, Washington. He was born in Norway, one of twelve children, all of whom were very well educated by a private tutor. His principal career was in the fish business, and he moved to Ketchikan in Alaska for this purpose.

Lem's mother had a great love of nature and plants. She would spend hours in her garden, and people came from miles away to see it. Lem inherited this passion. It expressed itself in many different ways, but not until he received a book on rhododendrons as a gift in the 1920s did his true calling emerge.[15] Gwen Bell, herself an important rhododendron figure, tells this story. He immediately joined the British Rhododendron Society. In 1934 he and his wife moved to Seattle to establish his own nursery.

Soon after settling in, he got to know another active rhododendron breeder in the area, Endre Ostbo. They began exchanging seed. He also received seed from an English breeder, Fred Rose of Southampton. Rapidly building a very large collection gave him a complex pool from which to choose crossings. This he proceeded to do, with gusto. As a friend commented, Halfdan would cross rhododendron with "everything except the chickens." Lem's notes indicated that he created more than two thousand crosses in any one year.

Lem was another breeder who chose whimsical names for his cultivars. There was *Rhododendron* 'Hello Dolly', named for his favorite tune, and *R.* 'Potato Peeler'. The latter evoked a customer who had said about a large bill one year, "Gosh, I shall have to peel a lot of potatoes to pay for this." The variety in question was a light yellow *R. caucasicum* hybrid. More of his cultivars are 'Hansel', 'Gretel', 'Lem's Fluorescent Pink', and 'Burgundy Rose'.

Lem was a very large and ebullient man. Even as he entered the terminal phase of the illness that killed him, he still attempted to potter about in his garden, oblivious to the cold and intent on taking care of his plants.

Hjalmar L. Larson

Hjalmar L. Larson (1897–1983) of Tacoma, Washington, was another master. Some of his cultivars were *Rhododendron* 'Double Winner', 'Elya', 'Helen Child', 'Hugtight' (with Fisher), and 'Karen Triplet'. Larson was of Swedish descent and had a Swedish-born uncle in Tacoma who encouraged him enthusiastically.

Like several other people who were attracted to the rhododendron in Washington state, Larson was not a trained horticulturist but turned to breeding rhododendron as a hobby. He earned his living in a sawmill. For years he roamed around, collecting plants and seeds.[16] To learn as much as he could, Larson corresponded with many well-known figures of the time, such as Dr. T. Rokujo in Japan and K. C. Pradhan in Sikkim. He also enjoyed the camaraderie of the other rhododendron fanatics in his community. Could we call them "rhododendriacs"?

In the 1930s, he began to create his own cultivars and continued for fifty years. Altogether, Larson left fifty named cultivars. Most of them are no longer in cultivation, but as Nelson puts it, they were "milestones." As with many of his colleagues, the hobby became a profession. He sold his hybrids in his own nursery. *Rhododendron strigillosum* led him to produce many beautiful red cultivars, such as 'Bert Larson', 'Double Winner', and 'Etta Burrows'.

The warm colors like red and orange attracted him at a time when cooler pinks were more fashionable. He bred a glorious large yellow cultivar, *Rhododendron* 'Mrs Lamott Copeland' and then crossed it with another yellow hybrid to create *R.* 'Pacific Gold'. This handsome plant had red buds and yellow flowers.

When he added *Rhododendron yakushimanum* to the mix in the late 1950s soon after its arrival in the region, the more compact 'Orange Marmalade' was the result. It had red buds, which became orange as the flowers opened.

The American Rhododendron Society recognized his achievements by giving him its gold medal in 1979.

RHODODENDRONS IN CONTINENTAL EUROPE

Germany

Hans Hachmann

Rhododendrons were popular in continental Europe.[17] One of the best-known breeders was Hans Hachmann of Barmstedt in Schleswig-Holstein, who lived from 1930 to 2004. He introduced dozens of prizewinning cultivars to the market. Here are a few of his varieties: *Rhododendron* 'Balalaika', 'Bariton', 'Barnstedt', 'Belona', 'Daniela', 'Hachmann's Feuerschein', and 'Hachmann's Polaris'.

Barmstedt is in the northern part of Germany, with very cold winters and hot summers. Hachmann's son, Holger, now runs the business. World War II prevented Hachmann from obtaining a sound education, but his passion for flowers started very early. At the age of twenty, he developed his first hybrid and did not cease until the year he died. Residual crosses were still being evaluated three years after his death, in 2007.

Hans Hachmann used *Rhododendron yakushimanum* to produce very abundantly flowering and compact hybrids such as *R.* 'Fantastica' and *R.* 'Rendezvous' in the 1970s. His cultivars *R.* 'Fantastica', 'Rendezvous', 'Hachmann's Marlis', 'Hachmann's Polaris', and 'Hachmann's Porzellan' all won Awards of Garden Merit at the Royal Horticultural Society's Wisley trials in the early 2000s. This set of trials was intended to find cultivars that performed very well in full sun, remained compact, and flowered well and consistently over a ten-year period.

Hachmann's output was prodigious. His son told me that he bred 4,947 cultivars in all and selected winners from among 5 million seedlings. Every year he crossbred at least 100 combinations, but he knew exactly which seedlings to select, and he had the necessary firmness to get rid of any less-than-perfect varieties. These are the key gifts.

Hans Hachmann with some of his signature rhododendron hybrids.
Reproduced by permission of Holger Hachmann

Dietrich Hobbie

Dietrich Hobbie (1899–1985) worked at his nursery in Linswege between the Ems and Weser near Hamburg. The soil is naturally acid with many layers of peat below the surface. In 1959, he published a description of his work in the *Rhododendron and Camellia Yearbook*. One of the reasons Hobbie took up breeding rhododendron in his district was the fact that a local nobleman, Herzog P. F. L. von Oldenburg, had planted rhododendron at his estate in the first years of the nineteenth century. Massive stands of *Rhododendron ponticum, R. catawbiense,* and *R. luteum* persisted into the twentieth century, setting the scene.

Many nurseries sprang up in that region, most of them concentrating on these older rhododendron varieties. Hobbie himself was encouraged to begin working with this plant in 1928 by G. D. Westerstedte. They planted the seedlings in a pine wood. In 1935 they received some of the new Japanese azaleas from England and watched as many of them failed because of the cold.

Hobbie visited Exbury and some of the Cornish estates in 1937 and really became serious about breeding new varieties. The English growers gave him seed and encouragement. He was also helped a great deal by Sir William Wright Smith of the Royal Botanical Garden at Edinburgh. Smith sent him seeds from the Ludlow and Sherriff collecting trips in Tibet in 1938. A Chinese botanist, Professor Hu, also sent seed that reached Hobbie. Apart from these valuable contacts, Hobbie basically taught himself everything.

For his first experiments, he used *Rhododendron* 'Britannia' and *R. williamsianum* to create *R.* 'Ammerlandse', and then he used 'Britannia' again, crossing it with *R. forrestii* var. *repens* to breed 'Linswegeanum'. The choice of *R. forrestii* var. *repens* was unexpected, as the species is not particularly attractive by itself.

Hobbie crystallized his goals in this article. He wanted to extend the flowering season and to create hardy compact shrubs with bright colors to enhance front gardens and the edges of roads. A few species can tolerate lime in the soil, and he wanted to extend this quality. Finally, Hobbie was fascinated by the idea of a handsome yellow rhododendron, and he also wanted to create plants with more fragrance.

By 1959 he had planted 250,000 seedlings in his pine forest, based on more than 600 crosses. He believed that *Rhododendron* 'Elizabeth Hobbie'

Dietrich Hobbie's nursery. Hobbie devoted his life to creating hardy rhododendrons that would flourish in northern Germany.
Reproduced by permission of Birgit Hobbie

was one of his best hybrids, bred from *R. forrestii* var. *repens*. He recalled the problem with other cultivars in which *R. forrestii* var. *repens* had been used. He carefully nurtured them for eight years until he realized they were useless. More than 90 percent of the buds failed to open, and 2,000 plants had to be burned. This insight into the harsh realities of plant breeding is valuable.

Some of his cultivars include *Rhododendron* 'Abendsonne', 'Baden Baden', 'Camille Schneider', and 'Goldflimmer' (with Hans Hachmann). The crosses based on Ludlow and Sherriff's *R. wardii* turned out to be very productive. The plants flowered later in the year and were fragrant.

Belgium

Ghent, in Belgium, was a center of azalea breeding, going back to 1820 (see azalea section below) To this day, the Ghent Series of deciduous azalea remains distinct, though it is seldom available in commercial nurseries. Hundreds of newer versions have superseded it.

The Netherlands

The Dutch, with a long tradition of plant breeding and horticulture, were also deeply involved with this group of plants. They began to crossbreed rhododendron in the 1860s. H. den Ouden and Son, Vuyk & C. B. van Nes(s) and Sons, L. J. Entz & Co., Felix & Dijkhuis, and A. Kluis all introduced outstanding rhododendrons and azaleas. These nurseries were in Boskoop, a town that is still the center of the Dutch nursery industry.

The high cost of crossbreeding rhododendron meant it was not a profitable crop but was done as a hobby. After World War II, the enormous destruction of the industry made the expense even greater. The value of the land increased, and so did the price of labor. Rhododendron breeding ceased even as a hobby. The Experimental Station for Arboriculture at Boskoop, really an association of nurserymen, took up the challenge, working with the Institute of Horticultural Plant Breeding at Wageningen.

Rhododendron 'Queen Wilhelmina', 'Britannia', and 'Earl of Athlone' (Van Ness); 'Dr. H. C. Dresselhuys' (den Ouden); 'Madame de Bruin', 'Mrs. Lindsay Smith', and 'America' (Koster); 'Dr. Arnold W. Endtz' (Endtz); and 'Kluis Sensation' (Kluis) were all still in cultivation in the 1970s.

One of the main contributions of the research was to reduce the long interval until a new seedling flowered, up to five years. By gathering the seed earlier in the season and drying it, breeders were now able to reach flowering a year sooner.

Koster Family

The best-known and perhaps most-prolific Dutch breeders were the Koster family. Koster introduced the first Dutch hybrid, *Rhododendron* 'Standard van Boskoop' in 1880. There was then a slight lull, but by 1890 work had started again. In 1896 'Hollandia' appeared, a cross between *R. japonicum* and *R. luteum.*

They introduced *Rhododendron* 'Nova Zembla' in 1902, and at least one nursery still carries it today. It is an intensely deep pink cross of *R. catawbiense* 'Parson's Grandiflorum' with an unnamed red *catawbiense.* Other cultivars include *R.* 'Betty Wormald', 'Fancy', 'Harvest Moon', and 'Lamplighter'. Another one of Koster's hybrids, originally introduced in 1895, was *R. occidentale* 'Irene Koster'. This cultivar won an Award of Garden Merit at the Royal Horticultural Society in 1993.

DEVELOPMENT OF RHODODENDRONS IN ASIA

India

Complicated reasons prevented Chinese and Indian gardeners from developing the rhododendron in spite of its being endemic in certain parts of those countries. The plants were distributed far from population centers, often in mountainous and inaccessible places. In China, the great "classical" plants such as roses, peonies, camellias, and magnolias occupied most of the attention.

Peter Cox, who had traveled and collected in Asia, believed that the absence of rhododendron breeding in China reflected ignorance of the best way to cultivate them. Whatever the reason was, with an indifferent public there is very little chance of a market and thus less incentive for breeders to create new varieties.

The Chinese did some work with azalea but the Japanese were more interested in these plants. Azaleas thrived in the hot plains of Japan, but rhododendrons did not. Because of this difficulty, rhododendrons are hard to find and very expensive in Japan.

Rhododendron does well only in a narrow segment of India. The plants flourish at modest altitude with slightly cooler temperatures, in regions such as the sides of the Western Ghats in southern India.

Viru Viraraghavan

One of the few rhododendron breeders in India at present is Viru Viraraghavan, at his hill station Kodaikanal. He works with his wife, Girija, a geneticist. The elevation there is 7,000 feet. In 1981, Dr. Viraraghavan set out to
breed roses that would withstand the hot and dusty Indian climate more effectively than the ones bred by Westerners for cold hardiness and disease
resistance. In a way, he is intentionally undoing the work of 150 years and
getting the rose back to its semitropical self. Part of his arsenal consists of
some native Indian roses with which he is making important crosses. These
confer some of the characteristics he is seeking.

While these experiments continue, he has studied the native *Rhododendron arboreum* ssp. *nilagaricum* found in the Palni hills, part of the Western
Ghats range. He used pollen from the American Rhododendron Society pollen bank to fertilize wild *R. arboreum* plants in the forest near his home. He
has also crossed some other species and hybrid varieties.

Working in the forest was complicated. For one thing, no matter how
carefully he marked the experimental shrubs, they were hard to find after
some time elapsed. The other problem was that local villagers wanted fire-
wood and often cut plants down.

Eventually he succeeded and registered the lovely pink *Rhododendron*
'Palni Princess' with the International Registration Authority at the Royal
Horticultural Society in London. The registrar told him this was the first
known rhododendron hybrid to come from India. 'Palni Princess' is a cross
between *Rhododendron arboreum* ssp. *nilagaricum* and R.{(Hawke × Idealist)
× Wheatley}.

Dr. Viraraghavan is still exploring the possibilities of the native rhododendron, crossing his own hybrid with *Rhododendron griersonianum* and a
few other hybrids. This work is currently at an intermediate stage.

Japan

Japan has many endemic species scattered around the islands that make up
its archipelago. Additional azaleas reached Japan from China and Korea. By
the late seventeenth century, there were probably about five thousand Chinese
plant species in Japan altogether. Japanese horticulturists classify the azalea

into two groups: the Tsutsuji, flowering early in the year, and the Satsuki, flowering later.

Descendants of Tsutsuji are the azaleas most commonly grown in the United States. A Japanese nurseryman, Itoh Ihei, wrote the first book anywhere in the world solely about azalea in 1692. It lists 332 species and varieties of both Japanese and Korean azaleas, divided into 171 Tsutsuji and 161 Satsuki.[18] The book was translated into English and published in 1984 with commentary by John Creech (1920–2009), azalea expert at the USDA. He later imported many Japanese varieties to incorporate into his breeding program.

Creech considered that the following set of species lay behind the bulk of Japanese hybridizing through the centuries: *Rhododendron kaempferi*, *R. kiusianum*, *R. sataense*, *R. macrosepalum*, *R.* × *mucronatum*, *R. scabrum*, and *R. yedoense* var. *poukhanense*. Creech also discussed the role of *R. japonicum* and *R. molle*. The latter is very tender and originated in subtropical China.

The Satsuki are evergreen. They have been developed in Japan for about five hundred years. They are thought to have arisen from a spontaneous crossing of *Rhododendron indicum* with *R. tamurae*. Some of the best known are the Kurume Series (see later discussion).

Koichiro Wada

Koichiro Wada (1907–1981) sent the first specimen of *Rhododendron yakushimanum*, one of the *R. degronianum* group, to England in 1934.[19] It had been identified in Japan in 1920. This species is found only in a minute niche at the very top of a tall mountain on Yaku Island. Wada was not himself a plant explorer but received new plants from men who were out in the wild.

There are many successful hybrids based on *Rhododendron yakushimanum*. Haworth-Booth lists several excellent azaleas of varying parentage that Wada had sent to England before World War II, including *R.* 'Asakanonare', 'Bungonishiki', and 'Chichibu'.[20] Quite soon after English breeders received *R. yakushimanum*, they shared it with colleagues on the Continent.

Koichiro Wada remains one of the most modern famous Japanese breeders. His father manufactured miso sauce and taught his son a great love of plants. Wada grew up in Numazu but later lived and worked in Yokohama. As a youth he bought his first rhododendron plant and was hooked for life.[21]

Koichiro Wada lost much of his family, as well as the results of so many years of patient labor, in World War II, but he evidently was able to restore his property and start again. Visitors recall that he did his work in a small cramped section behind his nursery but noted his good humor and kindliness at all times.[22]

While his English was not completely certain, he did write several useful articles on his work for the *Quarterly Bulletin of the American Rhododendron Society* (ARS). Various members helped him to polish them and made sure the piece said what he meant. The aggregate of his azalea breeding work was so impressive that the ARS awarded him its Gold Medal in 1970.

Before the Second World War, he had imported rhododendrons from England and Europe and found that most of them failed to thrive in the hot and humid climate around Yokohama. Wada began to breed new cultivars for the opposite qualities usually sought by Western growers, that is, he wanted them to tolerate heat and humidity. His colleague and friend Hideo Suzuki, almost ninety years old in 2008, told me that Mr. Wada had a nursery about sixty miles away in the Amaji Mountains, on the Izu Peninsula.[23]

Wada was also interested in magnolia and bred several named varieties that are still being grown. He registered *Magnolia* 'Wada's Snow White' in 1979. It has a pure white, very fragrant blossom.

Hideo Suzuki

Mr. Suzuki has bred many azaleas and is the honorary life president of the Japanese Rhododendron Society. In 1982, Mr. Suzuki also received the ARS Gold Medal for his contributions. This came as a complete surprise to him. The only hint was that the then-president of the ARS had strongly urged him to attend the annual conference in Washington, D.C., that year.

In contrast, when the Royal Horticultural Society awarded Mr. Suzuki the Veitch Memorial Gold Medal in London in 1994, they told him in advance but instructed him to keep it a secret. Mr. Suzuki was so enthusiastic about the Royal Horticultural Society that he and a friend obtained permission to develop a branch of the organization in Japan. This branch is still active and is headquartered in Tokyo.

Rhododendron 'Gibraltar', an Exbury cultivar.
Reproduced by permission of John Elsley

MORE ABOUT AZALEAS

For an idea of the range of azalea hybrids, one can look at the table of the Royal Botanic Gardens at Kew's azalea beds: this section presents them by horticultural class rather than by individual breeder.

Deciduous

- **Ghent hybrids:** These were started by P. Mortier, a Belgian baker in Ghent who probably used the heat of his ovens to bring on late-flowering species so he could combine them with early-flowering species. He used *Rhododendron indicum*, among others, and the series was sometimes called Southern Indicas. Mortier worked in the 1830s. He sold his collection to Louis Verschaffelt in about 1840. Very little else is known about him.
- **Mollis hybrids:** Louis Van Houtte worked with *Rhododendron japonicum* from about 1861, using seed collected in Japan.

- **Occidentale hybrids:** *Rhododendron occidentale* seed was sent from western North America in the 1850s to the Veitch nursery. It had been discovered in 1827, probably by David Douglas.
- **Knap Hill hybrids:** The Waterer family began their work to improve the Ghent Series.
- **Exbury hybrids:** Lionel de Rothschild worked with Knap Hill crosses for fifteen years, from 1922 to 1937.
- **Ilam hybrids:** Edgar Stead in Ilam, New Zealand, combined Knap Hill hybrids with species from the *Rhododendron luteum* series. Stead was a devoted amateur who founded the New Zealand Rhododendron Association in 1944.
- **Windsor hybrids:** Sir Eric Savill managed the queen's gardens at Windsor. In 1932 he planted a large number of Exbury azaleas, constantly refining and selecting the best ones over the years.
- **Rustica Flore Pleno hybrids:** In 1890, Charles Vuylsteke introduced this slightly mysterious series in Belgium. They are thought to have resulted from a cross between double Ghent cultivars and Mollis hybrids.
- **Slonecker hybrids:** These were created by Howard Slonecker in the American Pacific Northwest to withstand extremely low temperatures.
- **Felix & Dijkhuis Viscosum hybrids:** These cultivars were developed at Boskoop in the Netherlands from about 1960.

Evergreen

- **Girard hybrids:** In Ohio, Peter Girard bred his evergreen azaleas for hardiness and resistance to disease.

SOME BREEDERS OF AZALEAS

Belgium

For much of the nineteenth century and part of the twentieth, Belgium was a leader of commercial floristry. It was not the small country we know today but the center of a large colonial enterprise.

The city of Ghent (Gand or Gand-Brugge in Flemish) supported several important dynasties of nurserymen who made valuable contributions to flower collecting and breeding. It inaugurated the great recurrent floral expositions, the Floralies Gantoises, which still take place every four or five years.

Ambroise Verschaffelt, scion of a horticultural dynasty, was particularly interested in azalea and camellia.
Reproduced by permission of Luc D'Haeze

P. M. Mortier

Mortier was not part of this network. He was a working baker in Ghent and used *Rhododendron luteum* as a seed parent, crossing it with some American varieties. He kept his work secret, and no notes of which azaleas he actually used have come down to us. From internal evidence, experts believe that he must also have used *R. calendulaceum, R. periclymenoides,* and *R. viscosum.* After his death, other Belgian and (later) English breeders took over. For more than one hundred years, his crosses have been exploited and developed.

Vershchaffelt Family

The Vershchaffelt family produced at least three generations of nurserymen and could be accounted a dynasty. The first Vershchaffelt to appear as a gardener was Pierre-Antoine (1764–1844). His three sons—Alexandre, Louis, and Jean—unfortunately were not long-lived like their father.

They carried the business forward, but the one who became really prominent was the grandson, Alexandre's eldest son, Ambroise. He died in 1886 at the age of sixty. This too would now be considered an early age. Ambroise received a large civic funeral befitting a man whose nursery had been graced by a visit from royalty.

Verschaffelt took over from Mortier very soon, using the latter's hybrids as a basis for his own work. He introduced *Rhododendron* 'Cardinal', 'Grandeur Triomphante', 'Guillaume II', 'Heureuse Surprise', 'Jenny Lind', and 'Prince Henri des Pays-Bas'. By 1859 he had five hundred hybrids.

Verschaffelt was also very active in accumulating and breeding camellia (see later discussion). He published an iconography of the camellia in thirteen volumes, from 1848 to 1860.

Louis Van Houtte

Louis Van Houtte was another contemporary in Ghent (see later discussion in camellia section). He owned an enormous nursery, unlike anything that had been seen previously, and used Mortier's stock to create the Mollis Series. A few of his hybrids at this period were *Rhododendron* 'Madame Gustave Guilmot', 'Quadricolor', 'Roi des Belges', 'Rose Marie', 'Van Houtte Flore Pleno', and 'Wilhelmine'.

Various Breeders

Frans van Cassell and De Coninck also worked on the Mortier series. Another Belgian breeder, Charles Vuylsteke, came across a double-flowered Ghent azalea and crossed it with one of the Mollis Series.

Waterer and Davies in England picked up the work, too. The key characteristic of the Ghent Series is an extraordinary range of color, with a very vivid upper petal. Only when Rothschild's Exbury Series emerged, with even larger flowers and brighter colors, did the Ghent Series slip in popularity. Of the roughly one hundred named Ghent cultivars, about twenty-five can still be found.

The Kurume Series of evergreen azaleas is an example of Japanese azalea breeding. Ernest Wilson was the first to introduce them to the West. The Kurume azaleas were developed by Motozo Sakamoto, a Japanese nurseryman. He raised and selected seedlings of azaleas growing on the sacred Mt. Kirishima.

After Sakamoto's death, the collection was passed on to Kokiro Akashi, a nurseryman from Kurume, a small town on the southern island of Kyushu,

Japan. Wilson saw these azaleas in 1914 and suggested that John Ames, a member of a wealthy Massachusetts family, buy some of them. They arrived in the United States in 1916.

More Kurume azaleas came when the Domoto brothers, who were invited to come to Oakland in California by Anthony Chabot to run his program for producing tea, brought specimens with them in 1917. Toichi Domoto, one of their descendants and a much-loved figure in California horticulture, died a few years ago at the age of 103. Unfortunately, growing or curing good tea in California proved impossible and Chabot had to give up the idea, but the Domotos established a famous nursery. The azaleas were an important part of their stock.

CAMELLIA

This most beautiful of shrubs with widely varied flowers was named for a scholarly Jesuit priest, Georg Kamel (1661–1706), a Moravian missionary in the Philippines who also explored the islands for plants. He went there while still quite young and began the first systematic collecting of medicinal plants in the archipelago. Kamel sent his findings to the distinguished English naturalist John Ray, and they were published in 1704.

The Reverend Kamel did not discover the plant, but Linnaeus knew of his work and wanted to commemorate him in a plant name. There was no direct connection between Kamel and the plant. Only one of the huge number of species is native to the Philippines.

Recently a Belgian scholar, Luc D'Haeze, has offered an interesting conjecture that Kamel might indeed have seen cultivated camellias in the Philippines and found them beautiful. At that time, they would have been known only by their Chinese names. Members of the large Chinese minority in the islands may have taken the plants with them from China.[1] This still does not mean that Father Kamel found the plants in the wild.

Camellia is endemic to Southeast Asia, mainly China and Japan, but has adapted well to conditions across the globe. Economically, the most important camellia is the plant from which we derive tea, *Camellia sinensis*. Its leaves have been dried and fermented for centuries to be used as the basis for a drink. Chinese texts suggest that it was known in the third century BCE.

The story of how this native of China, so closely guarded by the authorities, came to be grown widely in India is very instructive. A close relative of this plant, *C. sinensis* var. *assamica,* is endemic to Assam. It would take a Nobel Prize–winning economist to tease out all the strands of modern tea growing. At least two major figures in the plant-collecting world were involved: Nathaniel Wallich and Robert Fortune.[2]

Tea was very costly. Apart from the beauty of the flowers, some of the intense interest in camellias originally stemmed from a quest to grow tea less expensively. Getting *Thea sinensis* (now *Camellia sinensis* (L.) Kuntze var. *sinensis*) and the Assam variant established in India was the first time anyone succeeded in that goal. Almost all the other smaller ventures failed. Recently someone has managed to grow good tea in Australia at a reasonable price by mechanizing the operations.

Centuries of breeding and experimentation in China and Japan led to the development of dozens of ornamental varieties. The first European collectors were not allowed to go into the countryside but found the modified plants in temple grounds, in pots at nursery gardens, and in the gardens of private homes. Wandering Buddhist monks carried camellias, and other plants, back and forth between China and Japan so frequently that the actual origin of some of them may never be known. The exquisite elegance of the plants and flowers played an important role in the Chinese and Japanese religion and culture. Camellias also symbolized longevity.

Scientists are still catching up on the identification of wild species. There are believed to be about three hundred species of camellia. The principal species that are the basis of modern hybridizing and commerce are *Camellia japonica, C. sasanqua,* and *C. reticulata.* Of these, *C. japonica* may be the most significant for breeding purposes. *C. japonica* flowers in late winter/ early spring, while *C. sasanqua* tends to flower in fall. Other basic species used for breeding include *C. saluenensis* and *C. lutchuensis,* a fragrant variety. The epithet "japonica" is slightly misleading, as the species is a native of China.

George Forrest sent *Camellia saluenensis* (named for the banks of the Salween River where he found it) to J. C. Williams in Cornwall in the 1920s. In 1930 Williams planted it in his garden at Caerhays and then sowed the seed it produced. Cross-pollination took place between the *C. saluenensis* and a neighboring *C. japonica,* giving rise to the first interspecific hybrid,

C. × *williamsii*. Other growers used these for further work, expanding their colors and styles. The amateur gardener enjoys a lot of choice.

These × *williamsii* hybrids have been very successful for many years. The plants grow well: they are productive and can tolerate some degree of cold. They flower for a long time, and when the blossoms die they drop off spontaneously, leaving the plant with a clean appearance at all times.

In the modern period, some cultivars bred by Dr. William Ackerman at the USDA National Arboretum based on *Camellia oleifera* have shown considerable cold hardiness. The winters of 1977–78 and 1978–79 were exceptionally cold in Maryland and Virginia, and almost the entire collection of historic japonica and sasanqua camellias at the National Arboretum was destroyed. Dr. Ackerman, the senior research horticulturist, observed that *C. oleifera* varieties had done much better. He began a program in which *C. oleifera* was crossed with the other species, and he later issued such hybrids as *C.* 'Winter's Rose', 'Winter's Waterlily', and 'Winter's Charm'.

At approximately the same time, Dr. Clifford Parks in South Carolina developed additional cold-hardy hybrids such as *Camellia* 'Survivor' and 'Mason Farm'.

Another species that is hoped to confer its traits on new hybrids is *C. nitidissima* (syn. *C. chrysantha*), a yellow-flowered type. So far these hopes have not been borne out very well. Almost all camellias are white, pink, or red or some combination thereof.

Stirling Macoboy writes that *Camellia sasanqua* is very versatile and easy to grow and can be used in various guises such as specimen shrubs, hedges, large trees, or even espaliered.[3] In Japan, sasanqua fruit was used for centuries to produce a clear cooking oil.

EARLY EUROPEAN HISTORY

Andreas Cleyer, a German physician with the Dutch East India Company, described the camellia in his two books about Chinese medicine before any other European. Alice Coats, author of several richly informative books about plant collecting, mentioned the fact that Cleyer was an inveterate smuggler and the cause of many Japanese men losing their lives—hardly an admirable character.[4]

James Cunningham, a Scottish physician attached to the East India Company's "factory" in Amoy, sent the earliest-known camellia to James Petiver in London at some time close to 1700. This was *Camellia japonica*. No more was heard of Cunningham after 1702. He may have died in the East.

One of his important accomplishments was to commission a set of colored drawings of different plants from a Chinese physician, Dr. Bun-Ko, showing the whole plant and its parts. Cunningham asked Charles Brewer to take the pictures, together with herbarium specimens, to James Petiver in 1701. Petiver was a scholarly apothecary who was very actively involved with the Chelsea Physic Garden. The pictures are still to be found in the British Museum.

On another collecting trip, Cunningham visited the island of Chusan and found a different camellia. This too went to London. It ended up with Leonard Plukenet, a distinguished naturalist of the period. This specimen turns out to have been *Camellia sasanqua*.

Not long afterward, Engelbert Kaempfer traveled to Japan as physician to the Dutch East India Company. He found several camellias: *C. sinensis, C. japonica,* and *C. sasanqua*. He reported on them in his book using the Japanese names he heard, "Tsubaki," but his drawings were so meticulous it is clear which plant he meant.

All these specimens were dried for the herbarium. It is not clear when seed or a living plant reached Europe. The eminent plant enthusiast Lord Petre of Essex grew the first known camellia in England somewhere about 1739. T. J. Savige, a distinguished camellia expert in Australia, has looked into how Lord Petre might have received this flower.[5] Because Lord Petre was a Catholic, his connection with the Jesuits in Macau is suggested as a possible route.

Religion was still a seriously divisive force in English life in the eighteenth century, and Catholics were considered to be renegades. They were not allowed to hold any public office or attend the ancient universities. It is a tribute to Lord Petre's qualities that men like the Quaker Peter Collinson held him in very high esteem.

Lord Petre's gardener, James Gordon, later set up his own nursery in London in 1742. He had at least one camellia plant, perhaps from Lord Petre's estate, and was able to propagate numerous camellias for sale. In 1768, Gordon advertised 118 varieties of green tea camellias in his catalogue and almost 200 other kinds of tea camellia.

An Italian historian placed the first camellias in Italy in 1760. A very old camellia plant, possibly from the eighteenth century, still thrives in Naples's Caserta Park. Savige has found a possible link between that plant and those in England. James Gordon had a partner for a few years, John Graefer, but in 1786, the latter became the queen of Naples's gardener and moved to Italy. The queen had created an English garden, Caserta Park. Savige believes that Graefer may have taken one of Gordon's camellias with him when he went.

The man in charge of the park was Sir William Hamilton, Charles Greville's uncle and Emma Hamilton's husband. Lady Hamilton and Lord Nelson's story is well known. The connection with a lovely camellia plant is less so.

In Western countries, camellia was to have more than one cycle of popularity followed by neglect. The original plants were not particularly attractive, and little notice was taken of them for many years. One of the issues of *Curtis's Botanical Magazine* for 1788 shows a single-flowered red camellia, possibly connected with Lord Petre's plant.

A few years later, things changed. In 1792, one of the East India Company's sea captains, Captain Connor, took a cargo containing new and much more exciting camellias to England. These flowers led to intense interest. The first double flower ever seen in the West, *Camellia alba plena,* was immensely popular.

Another British sea captain, Richard Rawes, subsequently carried the first *Camellia reticulata* to England. It bloomed in Kent in 1826. Robert Fortune found another variety of the species in China and sent it back in 1847. Both these flowers were rich shades of red, but neither was fertile. They were very tender, needing a warm environment, and could only be propagated by grafting. This made them costly indulgences for the wealthy.

The secretary of the Royal Horticultural Society, John Lindley, named the new species "reticulata" because of the veining on the leaves. He was aware that the plant he had might not have been a true species, but he went ahead with the name anyway. Now it is known that most of these plants were ancient and complex cultivars.

For the next sixty years, "camellia fever" raged across Europe, spurred by these new arrivals. The plants crossed the Channel very fast, and nurseries in France and Belgium took them up rapidly. France became the epicenter of camellia popularity. Fashionable young men would not leave home without a camellia in their lapel. The flowers were snapped up as fast as they could be produced.

Many nurserymen were deeply involved, as were legions of devoted amateurs. One by-product was the fabric "chintz." It was splattered with gigantic images of camellias and used for curtains and upholstery by all classes.

Camellia formed a significant part of Louis Van Houtte's stock when he opened his nursery in Ghent. Several other Belgian nurseries became known for camellias, among them Verschaffelt. Roger de Bisschop owned a giant nursery, issuing camellias on an industrial scale.

In France, Henri Guichard sold thousands of them. Guichard's granddaughters took over the business in 1911. It became known as Guichard Soeurs. The company was still flourishing in the 1970s under the management of Claude Thoby. Guichard Soeurs introduced several varieties of *Camellia japonica,* including 'Kenny', 'Jubilee', and 'Herme'.

One reason all this could succeed was the use of *Camellia* 'Donckelarii', named for the director of the Royal Gardens of Ghent, Monsieur Donckelaar. This *Camellia reticulata* cultivar came into Europe at a very troubled time and barely missed being destroyed at the docks. Philipp von Siebold had sent it from Japan in a large shipment. *C.* 'Donckelarii' turned out to do very well in the French climate and gave rise to several excellent cultivars in its turn.

The camellia was also very popular in Germany.[6] A single family seems to have been responsible for disseminating the plants throughout Germany and parts of Europe. Johann Heinrich Seidel (1744–1815) was the eldest of five sons of the mayor of Radeburg. Johann Heinrich learned his trade in several countries and became the head gardener at the Royal Gardens in Dresden. Saxony had been an electorate and a duchy, but in 1806 it became a kingdom as a result of Napoleon's edicts. A later duke of Saxony was Albert, who later became prince consort to Queen Victoria. While working for the duke, Johann Heinrich met the great German scientist and poet Johann Wolfgang Goethe. They had interesting discussions about many topics, including plants and gardens.

Out of Johann Heinrich's ten children, four sons were gardeners. Two of the brothers, Traugott Leberecht (1775–1585) and Friedrich Jacob (1789–1860) opened a nursery in Dresden after being trained abroad. A few years later, Traugott opened his own nursery in Vienna.

P. Stroobant, ad. nat. pinx. in Horto Versch.   Etab. Lith. de I. Stroobant, à Gand.

CAMELLIA CONTESSA TOZZONI.

Semis-Italie. (Serre-froide.)

A. Verschaffelt publ.

Camellia 'Contessa Tozzoni', an early nineteenth-century camellia hybrid.
Reproduced by permission of Luc D'Haeze

Another brother, Carl August, emigrated to Australia and settled in Victoria. One of his descendants prepared a brief family history and deposited it with the Australian National Library.[7]

Friedrich was stationed in Paris for two years, at the Jardin des Plantes. He is said to have taken three of the Empress Josephine's camellias in his rucksack as far as Erfurt in 1813. After returning to Dresden, he then used them as the basis of his business. This story has not been substantiated. At one point, the French military police were said to have been chasing him and his brother.

Camellias were initially introduced into Germany in different ways. Once was in 1799, when the tsarina of Russia sent plants to Dresden, to Schonbrunn in Vienna, and to the Royal Botanic Gardens at Kew. Johann Heinrich Seidel recorded them in his garden. Another plant was received by a gardener named Teschnik in 1804. French and Belgian nurseries stocked the camellia at the time, and many early camellias in Germany came from those countries. The 1820 Seidel catalogue listed six types of camellia.

Seidel's descendants continued to run the nursery. Finally it passed into the hands of a son-in-law, Ludwig Schroder, in 1986. His son, Christian, runs the firm of T. J. Rudolf Seidel in Grüngräbschen. T. J. Rudolf Seidel now specializes in rhododendron and azalea.

The eastern part of Germany does not immediately come to mind as camellia territory, with its Continental climate of very cold winters and hot, fairly dry summers, yet the Seidel enterprise flourished. Erfurt is a great horticultural center in Thuringia, many miles west of Dresden, with dozens of large wholesale nurseries founded many years ago. Soil and water are both ideally suited to growing flowers. Dresden is much closer to the Polish border.

There was then another hiatus in the entire camellia story, as well as the reticulata story. In the last quarter of the nineteenth century, fashionable interest fell off completely. Everyone was going into begonias and sweet peas. Camellia plants were still grown in suburbia and outlandish foreign parts, but high society yawned.

Lots of reasons were given, one of which was that it was getting too easy to buy and grow. Hoi polloi were ruining its mystique. One author attributes the onset of this decline to the notorious novel *La dame aux camellias* by Alexandre Dumas, *fils*.[8] The model for this character was the ill-fated, rather scandalous Alphonsine Plessis (alias "Marie Duplessis" and called Marguerite in the novel), a high-class courtesan in Paris. For three weeks out of the month she was adorned by a white camellia, but for five days she wore a red one. Alphonsine died at the age of twenty-three.

Seidel's nursery reported brisk sales in Argentina and Costa Rica at that time but very few in Britain or Europe. The other places where camellias thrived were Australia and New Zealand. The New Zealand climate seems to have been perfect for this genus. Australia has too many hot, dry days in some regions.

Almost one hundred years after Fortune's great introduction and crowning the efforts of three intrepid horticulturists, a new set of *Camellia reticulata* varieties arrived in the United States in 1948. Enthusiasm for the camellia was rekindled. Ralph Peer, a noted amateur camellia enthusiast; Walter Hazlewood, an Australian nurseryman; and Dr. Walter Lammerts, a California rosarian and noted plant breeder, independently imported these new plants from Yunnan. These were collectively known as the Kunming Group and jump-started the camellia revival after World War II.

Camellia history in that Chinese province goes back at least one thousand years. In spite of very serious political obstacles, Walter Hazlewood had been able to communicate with Professor Tsai, director of the Yunnan Botanical Institute, in 1947. The professor revealed the depth and riches of his collection, something no Westerner had known about previously. Hazelwood then suggested that Ralph Peer meet with Professor Tsai during one of his journeys to China. The meeting never took place, but the camellias were exported safely.

Very soon after the plants arrived, California gardeners began crossing them with other species to develop whole new races of plants. The breeders quickly found that these plants were very tender and shy in setting seed. Ignorance of the best way to grow the plants and slight inadequacies in California's climate and terrain affected them in some instances.

When the breeders improved their cultural practices, vigorous new hybrids emerged. Although their home in Yunnan is in the mountains, the latitude is almost equatorial. Things went much better in Australia and New Zealand. In the current period, the majority of significant new camellia varieties come from the East and West Coasts of the United States as well as from Australia and New Zealand.

Looking over this field as a whole from a distance, one can clearly see that the nineteenth-century fervor stemmed from more than any one flower.

There was a mood afoot. It was not only camellia fever, it was azalea fever, rose fever, pelargonium fever, begonia fever, fern fever, and so many more.

A series of events coincided to make horticulture extremely rewarding: large new fortunes based on new industries; the end of the Napoleonic wars and the onset of a prolonged period of peace; the ability to travel to formerly closed countries and slight loosening of the social fabric. New money could insinuate itself into higher social circles gracefully. Beautiful flowers cleansed the stain off money tainted by trade. Horticulture was all part of a triumphal declaration of progress and reveling in the opulence of wealth.

Abbé Lorenzo Berlèse

The Italian Abbé Lorenzo Berlèse (1784–1863) was probably the greatest authority on the camellia in the nineteenth century. He published *Monographie du genre Camellia* in 1840.[9] This was followed by his magisterial *Iconographie du genre Camellia* in three volumes.[10] The latter appeared from 1841 to 1843.

Berlèse was a very wealthy man who took holy orders and then moved to Paris to be a chaplain. Once there, he established a great estate. As the numbers of camellia varieties multiplied, he sought ways to simplify the discourse by putting them into groups. His first attempt was to do it by color, but he soon felt that this was inadequate. His next idea was to classify the flower heads by their resemblance to other flowers, such as anemones or roses. All these categories are laid out in H. Harold Hume's *Camellias*.[11] (This was later done with the begonia as well.)

Berlèse also believed that there were great possibilities for breeding the camellia species. Four or five French nurseries specialized in camellia breeding at the time: Bertin in Versailles, Cels, Paillet, Truffault and Boursault in Paris, and Cochet and Leroy in Angers. At the same time, Cochet also paid a lot of attention to roses and is far better known for them (see Roses later in this chapter).

The modern classification, created by the American Camellia Society in 1942, comprises three sections, with two kinds in the "Simple" group, three in the "Incomplete Double" group, and four in the "Complete Double" group.[12]

Berlèse's books mentioned 282 varieties of the flower. Ambroise Verschaffelt in Ghent followed Berlèse and played an important part in sorting out the different camellias, recording the situation in the mid-nineteenth century. Over the thirteen years that Verschaffelt brought out his books, he covered a total of 623 cultivars.[13]

Verschaffelt's American translator, E. A. McIlhenny, counted the different types of flower that Berlèse listed.[14] He created five classes for them. There were 43 single flowered, 44 semidoubles, 95 doubles with stamens and petaloids, 43 fully imbricated, and 53 full doubles. McIlhenny was a successful businessman, the originator of Tabasco sauce and a great camellia lover himself.

He then stated that Verschaffelt had left out the singles and semidoubles, no doubt because he felt they had been thoroughly covered by Berlèse. Their work overlapped in only six cases. In spite of the importance of the Verschaffelt series of pictures, they are now valuable more for their aesthetic content than for their botanical significance. Verschaffelt did not include any varieties bred by people with whom he competed locally. Many of the plants he illustrated came from Italy or France, with only a few from other countries. It was up to Louis Van Houtte to blow his own trumpet in *Flore des Serres*.

The interest in this plant was intense for many years, and anything that was published would succeed. Then, quite suddenly, after having made this fine contribution to horticultural science, the abbé seemingly inexplicably gave it all up in 1846, sold his collection, and moved back to Italy. Perhaps the church re-exerted its authority over his life with its iron insistence on obedience. He died in 1863 at his monastery. Verschaffelt took on the task of illuminating the world of camellias after Berlèse moved away.

INTRODUCTION OF THE CAMELLIA INTO THE UNITED STATES

The camellia was first introduced into the United States in the late 1790s. A Hoboken man, John Stevens, received a red camellia from England. In 1800 a friend of his from Devonshire, Michael Floy, brought him another plant, *Camellia alba plena*. Floy remained in America, opening two nurseries in Manhattan: one in the Bowery and the other in Harlem. He successfully grew camellias from seed and was considered to be an expert by other New York nurserymen, such as Grant Thorburn, Thomas Hogg, and William Prince, all of whom stocked the camellia. Whether any of them created any new varieties is not clear.

Camellia fancying was active in New York, but the principal center in America at the time was Philadelphia, with Boston a close second. Marshal Wilder in Boston bred a fairly large number of seedlings, and at least two were successful. He also imported a lot of plants from Europe and at one time was said to have three hundred camellias. Colonel J. L. F. Warren, a nurseryman in Brighton, Massachusetts, sold camellias in England. When he emigrated to California in 1849, he took the first camellias to that state.

C. M. Hovey, the man who started the *Magazine of Horticulture,* and an important figure in early American horticulture, also bred new varieties. This interest was fostered by the Massachusetts Horticultural Society, which held annual camellia shows.

In Philadelphia, camellia growing was even more active and advanced. A Scottish nurseryman, Robert Buist, who had immigrated in 1828, listed twenty thousand camellias in his inventory when he retired in 1875. This, and other nurseries such as that of David Landreth, supplied the rest of the country, North and South, and also sent plants to Europe.

Camellias moved south via Baltimore, a city not too far from Philadelphia. Farther south, Magnolia Gardens near Charleston, South Carolina, introduced a good number of *Camellia japonica* varieties: *C.* 'Catherine Cathcart', 'Debutante', 'Duchess of Sutherland', 'Eleanor Hagood', 'Elizabeth Boardman', 'Jessie Katz', 'Mrs. Charles Cobb', 'Prima Donna', 'Reverend John Bennett', and 'Reverend John D. Drayton'.

Berckmans Family

Camellias took stronger hold in the South when Dr. Louis Edouard Matthieu Berckmans (1801–1883), a physician and noted plantsman, left his native Belgium for political and religious reasons.[15] Although he came from an old aristocratic family, he was very radical, and the events of 1848 left him vulnerable to political retaliation. In keeping with his principles, he married a poor young woman from the Brabant countryside, Marie Gaudins, and not the noble heiress his family expected. The family was highly displeased and shunned both him and his wife. It was tragic that she died immediately after giving birth to his son, Prosper.

A few years later, Dr. Berckmans made the "proper" match they wanted. His bride was a descendant of Peter Paul Rubens the painter. This marriage

Dr. Berckmans's son Prosper and his wife (née Craig) with sons.
Reproduced by permission of Kenan Research Center/Atlanta History Center

was not a success, and they were divorced quite soon. The Berckmans did have a child, Prosper's half brother. Emile was Elizabeth Rubens Berckmans' son.

In 1850 Dr. Berckmans sent his elder son to prospect for him in America and find a place where they could settle safely and open a nursery. Prosper kept a meticulous diary of his journey; the family saved the diary and eventually bequeathed it to the Kenan Research Library at the Atlanta History Center. Georgia, particularly Augusta, appealed to Prosper. It had good land, an excellent climate, plenty of water, and proximity to transportation. How many nineteen-year-olds could do such a masterly survey?

Dr. Berckmans moved first to Plainfield, New Jersey, in 1851 with many of his valuable plants. He established a noted nursery in Plainfield with hundreds of varieties of pears. New Jersey was good as an interim place to settle, but it was too cold for all the plants they wanted to grow. They decided to try Augusta, Georgia. Part of its attraction was the fact that another set of expatriate Belgians had formed an agricultural colony nearby in Rome, Georgia.

In 1857, just before the Civil War broke out, Dr. Berckmans, with his son and daughter-in-law, Mary Craig Berckmans, bought a half share in the

Fruitland Nursery from D. Redmond and moved the family to Augusta. The younger son, Emile, did not stay there long and returned to Plainfield with his mother. Redmond was an indigo and cotton planter and editor of the *Southern Cultivator*. P. J. A. Berckmans edited the magazine once he became established.

Prosper Jules Alphonse Berckmans was born in 1821 and died in 1910. He and his wife, Mary Craig (the niece of Governor George C. Ludlow of New Jersey), had three sons: Prosper Jr. (always known as "Allie"), Louis, and Robert. Prosper Jr. later ran the family business, and Louis became a noted landscape architect. Robert also worked in the business. None of them was a horticulturist like their father and grandfather.

The nursery supplied camellias very widely. In 1858 the Berckmans family bought out D. Redmond and became sole owners of the firm. By 1861, their catalogue listed over one hundred varieties of azalea and camellia. It was one of the first large commercial nurseries in the South.

Another document lovingly cherished and handed down to the library was P. J. A. Berckmans' order book for 1858. Every order was carefully entered and checked off when the goods were dispatched. Among the customers was the firm of Ellwanger and Barry in Rochester, New York (see chapter 4). On two occasions, Ellwanger and Barry ordered several dozen grafted apple trees.

Fruitland Nursery received much of its ornamental stock, in particular the camellias and azaleas, from Belgium. The individual varieties of camellia were not named in their catalogues. For the rest of the nineteenth century, they continued to offer an equally large choice in camellias, distinguishing between those they imported and those that were homegrown.

One of the major suppliers of camellias in the second half of the nineteenth century was the family of Seidel in Dresden, Germany. While the catalogues do not name the suppliers, Robert Berckmans noted that he had traveled through Germany and imported *Camellia* 'Pink Perfection'. This was the American name for *C.* 'Frau Minna Seidel'. Minne Seidel was T. C. Seidel's wife.

At the same time, they also imported many rhododendrons and azaleas from France, Belgium, Japan, and Germany. This led to the azalea's increasing popularity in the South.

It is not clear why the camellias were unnamed while the Berckmans family ran the nursery, but it may have been because they were not regis-

Prosper Berckmans with his sons.
Reproduced by permission of Kenan Research Center/Atlanta History Center

tered with any camellia society. The first time named camellias appeared in the Fruitland Nursery's catalogue was 1931. This may simply represent a change in policy, listing cultivars the firm had created through the years but never named commercially, rather than necessarily reflecting new hybridizing being done in that decade. The Berckmans frequently referred to the thousands of camellias they grew at the nursery but did not make it clear whether these were new cultivars.

Someone named a camellia cultivar for Charles Sprague Sargent, director of the Arnold Arboretum in Jamaica Plains, Massachusetts. It made its first

The front cover of the
Berckmans catalogue,
1937/38.
*Reproduced by permission of
Kenan Research Center/
Atlanta History Center*

Berckmans camellias on
the back cover of the 1938
catalogue.
*Reproduced by permission
of Kenan Research Center/
Atlanta History Center*

appearance in the catalogue in 1931. Dr. Sargent had corresponded with P. J. A. Berckmans. It has not been possible to find out who bred the cultivar. The nursery changed hands twice in the 1920s. Sigmund Tarnok bought the business in 1920. One year later he sold it to Baillie and Gwin. The Kenan Research Library has the Berckmans archives and catalogues of the successor owners, but information about a specific breeder was not in them.

During the remainder of the 1930s, the catalogues emphasized camellia, with beautiful colored pictures on the front and back covers as well as both black and white and colored photographs in the body of the text.

P. J. A. Berckmans was a founder of the Georgia Horticultural Society in 1876 and an active member of the American Pomological Society.[16] He was a leader in experimental horticulture, introducing many new fruit trees and ornamental plants. The 'Elberta' peach, bred from the Chinese Cling Peach, may be one of his most lasting legacies, even though it has now been superseded by other more modern varieties. Samuel Rumph made the final improvements to the Elberta peach, which led to its gigantic popularity with canners. Elberta was Mrs. Rumph's name.

Berckmans' reputation and influence were so profound that his name was bandied about as a possible candidate to become the first secretary of agriculture. That did not happen: he had been born abroad and was a Democrat, both disabling characteristics.

There are a few interesting questions to be answered about this Georgia nursery and the Civil War. Did General Sherman march through the grounds? How did they handle the naval blockade of all the Southern ports? As far as one can tell from the family's papers and contemporary news reports, the nursery was not attacked. The family grew essential fruit and vegetables for the Confederate army. (This was how the Benarys escaped certain annihilation during the Nazi era in Germany; see chapter 4.)

There is no reference to the Southern blockades, but conditions were so unsettled in the 1860s that it is doubtful that the Berckmans were even trying to import ornamental plants during the conflict. There is a break in the catalogues from 1859 to 1869, which could reflect actual business conditions or simply be an artefact of preservation.

Fifty years after the Civil War, the First World War brought more difficulties. The catalogue for 1916 notes that European camellias were very scarce that year. Only the intercession of close friends in Belgium enabled the Berckmans to find a few choice plants. Later in the war, the U.S. government put a complete embargo on all imports of European seeds and plants.

Before horticultural and specialty societies became commonplace, Berckmans' personal correspondence with dozens of nurserymen and growers throughout the United States and other countries was responsible for spreading an enormous amount of knowledge and skill very widely. One of his correspondents was Adolph Sutro, mayor of San Francisco and a fellow immigrant with the Berckmans family in 1851. Sutro invited P. J. A. Berckmans to lunch when the latter visited San Francisco.

The property was sold in 1931 and is now the site of the Augusta National Golf Club, home of the Masters Golf Tournament. The company name was sold to Baillie and Gwin in the 1920s, and they operated the nursery until the 1960s.

Louis and Prosper Berckmans were both employed by the golf club. Louis laid out the ornamental grounds, and Prosper became the manager. They worked very diligently to save thousands of trees and shrubs their late father had planted. Each hole is named for a plant and is surrounded by the actual plants, such as camellia and azalea. This is one of the most beautiful golf courses in the country.

CAMELLIAS IN CALIFORNIA

After Colonel Warren took camellias to California in 1849, the plants spread widely and became very popular. The climate suited them. They continued to be imported, but within a fairly short period of time they were bred locally. By the mid-twentieth century, one nursery in particular, the Nuccios, became expert in breeding new varieties.

The Domotos, the Japanese experts encouraged by Antoine Chabot to move to California to produce tea on a very large scale, made a huge mark in camellia breeding, as well as in so many other plants. The tea program did not work out, but their nursery left a legacy of excellence. The California Flower Market in San Francisco was a cooperative effort by all the Japanese nurserymen in the region in the early 1920s, seeking an outlet for their wares. It is still very active.

Domoto either bred or introduced some handsome *Camellia japonica* cultivars: 'Akebono', 'Alba Gigantea', 'Flame', 'Hakurakuten', 'Pink Star', 'Shiragiku', and 'Snow Drift'. This is only a partial listing.

Nuccio Family

Joseph and Giulio ("Julius") Nuccio established a nursery in Alhambra, California, in 1935. This is in Alameda County, the northern part of the state, about forty miles east of San Francisco.[17]

A year after World War II ended, Joseph and Giulio's father bought a large tract of land in Altadena, near Pasadena in southern California. The nursery is now owned and managed by the children and grandchildren.

The cultivars that they bred are legion. Many of these plants won prizes and are still cherished today. Listing the Nuccio introductions is a serious task. In japonicas alone, I gave up at *M,* after counting more than 24 camellias. Over the years, they issued more than 130 camellias and 150 azaleas.

ANOTHER nursery close by in Pasadena, McCaskill, gave the Nuccios a good run for their money. McCaskill bred a very large number of handsome camellias, principally japonicas.

The Huntington Gardens in San Marino, California, a small town that is really part of Pasadena, has one of the finest collections of camellias anywhere. William Hertrich, Mr. Huntington's gardener and eventual business manager, issued new camellias starting in 1912 and named one for his wife, Margarete. The American Camellia Society offers a Margarete Hertrich prize every year.

Hertrich was passionate about camellias. At the end of his long career, he published the three-volume *Camellias in the Huntington Gardens.*[18] The collection, which is an internationally prized resource, contains about one hundred of the Nuccio cultivars. It was named an International Camellia Garden of Excellence by the International Camellia Society. There are only four other such gardens in the world.

HYDRANGEA

This beautiful shrub has a relatively short history in cultivation compared to the ancient story of roses, camellias, and azaleas. Its modern history can be said to start in Japan in the eighteenth century, although the plant was used in their gardens long before that.

Carl Thunberg described five species of hydrangea in *Flora Japonica,* 1784. He put them in the genus *Viburnum.*[1] There are about eighty species all told, found in East Asia and North and South America. The oakleaf hydrangea, *Hydrangea quercifolia,* is native to North America. At least two species have also been found in South America.

Most modern garden hybrids, the "Hortensias," come from French breeding based on varieties of *Hydrangea macrophylla, H. maritima,* and *H. japonica.* The terms *H. maritima* and *H. japonica* are now obsolete. Haworth-Booth, an English expert and devotee of the plant, named a species *H. maritima,* but it has been subsumed into *H. macrophylla.* The first specimen to reach England from China was named *H. macrophylla* 'Sir Joseph Banks', and that seems to be the one under the rubric of *H. maritima.* *H. japonica* was a term used by Siebold and by Regel, but it is no longer considered to be a separate species.[2]

Philipp Franz von Siebold brought *Hydrangea macrophylla* var. *otaksa* from Japan in the 1830s. He had been expelled for meddling too much in Japanese affairs. As he was packing up to leave, someone gave him this plant as a gift. The name "hortensia" comes from Siebold's era and is the vernacular name for the plant in France and Germany. Its origin is unclear.

Additional species used in the initial breeding in Japan were *Hydrangea acuminata* and *H. thunbergii.* Each contributed its very particular qualities. *H. maritima* provided hardiness in a coastal environment. It stands up to strong winds very well.

The classification of the hydrangea is very complex, to say the least. Most recently Dan Hinkley laid out the results of his research in Japan and challenged some of the accepted order. The Van Gelderens of Boskoop in the Netherlands have made important contributions to the field, publishing a valuable illustrated monograph.[3]

In the 1980s, seeing an opportunity to promote the country's horticultural trade, the Swiss government invested in developing a race of hardy hybrids: the Tellers. Each cultivar was named for a different bird, such as *Hydrangea* 'Pheasant' and *H.* 'Nightingale'. This period ended in 1992 with the death of Fritz Meier, the principal hybridist. Two other men, Fritz Kobel and Fritz Schütz, were active in that work, but they died many years ago. That department has been folded into a larger section of the Swiss agricultural endeavor.[4] The German government also did something rather similar in the 1990s, with the Friesdorf Series.

Hydrangeas are enjoyed in two main ways. One is as a pot plant. The other is as a garden shrub. Hardiness is always an issue with the latter. Different cultivars fill these niches effectively.

The history of developing new cultivars tends to involve many of the same people we have met in other contexts, such as Emile Lemoine, but there were also those who concentrated on this shrub: F. Matthes in Germany, E. Haller in Switzerland, the Moll brothers in Switzerland, and the Moulière family in France. Hydrangea is particularly admired in Germany and Switzerland, as well as in Japan.

The pattern for modern breeding was set by the Lemoines in the 1890s. In 1894, they released *Hydrangea* 'Otaksa Monstruosa', a cross between Siebold's cultivar *otaksa* and *H.* 'Intermedia'. The Veitch nursery introduced three varieties between 1904 and 1909: *H.* 'Mariesii Grandiflora', 'Mariesii Perfecta', and 'Mariesii Lilacina', based on Charles Maries's specimens from Japan in 1879. Haworth-Booth renamed *H.* 'Mariesii Perfecta'; it is now known as *H.* 'Blue Wave'.[5]

Different species and varieties have different chromosome counts. This, and the fact that so many florets are unopened, makes viable crosses very hard to obtain. The charming "lace cap" appearance means that there is very little pollen.

F. Matthes

Matthes worked in Saxony during the 1920s and bred very large and showy blooms. *Hydrangea* 'Gertrud Glahn', with mixed pink and blue florets, is still in commerce.

LILAC

The devotion to hybridizing and breeding of plants can be seen as a benign form of monomania. I had been calling it an obsession, but my psychiatrist son tells me that is too harsh a diagnosis. All the same comments that apply to the other genera also apply to lilac, but it does have some twists of its own, some having to do with the anatomy of the flower.

FRANCE

Madame Victor Lemoine contended with these anatomical problems in 1870 (for details, see chapter 3). The whole race of French hybrid lilacs was developed from her modest beginning. In 1878 the new varieties were introduced to the world at the Exposition Universelle in Paris. The skill with crossing lilac was passed down to their son and grandson. After Victor's death, the family still introduced new varieties but not many beyond the 1930s.

Lemoine Family

Some of the cultivars were hybridized by Madame Lemoine and some by Emile, their son. Even during the devastation of the First World War, new hybrids appeared. The execution of the heroic English nurse Edith Cavell was commemorated in *Syringa* 'Edith Cavell', a double white cultivar. *S.* 'Edith Cavell' was to prove very useful as a parent in hybridizing later. Nurse Cavell was also commemorated by the naming of a rose in the Netherlands.

The family honored another woman some years later. Mrs. Alice Harding (1886–1938), an American expert on peonies but also very knowledgeable about lilac, visited the Lemoine nursery on several occasions. She was the consummate amateur and had written the very first book about peonies in the United States, in 1917. Her book on lilac appeared in 1933.[1]

Emile showed her some of his latest lilac cultivars during a visit in the 1920s and asked her to select one of them. He gave her name to the one she chose, *Syringa* 'Alice Harding'. Besides lilac, Mrs. Harding and the Lemoines had something else in common. The Lemoines also bred spectacular peonies.

They finally introduced 129 *Syringa* cultivars. Most of them were *S. vulgaris* flore pleno, descendants of those first crosses between *S. vulgaris, S. oblata,* and *S. vulgaris* azurea pleno, but there were also many *S. × hyacinthiflora* types. Emile and later Henri also experimented with a few other *Syringa* species, such as *S. henryi* Schneid. and *S. sweginzowi* Koehne et Linglelsh.

RUSSIA

Leonid Kolesnikov

Leonid Kolesnikov (1893–1973), a Russian amateur who devoted himself to this flower, took up lilac breeding in middle life, though he had been attracted to nature and gardens since childhood.[2] He was very active during all the turmoil over genetics in the Soviet Union and while Lysenko was cynically destroying Vavilov's career. Perhaps Kolesnikov was protected by the fact that he adhered to the ideas of Ivan Michurin (1855–1935), a poorly educated plantsman who had created many hybrids and invented a theory to make sense of what he had done.

Trofim Lysenko seized on Michurin's theories to claw his way to the top of Soviet agriculture. Kolesnikov was introduced to Michurin's work in the 1920s by a very senior botanist at the Moscow Botanical Gardens, N. P. Nagibina. It is possible that Kolesnikov was not aware of the dastardly way in which Lysenko was rising to power.

The booklet he wrote in 1955, *Lilac,* contains several very laudatory remarks about Michurin's wisdom. Kolesnikov notes that as a young man he had "got down to a thorough study of Timiryazev, Michurin, Lysenko and their followers. The works of the founders of Soviet agrobiology became my everyday friends and advisers." For example, at one point when he had trouble with a hybrid's growth, he wrote, "In such cases I often resort to Michurin's mentor method, grafting the hybrid's head with a strain I consider will weaken or strengthen this or that feature."

Politics was a very sensitive subject for anyone living in Soviet Russia. One cannot know what he really believed. Kolesnikov became the director of a botanical research institute, the Experimental and Model Selection Nursery,

lilac breeders have come from Scotland, which is hardly surprising given the rich heritage of horticulture and gardening in that country.

James Dougall (1810–1886) left Scotland and joined his elder brother, John, in Montreal in 1826. They later opened Windsor Nurseries in Windsor, Ontario, together. They primarily sold fruit trees but offered roses and lilacs imported from Europe. James Dougall selected and named about seven varieties of lilac from open-pollinated seedlings. These were the first of their kind in North America.

John Dunbar (1859–1927) emigrated from a small town in Elginshire, Scotland, and eventually became superintendent of parks in Rochester, New York. He was thirty-two years old when he planted one hundred lilac bushes in Highland Park, starting a secondary career as a lilac breeder. Most of his work was in selecting open-pollinated seedlings.

The lilac became a great draw for people to visit the park and was the origin of several lilac festivals in Rochester. Dunbar was most proud of *Syringa* 'General Sherman', a deep lavender blossom that opens to a lighter lavender and derived from a very old cultivar, 'Marlyensis Pallida'.

Isabella Preston

Isabella Preston (1881–1965) was very well known for her work in breeding exceptional lilies. What is less well known is her success in crossing lilac, though Vrugtman considers her lilac cultivars to be her greatest achievements.[4]

Isabella Preston grew up in Lancaster, a town in Lancashire. She was the youngest of five children and very devoted to her parents. Her father was a silversmith who could afford to send her to private schools. The family also worked together in a large garden, and Isabella learned a great deal simply by following her father around. She picked up potatoes as he dug them, and he let her have her own little patch to grow flowers.

When she was thirty-one, she left Lancaster. Both parents had died. Her married sister, Margaret, was emigrating to Canada with her husband and suggested that Isabella move to Ontario with them. It turns out to have been a good move in many ways, not only because England suffered atrociously during World War I. Even with all the obstacles, Preston had a much better opportunity for a career in Canada than she ever could have had in England.

Isabella Preston, one of the few professional women plant breeders in the twentieth century. She was known for her lilies and lilacs.
Reproduced by permission of I. Preston Collection, Royal Botanic Gardens, Hamilton, Ontario

As a spinster, she was responsible for many of the housekeeping duties once her sisters married and left home, but she did try to find a little time for horticulture in 1906. She enrolled at Swanley Horticultural College for a short while, but her real training and experience came after her emigration. She entered Ontario Agricultural College in Guelph a year after arriving in Canada, but academic courses were not what she really wanted to do. Instead, she attached herself to W. J. Crow, a noted lily breeder. *Lilium × princeps* 'Paul Creelman' resulted from her work with Crow at that time (for more about lilies, see chapter 6).

Her preference for practical work does not mean that she failed to learn the important basics about horticulture. It was simply that she wanted to do it in her own way. Preston spent a lot of time in the library absorbing everything that was significant.

Some years later, the Central Experimental Farm at Ottawa took her on as a "day labourer" at fifty cents an hour to establish a program breeding new ornamental plant varieties. This farm was the major experimental center for Ontario, part of the Dominion-wide experimental farm system intended to improve Canadian agriculture. At the end of World War I, the Canadian authorities wanted to diminish their dependence on English and European plants and breed new hardier varieties for their difficult climate.

At first the scientists concentrated on fruits and vegetables, but the idea of improving ornamental horticulture was part of a "City Beautiful" movement spreading across North America in the early years of the twentieth century. There was also a notion that working with flowers had a redemptive effect on ordinary citizens living in crowded cities.

It took more than two years before Preston was promoted to be a "Specialist in Ornamental Horticulture." The position had to be created especially for her. As a woman in very complicated times, her career was hostage to the peculiar balancing act that organizations went through, pitting the loss of men in World War I against generic prejudice toward women. The latter were considered suitable only for low-level jobs.

Her supervisor, William Tyrrell Macoun, realized just how remarkable she was and lobbied hard to get her promoted to a rank that recognized her skill and effectiveness. Her lack of a formal diploma or degree was a drawback, but eventually the job description was worded to everyone's satisfaction.

The trust the Ontario authorities reposed in her was not misplaced. To put it crudely, she gave good value for money. Isabella Preston was instructed to work on lilies, roses, lilacs, Siberian irises, flowering crab apples and aquilegias. She bred numerous cultivars in each category, any one of which would be worth a separate discussion.

In spite of his recognition of Preston's talent, Macoun did not hesitate to betray her at one point. As he made his annual tour of Canadian agricultural stations, he told several people how she planned to carry out some of her crosses. Not surprisingly, she was quite upset about this. The nurseryman Frank Skinner benefitted from the advance notice. Skinner was a worthy competitor for Miss Preston. He later bred many excellent cultivars of clematis.

Eventually Preston bred and selected more than 120 varieties of lilac. She began her career with *Syringa reflexa* × *S. villosa*. Both species are hardy in Ontario. The very vigorous seedlings had some attractive plants among them, but none was fragrant. The exceptional number of trusses on each branch helped to overcome this potential disadvantage.

Word spread fast. Vita Sackville West wrote about the new lilacs in her gardening column in 1928. Susan Delano McKelvey, a cousin of Franklin

Delano Roosevelt's, was an expert in lilac and visited Miss Preston to see the new cultivars for herself before any of them even had a name.

They appear to have got on very well together. Edwinna von Baeyer writes that they each named a new variety for the other, as well as one for Macoun. This was very nice, but his fame rests more on the apples he bred. The very successful Macoun apple is still in commerce, though the final version was bred by someone else and given his name. It was prudent of Miss Preston to name a lilac for him, but her annoyance over his trumpeting her plans to all and sundry was vindicated when Frank Skinner came out with a set of cultivars based on the same species soon after.

She used the names of Shakespeare's heroines for the rest of that series. One cynical nurseryman, when confronted with the huge range of varieties, scoffed and said, "One dark and one light lilac is all that will sell. People do not care a hoot about varieties."

Another inspired cross was *Syringa vulgaris* 'Negro' × *S. hyacinthiflora* 'Lamartine'. Two of the cultivars from that crossing are still being grown: *S.* 'Muriel' and *S.* 'Norah'. Freek Vrugtman, who is the International Lilac Registrar, covers her output very thoroughly and points out problems in nomenclature. None of this diminishes her contributions.

In addition to her fairly heavy responsibilities at the center, Preston wrote many professional articles and two useful books about lilies. She wrote dozens of letters, including every other day to her sister Margaret. They visited each other several times a year. The family meant a lot to Isabella, and she followed the activities of her nieces and nephews closely.

Most of the time she did not suffer from being a woman in a man's world, but von Baeyer tells one humorous anecdote about an occasion when it did matter. The Trappist monks at Oka in Quebec requested a consultation from the Central Experimental Farm for some horticultural problem they faced. It never dawned on them that the consultant might be a woman.

Trappists do not even allow hens or ewes on their property, much less women. When she landed in the ferry, they could barely contain their shock and dismay, but it is said that they behaved like perfect gentlemen, strolling around with her outside their grounds, chatting about inconsequential matters, and rapidly bundling her back on the return ferry as soon as they decently could.

The toughness and determination that carried her forward also led her to be a little overbearing in person at times. There was the occasional grumbling about her monopolizing the conversation, leading to some awkwardness socially. The only other complaint about her was that she introduced too many varieties of the same plant, leading to difficulty in telling some of them apart. Something similar was said about Lemoine, but none of these flaws made any difference to her splendid reputation. Canadian nurseries still offer a few of her cultivars for sale.

Isabella Preston retired in 1946 and died in Georgetown, Ontario, in 1965. The Royal Horticultural Society had recognized her work and awarded her the Veitch Memorial Medal in 1938. During her retirement, she concentrated on her own garden, laying it out as a miniature of the Central Farm's grounds but free from any bureaucratic interference.

Frank Skinner

Frank Skinner (1882–1967) emigrated from Scotland as a youth and worked on his father's farm in northwestern Manitoba. When he was almost thirty, he had a very serious bout of pneumonia and lost part of his lung. He could no longer manage the same long hours at a hard outdoor job and turned to gardening and plants. This led to him becoming an active plant breeder, and in 1925 he gave up general farming for good. Roses were his principal love, but he spent a lot of time on lilac.

Skinner married for the first time very late at the age of sixty-five. He and his wife had five children. Their son Hugh subsequently managed the family nursery. The work with lilac began after Frank Skinner visited the Arnold Arboretum in 1918. The director, Charles Sprague Sargent, gave him seedlings of *Syringa oblata* ssp. *dilatata* and *S. pubescens* ssp. *patula*. The *S. oblata* variety came from Ernest Wilson's specimens. Four years later, these plants bloomed. Skinner took pollen from this species to impregnate several varieties of *S. vulgaris*. There was a hiatus of eleven years, but the American Hybrid Series prospered.

The first cultivars, *Syringa* 'Asessippi' and 'Minnehaha', were ready for introduction in 1932. Thirty years later, Skinner introduced his last hybrid, *S.* 'Maiden's Blush'. This may be his most outstanding variety, though Vrugtman also recommends *S.* 'Pocahontas'. *S.* 'Asessippi' is a rich warm violet in color.

Frank Skinner too received many prizes and awards for lifetime achievements. Just before he died at the age of eighty-six, he published a book entitled *Horticultural Horizons*.[5] This is a fitting memorial to his work at Hardy Plant Nursery.

Father John Fiala

John Fiala (1924–1990) was a Jesuit priest who taught education and psychology at the John Carroll University in Cleveland, Ohio; worked as district secretary to his bishop; and still found time to breed many cultivars of lilac. He was a founding member of the International Lilac Society and wrote an important monograph on *Syringa* that has recently been augmented and reissued by Freek Vrugtman.[6]

For forty-five years, Father Fiala worked on land his family made available to him. He was profoundly interested in many genera, but *Malus* and *Syringa* were his favorites. Teaching psychology required him to understand and propound on genetics. He used the fact that he was constantly crossing plants to illustrate his lectures. It was one of the reasons he studied the effects of colchicine.

Colchicine is a chemical agent that alters the numbers of chromosomes in the nucleus. It is somewhat toxic and hard to obtain without a medical license, but he persisted and used it several times to cause polyploidy in his seeds. In the end, Vrugtman indicates, these experiments did not produce much in the way of results.

Fiala left a legacy of about fifty named cultivars of lilac and received the Thomas Roland Medal of the Massachusetts Horticultural Society for his lifetime achievements. One of his most valuable contributions was to leave precise notes of his crosses, allowing other people to repeat them and to understand how he bred the cultivars. For the last eight years of his life, he was a rather sick man but still continued to work with his plants.

Alice Harding

Alice Harding (1886–1938) of Plainfield, New Jersey, is relevant because she wrote one of the earliest monographs on lilac in the United States. (It was not the very first one, however; that achievement belonged to Susan Delano McKelvey in 1928.)[7] Mrs. Harding was recording the choices she had made in her own garden, helped by Emile Lemoine. Here was a direct link between Nancy in France and the United States.

Lemoine wrote the foreword for her book. This book is also valuable for capturing a moment in time, a point at which some of the great masters were still active and yet enough time had passed to see which varieties would last.

Mrs. Harding also had a superb reputation in the field of the peony, writing a small monograph on that plant, too (see chapter 6). Both books are brief and unpretentious yet contain a wealth of information not previously available. One could compare them with Eva Kenworthy Gray's book about the begonia in 1932 (see chapter 6), written with great authority based on daily practice and meticulous observation.

The French government recognized Mrs. Harding's contributions in 1928 with the award of Chevalier du Merite Agricole. She had more than five hundred cultivars of lilac in her garden. She listed eight varieties of *Syringa oblata* from the Lemoine nursery that were worth growing. Mrs. Harding called them *S. giraldii* (syn. *S. hyacinthiflora*). They had been introduced over a period of fifteen years, from 1911 to 1926. Some were single and others double.

One of Mrs. Harding's chapters is devoted to the "French lilacs." She took quite a tough-minded approach: if something new was better, then it made sense to get rid of the older version. The lilacs are presented as single or double and then in color groups: white, pink, purple, red, and even gray.

The gray flower was *Syringa* 'Comtesse Horace de Choiseul', introduced in 1892. Mrs. Harding did not record the breeder, but it was by Emile Lemoine.

She liked Isabella Preston's cultivars. Two of John Dunbar's Highland Park varieties were also included in her list. Mrs. Harding thought that his cultivar *Syringa* 'President Lincoln' was the very best one he created.

Mrs. Harding bred quite a few new varieties of lilac, peony, and other genera herself but never exhibited them in public. She was shy and did not care to push herself forward.

MAGNOLIA

The extraordinary beauty of magnolia blossoms has beguiled gardeners for centuries. Even in very chilly climates, the flower comes early in the spring, before the tree's own leaves appear, and symbolizes as nothing else can the rejuvenation of the year. As new deciduous specimens were imported and trees turned luminously pink and white without any green leaves to balance the effect, this display struck some stuffy Victorian gardeners as vulgar! They turned their faces against the new magnolias and preferred the older, ever-green versions. It took a decade or more until they came to their senses.

Magnolia is another genus, like *Acer*, that is found in both North America and Asia, signifying its ancient origin when the continents had not yet split apart. It is one of the oldest known vascular plants, with fossil remains going back approximately 30,000,000 years. The appearance of the polar ice cap at that stage wiped out thousands of plant species across the Northern Hemisphere, leaving only China, Japan, Korea, and parts of North America able to support them.

The restless curiosity that has stamped the past few hundred years as "modern" soon made sure that magnolia was transferred from its ancestral sources to other sites. The "proto-magnolia" arose in India, but wandering Buddhist monks took its seeds to China and Japan before written records were kept.

The first magnolias to be distributed to Western countries were the North American ones, exported by English and French settlers. In London, Bishop Compton was the first person to receive a gorgeous new American tree, *Magnolia virginiana,* sent by John Banister in 1687. Compton had sponsored Banister's travels and thus received the first fruits of them. *Magnolia grandiflora* arrived in England in 1730. These were the evergreen magnolias.

When Western plant collectors came across the magnolia in China, it had already been established for generations, and no one told them that it was an immigrant plant. A specimen of the "yulan," *Magnolia denudata,* reached Sir Joseph Banks in 1780. Robert Fortune found others in his first trip to China in 1843.

The Duke of Portland seems to have been the first Englishman to grow *Magnolia liliiflora,* though it had been known in China for centuries. At some point, this tree traveled to France; in the 1820s, a French war veteran, Étienne Soulange-Bodin, introduced the first intentional magnolia hybrid, *M. × soulangeana.* He crossed *M. denudata* with *M. liliiflora.* The new variety appeared in England in 1828.

HORTICULTURE IN FRANCE

Étienne Soulange-Bodin

Étienne Soulange-Bodin (1774–1846) was a very serious horticulturist. He founded the Royal Institute of Horticulture at Fromont, near Paris, in 1829 and served as its first director for many years. The institute was the first formal horticultural training school in France, making use of new scientific information as it appeared.

This was approximately the time when Victor Lemoine was beginning his education in horticulture. He knew of Van Houtte in Ghent and the Baumanns and Miellez in France but either did not know about Soulange-Bodin and his institute or could not afford to pay any fees. At all the other establishments, he learned while working.

Soulange-Bodin also set up the first flower shows at the Louvre, during his term as president of the Linnean Society of Paris. In France he is considered to be the source of the Empress Josephine's violent passion for plants in general and roses in particular, through his friendship with her brother, Eugène de Beauharnais.

This cultivar, *Magnolia × soulangeana,* is perhaps the best known and most widely grown of all of them. Dorothy J. Callaway comments that most gardeners do not know of any other kind of magnolia tree.[1]

DISSEMINATION OF MAGNOLIAS

More magnolias kept coming west throughout the nineteenth century. Joseph Hooker sent *Magnolia campbellii,* a very large and imposing tree, from the Himalayan region to England in 1849. He did not know that W. Griffith, Nathaniel Wallich's nemesis, had come across it in 1838, so Hooker assumed that he was the first to find it. Hooker named it "campbellii" for a Scottish civil servant in charge of an Indian district. Hooker recorded that entire hillsides were covered with these trees and turned pink during the spring.

The Japanese *Magnolia stellata,* replete with exquisite open-petaled blossoms and very fragrant, came to England in 1877. The Veitch collector Charles Maries probably sent it to their Coombe Wood nursery in Devon from Japan. Dr. George Rogers Hall had sent it to New York ten years earlier.

Magnolia × *soulangeana* 'Coates'. *Magnolia* × *soulangeana* was the first intentional magnolia hybrid. 'Coates' is a modern variant.
Reproduced by permission of Dr. Jim Gardiner, Director of Horticulture, Royal Horticultural Society at Wisley (photographer)

James A. Gardiner points out that because the plant evolved so long ago, it predated the development of the hymenoptera.[2] Beetles, not wasps or bees, are the pollinators in the wild. Occasionally honeybees are seen to explore the flowers, and Suzanne Treseder noted that some experts believe that the flowers may still be evolving to accommodate this new process.[3] Magnolia leaves are very tough and impervious. This is said to be because the beetles might otherwise damage them as they crawl up to the flowers.

There is the usual mild disagreement about the number of genera and species, but there may be between six and ten genera and about eighty to one hundred species. An enormous number of hybrids have been developed even though the trees take a long time to mature and need a lot of space to grow. These requirements mean that the work of breeding magnolia tends to be confined to very wealthy people or large institutions. In that respect, it is not unlike breeding rhododendron.

UNITED KINGDOM

One of the prime regions in which this work has been done since about 1900 is Cornwall in England. Valentine and Jean Paton published a very beautiful book in 2001, *Magnolias in Cornish Gardens,* which lays out this history. The text is accompanied by painstaking and detailed watercolor paintings of each variety and the parts of each blossom.[4] The Patons include information about hybrids that may have originated in other parts of the United Kingdom or abroad but took root in Cornwall.

Besides Caerhays, the leading center, there is Trewithen, where Colonel George Johnstone bred magnolia and wrote a classic text on Asian magnolias as well as the Treseder Nurseries. The nursery lasted until the fourth generation.

Treseder Family

Neil Treseder published *The Book of Magnolias* with illustrations by Margaret Blamey in 1981. It is a very detailed and careful account of the species and their modification over time. No one had written such a monograph on magnolia since John Millais' son, John Guille Millais, in 1928.[5] Millais' book established what was known at the time before the large number of Asian varieties began appearing.

Neil Treseder died in 1983. His daughter, Suzanne, has left a fascinating account of the family's movements and achievements since 1857.[6] At one time, Treseders rivaled Veitch for complexity of inventory and the number of exotic plants offered for sale.

The three Treseder brothers left Cornwall for Australia in 1857, joining the gold rush. John Garland Treseder took vegetable seeds with him. His modest market garden prospered, and he expanded to larger nurseries and shops in Sydney. Eventually he decided to return to Cornwall and established a very successful nursery. He imported wonderful exotic plants from Australia and New Zealand and then sent them out to customers in many parts of the world. His great-grandson Neil Garland Treseder became an expert in magnolia and camellia, naming about sixty varieties of magnolia over his career.

John Charles Williams

John Charles Williams (1861–1939), owner of Caerhays Castle near St. Austell, was one of the leaders in plant collecting and development. His name is forever associated with magnolia, camellia, and rhododendron, but he had very broad interests in many plant genera beside these. Williams's first forays into plant breeding were with daffodils. William Robinson's book *The English Flower Garden* made a deep impact on him and was one reason Williams focused on spring bulbs for some time.

He began his daffodil program in 1897, working with his cousin (and friend) Philip Williams and the Reverend George Herbert Engleheart. It took about seven years for the program to peak. The daffodils were very successful commercially. Early spring (really, late winter) flowers come from the southwest corner of England and the Scilly Isles, just off the coast, several weeks before any flowers are ready on the mainland. This gives them a good share of the cut flower market. The islands' climate is influenced by the Gulf Stream. The famous gardens at Tresco Abbey support an almost-tropical flora.

J. C. Williams moved on to collecting and breeding larger trees and shrubs, but his cousin Philip continued to work on the bulbs. J. C. Williams's grandfather bought the large imposing Victorian "castle" in the 1840s, and his family is still connected with the estate. Williams invested in many syndicates that supported plant explorers in China and the Himalayas. He and Philip Williams worked together in many of these enterprises. Two of their partners were Lionel Rothschild and Lord Aberconway of Bodnant, both college friends.

Modern gardeners can only envy the scale of his operations. Williams employed sixty gardeners on his estate. Today there are five, plus the head gardener, Jaimie Parsons. When George Forrest began sending very large numbers of new Chinese specimens and seeds, Williams devoted himself to making sure they thrived. Growing them and keeping them alive were the first but perhaps most important steps. He used some of these new varieties to great effect at his other home, Wirrington House, planting an exquisite Chinese garden there. Williams also shared much of the Forrest material with four or five other friends.

J. C. Williams turned to magnolia later. Very little happened during the war years, 1914–18, but then *Magnolia mollicomata* flowered for him in 1918. It was an important moment.

His great-nephew Charles Williams is the current owner. Charles Williams not only maintains Caerhays but also runs a very specialized nursery for exotic plants nearby in Burncoose. He received me most graciously on a cold windy day in March, never indicating by a whisker that he might have had much more important things to do.

The National Council for the Conservation of Plants and Gardens (NCCPG) in the United Kingdom has designated the collection of magnolias at Caerhays as one of its holdings. There is always a risk that a collection can be lost because of natural disasters or other causes. The NCCPG has three other magnolia holdings across the United Kingdom as "insurance": Bodnant in North Wales, Windsor Great Park, and Wentworth Castle in Yorkshire. The great storm of 1990 was just such a terrible event. Hundreds of large trees at Caerhays were toppled and destroyed without much warning.

The estate has more than 40 species of magnolia, michelia, and maglietia (the latter two are related species but all in the family Magnoliaceae), 170 named cultivars, and another 250 unnamed seedlings growing. A very few of Forrest's and Wilson's original plants still survive. The present head gardener, Jaimie Parsons, has contributed a great deal to the value of the collection by clearly labelling everything and drawing up accurate lists. He too breeds rhododendron and has already registered five new varieties on his own. The estate has registered twenty new cultivars in the past few years. In spite of the fact that Cornwall is milder than the rest of England, they still have trouble with the plants setting seed.

Jaimie's predecessor, Philip Tregunna, developed one of the most handsome cultivars of magnolia, *Magnolia* 'Philip Tregunna'. There were only two other head gardeners before Tregunna, both exceptionally able men.

Caerhays is unusual in that it is right on the coast. The restful susurration of the waves can be heard in the background, but strong winds blow off the Channel much of the time. That made it hard to decide where to put fragile new plants on the site. Once these very exacting requirements were met, J. C. Williams began his programs of hybridizing that went on until he died in 1939. The magnolia hybrid *M.* × 'Caerhays Belle' is a very well known result of his work.

Other Significant Individuals

A more minor figure in the Cornwall story is Sir Charles Lemon, of Carclew. Joseph Hooker sent him rhododendron seeds in 1850 before anyone else, and Lemon bred a new variety, 'Sir Charles Lemon'. His main claim to fame now is that he employed William Lobb as one of his gardeners. Quite probably the actual work of creating the hybrid and getting it to grow was done by his previous gardener, Lobb's father.

Lobb and his brother James both grew up on the estate. Lemon saw that the boys were keen and permitted them more liberty than was usual in the still-feudal English countryside at the time. They were allowed to learn horticulture and work at complicated tasks at a young age. The exotic plants in the greenhouses enchanted them. It also meant that when the brothers were in different tropical cultures they excelled at spotting good plants and estimating whether they would grow, because they had seen others like them.

William listened to sailors talking about foreign parts in the local waterfront pubs and yearned to travel. He could not afford to do so on his pay, but when James Veitch asked his employee, young Thomas Lobb, if he knew anyone who would like to explore for the firm, Thomas immediately suggested William. He knew how much William wanted to see the world. In the end, both of them collected for Veitch—though with quite unhappy endings in each case.

Amos Pickard, Charles Raffill, Philip Savage, August Kehr, and Todd Gresham were perhaps the most noted hybridizers of magnolia in the recent past, as well as Williams. Callaway adds the names of Evamarie Sperber, Joseph C. McDaniel, and two men in New Zealand, Oswald Blumhardt and Mark Jury.

Amos Pickard had a nursery in Canterbury, Kent. He introduced elegant magnolia cultivars, such as *Magnolia* 'Pickard's Stardust', based on *M. kobus*.

Charles P. Raffill (1876–1951) was born near Newport, South Wales, and worked for many years at the Royal Botanic Gardens, Kew, becoming assistant curator. Raffill chiefly bred iris and lilies. When he died, the iris and lily societies both published obituaries about him. He also liked magnolias and began a breeding program in the 1940s. Raffill crossed *Magnolia campbellii* and *M. mollicomata* and distributed the resulting seedlings widely. He introduced nine hybrids based on this work. Almost all of them have the rich dark pink of the campbellii strain.

One of them flourished in Windsor Great Park, and Sir Eric Savill, deputy ranger of the park, named it for Raffill. The tree is still doing very well. A section of the park is now the Savill Garden. Raffill was awarded the Victoria Medal of Honour by the Royal Horticultural Society and made a Member of the Order of the British Empire by the king.

UNITED STATES

August Kehr

August Kehr (1914–2001) was a geneticist who bred the larger shrubs, rhododendron, camellia, and magnolia, even after he retired to North Carolina. He earned his doctorate at Cornell, then worked at Louisiana State University, the U.S. Department of Agriculture, and later the Agricultural Research Service. Kehr advocated using colchicine to obtain polyploidy. What he really wanted to do was to create a truly yellow magnolia. *Magnolia* 'Solar Flare' came very close.

In spite of breeding many hybrids, he finally registered only thirty-one magnolias, together with eleven azaleas and fourteen rhododendrons. He was known to be a gentle and kindly man.

Phil Savage

Phil Savage (1917–2002) was one of the founding members of the Magnolia Society in October 1963. He introduced numerous cultivars, but perhaps the most striking is *Magnolia* 'Butterflies.' Its blossom has a richer and more lasting yellow color than any that came before. Savage was always concerned about cold hardiness. He grew up in Detroit and was a graduate of the University of Michigan at Ann Arbor. Savage made his living selling horticultural supplies, but his heart was in magnolias.

D. Todd Gresham

D. Todd Gresham lived from 1909 to 1969. He was another founding member of the Magnolia Society. Although he made hundreds of crosses, he distributed their offspring to many other centers for development and introduced only a small number himself. He sent a great many seedlings to the Dodd family. Gresham used *Magnolia* × *veitchii*, *M. liliiflora*, and *M.* × *soulangeana* for his work. Some of his cultivars were very dark pink (these were called the "svelte brunettes") and others were very pale, fleshy, and delicately colored (these were known as the "buxom blondes").

Other Breeders

William Kosar (1913–1985), at the United States National Arboretum near Washington, D.C., was a very significant magnolia breeder. In addition to this important work, Kosar is also claimed by the holly fraternity for his work on *Ilex*.

Evamarie Sperber worked at the Brooklyn Botanic Garden. In 1957, she planted the seeds of a cross between *Magnolia acuminata* and *M. denudata*. It flowered in 1972. The results were worth the wait. Dr. Sperber patented the new variety in 1977 under the name of *M.* 'Elizabeth', in honor of the patron of the Brooklyn Botanic Garden, Elizabeth van Brunt. This cultivar has light-yellow flowers with a faint tinge of green at the bases of the tepals. Specimens can be seen in many botanical gardens and parks.

ROSE

The hybridization of roses in both China and the West deserves a book all to itself. I can only sketch a few highlights and refer the reader to useful texts to fill in the gaps.[1] The vagaries of history have led to this juxtaposition of China and the West for rose growing. Explorers went to China for silk and jewels. They came back with specimens of glorious plants they had never seen before, among them a few types of rose previously unknown in the West. New hybrid flowers were a by-product of those expeditions and in turn led to new forms of floral commerce, culminating in today's vertically integrated plant companies and ubiquitous garden centers. Many of their discoveries were roses, initially as cultivated plants in pots and later as the wild forms.

There is a substantial history of interest in roses in Western Europe. The Romans were fanatical about them. They not only used the petals for fragrance and decoration but also ate them and together with many other peoples used the hips for medicine. During World War II when England could not import citrus and there was the risk of vitamin C deficiency, rose hip syrup was a very effective substitute.

Almost all the European countries had rose fables and legends of one sort or another. In France, *Le roman de la rose* ("The Romance of the Rose"), a medieval allegory, charmed people for centuries.

In China, religion and philosophy guaranteed that roses would be of central importance to the way of life. When the two cultures met and the vast number of different roses growing in China was recognized, there was considerable excitement.

Roses have always had a powerful romantic appeal for the public, non-gardeners as well as gardeners. Other plants are as beautiful and many are fragrant, but the exquisite appearance of fragility and the difficulties in growing them to perfection add to the allure.

Countless generations of gardeners in China had modified the rose's form to their own satisfaction. Western plant collectors were not aware of this when they sent specimens of newly found roses back to Europe. They assumed they were sending new species, but in fact some were subspecies, others were horticultural varieties, and quite a few were naturally occurring hybrids, or to put it more precisely, hybrids whose origins go so far back into history as to be unknown. China roses began arriving in the West in the eighteenth century, but Western botanists did not unequivocally identify some of the key species in the Chinese countryside until much later.

The number of species in the world as a whole may be between one hundred and two hundred. Currently the best thinking is that there are two hundred Chinese species.[2] There is no agreement among experts as to the precise number. One reason is that some rose groups, such as the Caninae, are still evolving. The elusive boundary between species is reflected in its shifting taxonomic number.

The other is that, astonishingly, John Lindley's aggregate listing in 1820, *Rosarum Monographia,* is only just now being updated.[3] The complete description on the title page is "A Botanical history of ROSES. To which is added, An Appendix, for the use of cultivators, in which the most remarkable garden varieties are systematically arranged." Lindley's monograph has certainly stood the test of time,

There are many species in western and central Asia and Europe, with fewer in North America. A few have arisen in India. It is probably safe to say that more rose species come from Asia, especially the Himalayas, China, and Japan, than any other continent. By contrast, only seventeen species are endemic in North America. Charles Quest-Ritson comments that in comparison to the European and Asian species, those from North America have not been exploited as fully as the others in the development of new hybrids.

Four prominent breeders—Jan Böhm, Rudolf Geschwind, Michael Horvath, and Isabella Preston—did use the Prairie Rose, *Rosa setigera,* one of the American species, as a parent to create vigorous hybrid climbing roses. Very little has been done with the other species, but a few early American nurserymen bred some new roses, not only with *R. setigera* but also with *R. sempervirens.* Samuel and John Feast in Baltimore, William Prince in Long Island, and Henry Ellwanger in Rochester, New York, used the Evergreen Rose for breeding. In France, Jacques-Louis Descemet, Jacques Antoine, and Jean-Pierre Vibert also used *R. sempervirens* for crosses.

Probably the best-known American hybrid, but one not containing any native rose genes, is *Rosa* 'Champney's Pink Cluster', sent from South Carolina by Philippe Noisette to his brother Louis in Paris, circa 1811. Philippe gave a specimen of 'Parson's Pink China' to his neighbor John Champney, a rice farmer. Champney then bred it with the Musk Rose, *Rosa moschata.*

Philippe Noisette (1773–1895) was a French horticulturist who became the distinguished director of the South Carolina Medical Society's physic garden in Charleston. Seed from Champney's cross sent to Paris by Philippe Noisette was identified as *Rosa* 'Blush Noisette'. The brothers' surname graces the noisette form in roses, referring to these antique forms known for fragrant clusters of loosely petaled, double roses from crosses of Musk and China Roses. The unusual breadth and hardy shrubbiness of the noisette roses, with a longer or remontant blooming season, were what so engaged the attention of nineteenth-century rosarians. 'Champney's Pink Cluster' remains an especially fragrant cultivar of a noisette rose even today.

In return for Noisette's generous gift, Champney gave him some of the new 'Pink Cluster' seedlings. Noisette planted their seeds and came up with 'Blush Noisette'. This was the variety that went to France. The French were thrilled with it. Very shortly afterward, it reached England, and Thomas Rivers descanted upon its virtues.

For a time, the American species roses were fashionable in Europe, and many nurseries sold them in their natural state, unimproved. Even though colonial settlers in North America enjoyed the native roses, the vast majority of roses grown in the United States and Canada today are of European and Asian origin.

The rose evolved primarily in the northern temperate zones. Paleontologists have found fossil roses dating back about 35,000,000 years, in places like Oregon and Washington state. No native rose species have been found in Africa or Australasia. School is out about the Arctic or Antarctic, as paleontological research may not yet have uncovered evidence of roses under their current ice sheets.

One naturally occurring hybrid, *Rosa* × *damascena* Mill., has considerable economic significance. It is found in Eastern Europe and western and central Asia and is grown for its aromatic petals. These are distilled into attar of roses. The petals contain fragrant oils, notably beta-damascenone, beta-damascone, beta-ionone, and rose oxide. This industry has a very long tradition, dating back to 1000 CE. About 80 percent of the world's attar currently comes from Bulgaria.

Until recently, no one knew the prior history of *Rosa* × *damascena* Mill. It is found only in cultivation. Travelers, perhaps Crusaders, were thought to have taken it back to the West in medieval times, possibly in the fourteenth century, together with varieties of *R. gallica*, but the puzzle was solved in 2000, when three Japanese scientists analyzed the DNA of *Rosa × damascena*, using randomly amplified polymorphic DNA (RAPD) technique to identify the parental ancestors for the oldest Damask Roses.

It was no surprise to confirm that the first crosses were between *Rosa gallica* and *R. moschata* and that *R. moschata* was the maternal parent. Both species were European in distribution. To rosarians' surprise, however, a third species was involved, as a parent to the hybrid cross *Rosa moschata × Rosa gallica*. This second cross involved not a European rose at all but one considerably farther to the east. *Rosa fedtschenkoana* is a wild rose native to central Asia and northwestern China, from Kazakhstan and Xinjiang. It is one of the few repeat-blooming, or remontant, wild roses, and its contribution to the Damask Roses can be seen in their gray-green foliage and the mossy hips (stipitate glandular hypanthia). How extraordinary it is to realize that European hybrid roses traveled along the Silk Road in time out of memory. Given the historic medicinal uses of roses, one can easily imagine astute merchants trading roses to augment the profit of their silken wares. We now have the genetic proof of such a long-ago event: the Rose of Damascus had three parents and represents a triparental cross from antiquity.

In the West, this chapter about rose breeding can be said to begin with the China Rose, *Rosa chinensis* var. *spontanea*. Wild roses grow all over Europe and the British Isles and were known and cherished from earliest times, but because we are primarily considering intentional hybridizing, the arrival of a repeating Chinese rose is the point of departure here.

Linnaeus's pupil Peter Osbeck found a cultivated variety of *Rosa chinensis* var. *spontanea* (Rehd. & Wils.) T.T. Yu & Ku in Canton at the Customs House in 1751. Because the rose was sent to England via Bengal in India, Linnaeus named this rose *R. indica*. It became known as 'Parson's Pink China' because a Mr. Parson grew it in his garden just outside London. This rose had pretty little pink flowers with a modest amount of scent, and nobody paid very much attention to it. They saw it blooming constantly, but the notion that there was any value in the repeat blooming did not strike them for a time. The first prerequisite for any advance is an idea.

Not until Sir George Staunton took another specimen back after the unfortunate Macartney expedition to China in the 1790s did collectors begin to capitalize on its amazing qualities. Sir Joseph Banks had it grown at Kew.

Most experts consider that these two roses, the initial import and Staunton's find, were identical. In London, James Colvill, a florist in Hammersmith, propagated this rose under the name of 'Pale China Rose'. Easy to grow, it spread very quickly to many gardens and even began to naturalize in hedgerows. Both these specimens from China are now known to have been cultivated plants.

The native European roses flowered for a few weeks in the summer and lay unadorned the rest of the year. *Rosa chinensis* produced beautifully formed, cupped flowers continuously throughout the warmer months. Then it dawned on someone: why could the two kinds of rose not be combined?

The first actual hybridizing was done in France.[4] Even though England and France were at war from the 1790s to 1815, rose fanciers did not let a little thing like that stop them. The British blockaded the French ports, and for a time the best of the new imports were not reaching the French growers, but obliging English sea captains smuggled the plants aboard their ships and managed to forward them to Paris. (For more about French rose breeders, see later section.)

In 1814, a Monsieur Ecoffey released the first known Hybrid China rose in St. Cloud, near Paris. He named it 'Vibert', for a colleague who later became very well known. He had pollinated *Rosa* × *damascena* with pollen from a China Rose. 'Vibert' did not quite do what he had expected, but it had plentiful blossoms and was very vigorous. Jean-Pierre Vibert himself then released more Hybrid Chinas in 1816: *Rosa* × 'Cerise Éclatante' and *Rosa* × 'La Philippine'. They were bred by his associate Monsieur Jantet. All these roses had gorgeous red flowers. Dozens more followed over the next two decades, but then they were superseded by other, more exciting, hybrids and went into abeyance.

The true wild type of *Rosa chinensis* was not discovered until a hundred years after it was first imported.[5] Augustine Henry found the robust shrubs with hooked prickles in a ravine running north from the Yangtze River near Ichang, where he worked in the 1880s. A century after that, in 1983, Mikinori Ogisu also found several stands of *R. chinensis* var. *spontanea* in the Ichang Gorge. The colors varied with altitude. Roger Phillips and Martyn Rix also found wild forms of the four "studs" in the early 1990s.

Another import of immense importance was *Rosa odorata* var. *gigantea* (Collett ex Crépin) Rehd. & Wils. (syn. *R. gigantea* Collett ex Crépin), also

An early French rose hybrid, *Rosa gallica* × *Rosa chinensis* Jacq. Breeder unknown.
Painting by Pierre-Joseph Redouté.

Reproduced by permission of University of Erlangen, Nuremberg

collected in China in its later, very sophisticated varieties. Sir Henry Collett discovered it in the Shan Hills of Burma in 1824, but it did not reach England until 1888. Long, silky white petals and exquisite fragrance rapidly endeared it to rose lovers. Almost all the modern hybrid roses of whatever type have some of these flowers' genes in them.

When genetics was in its infancy at the turn of the twentieth century (really, before the subject even had that name), a capable scientist, Major Clifford C. Hurst (1870–1947), set out to untangle the strands of the rose story using the latest modern techniques, creating a putative genealogy. Mendel's work had just been rediscovered, and Hurst was inspired by it. The John Innes Horticultural Institution provided him with the resources to use cytology and chromosome analysis in his research.

Hurst's work has not been seriously challenged to date, in spite of new developments in molecular biology and other investigative methods. Working with Robert Allen Rolfe at Kew, he also elucidated the story of modern orchids in a similar fashion.

Based on what he could find out about the chromosomes of the significant garden roses and using very considerable powers of deduction and imagination, Hurst drew up a tentative framework for the known characteristics of the garden roses to date. Paintings and drawings of lost roses also helped him put things together.

Hurst knew about *Rosa chinensis* var. *spontanea* and *R. gigantea.* In addition, he considered the impact of 'Slater's Crimson China' (imported by Gilbert Slater of the East India Company) and Parks's yellow variety (introduced by John Parks, collecting for the Horticultural Society), bought in Canton a few years later. He named these four important roses "Studs." This term does not mean that they were used only as pollen parents but is simply a shorthand way of referring to them collectively. Parson's 'Pale Pink China' had survived in a few remote cottage gardens, and the Slater and Parks roses were also extant, though barely, when Hurst started his work. *R. gigantea* as such was not to be found in the British Isles, but he deduced its role from descriptions and paintings.

Hurst believed that five roses, *R. gallica, R. moschata, R. damascena, R. centifolia,* and *R. alba,* were the "Ancestors" of all the modern hybrids. The "Studs" and "Ancestors" were themselves hybrids but, apart from *R. centifolia,* still more or less fertile.

He started the Burbage Experiment Station for Genetics in Leicestershire, but the First World War put an end to his work for the duration. The buildings were allowed to run down, and his staff was called up to serve in the army. He started again at Cambridge in the mid-1920s and moved forward as soon as he could.

Despite his resilience and courageous efforts, Hurst was fated not to see his work through. He died before it could be completed. His wife, Rona, also a botanist, knew enough about the work to edit his notes and issue several papers.[6]

This is the scientific background to a huge endeavor that is still going on in the present. Roses present a constant challenge because they are beautiful and fragrant yet have many weaknesses that make it hard for nonexperts to grow them. Hope and optimism drive the almost-continual effort to breed the ideal rose: handsome and fragrant flowers on plants resistant to pests and independent of the climate, to say nothing of the quest for a pure blue rose.

FRENCH ROSE BREEDERS

Modern European rose breeding originated in France in the late eighteenth century. The native European roses had been augmented by imports from western Asia and other accessible places over centuries. The Dutch developed long series of varieties using the very fragrant hybrid *Rosa × centifolia* and exported them across Europe.[7] "Centifolia" refers to the numerous petals in the globe-shaped blossoms. This is also the humble Cabbage Rose.

These roses had been in Europe so long, their origins were blurred by time. Linnaeus named species according to the place from which he received them. He named *Rosa gallica* in the same way he named *Rosa indica* and *Azalea indica*, not giving any thought to the possibility that these plants were not native to those places.

At first, new varieties were chosen by selection, particularly of sports and mutations. Many of the old roses, especially the gallicas, were very fertile. Planting their seeds provided a cornucopia of new possibilities. *Rosa centifolia* was not as fertile, since the additional petals were modified stamens. *R. gallica* was exploited very effectively in the Netherlands but much less so in France.

Elaborate variations on the gallicas were not yet important to French rose lovers or breeders. That would change as the war engendered between England and France by the French Revolution stretched out into the Napoleonic wars, roughly between 1799 and 1814. In the Netherlands, breeding gallicas had been going on for many years. Claude-Antonin Thory (1759–1827), the botanist who wrote the text for Pierre-Joseph Redouté's paintings, noted that the Dutch rose catalogues listed as many as five hundred varieties of *R. gallica* as well as myriad centifolias. Thory was a "rosomane," to use François Joyaux's expression. His love of roses was second only to his immersion in Freemasonry.

In 1829 he published a monograph on the genus rose, *Monographie; ou, Histoire naturelle du genre groseillier.*[8] He had also published *Prodrome de la monographie des espèces et variétés connues du genre rosier.*[9]

Thory established names for divisions within the rose spectrum that are still used today. His use of the term *preliminary* was very prescient in recognizing that there was a lot more work to be done in classifying roses.[10]

Once the idea that crossings should be controlled emerged, different rose breeders took it up very enthusiastically. How it was actually done is not perfectly clear at present, but several scholars are working on the question. (See chapter 1 for a discussion of early hybridizing.) Using the pollen of one rose to fertilize the stigma of another rose intentionally clearly took place in the nineteenth century. Henry Bennett in Wiltshire was thought to be the first to do it, but there are tantalizing hints suggesting that men such as Louis Noisette, Jean-Pierre Vibert, and the Verdiers also pollinated their roses this way, as far back as the 1820s. Dr. J. H. Nicolas thought that André Dupont hand pollinated his crosses.[11] This is an important point, as both Descemet and Vibert learned a great deal from Dupont.

Ingrid Verdegem has found out that some breeders held two flowers tightly together to transfer the pollen. The Feast brothers in Baltimore controlled the pollination in their crosses between *R. setigera* and *R. gallica*, but which method they used is not clear. That was in the 1830s.

The early hybridists believed that they had to protect the newly fertilized female recipient of pollen from being contaminated by stray "farina," to use the old term. More recently, scientists have recognized that a stripped-down flower without petals or other attractive characteristics is of negligible interest to passing insects. Fewer breeders use the little protectors, or cotton "bonnets."

For much of the nineteenth century, Lyon was considered to be the "rose capital of the world," though as can be seen in the following discussion, much excellent work took place in Paris and other cities. The reliably warm climate in the south of France provided the basis of the perfume industry, which was dependent on roses. Whole hillsides in Provence were covered with very tough roses grown for their scent. Rose breeders were not far away, planning to change and improve their stock.

The precise dates when China Roses arrived in France are not available, but this seems to have taken place in the last quarter of the eighteenth century. At that point, politics, not usually associated with a peaceful pursuit such as horticulture, became overwhelming. In 1789 the French Revolution broke out, and England went to yet another interminable war with France. One of England's principal weapons was a maritime blockade of the French ports.

A few breeders were tempted by the new imported roses and began creating a series of Hybrid Chinas. Their goal was to combine the remontant character of the China Rose with the highly decorative older roses in their gardens. Sadly for them, this did not happen. The new Hybrid China roses were unexpectedly attractive, with upright canes and voluminous quantities of flowers, but almost none of them bloomed more than once. With more new specimens from America and Asia appearing, roses grew much more popular and demand grew. Nurserymen sold American species as novelties on their own, but with the tightening of the blockade, French breeders had increasing difficulty in obtaining the new roses.

The pendulum in rose breeding swung to England, as English horticulturists gained a virtual monopoly on the new flowers. One result was that the French breeders turned back to the European gallicas almost out of desperation.

A big incentive for all this effort was the Empress Josephine's fervent admiration for roses and insatiable desire to have as many as she could. Not only would she buy the rose, but nurserymen merely telling their other customers she had done so was a powerful marketing tool on both sides of the Channel. Her collection at Malmaison was said to be the largest in the world. François Joyaux and others lament the fact that no formal inventory of the

Malmaison roses other than legend and the Redouté paintings has come down to the modern era.[12]

Skeptical modern scholars even question the very existence of such a collection. In 1900, Jules Gravereaux issued the list of roses he thought had been in that collection, and this was used in the restoration.

The ancient love-hate relationship between Great Britain and France is mirrored in the rose world. Claims and counterclaims of priority in discoveries and introductions raged throughout the whole period under consideration. That slightly prickly relationship still exists today and includes the other Anglophone countries within it.

THE FOLLOWING section mentions some of the most notable of the great nineteenth-century French breeders. This list is by no means exhaustive.

Barbiers

Les Frères Barbier began their firm in Olivet, a small village near Orléans. They are remembered because they were among the first to use a Chinese rose sometimes called the Crépin rose after the botanist who described it in 1886. *Rosa wichurana* (originally misspelled as *R. wichuraiana*) allowed them to breed impressive rambling roses unlike any others seen before. *R. wichurana* was used as a parent rose with *R. chinensis,* particularly the 'Old Blush' cultivar, because these crosses produced fertile offspring. This white-petaled rose, two to three centimeters in diameter, does not take its name from its native location but rather honors the Prussian botanist Max Ernst Wichura (1817–1866), who journeyed to eastern Asia in 1855. In its native range, *Rosa wichurana* occurs in sprawling thickets three to five meters high, with prostrate prickly branches, which would be visible on seaside limestone cliffs in China. This rose today is also known as *Rosa luciae* Franch. & Roche. (1871). According to the international rules on nomenclatural priority, the name used first must be given priority.

Jean-Alexandre Bernaix

Jean-Alexandre Bernaix (1831–1905) founded his nursery in Lyon in 1860. He took his time in setting up rose breeding protocols. Three of his introductions were *Rosa moschata* × *polyantha, R. polyantha* × *grandiflora,* and 'Mme. Ocker Ferencz', a Tea Rose (*Rosa* × *odorata*).

Between 1886 and 1897, Bernaix issued thirty rose cultivars and was noted for his grafting techniques, often preferring *Rosa polyantha* rootstock, a rambler that is not used so often now. Bernaix used *Rosa moschata* × *Rosa polyantha* and *Rosa polyantha* × *Rosa grandiflora* as well as the Tea Rose cultivar *R.* 'Mme Ocker Ferencz' as parents. Perhaps best known and exhibited under the name *Rosa polyantha* × *grandiflora,* this climbing rose for Bernaix would win the 1886 silver medal in Lyon. (This exhibition name has been referred by some to *Rosa gentiliana* H. Lév. & Vaniot.) Among the parents in Bernaix's crosses, the Musk Rose, *R. moschata,* had its probable origins in the Himalayas yet had been cultivated in Europe since the sixteenth century, prized for its remontant habit and musky fragrance of the stamens. This white-petaled Musk Rose also lies behind the origins of the Damask and noisette roses. *R. polyantha* was first described by Philipp Franz von Siebold and Joseph Gerhard Zuccarini in their *Flora Japonicae familiae naturales.*[13] Although not originally described as a hybrid, *R. polyantha* has been discussed as a natural cross between *R. chinensis* and *R. multiflora* Thunb., both roses native to eastern Asia (China, Japan, and Korea). Today, Polyanthas, as climbing or rambler roses known for their abundant sprays of double, light-pink flowers and a long blooming season, are sometimes called Sweetheart Roses when in miniature form.

Cochets

Christophe Cochet founded his nursery in a tiny village, Suisnes, in the Brie district. He was Admiral Count Bougainville's chief gardener, and the admiral supported him generously. Joyaux notes that Christophe disappeared in 1819. His son, Pierre Cochet (1794–1853), took over his nursery and breeding program and went on to introduce several well-known varieties. Subsequent Cochet sons and grandsons continued to breed new roses well into the twentieth century. New gallicas included the fragrant cultivars 'Provins Ancien' (P. Cochet, 1906, light-pink, fragrant roses) and 'Rosier des Parfumeurs'. Both were developed from the European *Rosa gallica* L., also known as the French or Gallic Rose, or Rose of Provins.

The Cochet nurserymen also hybridized among the rugosa group, shrub roses known for the distinctive impressed or rugose venation of their leaflets.

Rosa rugosa Thunb. was used as a hybrid parent to develop the remarkable cultivars *R. rugosa* 'Roseraie de l'Hay' (fragrant, deep-purple blooms, introduced by Cochet-Cochet, 1901), *R. rugosa* 'Adiantifolia' (white flowers with pink shading, Cochet-Cochet, 1907), and the cultivar 'Heterophylla' from the cross *Rosa rugosa* Thunb. × *Rosa lutea* Mill. (semidouble white blooms, Cochet-Cochet, 1899).

Pierre had good business sense. He recognized the value of wealthy and famous customers and supplied Salomon Rothschild and Prince Napoleon of Wagram with roses. With each generation, the modest establishment expanded, taking on a larger number of skilled workmen and growing roses by the thousands. In about 1900, La Maison Cochet became Cochet-Cochet.

Descemets

In the eighteenth century, fashionable gardeners in Paris promoted *Rosa centifolia,* the Cabbage Rose. It was already an antique hybrid by then. Its source was unknown, but the French received it from the Netherlands more than a hundred years before. With three or four other stalwarts such as *Rosa × alba, R. moschata,* and *R. gallica,* these comprised the rose repertoire of the age. Roses were not yet the stars of ornamental gardens they were to become. There was a very respectable number of varieties to be had, but the glamour was in the future.

Jacques-Louis Descemet (1761–1839), descended from a long line of master gardeners in charge of the French Society of Apothecaries' gardens, was an important figure in the transformation of the rose.[14] Descemet's name is relatively unknown today, but French rose breeders consider him to be the first true creator of the modern rose.

The Descemets grew four kinds of rose in the gardens: *Rosa moschata, R. gallica* (or Rose de Provins), "La Rose Pale" (also known as "Rose de quatre saisons"), and *R. canina* (eglantine or wild rose). In England, *R. gallica* was called the "apothecary's rose" because the apothecaries used it in compounding the (often nauseating) drug mixtures of the day. These roses were accounted to be old-fashioned even back then.

Descemet ran a commercial nursery in St. Denis as well as working for the royal family. He was the one who maintained the magnificent royal display gardens. In 1785 he offered an extensive array of plants, including forty roses, mainly varieties of *R. centifolia*, in his catalogue. None of these catalogues contained the China Rose yet.

The French Revolution destroyed his clientele and ruined his living, but he managed to start up again in St. Denis in 1792. He produced dozens of new roses between 1804 and 1818. These were so prized among rose fanciers that other nurseries sold Descemet roses. Vibert offered 176 varieties of them. This could be said to be Descemet's "golden age." Descemet planted long beds of gallicas and then followed up by growing the seeds they produced.

Poor Descemet then met with another disaster. Rampaging foreign soldiers demolished his nursery in 1814. Still resilient, he washed his hands of France and moved to Russia. The Russian government recognized his skill and appointed him the director of a new botanical garden in Odessa. To pay for his journey, he sold what was left of his rose plants to Jean-Pierre Vibert in Chennevières-sur-Marne; Vibert had formerly been his neighbor in St. Denis.

Brent C. Dickerson gives a very long list of Descemet's introductions, the majority of them gallicas.[15] The list starts circa 1808 with 'Rouge', a pimpinellifolia, and ends in the early 1820s with 'Triomphe de Flore', a gallica. Dickerson points out that his list is not exhaustive but reflects only those cultivars he decided to include in his books.

Verdiers

The Verdier family of rose breeders spanned several generations. Eugène, Victor Verdier's son, released the most new cultivars, curiously naming one for himself and three for Englishmen: 'James Cranston', 'James Mitchell', and 'James Veitch'. Presumably the hatchet was buried for a time.

The first two were moss roses. These arose within the centifolia group and are distinguished by the mossy or glandular hairs on the calyces and pedicels below the flowers. This mossy covering releases its own fragrance when the glandular hairs are brushed. The moss rose cultivar 'James Cranston' was introduced by Eugène Verdier in 1862 and has fragrant, violet-red blossoms. The moss rose cultivar 'James Mitchell' dated from 1861 and had paler, pink flowers. Introduced in 1854 by Verdier, the third cultivar, *Rosa centifolia* 'James Veitch', is also a fragrant moss rose, with deep-red petals, but it is a moss rose from a mutation among the Portland roses, the first repeat-blooming roses bred in Europe. Sometimes identified as Damask Perpetual roses, the Portland roses are named for the English Duchess of Portland. Her original plant was sent from Italy circa 1800 and lies behind all Portland roses. DNA evidence now indicates that these originated from a cross between Damask and gallica roses.

Henry Ellwanger paid attention to how many cultivars were released each year in France.[16] He pointed out that every year between 1872 and 1879 the Verdiers promoted an average of forty new varieties, of which between eight and twelve were of their own breeding. He added very drily, "There are of course several new sorts each year which M. Verdier does not get hold of. Perhaps 1/5 of them are worth growing, certainly not more. The rest are ultimately consigned to the rubbish heap."

In Ellwanger's opinion, the Hybrid Perpetuals were the most important class. The Hybrid Tea was just becoming known, but the class still remained very tiny. He considered only 'La France', 'Cheshunt Hybrid', and 'Beauty of Stapleford' to be Hybrid Teas.

Jean-Pierre Vibert

Jean-Pierre Vibert (1777–1866) bred many fine roses himself but was scrupulous about indicating which ones had been developed by Descemet. A few years after Descemet left, Vibert introduced 'Aimée Vibert', named for his daughter. This was the white-flowered result of a fragrant noisette rose crossed to 'Crimson Climber'. Reflecting its ancestry, the buds and flowers are edged in red, unfurling to pure white. *Rosa* 'Aimée Vibert' is still prized as an heirloom rose today.

In 1845, Vibert would release the cultivar 'De la Grifferaie', a cross between *Rosa multiflora* 'Platyphylla' and *R. gallica*. This hybrid Multiflora Rose is identified by its highly dissected stipules and crimson blooms that fade to paler pinks and lavenders. Rudolf Geschwind would later base many of his crosses on this hybrid multiflora. *Rosa* 'De la Grifferaie' was especially used in England as a rootstock for grafted roses in the late nineteenth century, and often the hardy rootstock of this climbing rose persists and naturalizes in the garden landscape.

Vibert was a veteran of Napoleon's army and had been wounded several times. After returning to Paris, he worked in an ironmonger's shop and eventually bought it. Unlike most of the other notable breeders, he had no previous experience with gardening.

Historians believe that he became interested in gardening and roses specifically because of that shop and its location. Paris was still quite rural, and many residents grew their own vegetables behind their houses. They bought their gardening tools from Vibert. An additional impetus to his development was that by chance Vibert's business was quite close to that of both Descemet and Dupont.

André Dupont was an important rose grower. He even supplied the Empress Josephine with plants. Vibert and he became close friends, and Vibert began to grow and collect roses himself. In 1814 Vibert decided to move to Chennevières-sur-Marne. He managed to take the residual plants from Descemet's collection to his new nursery in 1815.

In 1816, Vibert issued his first catalogue. His young wife had died the year before and he bred a gallica rose in her memory, 'Adele Heu'. Some years later he moved again, to Angers, to escape various pests that attacked his rosebushes. Ultimately he returned to Paris and spent his retirement organizing his thoughts and ideas.

Vibert was very astute. He imported valuable breeding stock from England, such as 'Park's Yellow Tea-scented China' and *Rosa banksia*. He traveled to England at least once, visiting William Paul and Thomas Rivers. When Rivers returned the visit, he arrived just as *R.* 'Chromatella', a brand-new cultivar not yet released, was coming into bloom. It took his breath away.

Vibert wrote articles and pamphlets about growing roses.[17] He developed very strict principles of rose breeding and exhorted his colleagues to take more care with their choice of parent flowers and more time in making sure the hybrid was really as good as it was supposed to be before releasing it on the market. He constantly culled his own collection and destroyed plants that he felt were not up to his standard. Even so, the total number of varieties that Vibert introduced runs into the hundreds.

Henri Jacotot and Antoine Levet

History is replete with the names of writers who produce one splendid book and then fade away. Nothing they ever write again is as good as that first book. Something of the sort operates in the rose breeding field too.

Henri Jacotot (1799–1883) was a florist in Dijon.[18] He specialized in cut flowers and grew his own Tea Roses to increase his stock. He released 'Gloire de Dijon', as a climbing Hybrid Tea, in 1851. It just sort of "happened." By the time he realized that he had an amazing cultivar on his hands, he had long forgotten who the parents were. Seventy years later, his granddaughter tried to reconstruct what might have taken place.

The family believed that he used the pollen of 'Souvenir de la Malmaison' on a yellow climbing Tea Rose. The blooms of 'Gloire de Dijon' are fully double and quartered, apricot, shading from cream to buff to pink tones. It was one of the first hardy climbing roses with yellow shading. Its remontant habit and fragrance come from a noisette ancestry, but the floral form is influenced by a Bourbon rose. It has been called variably a Tea Rose or a Tea-Noisette climber, and despite the uncertainty of its parentage, this rose is hailed as a classic and is honored as one of the World Federation of Rose Societies (WFRS) Rose Hall of Fame. Its likely parentage (of three) includes the yellow noisette rose 'Desprez à Fleur Jaune', itself crossed with an unknown Tea Rose fertilized with either of the two Bourbon roses 'Souvenir de la Malmaison' or 'Madame Desprez', both with pink blooms.

The rose is now classified as a Climbing Tea, but there have been many arguments about in which class it belongs. Most breeders spend years introducing more and more cultivars. Jacotot left only the one.

Not only has 'Gloire de Dijon' continued to thrive in modern gardens, but it has also been a stalwart ancestor to dozens of handsome and effective roses. To give some idea of how it affected the rose world, Dean Hole said that if he were ever condemned to choose only one "rose-tree" for the rest of his life, this would be it. 'Gloire de Dijon' blooms almost the entire year in temperate climates and all year long in the subtropics. It is remarkably tough and withstands pests and bad weather easily. A more recent expert, Graham Stuart Thomas, echoed Dean Hole's praise, saying that it was "the most popular and satisfactory of all old climbing roses."[19]

Antoine Levet (1818–1891) was said to be very charming and unassuming and not at all businesslike. He lived and worked in the nurseryman's quarter of Lyon, which has since been taken over by unattractive industry. By the end of his life, he suffered from great poverty. He took 'Gloire de Dijon' and bred some glorious progeny. 'Belle Lyonnaise' was one, vigorous and fragrant but not much like the parent in form or color. 'Madame Bérard' was another success.

Once Levet issued a successful flower and people took to it in droves, the often even more beautiful and satisfactory later ones were ignored. That difficulty was not unique to him, but he suffered badly from it. Successful roses last a long time, and even the gardens of the wealthy eventually get filled up.

Ellwanger kept a list of those whom he thought bred and grew the best roses. Sixteen of Levet's roses, from 'Mademoiselle Thérèse Levet' in 1866 to 'François Levet' in 1890, were on Ellwanger's list. 'Madame Bérard' appeared in 1870.

Ellwanger's choices included the following:

'Mademoiselle Thérèse Levet', Hybrid Remontant, 1866

'Belle Lyonnaise', Climbing Tea, 1869

'Madame Trifle', Climbing Tea, 1869

'Paul Neyron', Hybrid Remontant, 1869

'Madame Bérard', Climbing Tea, 1870

'Madame Jules Margottin', Tea Rose, 1871

'François Michelon', Hybrid Remontant, 1871

'Madame François Janin', Tea Rose, 1872

'Perle des Jardins', Tea Rose, 1874

'Antoine Mouton', Hybrid Remontant, 1874

'Marie Berton', Climbing Tea, 1878

'Madame Etienne Levet', Hybrid Tea, 1878

'Mademoiselle Brigitte Violet', Hybrid Tea, 1878

'Reine Marie Henriette', Climbing Tea, 1878

'Madame Ducher', Hybrid Remontant, 1879

'François Levet', Hybrid Remontant, 1880

Guillots

There were two Jean-Baptiste Guillots, father and son. Jean-Baptiste Guillot, *père*, was born in 1803 and died in 1882. His son, Jean-Baptiste Guillot, *fils*, lived from 1827 to 1893. In 1867, the son became famous for introducing 'La France', considered by many to be the first Hybrid Tea.

Rosa 'La France' was a striking discovery, from unknown parentage. It unmistakably presages the modern Tea Roses, with long, pointed buds that unfurl to high, double flowers. The blossoms are quite fragrant, a light pink in color that matures to silvery white with lilac pink shading, on bushes that bloom repeatedly, but like so many other teas, its leaves are susceptible to fungal black spot and require spraying.

The father laid down the basis for later success. He opened a nursery in Lyon as a young man and very quickly offered a catalogue with hundreds of rose varieties. His business prospered.

In 1871 he sold it to Joseph Schwartz, an excellent rose breeder from Vienna. Schwartz is chiefly remembered for the beautiful white climbing noisette 'Mme Alfred Carrière'. It is still in demand today.

Guillot's son had his own nursery and developed a better technique for grafting, which continues to be used. Both father and son bred dozens of new cultivars before the signal achievement of 'La France'. Guillots are still breeding roses in the twenty-first century.

Alexandre Hardy

Alexandre Hardy (1787–1876) was born into a family of gardeners, and like so many boys of the same class, he needed to earn a living quickly. At the age of fifteen, he went to Paris and worked for Jacques-Martin Cels, a noted nurseryman. Cels and his son, François, recommended Hardy for a position at the Jardin de Luxembourg, where he worked for almost the rest of his life. He retired in 1859.

Hardy's primary interests were in fruit trees, and he was considered to be an amateur in rose breeding. His career was very similar to that of John Dunbar in Rochester, New York. Dunbar was the superintendent of parks but bred extraordinary lilacs in his "spare" time.

Hardy collected almost two thousand varieties of fruit trees but this collection was dispersed when Baron Georges-Eugène Haussman began rebuilding Paris in the 1860s. The authorities cut the collection out of the budget, a familiar piece of governmental myopia.

Hardy introduced his cultivars over about a thirty-year period between 1819 and 1848. Almost everyone has heard of 'Felicité Hardy', a gorgeous white Damask Rose named for his wife and released in 1832. Although he worked with gallicas and centifolias, his deepest interest lay in the China Rose. He went to London and brought back a 'Park's Yellow Tea-scented China' in 1825.

Hardy left more than eighty cultivars with China Rose genes in them. As a result, Joyaux considers him to be a major figure in nineteenth-century French rose breeding.

He was very curious and thoughtful and shared the editorship of *Journal des Jardins ou Revue Horticulturale* with Pierre Boitard. Alexandre's son, Auguste, was sent to agricultural school at Grignon; he worked for two years with his father but then devoted the rest of his life to the Potager at Versailles. He too was an expert in the care of fruit trees.

François Lacharme

François Lacharme (1817–1887) introduced new roses from 1852 until 1879. In 1869 he named a rose for Louis Van Houtte in Ghent. He also named two roses for the relatives of Pierre Soupert in Luxembourg. [20]

The rose fever seized him as a very young man. Like so many others, he began by studying general horticulture with a local nurseryman but quickly moved to a larger place and eventually took over a well-known nursery in Lyon: Plantier. Plantier must have had his eye on Lacharme for some time. He gave the boy letters of introduction to Hardy and Verdier, significant rose growers in Paris. Lacharme was mesmerized by the rose collection at the Jardin du Luxembourg.

Lacharme was a favorite with the English rose fraternity, as well as in the United States. He had a quiet but tenacious personality. He never named a rose for himself but stood up and argued for things he considered important. Just as Ellwanger placed him first in one of the lists always being made, so too did the English garden writer Shirley Hibberd. (In spite of the feminine-sounding name, Shirley Hibberd was a man. Until fairly recently the name was used for both men and women in the United Kingdom.)

Jean Laffay

Jean Laffay (1794–1878) bred the first Hybrid Perpetual, 'Princesse Hélène'. He had worked at Neuilly for the Duc d'Orléans as the head gardener before marrying in 1829 and opening his own nursery in Auteuil. His interest in roses grew, and in 1835 he imported a specimen of the remontant pimpinellifolia (*R. spinossima*) 'Stanford Perpetual' from England. Laffay's nursery flourished, doubtless helped by his connection to His Grace the duke. Laffay bred about forty cultivars, many of them moss roses.

In 1859 he seemingly abruptly left France for Kouba in Algeria and remained there for nearly twenty years. Just as strangely, he returned to Paris in 1877 and died a year later, leaving no explanation for his behavoir.

Before leaving for North Africa, he issued *Rosa* 'William Lobb' in 1855. William Lobb, the ill-fated collector for the Veitches in London, first set sail for South America in 1840 and traveled extensively in the western parts of both North and South America. He sent back incredible discoveries, perhaps the best known of which were the great sequoias, known as 'Wellingtonia' in England. His fame must have spread to the Continent. Lobb died a sad and lonely death in San Francisco, reviled by his formerly enthusiastic employer.

Meillands

The Meilland family has continued to breed roses into the present. Antoine Meilland (1884–1971) grew up with a hardworking father and a mother who had an indomitable spirit.[21] They barely made a living on a smallholding not too far from Lyon. Antoine did well in school and also learned avidly from a neighbor who taught him how to bud roses while he was still a small boy. He was proud of this skill and told his family that he wanted to be a rose grower. Jack Harkness recounts the story that Antoine saved every sou he could find and bought a budding knife when he finally amassed thirty sous.

His father was concerned because he knew what happened in hard times and believed that the only safe occupation was growing food. Food would never go out of style, but flowers might. Clearly, however, they could not dissuade their son from his obsession with roses even though he was only twelve. Antoine spent a few years learning the general nursery trade close to home and at sixteen went to work for François Dubreuil in Lyon.

Dubreuil took up roses after many years as a tailor. Being in or around Lyon in 1900 no doubt did that to one. When he left his apprenticeship, Antoine worked hard, married, and tried to survive as a rose grower on his own. His son, Francis, was the one who produced the rose that ultimately became known as 'Peace'.

Like 'Gloire de Dijon', it had a slightly hazy start, but once the Conard Pyle Company released it in the United States in May 1945 when the peace agreement with Germany was signed, no one bothered very much about its parents. Its beauty was breathtaking.

Francis had started to work on it in 1935. By 1939 Francis Meilland foresaw the coming German invasion of France and was concerned about the survival of the outstanding new rose he and his father had been working on since 1935. The seed parent was {George Dickson × Souvenir de Claudius Pernet} × {Joanna Hill × Charles P. Kilham}. Pollen came from 'Margaret McGredy'. It was a Hybrid Tea with soft shades of peach and yellow. People who visited the Meilland nursery in Lyon knew that it was quite out of the ordinary. Meilland sent eyes to three or four rose growers in different countries, including Conard Pyle. He knew they would be handled with integrity. Conard Pyle named it 'Peace' and released it in 1945 on the day that Berlin fell. When the rose was ready for release in 1939, Francis named it 'Madame A Meilland' for his mother. According to the rules, this is the correct botanical name. In 1945 the rose was introduced in France as R. 'Madame A. Meilland'.

Nabonnands

The house of Nabonnand was founded by Gilbert Nabonnand (1828–1903). He was followed in turn by his sons Paul (1860–1937) and Clément (1864–1949). They lived and worked in Golfe Juan on the Mediterranean coast of France. They currently list an aggregate of 220 prizes and medals for their roses.

Gilbert apprenticed himself at sixteen to the Guillots and learned everything he could about roses. He then returned home to seek work. An enthusiastic Englishman, Lord Brougham, bought a large piece of property in Cannes in 1855 with the idea of making its garden a showplace. He chose Nabonnand to take charge. A few years later, in 1864, Nabonnand opened his rose nursery near Cannes, Les Roses de Golfe Juan. His sons took it over as Etablissement Paul et Clément Nabonnand.

Gilbert bred a very wide range of flowers, not only roses, and influenced the development of horticulture along the Cote d'Azur, but he remains best known for his roses. Gilbert probably introduced about three hundred cultivars.

His sons worked together at first but later separated. Paul also bred many exotic and semitropical plants, but he too devoted a great deal of his energy to roses. Paul's nursery was Aux Roses de la Côte d'Azur, Cannes

Eden. He was particularly interested in using *Rosa gigantea* as the base of his crosses. Paul wrote "Les rosiers thés sur la Côte d'Azur et sous les climats froids" in 1935.

Clément opened his nursery first in Mandelieu. There he introduced *Rosa* 'Estérel-Parc'; subsequently, in Villeneuve-Loubet, he introduced *R.* 'Mas dou Loubet' and *R.* 'Lou Mas di Roso'. He too bred roses suited to the Mediterranean climate and wrote an article about the flower in 1935, "Les hybrides de Thé et de Lutéa sur la Côte-d'Azur." Clement bred many roses of his own.

Like Ellwanger, Clément was tough about novelty for its own sake. He too commented that far too many new roses came out each year and that only a few of them stood the test of time in his region. Interestingly, he recommended two Morse roses. While this nursery is no longer widely known, Jack Harkness, the prominent rosarian and author, was an apprentice at the Morse Brothers Nursery. The firm has survived to the present and still offers a huge selection of roses.

Pernet-Ducher

Joseph Pernet (1858–1928) was a very enterprising youth. His father sent him to be an apprentice with Alphonse Alegatière in Lyons, a man primarily involved in breeding carnations but very much respected as a teacher. Later Pernet started to work for Claude Ducher, a prominent nurseryman. In 1881 Joseph married the latter's daughter, Marie, and thus was in line to inherit the business. Good solid French bourgeois common sense was at work. Joseph agreed to append the name "Ducher" to his own and was known as "Pernet-Ducher" for the rest of his life. Claude's widow, La Veuve Ducher, introduced the vigorous climbing Polyantha 'Mlle Cécile Brunner', which is still widely grown.

Pernet-Ducher worked with his father to breed a new Tea Rose with a strong yellow tint, 'Soleil d'Or', released in 1900. The parents were *Rosa foetida*, known as the "Persian rose," and a red Hybrid Perpetual. His father died before it was ready for display. Joseph's reaction on seeing the first blossom was said to be ecstatic. There had been no such yellow roses before that. This breakthrough allowed him to pursue other warm tones such as light orange and scarlet, a whole new palette.

Pernet-Ducher controlled his pollination very carefully to reduce the risk of error. For a long time, his roses were considered to be a separate race and were known as the Pernetianas. 'Soleil d'Or' was an ancestor of the famous Meilland rose 'Peace'.

Pernet-Ducher will always be remembered for 'Mme Caroline Testout', 1890, a lively pink Hybrid Tea rose that has been in the garden repertoire for more than a century. In the early 1900s, the city of Portland, Oregon, planted ten thousand bushes of this rose in its streets. Many experts consider it to be their favorite Tea Rose. The real Madame Testout was a feisty business-woman who ran a successful millinery. She paid Pernet-Ducher for the privi-lege of having a rose in her name.

Throughout his career, Pernet-Ducher won more than thirteen gold medals at the Concours de Bagatelle, the international rose show in Paris. In spite of these triumphs, his life was crushed by the death of both his sons in World War I. He named roses for each one, 'Souvenir de Claudius Pernet' and 'Souvenir de Georges Pernet', but one can imagine that everything turned to ashes for him with the loss of his sons. This insight is borne out by the notes David Fairchild made during his journey around France in 1925.

The Fairchilds wanted to visit significant horticultural places, and Pernet-Ducher was high on their list. They were startled to find him in a rather small and dilapidated house without much land around it in a nondescript section of Lyon. He looked thin and worn. He told them that he had never made very much money from all the marvelous roses he created.

When they mentioned his sons, Fairchild commented that all the fire went out of Pernet's eyes. He turned back to the dull task they had inter-rupted, and the interview was over. If Fairchild had not been a reliable eye-witness, this description would be almost unbelievable. When Joseph died, his son-in-law, Jean Gaujard, took over the business.

ENGLISH ROSE BREEDERS

Henry Bennett

Henry Bennett (1823–1890) was a very divisive figure. Contrary to the prin-ciples of the high-minded deans, canons, and prebendaries who constituted the National Rose Society, Bennett was anxious to make money quickly. That was the only reason he gave for becoming a breeder of roses: roses paid bet-ter than cattle or wheat.

He started out with the same idea as one does in breeding a prize cow: select good strong parents, and use pollen from the preferred male to fertilize the plant chosen to be the mother directly. After many disappointing failures, he came up with ten seemingly excellent varieties and showed them in 1878. They caused a sensation, followed by an immediate uproar.

Bennett transferred the pollen with a small paintbrush. It is quite possible that this had been done previously, but it is hard to know with any certainty. Geschwind described a similar process.[22] The noted rosarian Ingrid Verdegem remembers funny old gentlemen (*geezers* was her actual word) being very coy about precisely how they created new varieties. Even as a child she thought they were very comical in their attempts to be secretive.[23]

Another of Bennett's innovations was to grow the seedling roses in a heated greenhouse. He traveled around France from 1870 to 1872. He visited the rose nurseries in Lyon looking for their "secret," making careful notes. He was scornful of their sloppy methods. No one was controlling pollination the way he thought it should be done. It was all "business as usual," selecting promising forms from the seedlings thrown up naturally.

The secret, if any, was really the long hours of warm sunshine in much of France. Bennett could not affect the English climate or reproduce the French sunshine, but he could protect the fragile new plants from the damp cold.

Once he went home, Bennett started to cross hardy Hybrid Perpetuals with Tea Roses. He chose yellow and white Hybrid Perpetuals and deep-crimson Teas but was somewhat surprised to find that he had given rise to pink hybrids. His white and yellow cultivars were not true Hybrid Perpetuals, and his red varieties were not true Teas. In spite of that, Charles Quest-Ritson, a distinguished English rosarian and author, believes that Bennett had created the first actual Hybrid Teas. This remains a hotly disputed claim.

All was not sweetness and light between the English and French rose breeders. The old British-French mutual suspicion was very much at work. When Jean Guillot, *fils*, introduced 'La France', said to be the first documented Hybrid Tea rose in 1867, the English growers challenged this claim very vigorously. Sniping went on for years.

Bennett had his own grievances against the French. He had bought cuttings in France. The nurseryman claimed that they were cut that very day in front of Bennett, evidence of that favorite modern term *transparency*. Bennett disagreed publicly. He wrote to the editor of the *Gardeners' Chronicle*, pointing out that the nursery made him wait for two days after he requested the plants and did not cut them in front of him.

Quest-Ritson reviews the evidence for and against the claims of priority.[24] He dismisses Guillot as an untrustworthy self-promoter. 'La France' was sent into the world as a Hybrid Perpetual, changing its designation to a Tea Rose only in 1877 and to a Hybrid Tea in 1880. Furthermore, Guillot could not identify its parents accurately. In 1864 he had sown a lot of seeds and not kept careful notes about each one.

In England the Paul & Sons Nursery in Cheshunt claimed they had bred a Hybrid Tea, 'Cheshunt Hybrid', in 1872. (This was not William Paul's nursery but his nephew's.) That claim quickly became a nonstarter. All this storm in a teacup is important only because of the enormous impact that the discovery of the Hybrid Tea roses made on rose growing as a whole.

Roses could now be bred in many more colors, and they could flower as long as there was warmth and sunshine, on a bush simply covered with blossoms. The bushes were quite versatile and could be used in various ways in the garden. Taste changed almost overnight.

Bennett worked to make his new plants stronger. The weaknesses of the first ones were bred out. The later ones no longer needed the protection of the greenhouse, though they were much more finicky in the cool British climate than farther south. Hybrid Teas do particularly well in California, Texas, and Arizona, as well as the warmer Mediterranean regions. *Rosa* 'Viscountess Folkstone', 'Mrs John Laing', and 'Her Majesty' became classics.

The use of the word *pedigree* startled the National Rose Society, reminding them too forcefully of the barnyard. They disliked Bennett's coarseness and commercial attitude, while he probably considered them to be a bunch of hypocrites. The National Rose Society's chilly notice of Bennett's death in 1890 reads, "Rosarians have to regret too, the loss of Mr Henry Bennett of Shepperton. He never, it is true, took kindly to the Society and it is as a raiser of new roses that he will most be missed."[25]

The Royal Horticultural Society was more open-minded. His work impressed them very deeply, and they invited him to join the society's Scientific Committee as a permanent member.

Bennett's reading of the economic conditions was accurate. He gave up his cattle farm and opened a rose nursery in Teddington, Middlesex. He prospered and made much more money than he would have done had he remained in farming.

Part of his legacy lay in inspiring dozens of British rose growers. They copied his work and outdid themselves in producing ever better roses. It is not far-fetched to say that he stimulated the development of an industry. Some call him the "Father of the Hybrid Tea."

It is sad to report that Bennett drank too much and died of cirrhosis of the liver.

Jack Harkness

Jack Harkness (1918–1994) was born in Surrey into a branch of a well-known family of nurserymen but at several removes. His parents were indifferent to gardens and plants but allowed Jack to leave school at sixteen and apprentice himself to an Irish firm, where he stayed for three years. Once back in England he started to work for his father's cousin, William Harkness. The sight of row upon row of extraordinary vigorous roses excited him. He realized how poorly tended the roses in the Irish nursery had been.

He planned to start breeding new roses for the firm but had to serve in World War II. In 1947 he set up his breeding stock again. While he had been away, an amateur rose breeder, Albert Norman, had consigned two new roses, 'Ena Harkness' and 'Frensham', to William Harkness, and these became extremely successful.

The name of Harkness was a significant one in the rose world. The first notable rose sent out by the firm of R. Harkness & Co had been 'Mrs Harkness' in 1893. It was a sport of 'Heinrich Schultheis', a Floribunda rose.

Jack Harkness's work was known and revered by all English rose fanciers. He ceased breeding roses when he retired and took up writing.

Dean Hole

Samuel Reynolds Hole (1819–1904), dean of Rochester, was one of the founders of the National Rose Society (now the Royal National Rose Society) in 1876.[26] He was a handsome, charming man of the cloth and very gifted in speaking and writing. His books were constantly in print, and his name has come down to modern times in very high repute. When one thinks of roses in England, one thinks of Dean Hole. One wonders whether some particle of the man and his style can be found in Trollope's Barchester books.

In 1844 he became enamored of a rose and chose to spend the rest of his life growing and studying these beautiful flowers. This reaction was similar to the one undergone by the Duke of Devonshire with an oncidium orchid. It trapped his soul.

Hole applied himself very diligently to his self-appointed task, reading every book and article he could find and visiting many nurseries and gardens. Poor workingmen in the vicinity were growing very fine blooms in very difficult circumstances and knew of his enthusiasm. Even before he had a single rose plant of his own, a group of them asked him to come and judge a competition. He was touched and humbled by their trust in him and redoubled his efforts to justify it.

Hole did all this at his vicarage in Caunton Manor, Nottinghamshire, moving away only when he was appointed dean of Rochester Cathedral at the age of sixty-eight. His *A Book about Roses* contained very valuable information about every aspect of growing roses, including how to prepare them for exhibition. At one point he had about five thousand rose plants in his garden, from not only Great Britain but all over Europe.

In 1858 he and the Reverend Henry Honywood D'Ombrain led the move to hold a national rose show. The first year, two thousand people attended. By the third year, that number had grown to sixteen thousand. Dean Hole is included in this chapter because of his significance in organizing rose growers into a coherent body. This was a major contribution, providing a forum for competition and debate. He did not breed new varieties of rose, but he encouraged the pursuit.

William and George Paul

William Paul (1823–1905) was a skillful nurseryman and great expert on roses. His father, Alex Paul, and his elder brother, George, were partners in a nursery in Cheshunt, Hertfordshire. After their father died in 1847, George made it clear that William could work with him but only for a limited time. They split up in 1860.

William moved a short distance away to Waltham Cross, one of the stations on the road taken by Eleanor of Castile's body after she died traveling to join her husband, Edward III. Edward was so crushed by her death that he caused a large cross to be built at each town and village where the cortège stopped.

William Paul was a very devout and earnest man, quite unlike the worldly dean. When a neighbor suggested that he name a rose 'Queen Mab', he very innocently asked whether she was a good woman.

Williams' brother George had a son, George Laing Paul. George Laing is a good example of how when a family becomes more prosperous, they have the resources to educate the next generation more formally. George Laing Paul studied in Germany and then joined Charles Fisher at Handsworth, near Sheffield. He was ready when his father died young and was able to step into his shoes easily.

William maintained a reasonably friendly rivalry with his nephew, each bringing out new roses every year. Both were very interested in climbing and rambling roses.

Quest-Ritson lists many of the Paul cultivars.[27] Most of them were introduced after both William and his nephew George had died, in the twentieth century. One of George's well-known climbers was 'Psyche'. William and his son, Arthur, employed a man named Easlea as a hybridist. Easlea subsequently went into business for himself. Many of the later cultivars issued as the Pauls' were really his work.

George Laing Paul won many medals and honors. He was awarded the Victoria Medal of Honour at the Royal Horticultural Society. This was hardly surprising. He had served notice of his skill at the very first National Rose Show in 1876, winning first place in more than one class.

As a tribute to Dean Hole, William Paul bred a glorious deep-red rose and named it 'S. Reynolds Hole'. The dean responded humorously that he had not known he would live to hear himself described as "a splendid maroon, dashed with crimson, large and globular, generally superb."

William Paul was something of an intellectual and wrote several books about roses. His first one, *The Rose Garden*, came out in 1848 when he was only twenty-five years old.[28] Paul was interested in the actual number of rose species known in his time. He devoted some space in his book to this question and showed that as time passed, more and more species were being discovered and listed.

Linnaeus counted 10 species. Philip Miller knew of 31. John Lindley prepared *Rosarum Monographia* in 1820 and mentioned 78 species (the great English rosarian Martyn Rix has been entrusted with updating this work). Sweet wrote *Hortus Britannicus* in 1827 and counted 107 species. Two catalogues of roses appeared in France in 1829, one by Narcisse Desportes and the other by Baronne Prévost; both listed about 2,000 varieties.

Clearly, the defining of species and a dizzying number of varieties is a very old problem. Paul also enlivened his book with slightly gossipy remarks about the French breeders and the superiority of English rose gardens over those of France. He traveled to France fairly frequently and corresponded with Jean Laffay and Alexandre Hardy. It was clear that he was familiar with Jacques-Louis Descemet and knew Jean-Pierre Vibert quite well. There is a freshness and immediacy to his book because he was writing about things that were important to him at the time. What started out as a dry duty became fun.

Thomas Rivers

Thomas Rivers (1798–1877) was an exemplary Victorian. He embodied all the virtues of industry and uprightness that characterized that era. Rivers inherited the fine property of Sawbridgeworth as a young man and spent his life turning it into an impeccable rose center. His book *The Rose Amateur's Guide* also ran into many editions.[29] He introduced many new roses himself and spread the word about other men's work very generously. His reputation in this field has almost overshadowed his other interest: fruit growing. Rivers was one of the founders of the British Pomological Society in 1854.

Rivers had the time and resources to travel extensively. In France he spent time with Laffay, and the latter bred a rich red Hybrid Perpetual and named it 'Rivers' in his honor. Moss roses were favorites of both of them. Unlike some curmudgeonly experts, Rivers thought that modern developments were most worthwhile and encouraged beginners enthusiastically. Laffay must have known Rivers quite well. Dark-red roses definitely attracted him most.

Rivers issued 'George IV' in 1820, another very rich, dark-colored rose. He fervently promoted two other roses with deep-red flowers: 'Géant de Batailles' (Nerard, 1846) and 'Général Jacqueminot' (Roussel, 1853). These were Hybrid

Perpetuals and had all the advantages and disadvantages of their tribe. Rivers was not alone in his enthusiasm. In the United States, the Philadelphia nurseryman Robert Buist raved about *Rosa* 'George IV' and the other two. The roses also sold well in Canada.

Rivers corresponded with Darwin about his breeding efforts. Darwin had written to ask him about the appearance of sports, and Rivers replied very quickly. Darwin was delighted and told Rivers that he had read everything the latter had ever written. It seems the only thing Darwin did not read and value was Mendel's work.

All Darwin's correspondence is indexed in the Darwin Project at Cambridge. Darwin was really more interested in Rivers's peaches and almonds than in the roses. They exchanged thirty-one letters in all.

Edward LeGrice

Edward LeGrice (1902–1977) remains well known for his interest in unusual colors and shapes of roses: the best known are 'Vespa', with a brownish flower; 'News' and 'Purple Splendour', both purple; and 'Grey Dawn'. He always had a very small business and did almost everything himself. His signature rose was 'Allgold', truly yellow through and through. Though it was passed over for a gold medal in favor of one that flopped after a couple of years in commerce, 'Allgold' became extremely popular.

LeGrice did not benefit financially from its success. This painful experience led him to be interested in the possibilities of patent protection. Despite his small output and retiring ways, his colleagues in the Royal National Rose Society held him in very high esteem and invited him to be the keynote speaker at their centenary event. He also wrote a very useful book in 1965, *Rose Growing Complete*. Peter Beales, another fine rose breeder, learned a great deal from LeGrice.

Joseph Pemberton

The Reverend Joseph Pemberton (1852–1926) was another of those clerical rose fanatics who combined religion with an innocent love of flowers. He and his sister, Florence, bred the series later called Hybrid Musks, though at first he tried to get them accepted as a form of Hybrid Tea. Joseph and Florence's beloved grandmother had grown roses, and they hoped to restore the fragrance of her old-fashioned blooms. Pemberton found that Peter Lambert's 'Trier' supplied the missing quality. He also wanted to extend their blooming season.

Joseph Pemberton was a founding member of the Royal National Rose Society, joining in 1876. He could be cavalier about its rules and evidently extremely tiresome when he chose. Clerical self-abnegation was not his strong suit.

The story is told that he showed up a day late with his entry for one of the shows and was turned away. This did not suit him, and he made such a fuss that he wore down the honorary secretary, Mr. D'Ombrain. Mr. D'Ombrain finally gave him the necessary card and told him to set up his display on the floor. Pemberton did that and even won the second prize. This does not sound as though he was very deeply imbued with the Christian virtues of patience and acceptance. As noted elsewhere, roses sometimes did bring out the worst in people.

The Reverend Pemberton was the vicar at Havering atte Bowe in Essex. In 1916 he opened his own nursery with his sister. They issued a long catalogue of their roses. All those cultivars are now obsolete. His gardener and the gardener's wife, Ann Bentall, were also skillful breeders. One of the best known of the Hybrid Musk Series, 'Buff Beauty', was actually created by Mrs. Bentall after Pemberton died. The Pembertons bequeathed their collection to the Bentalls, who opened their own nursery once both Joseph and Florence were dead.

IRISH ROSE BREEDERS

Dicksons

The Dicksons were originally from Scotland, but the first one to own a nursery had moved to Northern Ireland looking for opportunity.[30] Alexander Dickson (1801–1880) opened his nursery in Newtownards, about ten miles from Belfast, in 1836. This was a prosperous time and business flourished. He and his wife, a former Miss McGredy, had two sons, George (1832–1914) and Hugh (1834–1904), both of whom would continue in the business. The boys joined their father as partners in 1853 in Alexander Dickson and Sons. In 1869, Hugh decided he wanted to be on his own and left. He established a very successful nursery in Belfast.

Alexander Dickson and Sons supplied both flower and vegetable seeds, as well as various sorts of rose. As George grew up, the gardening public was becoming very interested in roses. George believed that roses were a lost cause in the cool damp Irish climate and was content to leave rose breeding to the French. He changed his mind in the late 1870s and decided to take them up seriously after seeing a display titled "Pedigree Hybrids of the Tea Rose" at a London show in 1878. As noted above, Bennett had applied his understanding of cattle breeding to the problem of developing better rose hybrids. It happened that these particular Bennett roses were not destined to last, but Dickson's reaction was that if a Wiltshire farmer could do such a good job, why could not he, an experienced nurseryman, do the same? He started straightaway, in 1879. He and his sons absorbed some of Bennett's ideas and chose the rose parents carefully.

They too made a lot of mistakes out of ignorance, but for the next fifteen years new Dickson roses appeared frequently and ultimately began to carry off the prizes. Dickson's ceased to be an obscure little nursery in Northern Ireland and became a national player. 'Mrs W. T. Grant', a pink Hybrid Tea, won the gold medal in 1892. It was the first Hybrid Tea rose to win this medal. The blossom was beautiful, but the plant lacked vigor. To use the jargon of the trade, its constitution was weak. In spite of that, people were so devoted to the rose that they put up with a lot of inconvenience to keep it going instead of just moving on.

Dicksons were also very conscious of money and its importance. They depended on their products for a livelihood. George Dickson pottered about with all sort of strange crosses, but his two sons (who by then were in charge) stuck very closely to varieties that sold reliably. They did not hold with art for art's sake.

The First and Second World Wars dealt heavy blows to Dicksons. In addition, a disastrous fire in 1921 destroyed all their records. Irish politics did not help, either. The firm and family went through many more vicissitudes but by the 1980s were once again introducing remarkable new roses. Colin Dickson is the sixth generation to run the business.

Speaking of the descendants of famous people—the great plant collector Frank Kingdon Ward's grandson, Oliver Tooley, told me that Dicksons named a rose for his late grandmother, Florinda Norman Thompson (Ward), in 1920. It was described as a full fragrant Hybrid Tea, delicately rose colored with a lemon ground. There is a printed record of it but no pictures. Mr. Tooley would have liked to see a picture of his grandmother's rose, but so far none has emerged despite far-flung inquiries.

The retired president of the Rose Society of Northern Ireland, Mr. J. Craig Wallace, knew of this rose. He found it in the Dickson catalogue for 1926–27. It was listed in the category "Modern Rose" in 1964 but was offered in commerce for only a few seasons. Mr. Wallace traced it in catalogues as late as 1934 but not after that.

McGredys

Unlike the Dicksons, the McGredys were local people in Northern Ireland. Sam McGredy (1828–1903) set the whole thing in motion with his little nursery in Portadown. In 1880 he gave up his secure post as a head gardener and leased ten acres on his own. There was a greenhouse on the property already. Sam I grew fruit and vegetables and took a great interest in pansies.

His son, Sam II (1861–1926), carried on the business. He realized that roses were the coming thing and quietly began dabbling in this flower in about 1895. Ten years later he entered some of his best roses at the show in London and won the gold medal for the salmon-pink *Rosa* 'Countess of Gosford' at his first attempt. He went on to win many more gold medals and was awarded the National Rose Society's Dean Hole Medal in 1921.

Sam II died unexpectedly young, when his son, Sam III, was only two years old. The family kept everything going until the child grew old enough to take on the work. The firm of McGredys grew larger, introducing numerous new cultivars and growing millions of seedlings every year.

During the last part of the twentieth century, life in Northern Ireland was very unpredictable. Portadown was the scene of many political marches and much strife. The current scion of the McGredys emigrated to New Zealand in 1972 to grow his roses in a more peaceful environment. Sam IV also recognized that the climate in New Zealand was more conducive to fine roses than was the chilly damp of Northern Ireland. He continues to breed extraordinary roses. His 'Sexy Rexy' is famous.

One of Sam IV's most important contributions was supporting the idea that a new plant should be patented. Sam IV's daughter now manages the firm.

AMERICAN ROSE BREEDERS

John Champney and Philippe Noisette were the first recorded people to breed new roses in America. As the great inundation of exotic plants proceeded through the nineteenth century, more and more were received in America, at first indirectly from Europe but later directly from all parts of the world.

Roses were a very important part of this movement. The plants flourished in the warmer parts of the country, like the South and the West, and breeders happily began crossing them with each other and occasionally with the native roses.

Henry B. Ellwanger

George Ellwanger had a son who followed closely in his footsteps. Henry Brook Ellwanger was born in Rochester, New York, in 1850. He died of typhoid fever in 1883, much too young. Henry was the second son in a family of four boys and paid particular attention to what was happening with roses. His book, *The Rose: A Treatise,* was published in 1882, the year before he died. Ellwanger and Barry grew an immense number of roses at the Mount Hope Nursery in Rochester. Henry recorded everything about them, as well as about roses from all parts of the world.

He was also passionate about music, especially church music. Henry Ellwanger founded the choir at St. Andrew's Episcopal Church in Rochester and was its director until his death. His sacred compositions are in the University of Rochester's Special Collections Department.

The Rose was reprinted in 1892 and again in 1914 with an introduction by his father, George Ellwanger. The principal value of considering this book is that it is a snapshot of the rose world in the 1890s. Henry and probably his father George Ellwanger had a low opinion of the French rose breeders. As a very upright citizen, Henry decried their habit of bringing out new roses simply for the sake of bringing out something new, regardless of whether or not it showed any improvement on its predecessors: "The incentive to produce new kinds, it should be remembered, is especially great in France, where twenty five francs apiece is demanded for a novelty which may be good, bad or indifferent but whose description is invariably *couleur de rose*."[31] This was a very harsh indictment but would have gone down well in England at the time. As noted elsewhere, there was no love lost between the English and French rose breeders.

Ellwanger carefully pointed out that most French breeders did not intend to deceive the public but that there was a great temptation to promote something new and thereby enhance one's income. He did not accuse the English breeders of being so mercenary, commenting that they "exercised better care and more reliability in selecting [new roses] than the French."

There is something novel and modern about the Ellwanger book. It is supplied with several very valuable tables. It is not clear whether the father updated them after his son's death, but as far as one can tell they were not changed. At the back of the book is a complete listing of all the rose cultivars in commerce at the time, about 1,500, with brief descriptions and cultural characteristics.

A smaller table consists of the names of those who bred and grew the best roses. Henry attempted to make his choices objective, basing his decisions on the growers' reputations. Thirty-two growers made the cut, but the thirty-second, Pierre Oger, was dismissed, not with faint praise but with no praise at all: "Last and least, is one of the oldest raisers who has sent out a large number of sorts, but the rose public, perhaps being prejudiced, have never seen merit in anything he has produced." So there. In spite of that, Oger roses are still in commerce. 'Madame Pierre Oger' is a delicate pink Bourbon rose, found as a sport of 'La Reine Victoria' by Oger in 1878. It is currently listed for sale on the Internet.

Ellwanger said much the same thing about Nabonnand, in position 23: "This gentleman has sent out some seventy varieties, mostly Teas, but for some reason, (is it lack of merit?), they have not taken well with the public." Perhaps there was a slight personal animus lurking in the background in both these instances.

He liked François Lacharme, putting him first. The reason was that Lacharme's output had very few failures. Jean-Baptiste Guillot, *fils,* and Eugene Verdier were second and third, respectively. He favored George Paul over William Paul, consigning the latter to the dust heap of the past: "Although this firm have sent out no roses of sensational beauty, they have given some that have been useful in their day." Useful? That is a very damning epithet.

Still, this all tallied pretty well with a poll taken by the *Journal of Horticulture* in October 1881. Lacharme, Verdier, and Guillot were in the top three positions, though Verdier was no. 1 and Lacharme no. 2.

John Cook

The history of the first Hybrid Tea rose in the world, 'La France', is very vexed, as readers to this point will be aware. In the United States, John Cook (1833–1928) created the first new American Hybrid Tea cultivar, 'Souvenir of Wootton'. Cook crossed 'Bon Silene', a Tea Rose, with 'Louis van Houtte', a red Hybrid Perpetual. He named the new flower "Wootton" to honor George Childs of Philadelphia. Cook had enjoyed a visit to Childs's estate, Wootton.

John Cook was the anglicized version of his real name, Johan Koch. He was born in Freiburg im Breisgau, in Germany. His father was a florist, and Johan was apprenticed to a nursery in 1847. Rather than serve in the German army, he emigrated to America and settled in New York. From there he went to Baltimore to become chief gardener at a large estate.

Once he married, he opened his own business and bred many more striking roses. Several won medals, but 'Radiance', a pink Hybrid Tea, is the best known. It won a silver medal at the American Rose Society show in 1914.

Cook set up a medal at the American Rose Society in 1928. It was won by many prominent breeders, such as Pedro Dot, Eugene Boerner, and Herb Swim, among others. His other memorial is a granite monument in Clifton Park in Baltimore.

Walter van Fleet

Walter van Fleet (1857–1922) worked for the U.S. Department of Agriculture (USDA) in Glenn Dale, Maryland, as a horticulturist. Like so many of his colleagues, he wanted to extend the blossoming season of roses in all parts of the country and allow the ordinary citizen to enjoy easily cared-for roses. He was one of the very first breeders to breed climbing roses specifically for the American garden. His own name for the series was "dooryard roses." Van Fleet recognized the importance of using native species, well adapted to the American soil and climate, as distinct from European roses.

Walter was born in New York into a family of Dutch origin. Initially van Fleet qualified in medicine, but he gave up practicing medicine to devote himself to breeding new roses. In 1905 he joined the USDA.

Van Fleet kept very careful records, and his work ran from 1895 to his death and even beyond it. His death came rather unexpectedly, and he left many new seedlings to be developed. According to the *New York Times* of January 28, 1922, he underwent surgery in Miami, Florida, and did not recover.

Two of his varieties were introduced as late as 1926 and 1927. He used a comparatively small number of species. More than two-thirds of his crosses were based on *Rosa wichurana,* and a few used *R. rugosa, R. setigera, R. multiflora,* and *R. moyesii.* The first hybrid he introduced was 'May Queen' in 1895. Its parents were *Rosa wichurana* Crép. synonym × 'Madame de Graw'. The last one to appear was 'Ruskin', in 1927. Its parents are unknown.

The very reliable *R. rugosa* hybrid 'Sarah van Fleet' came out in 1926. Van Fleet's 'Mary Wallace' (1921), named for Secretary of Agriculture Henry Wallace's daughter, was the first shrub rose that could resist multiple pests. In 1928 it was voted the most popular rose in the country. It is still said to be for sale today. The rose that was introduced in 1920, 'Dr van Fleet', is very vigorous even in cold climates and is very fragrant. The name was not his idea. He was not a self-regarding narcissist and did not name it for himself. Van Fleet called it 'Daybreak', but he gave the seedling to Peter Henderson's company to develop in 1908, and someone in that firm decided to change the name.

Fred Howard

If it were not for the prodigious exertions of dedicated rosarians like William Grant of Aptos, California, little would be known about Fred Howard today.[32] Howard (1873–1947) became famous after winning the gold medal at the Paris competition in 1918 for his Hybrid Tea 'Los Angeles' (parentage: 'Mme Segond Weber' [seed], 'Lyon Rose' [pollen]). In 1921 he won the medal again, this time for 'Miss Lolita Armour'. The roses were shown at Bagatelle in the Bois de Boulogne in the dreadful aftermath of the First World War.

Fred Howard was the son of an English physician who moved to Los Angeles when it was still a very small town. The Howards were a gardening family, and one of their friends, George Smith, was equally enthusiastic. Fred and George opened a nursery together in 1890. The business prospered. Howard understood how to propagate on a very large scale. In addition to cannas, gerberas, and numerous other attractive herbaceous plants, Howard and Smith sold vast numbers of roses. To gain more space, they moved their business to Santa Barbara, but in 1914 Howard bought Smith's share. After that, Fred Howard ran the business with three of his brothers.

Rosa 'Los Angeles' remained available in commerce, as did another one of his successes, 'The Doctor', named for J. Horace McFarland. Howard insisted that any new hybrid had to be not only beautiful but also vigorous. Even with his high standards, the vast majority of his introductions faded away, but the American Rose Society honored him with its gold medal in 1941 for his years of service to the industry.

Father Georg Schoener

William Grant has also written about Father Schoener (1864–1941).[33] Schoener spent much of his life in Santa Barbara, though his order had exiled him to Portland, Oregon, for a time. His legacy consists of two very different roses: 'Arrillaga', descended from 'Frau Karl Druschki' and *Rosa centifolia;* and 'Schoener's Nutkana'. In Grant's account, the "Padre of the Roses" emerges as a disappointed and complex man, riven with inconsistencies.

'Schoener's Nutkana' was a cross between the wild *Rosa nutkana* and 'Paul Neyron', a Hybrid Perpetual. Schoener liked to use American species roses for his crosses. He left other cultivars, but they have not been found.

Herbert C. Swim

Herbert Swim (1907–1989) worked for Armstrong Nurseries much of his professional life.[34] John Armstrong, a Canadian from Ontario Province, founded his nursery in Ontario, Riverside County, California, to grow and sell orchard trees. His doctors told him that he had to live in a warm climate to prevent his tuberculosis from getting worse. Armstrong and his son, John, were both active plant breeders themselves. The nursery became very well known for its concentration on the olive tree, issuing a valuable pamphlet describing the best way to care for them.[35]

As the olive epoch wound down, Armstrong turned to breeding roses in the early 1920s. In his careful and thorough way, Armstrong made sure he had excellent breeders working for him. Dr. Walter Lammerts was in charge initially. He was followed by Swim, Jack Christensen, and Tom Carruth.

Each of these men introduced important roses for Armstrong and his son. Walter Lammerts may be best known for 'Charlotte Armstrong', his first successful rose, and 'Queen Elizabeth', a cross between a Hybrid Tea and a Floribunda. The American Rose Society set up a new class, Grandiflora, to accommodate this new variety. Lammerts was not a prolific breeder, but each rose he created was of extremely high quality.

Swim insisted on several characteristics in a new rose. The petals had to cope with the hot sun; they had to drop off when they were finished blooming; and the foliage had to tolerate heat: otherwise there was no point to introducing yet another new variety. This all underlay his drive to find a rose that would win prizes and thus build commercial success. Novelty is the lifeblood of the rose business.

He crossed 'Charlotte Armstrong' with 'Contrast' and created two cultivars that came close to meeting his goals: 'Forty-niner' and 'Applause'.

In 1988, Herb Swim published his memoir, *Roses: From Dreams to Reality*, and ended its foreword by saying, "[S]ome ego indulgence has been involved in the production of this treatise. One does not relish the thought of life's work being lost in the mists of time."

Swim grew up on a farm in north-central Oklahoma, and there were always roses in his mother's garden. After a solid education in agriculture and horticulture, Swim took a variety of related jobs to survive the Depression and in 1934 went to work for the Armstrong Nursery. By then he knew that roses were to be his life's work.

Dr. Lammerts was still primarily a pomologist and had not yet started his great work on roses. He was in charge of the research department at the time, evaluating peach trees for tolerance of low rainfall and warmer winters, in other words, the Southern California climate. The Armstrongs then wanted him to turn his attention to roses.

A Walter Lammerts hybrid rose, *Rosa* 'American Heritage', 1965.
Reproduced by permission of Dr. Z. Zhang

Lammerts used his encyclopedic knowledge of genetics to start an innovative rose breeding program. Swim succeeded Lammerts and in 1939 worked with his employer, Robert Pyle of Conard Pyle, and others like Fred Howard to put together the All-American Rose Selections Inc. (AARS), a professional organization to stimulate excellence in rose breeding. One of their major tasks was to describe and assess the dozens of new roses coming to the United States each year, often accompanied by very misleading marketing information, closer to propaganda than fact. If the AARS recommended a plant, the buyer was guaranteed that it would succeed.

Reading Swim's book is character-building. Swim describes the amazing success that led to 'Charlotte Armstrong', but whereas most people would sit and admire their handiwork and think they were done, he saw what it lacked and got busy repairing those (minute) deficits. Never being satisfied is a mark of a great creator in any field.

A yellow hybrid rose, *Rosa* 'Brandy', bred by Herb Swim in 1981.
Reproduced by permission of Dr. Z. Zhang

In 1955, Swim joined Ollie Weeks to expand Weeks's wholesale rose business into one that included breeding their own new cultivars. As he summed up his career in his book, he thought that his best roses were 'Sutter's Gold', 'Circus', 'Mister Lincoln', 'Angel Face', 'Double Delight', and 'Brandy'. All of them won AARS awards. Swim moved back to Armstrong on a part-time basis as he grew older and set about finding a worthy successor. Jack Christensen had joined Armstrong as an assistant to Arnold Ellis, and Swim trained him for the post.

The last three chapters of Swim's book include a brief treatise by Walter Lammerts on the best way to breed new roses and a fascinating list of crosses that Swim would have made if he had had enough time. The final one is a chronological list of the roses Swim introduced himself, 125 in all.

Their intellectual heir, Tom Carruth, has gone on to a stellar career in rose breeding partly based on what he learned from these impressive men.

Francis E. Lester

Francis E. Lester (1868–1945) was born in the English Lake District and moved to the United States in about 1900. After living and working for more than twenty-five years in New Mexico, he and his wife, Marjorie, moved to California. They found an ideal setting for their purposes in Corralitos, near Santa Cruz, and established a commercial nursery devoted to old roses.

Lester died of leukemia and was buried in Watsonville. His widow released a very hardy rambling *Rosa moschata* cultivar, 'Francis E. Lester', in 1946. Lester had bred it from *R*. 'Kathleen' crossed with an unknown seedling but died before it could be introduced.

Lester was a devotee of old roses and rambled among the ghost towns of the gold country recording the various treasures he found.[36] One could say he was a proto–"rose rustler" before that term was coined. Lester took cuttings and raised some of the hardier roses he found, intending to make use of this characteristic. He found 'Harison's Yellow' most often: "[M]ost interesting of all were the Old Roses. Chief among them was Harison's Yellow." He went on, "[A]lthough they have been neglected for fifty years, they still live." Lester also pondered the fact that when the miners and their wives traveled to California, 'Harison's Yellow' was still a relatively recent rose (it had been released in 1830).

Lester's catalogue listed many of the heirloom roses discussed in the foregoing pages: 'Général Jacqueminot', 'Gloire de Dijon', 'Frau Karl Druschki', and many of the same sort. He was almost alone in doing this so early. Nowadays, since the heroic efforts of people like Miriam Hopkins, growing and selling old roses is no longer an exotic enterprise.

After Lester's death, Mrs. Lester ran the nursery with Will Tillotson, their manager, until she died. Will Tillotson took it over, but he had no close family. When he died, he bequeathed the business to his assistant, Dorothy Stemler, and the firm remains in the hands of the Stemler family. Dorothy's daughter, Pat Wiley, and her husband, Newt, retired and handed the business on to their sons, Andy and Jack. Guinivere and Jack Wiley are now the owners. Jack takes the photographs, and Guinivere arranges the bouquets for their gorgeous catalogues.

Conard Pyle Company

Alfred F. Conard (1835–1906) was born on a farm in West Grove, Pennsylvania. At first he worked with his brother in the nursery business, but in 1862 he joined with Charles Dingee to open the Harmony Grove Nursery. Dingee and Conard employed Antoine Wintzer, originally from Alsace, to do their hybridizing. Conard took Wintzer with him when he created a new firm, Conard and Jones, in 1897.

Antoine Wintzer (ca. 1848–1925) was a skilful and sophisticated breeder.[37] In addition to roses, he worked for many years on the canna and released an important dwarf yellow canna, 'Buttercup'. In the 1897 catalogue, Conard announced that Wintzer had joined the firm, bringing more than twenty years of experience in the floral mail-order business. Wintzer rose to become vice president of the company.

They had several valuable new ideas that made the company profitable. Wintzer used a new system to propagate his roses very successfully, and Conard thought of selling their plants through the mail. One of their less-attractive ideas was to use the swastika as the emblem of the cannas in 1915. It was done entirely innocently. They could not possibly know the way it would be appropriated by the Nazi criminals a few years later, but it still gives one a shock to see it displayed so prominently in their literature.

Robert Pyle (1877–1951) joined the company in 1898 and after Conard's death bought the majority share. When Wintzer died in 1925, Sydney Hutton became the head nurseryman. Throughout the company's whole history, roses were the principal focus. Pyle took the business to another level, selling grafted two-year plants, which blossomed the following year. These plants cost more, but the public was excited about flowers coming so soon and paid the premium.

In the 1925 catalogue, Pyle wrote about Wintzer: "[He] was the first man in America to grow roses in quantity for a mail order business, a greater-than-Burbank with cannas, his 77 years of life have established him in the esteem of customers and associates."

The following year he wrote this brief elegy: "Antoine Wintzer's work among his Cannas is finished. Early in 1925 he left us for the higher life. His contribution to mankind was certainly an "added beauty to the earth."

ANTOINE WINTZER,
Originator of the C. & J. Improved Cannas

When the history of the American Canna
comes to be written, Antoine Wintzer, Vice-
President of The Conard & Jones Co., will
occupy a prominent place, as through his untir-
ing efforts the world has been made richer in
beauty with flowers, in manifold shades and
colors formerly unknown or even dreamt of,
when he took up the improvement of the Canna.

"The greatest breeder of new American Cannas is
Mr. Antoine Wintzer, who has raised nearly 40,000
crosses."—From *Garden Magazine*, 1907.

Antoine Wintzer, whose
work established Conard
and Jones as a major firm.
*Reproduced by permission of
Special Collections, University
of Delaware*

Like McFarland, Pyle built institutions and contributed powerfully to the development of the rose industry. He traveled to Europe and was impressed by the Meilland family. It was he who arranged for Francis to cross America by car and see everything he could about the rose business in the United States.

By 1939 Meilland foresaw the coming German invasion of France and was concerned about the survival of the outstanding new rose he and his father had been working on since 1936. People who visited their nursery in Lyon

C. & J. NEW LILY-CANNAS 1915

KING OF BEDDING PLANTS

To have doubled, and more, the size of a flower;

To have trebled the variety of colors;

To have increased the endurance of the bloom;

To have given bronze foliage to flowers that before had only green;

After twenty years of faithful, enthusiastic hybridizing is the record of our Vice-President, Antoine Wintzer, America's Canna Wizard.

☸

C. & J. SWASTIKA INDICATES THE VARIETIES ORIGINATED BY THE CONARD & JONES CO.

To have won for these improved flowers leading awards at the great expositions in America;

To have won for America the majority of the awards against all competing nations of Europe in a two-year international competitive test by the Royal Horticultural Society of England;

To have the superiority of C. & J. Cannas recognized and to have them used by the leading parks of our country;

Is evidence conclusive that C. & J. Improved Lily-Cannas are superior to all other existing sorts, and that they have, by merit alone, won the title of "The Finest Cannas in the World."

HAD YOU BEEN PASSING HERE

IN YOUR FLYING - MACHINE

last summer, there would have burst upon your gaze a spot of earth ablaze with color (the acres of Cannas of The Conard & Jones Co.); but had you come nearer you would have seen that this color is made up of row upon row in solid separate colors, waving like broad ribbons across the field. (See illustration on page 44.) In appearance one section is a real floral kaleidoscope. Dismount and enter this carefully guarded collection, and if you were attracted by the first sight, you will marvel at *this* wealth of color in riotous array. Visitors invariably are enthused, then enraptured, at the beauty and size, the shades and combinations and abundance of bloom of our wonderful seedlings.

Remember that for nearly twenty years our Vice-President, Antoine Wintzer, has been selecting and cross-breeding the finest specimens from this unusual race, and from these thousands of his flower-children we have picked out for you just five superior new sorts, listed below and deserving a place in every up-to-date collection.

POCAHONTAS (4½ feet)

(Bronze Olympic) No. 4279

The large, orient red flowers are borne on firm, upright stems, just enough above the foliage to show the entire head. The foliage itself is a *dark bronze-green* with emerald shadings, the ribs a darker bronze. Single roots of this Canna produce from five to twelve grand bloom-stalks in a season, and each stalk makes two or three bloom-heads, with from twenty to thirty perfect flowers on each. A truly magnificent sort, an early and continuous bloomer. Strong plants, $2.50 each, postpaid.

FLAG OF TRUCE (4 feet) No. 4311

A large-flowered, green-leaved, cream-white Canna with faint pink dots on each petal and a sulphur-colored tongue. When a short distance from the flowers they appear pure white. The heads average eight to twelve blooms on each, and each bloom-stalk generally has three heads of flowers, which bloom in succession, thus keeping the plant in bloom all the time. Strong plants, $2.50 each, postpaid.

DRAGON (3 to 4 feet) No. 2527

If it were not for "Beacon," which we introduced in 1912, this Canna would be in a class by itself. It blooms incessantly and keeps sending up new bloom-stalks about every week, until cut down by frost. Dark ox-blood-red, and especially suitable for mass planting. Strong plants, $2.50 each, postpaid.

PRINCETON (3 to 4 feet) No. 4063

An intense bright yellow flower with a decided dash of red in the throat, extending well up on the petals and showing on the tongue also. Its principal value lies in its ability to resist bleaching better than any other yellow Canna. It flowers early. Strong plants, $2.50 each, postpaid.

GAIETY (5 feet) No. 4252

Color is reddish orange, mottled with carmine and edged with yellow. The tongue is yellow and densely spotted with carmine. When planted in solid beds or rows produces a dazzling effect. Strong plants, $2.50 each, postpaid.

THREE MAGNIFICENT C. & J. LILY-CANNAS

SEE IN COLOR ON OPPOSITE PAGE

☸**MRS. ALFRED F. CONARD.** 4 ft. The most popular pink Canna ever introduced and unsurpassed for planting either singly or in large beds. The exquisite salmon-pink flowers are of largest size and so freely produced as to keep up a superb showing for months. 35c. ea.; choice potted plants (ready April 15), 45c. ea., postpaid.

☸**KATE F. DEEMER.** 4 ft. The grand flowers open a rich oriole-yellow, which gradually gives place to turkey-red in the center and throat of the flower, the rest of the blossom turning almost white. Buds are rich yellow on reddish brown stems. 30 cts. each; choice potted plants (ready April 15), 40 cts. each, postpaid.

☸**METEOR (Wintzer's).** 5 ft. The almost solid mass of deep, dazzling crimson bloom produced is spectacular. Judges at the S. A. F. National Convention, 1913, pronounced this the best red Canna on the grounds. 35 cts. each; choice potted plants (ready April 15), 45 cts. each, postpaid.

OFFER 40 One each of the 3 Cannas shown in color on opposite page, in dormant roots, 75 cts.; or the 3 in potted plants, $1, postpaid.

OFFER 40a The above 3 Cannas and the 3 offered on the back cover—6 superb sorts, in dormant roots, $1.90; or the 6 in potted plants, $2.25, postpaid.

The front cover of a Conard Pyle catalogue showing the Wintzer cannas with the ancient Chinese swastika symbol chosen as a logo.
Reproduced by permission of Starr Roses

knew it was quite out of the ordinary. Meilland sent eyes to three or four rose growers in different countries, including Conard Pyle. He knew they would be handled with integrity. Conard Pyle named it 'Peace' and released it on the day that Berlin fell.

Today the company lives on in West Grove with its Star roses.

Jackson & Perkins

Jackson & Perkins began as a fairly small nursery in Newark, New York, when Charles Perkins joined his father-in-law, Albert Jackson, in business in 1872. The two men grew grapes and berries for the local market as a sideline. Perkins was primarily an attorney, but his life changed when he read Henry Ellwanger's book *The Rose*. Perkins became fascinated by roses. He stopped practicing law and went into the nursery business full time.

In 1884 they took on E. Alvin Miller (or Alvin E. Miller: the records vary) as a hybridizer, barely two years after Ellwanger's book was published. At the same time, the very young firm leased another fifty acres of land and built a new greenhouse. This first greenhouse was glazed with recycled church windows. It is hardly surprising that they found Miller at Ellwanger and Barry. Newark is in the Rochester orbit.

Alvin Miller was born in Germany in 1857 and learned his métier in the impressive German system of apprenticeship. He was barely twenty-eight years old when he went to Newark. Miller and his wife lived in Arcadia Township near Newark for many years, appearing in three censuses. The census takers listed him baldly as a "gardener." Without Miller, the company might not have succeeded so well so quickly. Some years later, the local business directory listed him as a nurseryman.

Miller was instructed to develop a new rose and made the firm's reputation with the exquisite climber 'Dorothy Perkins', named for Perkins's granddaughter. It was released in 1901 and went on to win prizes for several years. (The success of the rose led to the name Dorothy Perkins being used for stores selling ladies' clothing in England.) Miller based his crosses on descendants of 'Turner's Crimson Rambler' and used the pollen of 'Mme Gabriel Luizet'.

Perkins's nephew, also named Charles, took the company more deeply into rose production. In 1928, they decided to appoint Dr. Jean H. Nicolas (1875–1937), a prominent French rose expert, to guide their development program.[38] He did not disappoint them. Of the fifteen or more excellent roses he introduced for the company, the most highly acclaimed variety was 'Eclipse'. This rose was introduced in 1935. It received the Portland Gold Medal and three other major prizes.

Jean Nicolas grew up amid roses. His father adored them, and rose fanciers came to their house all the time. Jules Gravereaux was only one of the people from whom he learned. After college and graduate school, Jean

Alvin Miller created the outstanding 'Dorothy Perkins' rose.

Reproduced by permission of Newark-Arcadia Historical Society, Newark, New York (photographer unknown)

E. ALVIN MILLER

Came to work for Jackson & Perkins in 1884 as propagator and foreman. His skill and success in the propagation of rose bushes and other ornamental nursery stock contributed in no small measure to the early success of the Jackson & Perkins business. It was Mr. Miller who did the actual hybridizing which resulted in the origination of the Dorothy Perkins rose.

Nicolas enrolled at the Polytechnic School of Artillery, in accord with the traditions of his family and class. His vision turned out not be acute enough, and he had to resign from the French army. He went to work for his father. Later he married an American woman and transferred his allegiance to the United States. He still visited France frequently and traveled very extensively as part of his work. By the time Perkins approached Nicolas, he already had an international reputation as a rose breeder.

Nicolas bred new roses to increase their cold hardiness. His family lived near Lille, but upstate New York has a much tougher climate. The names of some of his creations give an idea of what he had in mind: *Rosa* 'Polar Bear',

Dorothy Perkins seen with the rose named for her.
Reproduced by permission of Newark-Arcadia Historical Society, Newark, New York

'Yosemite', and 'Snowbank. These names do not only describe the color of their petals. His three books remain very readable. A *Rose Odyssey* has first-hand accounts of many major figures in "rose-dom."

After Nicolas's death, Jackson & Perkins took on Eugene ("Papa") Boerner as their chief hybridist in 1939. It was an inspired choice. Boerner developed the Floribunda rose to its peak. In subsequent years, the company was bought and sold several times. The rose breeding facility moved first to Tustin in California and then to Somis. Currently Donald and Glenda Hachenberger's investment group owns Jackson & Perkins.

Peter Reinberg

Peter Reinberg (1857–1921) was born in the United States of Lithuanian immigrant parents. His father built up a very successful wholesale florist business in Chicago, and Peter inherited it after his father died. His father seems also to have dabbled in rose breeding.

In 1906, Peter released a red Hybrid Tea rose, 'Mrs Marshall Field', named for the Chicago department store magnate's wife. Peter Reinberg went into local Illinois politics and clearly knew how to proceed, as he rose through the municipal ranks. A few years before he died, he was president of the Cook County Board of Supervisors.

His rose is no longer in commerce, and it took considerable effort on the part of the author's friends to find it. Like so many others of that epoch, it had found a home at Sangerhausen. That did not last either. In 2002, the rose was removed.

Eugene Boerner

Eugene Boerner (1898–1966) was born in Cedarburg, Wisconsin. His family was comfortable if not prosperous. An uncle had a nursery, and Eugene learned a good deal from him. His grandfather had bought orchard trees and shrubs from Ellwanger and Barry for twenty-five cents apiece.

There was enough money to send him to college in Madison, Wisconsin, but he disliked the engineering courses. He left college and went to work for a large wholesale nursery in Council Bluffs, Iowa. Boerner was briefly in the armed forces at the end of World War I. A year after he was demobilized, he answered an advertisement from Jackson & Perkins for a college-educated man to handle plant diseases in their nursery.

He moved to Seneca Lake near Newark and stayed with the company until he died in 1966. Boerner never married but was universally known as "Papa" because of his warm and jovial disposition.[39] Each morning he marched off to review his "children" and picked a promising bud very early before the sun rose too high. Boerner placed the bud under his hat. This slight degree

The floribunda rose 'Little Darling'. Eugene Boerner of Jackson & Perkins expanded this class of roses. *Rosa* 'Little Darling' was bred by Carl G. Duehrsen. *Reproduced by permission of Dr. Z. Zhang*

of warming brought out any latent fragrance. By the end of the day, he knew which roses would be worth pursuing.

Eugene Boerner moved up the ranks at Jackson & Perkins. He saved enough of his salary to buy a modest share in the company. Another key milestone was when new plants were protected under the patent laws; for the first time, the originator of a new cultivar was able to collect royalties on his work.

When Jean Nicolas joined the firm, Boerner learned from him. Nicolas had seen what Wilhelm Kordes was doing at Sparrieshoop in Germany. The Floribunda idea originated with Kordes, and the Germans used it very creatively. Boerner took the concept and developed it to its finest pitch as a landscape rose. The group lies somewhere between the Hybrid Teas and the Polyanthas. For a long time the American Rose Society called them "large-flowered polyantha hybrids."

The term "Floribunda" indicates the abundance of the flowers. Boerner used many related cultivars from experts like Kordes and Poulsen to come up with his successful introductions. One of these was 'Golden Masterpiece', a yellow-flowered Floribunda that did well in ordinary home gardens. Up until then the American rose growers had focused on the greenhouse and cut flower aspects of the trade, but the Europeans always kept the amateur gardener in mind.

Griffith Buck

Dr. Griffith Buck (1915–1991), a professor of horticulture at Iowa State University for almost forty years, became enamored of roses as a very young person in a most unusual manner. Quite by chance he started up a correspondence with a Spanish pen pal who turned out to be Pedro Dot. Dot asked his niece Maria to reply for him and sent a constant stream of information about roses to the young man. It did not take long before Buck was hooked. One of his earliest cultivars was *Rosa* 'El Catala', named for Dot, a Catalan.

As noted earlier in this work, Buck had no grant funds for his research and had to do the best he could. Only a few rosebushes survived being left outside in the Iowa winter in 1947 without any protection, but he took those and bred them as a start. From this small beginning he created many fine roses that were extremely tough and yet still very beautiful. The additional benefit was that they withstood disease and pests very effectively, too; the extreme cold killed everything off. One variety has very long stems and is suitable for the cut flower industry.

The reverse also turned out to be true. Some Buck roses, such as 'Carefree Beauty', will do very well in the heat and humidity of Texas. He left altogether about ninety cultivars. At first he used Hybrid Teas, but he later worked with some old roses.

The original Buck rosebushes were all dispersed, but a devoted team is reassembling them in the Reiman Gardens at Iowa State University. At last count they had found all except eight of them.

J. Horace McFarland

J. Horace McFarland (1859–1948) is mentioned in this chapter for the same reasons as Dean Hole and Henry Ellwanger, men who may not have bred new varieties of rose themselves but whose insights and tremendous efforts made roses more accessible and led to important changes. McFarland was one of the founding members of the American Rose Society and edited its annual for many years. The National Agricultural Library in College Park, Maryland, has all his papers and photographs in its archives.

GERMAN ROSE BREEDERS

Kordes Family

The first Wilhelm Kordes (1865–1935) founded a dynasty. He braved the wrath of his family and became a rose grower in Schleswig-Holstein. His son, Wilhelm Kordes II (1891–1976), discovered the work of Gregor Mendel as a youth and determined that he would grow roses in a thoroughly scientific manner.

The younger Kordes was caught in England at the outbreak of the First World War and was interned on the Isle of Man as an enemy alien. He and a German friend had opened a rose nursery in Surrey in 1913. It ran for only a short time before they were arrested. Although this was of course highly inconvenient, he used the enforced idleness to improve his education. Being there also probably saved his life.

His father exemplified the idea of vision, which is used as the title of this book. Father Wilhelm loved 'Mme Caroline Testout' above all other roses, but he told his sons it would be utterly perfect if it could be bred into a deep red instead of pink. Wilhelm II tried to do what his father wanted. He crossed 'Mme Caroline Testout' with 'Général Jacqueminot' and other dark-red roses but was very disappointed in the results.

Back in Germany in 1920, a very dark time, he established himself as an expert breeder of roses at a new nursery in Sparrieshoop with his brother Hermann. Harkness likens summarizing Wilhelm Kordes's work to condensing the writings of Shakespeare in a nutshell.[40]

I will focus on just one rose. Wilhelm picked up his father's challenge again but this time realized that he could not tackle it directly. His reading had shown him how to do it indirectly. A descendant of 'Caroline Testout' named 'Superb', introduced by Evans of Brighton, offered a glimpse of what he wanted. He fertilized this rose with pollen from the dark-red 'Sensation', bred by the Joseph Hill Co. in Richmond, Indiana. Most of the seedlings were still pink, but one was not. The result was 'Catherine Kordes'.

Kordes was still not satisfied, because this very handsome rose had very little scent and could even have been a bit redder still. He returned to the bench and crossed 'Catherine Kordes' with 'W E Chaplin', an introduction by the English firm Chaplin Brothers in 1929. He then achieved what he had set out to do. This was a rich red rose, 'Crimson Glory', everything he wanted it to be.

Wilhelm's children and grandchildren continue to breed roses. Wilhelm IV is in charge of the firm. They have moved into organic and sustainable methods of growing their roses, no longer using any artificial chemicals.

Peter Lambert

When people do their work too well, they are at risk of being forgotten. Their accomplishments become accepted wisdom and seem always to have been part of the scenery. Peter Lambert (1859–1939) fits this description. The Lamberts were nurserymen and horticulturists in Trier for many generations. This gave him a good start. Peter studied at the Prussian horticultural college at Potsdam and then spent several years gaining polish at nurseries in England and France.

There were no professional rose breeders in Germany at the time, but he knew very early that he wanted to breed new roses. Working at his family firm back in Trier, he spent most of the rest of his life breeding hardy new roses suitable for the tough German climate.

Perhaps the best known was 'Frau Karl Druschki', a white Hybrid Perpetual still grown today. Mrs. Druschki was the wife of the president of the Verein Deutche Rosenfreunde, a merchant called Karl Druschki. The name has had many incarnations in the century since its release because the German one sounds harsh to English ears: 'Reine de Neige', 'Snow Queen', and 'White American Beauty', among others.

One of Lambert's most valuable achievements was to found the German Rose Society, Verein Deutsche Rosenfreunde, in 1883 with Heinrich Schultheis, Johan Lambert, Heinrich Drögemuller, and Friedrich Harms.

The terrible aftermath of World War I for Germany clouded the end of his life. Lambert was not able to cope with the distress and humiliation and struggled to keep his rose breeding afloat.

Tantau Family

Mathias Tantau (1882–1953) started out with a tree nursery. He also planted the seeds of Polyantha roses and watched what resulted. He gradually realized that he was more interested in his roses than his trees. With that recognition, he spent a year in Trier at Peter Lambert's nursery as a trainee and short stints at other important centers.

Mathias Tantau had a very long hard slog to overcome the disaster of the 1914–18 war, but by 1928 he had introduced 'Joanna Tantau', a rose he called a Polyantha but which now is known as a Floribunda. His breeding plans were always laid well into the future. His son, Mathias II, was born in 1912, and he taught the boy everything he knew.

Twenty years was not too long a time over which to accomplish what he wanted using *R. multibracteata,* a wild rose from China. Even though the Second World War led to enormous hardships, the family continued to breed new roses. Some were released in 1942 and others in 1946 and 1947.

Tantau roses are almost always fragrant. In 1960, 'Super Star' finally emerged. It was the culmination of the Chinese rose program, twenty-three years after they began crossing it. It was a "rosy vermilion" Hybrid Tea, completely new in its day. Harkness also points out that Kordes was a close neighbor of Tantau's. They had a very constructive friendship. Tantau used several Kordes hybrids for his own purposes.

After his father's death in 1953, Mathius II rebuilt the business because so much was in ruin. Mathias II steadily introduced a stream of winning roses almost every year until 1972. In the mid-1980s, longtime employee Hans Jürgen Evers took over the company, followed by his son, Christian, in 2000. Their recent introductions include 'Diadem' and 'Monica', both useful as cutting roses.

CZECH ROSE BREEDERS

Rudolf Geschwind

Rudolf Geschwind (1829–1910) was a Czech forester whose passion was roses. He was born in a village near Teplitz when the Czech lands were still part of the Austro-Hungarian empire. He was educated at the Technical University in Prague and entered the royal forestry service. His superiors transferred him frequently. One wonders how he maintained his rose collection in these circumstances, but he worked alone in his garden in Krupina, Slovakia, whenever he could.[41]

Geschwind traced his love of roses back to childhood. One of his uncles wanted to throw out an early Hybrid China rose, 'Malton', but Rudolf took cuttings from the plant and budded them onto *Rosa canina*, where they flourished.

The winter in central Europe can be brutal, and Geschwind was determined to breed hardy roses that could tolerate the climate. Climbing roses fascinated him. Because he moved frequently, was an amateur in central Europe rather than London or Paris, and named his roses in "difficult" German phrases rather than English or French, his work was almost lost until one or two devoted scholars realized what was happening and stopped the decline.

Geschwind was first noticed in 1886 when he exhibited a collection of climbing roses at the Paris World's Fair. Some of his best-known climbers were the Nordlandrosen Series. 'Nordlandrose no 1' is perhaps the best known of that group. Its silvery-pink flowers reappear in autumn, a rare occurrence. Austrian rosarian Eric Unmuth notes that Geschwind based many hybrids on 'De la Grifferaie', a hybrid introduced by Vibert in 1845. Some of these crosses were introduced as 'Erlkönig', 'Ernst Dörell', and 'Nymphe Tepla'.[42]

Then there was 'Grüss am Teplitz'. This name does not trip off the Anglophone tongue, but there is no more beautiful and hardy red shrub rose. It is also very fragrant. Geschwind introduced it in 1897. William Grant and Eric Unmuth deserve much credit for restoring as much as can be known about this important figure. Additional factors making Geschwind "invisible" were the depredations of two world wars and the rise of communism.

Despite all that, at least 3 roses out of the 140 cultivars he is known to have bred have remained current. At the time he began to work on rose breeding seriously, most breeders used well-known roses as parents, especially elegant Hybrid Tea roses, assuming that the offspring would reveal the ideal combination of both sides. Gregor Mendel was just starting his studies, and the scientific world did not yet know anything about heredity.

Geschwind noticed that many highly touted new roses were very short lived, failing rapidly after one or two seasons. This was why he was determined to breed for hardiness. He recognized that two gorgeous parents were no guarantee of successful offspring and that it was only a matter of chance whether any of them inherited good qualities from either one. The logical next step was to use an earlier generation as parent rather than the complicated double and triple hybrids that were fashionable.

Geschwind was one of the most important breeders to turn to species roses as parents. He was unusual in choosing many North American species when almost no one else was doing that. His garden contained *Rosa californica, R. canina, R. roxburghii,* and *R. setigera* together with *R. × alba.* He probably bought them from the French rose nurseries like Laffay, which sold American species roses.

Immediately after his death, his collection was transplanted into the garden of the Countess Chotek, his patroness. Geschwind's roses did not survive the upheavals of the 1920s and 1930s, and if it were not for the fact that enough specimens had made their way into large rosaria such as Sangerhausen and Cavriglia, nothing of his would have been around any longer. Today, there is a collection of his roses in the Austrian Rosarium in Baden (near Vienna) and another one in the Czech town of Zvolen.

Geschwind was very thoughtful and had been well educated. He wrote three books in German about the hybridizing of roses: *Hybridizing and Growing Roses from Seeds, The Tea Rose and Its Hybrids,* and *Roses in Winter.* They outlined his theories about the choice of parent and emphasized his concern with hardiness and vigorous flowering.

During their heyday, Ketten Frères of Luxembourg introduced many Geschwind roses for sale.

Jan Böhm

Jan Böhm (1885–1959) grew up knowing he would be a gardener. Son of a very well known rosarian, he gravitated into breeding roses almost as a matter of course. In the 1920s he established his own nursery in Blatná. He not only created many new hybrids himself but also carried some of Geschwind's roses. Böhm left more than seventy new roses, fourteen of which won gold medals at major shows.

With the advent of communism after World War II, the nursery was expropriated by the Czech government in 1952. The new management was not expert, and the nursery faltered. After the end of the regime, the family reclaimed the house, but the land had been sold for building lots. The Böhms bought new land in another district of Blatná and started again.

Böhm incorporated *R. setigera* into some of his roses. He was heavily influenced by Geschwind and based some of his crosses on the Geschwind hybrids. He understood the value of this species. Böhm introduced 'Stratosfera' in 1934 and 'Tolstoi' in 1938, both containing *R. setigera* genes. His rambler 'Demokracie' is listed in Western rose catalogues for its gorgeous vermillion blossoms and vigorous growth.

BELGIAN ROSE BREEDERS

Louis Lens

Louis Lens (1924–2001) bred many extraordinary roses over his long career, at least one of which is in the World Top Ten: a white Hybrid Tea, 'Pascali'. His father, Victor Lens, also bred roses. At one time, Pepinières Lens was the largest wholesale nursery in Belgium, selling literally millions of rosebushes at lower prices than the others could match. That led to a lot of resentment, and J. H. Nicolas dismissed them very cavalierly. He did allow that *Rosa* 'Madame Louis Lens', later named 'White Briarcliff' in the United States, was a passable flower.

According to Charles Quest-Ritson, Louis Lens stood apart from his family's powerful concern with money and bred his flowers for their beauty alone.[43] As he got older, Lens explored the possibilities in species roses seldom used by other breeders. *Rosa bracteata* led to 'Pink Surprise' and 'Jelena de Belder', and *Rosa filipes* gave 'Pleine de Grace', 'Dentelle de Malines', and 'Dentelle de Bruxelles'.

ROSE BREEDERS OF LUXEMBOURG

Soupert & Notting

Pierre Notting (1825–1895) started out as an apprentice to the nurseryman Constantin Wilhelm in 1845. In 1855, he and Jean Soupert (1834–1910), another of Wilhelm's apprentices, joined forces and opened their own business in Limpertsberg. This connection was further cemented by Soupert marrying Notting's sister, Anne Marie, in 1857. The fledgling firm introduced three striking roses: 'Tour de Malakoff', 'La Noblesse', and 'Duc de Constantine' in 1856.

Over the next fifty years, they won so many gold medals for their roses that the numismatic department of the National Museum of History and Art put them on display. Their French counterparts paid a lot of attention to what was happening in Luxembourg. In 1874, Pernet-Ducher named one of his new remontant moss roses 'Soupert & Notting'.

Soupert & Notting supplied roses to the Grand Duke of Luxembourg and sent them as gifts to Queen Wilhemina of the Netherlands. Each man received all sorts of awards and honors, but Soupert never quite recovered from the death of his partner in 1895. In the end, his three sons took over for him. Jean-Constant Soupert was a genius at breeding Hybrid Teas. When he died in 1942, the business came to an end.

"Constant," as he was known, released *Rosa* 'Mme Segond-Weber' in 1906 as a tribute to a noted French actress. This rose won prizes in 1907 and 1908 and went on to win the grand prize at the Concours Bagatelle in 1909. In 2009, members of the Luxembourg Rose Society dedicated a Soupert & Notting rose they found at the Sangerhausen Rosarium, 'Bagatelle', to commemorate this centenary.[44]

Ketten Frères

Jean Ketten (1841–1922) and his brother, Evrard (1842–1912), also began their business in Limpertsberg, in either 1864 or 1867, depending on which source is correct. They had been apprentices of Soupert & Notting. One of Evrard's sons, Jean (1875–1937), carried on the family rose breeding.

ROSE BREEDERS OF THE NETHERLANDS

Jan Spek bred roses in Boskoop. He was not particularly well known, but he did introduce *Rosa* 'Edith Cavell' in 1917. The coldblooded execution of Nurse Cavell by the Germans touched many throughout Europe, even in the midst of an unprecedentedly terrible war. More than one flower breeder introduced a plant named for her.

DANISH ROSE BREEDERS

Poulsens

Just as Germany, with its harsh climate, should have been a slightly unlikely place for the serious culture of roses, so too is Denmark. Dines Poulsen (1879–1940) was the eldest of three brothers who were all thoroughly grounded in horticulture by their nurseryman father.[45] He sent Dines to learn from Peter Lambert in Trier and then to England. He returned to work on one of his father's farms, where he principally grew fruit trees but also experimented with roses. Poulsen introduced a semidouble red rose, 'Rödhätte', in 1912. It can be considered a forerunner to the Floribunda class.

Dines decided to stick to orchard trees and left it to his younger brother Svend Poulsen (1884–1974) to work on the roses. In 1924, Svend introduced two new roses that were in a different class from any that had gone before: 'Else Poulsen' (very bright pink) and 'Kirsten Poulsen' (cherry red). Both were very hardy, an important characteristic for northern Europe. They had clusters of flowers, but the individual blossoms were much larger than on any previous Polyantha truss. After the usual to-ing and fro-ing of the nomen-claturists, a new class, Hybrid Polyantha, was created to contain them. For the rest of the world, they were simply known as "Poulsen roses."

Svend continued to introduce new and wonderful roses but then turned to cherries in his late seventies. He died at the age of ninety. Svend's son, and later granddaughter, managed the firm. It is still very active.

Svend Poulsen and Francis Meilland were both deeply concerned about the piracy of their work. Svend was outraged at a National Rose Society Show in London in 1934 when he saw another firm displaying his work as their own. Sam Davison McGredy was concerned that Poulsen might create an unfortunate incident that he would later regret. He told Poulsen that he would sign a contract to market Poulsen roses in the United Kingdom and pay him a royalty for three years. Meilland led the international fight to patent plant products.

SPANISH ROSE BREEDERS

Pedro Dot

Pedro Dot (1885–1976) came from a family of gardeners and was apprenticed to the firm of Joaquin Aldrufeu, the only man who bred roses in northern Spain in the early 1900s. Aldrufeu died before Dot started, but the business was still deeply involved with roses. After learning all he could at this firm, Dot spent very valuable time in France just before the First World War. By 1915 he could go back to Spain and begin his own experiments.

One very important one was in the process of pollination. He devised a system that covered the mother flower with the male one, under a paper cone. Until then, this had been a two-stage operation, but Dot streamlined it, reducing the amount of work needed for this task.

The goals he set were to breed strong, healthy plants with very brightly colored flowers that would survive the Spanish sunlight. He did this work at his father's nursery in San Filieu de Llobregat, with its perfect microclimate for rose growing.

In 1923, he introduced *Rosa* 'Francisco Cubera', salmon pink and yellow. Dot went on to breed more brilliantly colored Hybrid Teas, followed by a spectacular white climber, 'Nevada'. In the United States, Robert Pyle, of Conard Pyle, picked up on what was happening very early and soon began importing Dot roses for the hot, dry climates of the American West and Southwest. For a time, "Spanish roses" had a considerable vogue.

The next climber in 1927 was a prizewinner, 'Spanish Beauty', a name chosen by Pyle for its allure in the American market. 'Spanish Beauty' was so thoroughly covered with large fragrant pink flowers that one could hardly see the stem.

Dot also bred miniature Hybrid Teas and worked until his eighties.

CHINESE ROSE BREEDERS

Although the China rose caused huge excitement in the Western world and its repeating qualities affected rose breeding very vigorously, it was not held in such high esteem in its own country. Several scholars, including Peter Valder, comment that it trailed after orchids, chrysanthemums, and peonies in the estimation of the Chinese elite. In spite of that, rose breeding went on for hundreds of years. It would not be the first time the public enjoyed something that the elite scorned. Chinese horticulturists saw the potential of a flower that bloomed more than once per season.

Valder quotes Wen Zhengming, a famous artist-scholar from the Ming period, who was considering climbing roses: "I once saw in someone's garden a screen made from bamboo, with five-coloured climbing roses trained across it. The Banks [sic] roses were trained on a wooden frame, called a 'rose arbour'. When they flowered he would sit beneath it—what difference is there between this and dining in the market place? However neither of them can be planted without a framework, so perhaps they should be planted around the women's quarters for the servant girls to pluck—this is just about acceptable."[46] Modern Western gardeners would disagree with this half-hearted praise.[47]

Valder notes that only one treatise devoted solely to roses existed as late as the eighteenth century.[48] He also comments that the old Chinese varieties are not as bright and glossy as the modern Western hybrids.[49] *The Treatise on the Monthly Rose* lists some of the romantic names they were given.

Hazel LeRougetel, a well-known English rosarian in the mid-twentieth century, spent much of her time trying to track the development of Chinese roses. She became aware of this book and discovered a family of Chinese horticulturists, the Shens in San Francisco, who helped her with the research.[50] One of the roses most frequently seen in paintings from the earliest times was very similar to 'Old Blush'. She provides the names of the ten old roses most esteemed. One appeared to have blue petals at its heart. Another resembled a golden bird in a fountain.

Mr. Shen grew *Rosa* 'Jin Ou Fan Lu' in his own garden and told Mrs. LeRougetel that its yellow blossoms had a "light green cold feeling" about them. This is a very nuanced description and is reflected in the ancient name.

Chinese gardeners still grow the old roses but add potted modern roses as accents. Balance and harmony are the keys to Chinese philosophy. New flowers are very exciting, but older ones, laden with poetic meaning, are just as important.

Robert Fortune found a Banksia rose with red, white, and striped flowers in a garden in Ningbo, possibly the "five-coloured" variety that Wen Zhengming scorned. It is still grown today. Many other old cultivars have been lost. Finding out who bred any of them is very difficult. There is no question about the existence of cultivars. Mikinori Ogisu lists forty-one of them growing in Luoyang at one time.[51] Connecting the names of the old cultivars with their modern descendants is very hard. Ogisu learned to be very patient and very skeptical.

In the early 1990s, two English rose experts, Roger Phillips and Martyn Rix, traveled to China to see whether they could find the fundamental species and learn where some of the Chinese hybrids had been bred. They went into less well populated country areas and found the species they sought as well as some of the hybrids, such as *Rosa multiflora* and *R. gigantea*, the sources of the roses of the past 150 years, and a white Tea-Scented Rose, *Rosa gigantea*, growing in a valley. They formed the impression that the early breeding had taken place in the western parts of China and not in the coastal cities visited by British and foreign collectors.

Very old varieties were still grown in small villages, but Phillips and Rix did not record the names of any particular breeders, probably because those names are not known any more. Banksia roses of many types were common along the hedges and roadsides. Phillips and Rix observed that there was usually only one variety of rose per village, unlike the Western tradition of having several types of the same plant available. This presumably reflects the long distances from larger centers and the isolation of small villages.

Zhang Zuo Shuang, the former director of the Beijing Botanical Garden, is also chairman of the Chinese Rose Society. He holds several other important posts in Chinese botany. Dr. Zhang has written a book about Chinese roses. He makes it quite clear that intentional cross-pollination of roses was not done in China before the European breeders introduced this method.[52]

The current director of the Shanghai Botanical Garden, Hu Yong-Hong, is a rosarian and interested in the history of the rose. Dr. Hu studies the potential of old roses for rose breeding in eastern China. His assistant, Zhang Ya-li, generously prepared a few notes for me about one of China's most notable rose breeders.

Jiang En-tian

Jiang En-tian (1908–1975) was known affectionately as the "Rose Lady" during her lifetime. She was born in Taicang, Jiangsu Province. Taicang lies near the Yangtse River and was an important shipbuilding city and port in the

A Chinese hybrid rose, *Rosa* 'Medallion', released by the Chinese Academy of Agriculture, 1982.
Reproduced by permission of Dr. Z. Zhang

A Chinese hybrid rose, *Rosa* 'Pink', bred by Yang Rose Company of Kunming, China, 2003.
Reproduced by permission of Dr. Z. Zhang

Paintings of different classical Chinese roses (artists unknown).
Reproduced by permission of Dr. Z. Zhang

fifteenth century. Admiral Zheng set off on his enormous voyages from this city in 1421 in the name of the emperor Zhu Di.

As a young woman, Jiang studied Western literature at Qinghua University (now Tsinghua University) in Beijing, but later in her life she worked exclusively on roses. From the 1950s, Jiang En-tian established many of the important bases of modern rose classification in China, identifying early cultivars as well as breeding new ones.

She began her career as the unexpected heir to an elderly physician, Dr. Wu Lai-xi. Dr. Wu had studied in England and had imported more than two hundred European rose cultivars over the years. As he grew older, he started to look for someone who cared deeply about roses, had enough space to keep all the plants in good condition, and knew English well enough to read his books about roses.

Jiang En-tian fitted these criteria. Dr. Wu died in 1951. Even though her husband's work took them away from Beijing to Tianjin, she successfully moved the roses to Tianjin and pursued her career. There were about four

The "Rose Lady" of Beijing.
Jiang En-tian planted her
hybrid roses in the gardens
of the Great Hall of the
People in Beijing.
Reproduced by permission of
Dean Chen, Jiang En-tian's son

hundred roses in Dr. Wu's collection. Within about five years she became expert, partly from the books and partly from her own experience.

One of her classmates at university rose through the political ranks to become the vice mayor of Beijing. He knew about her work and in 1958 asked her to create a rose garden at the Great Hall of the People to celebrate the tenth anniversary of the New China. In a fairly short time, Jiang built four rose gardens: one in Beijing and the others close by. She spent more than seven years commuting between Tianjin and Beijing every week and accepted no pay from the Chinese government.

She must have been very adept at politics. Both husband and wife suffered from the Japanese invasion and brutal occupation of China. This was hardly over when the Maoist movement spread and the Communists seized power. As an educated person, she was always at risk of being sent away into the depths of the countryside for "re-education." Jiang En-tian's son recorded the tribulations of his parents when he moved to the United States.

The next thing we know is that she donated all her roses to the people of China. She bred more than three thousand cultivars and placed the best of them at the Great Hall of the People. To commemorate her work, Taicang created the Entian Rose Garden. A senior official of the China Biodiversity Conservation Foundation planted a specimen of *Rosa* 'Entian Lady' in the park. This official may well have been Zhang Zuo Shuang, the current chairman of the Chinese Rose Society and a member of the foundation's botanical committee.

Jiang En-tian also worked in the gardens around the Temple of Heaven, the fifteenth-century monument in Beijing near the Forbidden City. These grounds provide a peaceful place in which the citizens of Beijing can relax and enjoy doing their exercises.

Jiang En-tian's son, Chen Di, showed his mother's roses to Hazel LeRougetel, a prominent English mid-twentieth-century rosarian, when Mrs. LeRougetel visited China in 1985. He remained in communication with her for a long time but eventually moved to the United States in 1987, to continue his work as an engineer.

Other Chinese Rose Breeders

Jiang En-tian was assisted by the gardener at the Temple of Heaven, Liu Hao-qin, who also bred many new cultivars. Between 1957 and 1989, Zong Rong-lin created forty new roses at the Hangzhou Nursery. He is best known for *Rosa* 'Green Clouds'. Other firms are the Kunming Yang Rose Gardening Company, Yunnan Lidu Flower Enterprise Development Company, and the Nangyang Rose Base. Li Hong-quan was another very active rose breeder.

6

Herbaceous Plants

BEGONIA

> Her essential Narcissism (pleasure of looking in a mirror) was
> met by his Begonia-ism (concept of the potted plant). Things got
> so that Woman spent *all* her time admiring herself in mirrors,
> and Man, discouraged, devoted himself quietly to raising
> begonias, which are fairly easy to raise. Sex atrophied.
>
> —James Thurber and E. B. White, *Is Sex Necessary?*

EGONIAS WERE originally found in warm climates, including the New World. They traveled to Europe and then were exported west to the United States several centuries later. One authority, the *USDA Germplasm Resources Information Network,* lists a total of 1,548 species at present.[1] Highly polymorphous, begonias have been found in all tropical and subtropical climates except for northern Australia.

The genus is subdivided into scientific botanical groups as well as horticultural ones. The American Begonia Society defines eight horticultural groups: cane-like, shrub-like, rhizomatous, semperflorens, tuberous, rex (a form of rhizomatous), trailing/scandent, and thick stemmed.[2] Different classifications are used in other parts of the world.

Because of this immense range, many begonias depend on the shade, a lot can be grown in direct sunlight, a very few are reasonably tolerant of the cold, and some are fragrant. These inherent qualities have been markedly affected by centuries of interbreeding and modification. For every cultivar needing to be in a lath house, another one flourishes outside in an open field.

English gardeners dote on the tuberous form, which offers them the greatest challenge and has the greatest appeal. In the United States, a much wider range of other very attractive types is grown in addition to the tuberous kind. The smaller annual forms, hybrids of *Begonia cucullata* Willd. (formerly *B. semperflorens* Link & Otto), are used everywhere for bedding out and are universally popular. Several forms treated as annuals in temperate climates are perennial in their countries of origin. Most of them have shiny, waxy-appearing leaves, giving rise to their commonest name, wax begonias.

It is not unlike the situation with *Impatiens*. The breeders have been so successful that the excitement and risks are reduced almost to zero. Wax begonias have become a cliché in some ways, but newer introductions are starting to revive interest in them.

THE BEGONIA REACHES EUROPE

Begonias first reached Europe from Central and South America and the Caribbean islands. In the sixteenth century, the Spanish physician and botanist Francisco Hernandez (1514–1587) described and illustrated a native Mexican plant that was clearly a begonia, using the Nahuatl name *Totoncaxoxo coyolin*. After ordering Hernandez to go to the New World in 1571, King Philip II left him to suffer in the tropical heat for eight years after he should have gone home and delayed the publication of his huge work. The treatise was not published until long after his death, in 1625.[3]

Charles Plumier (1646–1706) found six species of *Begonia*, naming the genus for the governor of the French Antilles, Michel Begon. One of these discoveries was the plant now known as *Begonia obliqua* L. This was the only begonia listed by Linnaeus in *Species Plantarum* under the rubric begonia. It is considered to be the "type" plant, the one with all the attributes of "begonia-ness."

These discoveries were first listed in a book published in 1700 by one of Plumier's colleagues. Since then, many more species have been found. Modern hybrids still mainly descend from *Begonia veitchii* Hook.f., *B. schmidtiana* Regel, and *B. socotrana* Hook.f., all collected in the latter part of the nineteenth century.

During that same epoch, the very efficient collector Richard Pearce worked for the Veitch nursery in Chelsea and discovered five truly seminal forms in Bolivia, Peru, and Chile: *Begonia boliviensis* A.DC., *B. veitchii* Hook.f., *B. davisii* Hook.f., *B. rosiflora* Hook.f. (as *B. rosaeflora*), and *B. pearcei* Hook.f. The latter supplies the indispensable yellow pigment for hybridizing.

James Veitch Jr., a brilliant but irascible man, did not release all of these flowers right away but sequestered some of them in his Devonshire greenhouses and allowed the hybridists John Heal and John Seden to work on them for a few years. When the hybrids were introduced, they were dazzling.

Veitch and Pearce did not see eye to eye over what have been described as Pearce's self-serving and devious ways (see chapter 3). After a fierce argument about Pearce selling unauthorized duplicates of the South American plants directly to Sir William Hooker at Kew, Pearce straightway transferred his loyalty to Veitch's competitor across the street in Chelsea, a most unfortunate business. Knowing how tightfisted and harsh the employers of plant collectors were, we may now regard Pearce's perfidy with more understanding. No one looked out for the collectors if they did not look out for themselves.

Begonia socotrana was discovered in Socotra, an island in the Indian Ocean about 150 miles off the coast of Somalia. The distinguished Scottish botanist Isaac Bailey Balfour found it in 1880. One of its characteristics was the ability to flower in the winter months, giving it immense importance in the hybridizing world. This quality is the basis of the group name, Hiemalis begonias.

Finding this plant was really a tour de force. It was thousands of miles away from any other specimens of the genus. The island is extremely arid, with the usual xerophytic flora such as *Dracaena cinnabari*. Stands of the begonia were perched at a high elevation near these trees. Recent research by scientists at the Royal Botanic Gardens at Edinburgh has suggested that these plants were probably relics of an evolutionary shift as the begonia moved from Asia to Africa.

Most begonias require a lot of water and are usually found in humid environments. *Begonia socotrana* has developed striking adaptations to the arid climate. The plants become dormant during the hottest months of the year, and small bulb-like structures at the base of the stems hold water and nutrients to tide them over.

Begonia schmidtiana Regel was discovered in Brazil by the collectors Scharff and Haage of the German firm Haage & Schmidt in Erfurt and introduced in 1879. Begonias were specialties of this and another leading Erfurt nursery, Ernst Benary Samenzucht, for many years. Benary produced the first semperflorens hybrid that could be reproduced faithfully from seed. This was a hugely important step.

Mark Tebbitt comments that the Chinese cultivated their own species of begonia, *Begonia grandis* Dryand, from about 1400 on.[4] By 1641, begonias were appearing in Japan.

The treatment of the begonia epitomizes the approach of late-nineteenth- and twentieth-century plantspeople: whatever could be crossed successfully was crossed. In spite of that, a great many species have never been tried. In 1892 the Royal Horticultural Society held a begonia conference, indicating its arrival as a plant of significance at that time.

It is odd that one of the few cold-hardy species, *Begonia grandis,* has not been widely used in breeding. The Chinese developed it over several hundred years, and in 1641 it was known to be in Japan. In 1691 Engelbert Kaempfer described it for the first time while working in Japan for the Dutch East India Company.

The dominant early names in hybridizing were Benary, Lemoine, Blackmore and Langdon, and Veitch, with numerous smaller nurseries and many individuals working during the same period. Begonia breeders in the past eighty years have built on the foundations laid down by their forerunners. In California, Frank Reinelt and Rudolf Ziesenhenne were the most noted.

THE BEGONIA REACHES CALIFORNIA

The begonia found a most congenial home in California, where its cultivation reached a peak. The state's fertile soils and equable climate were ideal for many species of this tropical and subtropical genus. How this came about is a curious and circuitous story, mirroring that of quite a few other plants. Begonias originally found in the New World made almost a complete circle and returned there. Begonias from Asia and Africa joined them as they traveled at least three thousand miles across the Atlantic Ocean and a further three thousand miles to the West Coast.

Harry Butterfield attributed the first begonias in California to William Walker of San Francisco (1858) followed by James Hutchison of Oakland (1874).[5] He credited Walker with stocking *Begonia manicata* Brongn. ex Cels and Hutchison with *B. semperflorens* Link & Otto (now known as *Begonia cucullata* Willd. var. *cucullata*). In 1969, the American Begonia Society awarded Harry Butterfield its Eva Kenworthy Gray medal, given to a member who offered the most help to novices in growing the flowers.

Begonias were a rich man's indulgence. During its heyday, from the 1870s to the 1920s, this flower was treated rather like the orchid. It needed heat and specialized care. Once it could be reliably grown from seed and became less finicky in its needs, the general public was able to enjoy it too.

To gain some perspective on the value of this crop, it is helpful to look at the USDA floriculture summary published each year. For the United States as a whole, ornamental horticulture contributes about four billion dollars to the GDP. In 2000, California begonias constituted about six million dollars of that aggregate. Curiously, Michigan, North Carolina, and the northeastern states are all larger suppliers of begonias now than California. Many California growers have transferred much of their activity to Central America or Mexico.

During the first phase of begonia collecting and breeding, the principal work was done in Europe, mainly Belgium, England, France, and Germany. The possibilities seemed limited, but the process began quite early. Helen Krauss listed I. von Warscewicz's hybrids of *Begonia manicata* Brongn. ex Cels and *B. dipetala* appearing in 1840 or 1841.[6] The earliest species had small and single flowers and came in tones of pink and white.

Victor Lemoine, and the firm of Crousse in Nancy, as well as Louis Van Houtte in Ghent, began to expand the choices. A double flower had been seen in England in 1872 and in Lyons in 1873. Lemoine issued a double begonia in 1876.[7] Classification began to stagger under the weight of new forms. Using the nomenclature suggested by Voss, Lemoine called his flowers *Begonia* × *tuberhybrida*.

This portmanteau term was adopted by experts such as Charles Chevalier, a professor at the Liège Professional School in Belgium who published an important monograph on begonias in 1938. Within that grouping, many horticultural subgroups were formed, with informal names such as "rose form," "camellia form," and "picotee."

Harry Butterfield credited Lemoine with four definite seminal introductions in the bedding class and at least three other probable ones, between about 1880 and 1900. Flower series named "Gloire de Lorraine" or "Gloire de Nancy" were a Lemoine hallmark even if his name did not appear. Another handful are simply listed as being "from France" and are either Lemoine or Crousse varieties. Lemoine's son, Emile, or his grandson, Henri, did the later work (see chapter 3).

The First World War was a turning point in this, as in so many other things. Shipping was restricted to essentials, and there was a great shortage of food. No seeds or plants could go to the United States from Europe. That led to a shift in the American nursery scene and stimulated local initiative.

American nurseries looked to the neighboring countries. Begonias began to arrive directly in the United States. The Central and South American sources were closer and more contiguous, but in spite of that, very little is known about the advent of particular begonias in California.

A review of early nursery catalogues reveals that the commercial choice of begonias was still extremely limited until after the First World War. The large seed companies such as Burpee offered a few species, an occasional hybrid, and very little else. In the 1890s, rex begonias were listed as "conservatory and parlor decorative" plants. People were fearful of planting them outdoors because they were so tender.

There was some hybridizing in early twentieth-century America, but nurseries were still importing European varieties. One of the notable Californian begonia breeders in that epoch was Mrs. Theodosia Burr Shepherd, a housewife of extremely modest means in Ventura.

In 1912 the San Francisco firm of C. C. Morse listed a new shipment of begonias from a "distinguished English breeder." Most probably that was Blackmore and Langdon. (C. C. Morse merged with the D. M. Ferry Seed Company in 1930 to create the Ferry Morse Seed Company long after both Charles Copeland Morse and Dexter M. Ferry had died.)

This combination of factors—namely, the absence of European imports and the recognition that California's climate was favorable for begonias—led to a profound change. The Vetterle Brothers in Capitola played a very important role in this transformation.

Alfred D. Robinson, one of the founders of the California begonia industry.
Reproduced by permission of KOLZ Begonia Research Center

American Begonia Society

The American Begonia Society began as the California Begonia Society in 1932. Aficionados got together at intervals and distributed an informal newsletter, a mimeographed *Monthly Bulletin* launched in January 1934, with valuable hints about the growth and culture of their favorite flower. By 1938, this simple sheet had become *The Begonian*.

Only a few knew much about this plant. There were problems with its classification, and species that are now commonplace had not yet been discovered. What was known was that it did flourish in California.

Herbert P. Dyckman started the organization, and the initial monthly meetings were held at his house in Long Beach. To survive during the Depression, he taught people how to grow their own vegetables at the Long Beach schools' Adult Education department.

A year or two later, there were enough people to set up a branch in Ventura, and by 1940 Santa Barbara had its own branch. This was a boon to members who lived a long way away. It was hard to travel back and forth to a meeting in the evening, getting home after midnight. The roads meandered through small towns, and the speed limit was 25 miles per hour. Freeways have their uses.

The members tended to be in Central and Southern California, with rather fewer in Northern California. This pattern followed the lines of climate. In 1935, Alfred D. Robinson recommended that they become a national society. Once that happened, begonia fanciers in the eastern United States rapidly joined the society. Now there are chapters in many states.

Developing California Begonias

Vetterle and Reinelt

The brothers J. Lowell (1892–1969) and Everett Vetterle (1899–1943) inherited a thriving nursery in Capitola from their father, John. John was a lawyer of Swiss descent from Michigan who had moved to California in 1910 to start a bulb business. Calla lilies were among their most important crops, but they also offered gloxinias, montbretias, anemones, and ranunculus. The Vetterle family was very civic minded. Some of them were elected to office in Capitola's government. They also owned property in the town.

Vetterles grew begonias fairly successfully in the 1920s in spite of the seed being almost microscopic and extremely hard to handle. Choices among begonias remained fairly narrow until the brothers' inspired move of taking Frank Reinelt on as their breeder and hybridizer in 1934 (see chapter 4).

The joint firm became a leader in the great expansion of the begonia palette for amateur growers and fanatical collectors alike. The public flocked to the nursery because of the extraordinary beauty of the premises. Their "Cathedral of Begonias" was breathtaking.

Everett died in an accident in 1943. His wife and two daughters joined Lowell and his wife, and Reinelt, to continue the firm. This partnership lasted until 1969. At that point, Frank Reinelt's arthritis interfered with his ability to work and he moved to Arizona, hoping that the warmer climate would relieve some of his pain and stiffness. Vetterle and Reinelt reverted to Vetterle Brothers. Two of Everett Vetterle's granddaughters, Sherrel Miller and Patricia Williams, helped me with this story.

Vetterle and Reinelt's "Cathedral of Begonias." Frank Reinelt's myriad cultivars of the tuberous begonia were shown very well in their "cathedral."
Reproduced by permission of Dick Turner/Aphra Reinelt Katzev

The business basically came to an end in 1973 when it was sold to Shasta Nursery, a large strawberry-growing concern. By then, Reinelt had retired to Las Vegas in Nevada and started to breed new forms of cactus. In this he was indeed following Luther Burbank's footsteps. Shasta moved the begonia grounds to Watsonville, but without its mainspring Vetterle and Reinelt ceased to operate.

The Begoniacs

What follows is a series of brief biographical sketches of some incomparable people. The epoch in which they lived constituted a "Golden Age" for the begonia in California.

It is almost impossible to do justice to all the important people who devoted themselves to breeding and producing ever more wonderful begonias in an essay of this length and invidious to mention some without including all of them. At the risk of causing some completely unintended distress, I will note the names of some of the more active ones, given to me by two tireless workers who are themselves utterly absorbed in this pursuit, Thelma O'Reilly and Michael Ludwig: Bob Cole, Mabel Corwin, Paul and Marge Lee, Irene Nuss, Barbara Phillip, and the man who set the stage for much that followed, Alfred D. Robinson.

Eva Kenworthy Gray

Eva Kenworthy Gray (1863–1951) wrote a small book about begonias that she published herself in 1931.[8] It was the first book devoted solely to the begonia in the United States. Mrs. Gray created the book entirely on her own. She grew the plants, wrote the text, drew and later photographed the seedlings at different stages, set the type, and made the copies on a hand press.

Eva Kenworthy was born in Booneville, Missouri. She was a university graduate at a time when few women were well educated. After her marriage, she lived in Pacific Beach, California. Her interest in the begonia seems to have been the result of a chance encounter. She met Constance Bower, an early enthusiast of the begonia, in 1920, and Mrs. Bower gave her two begonia cuttings.

Successfully growing the begonias sparked her energies and enthusiasm. Flowers became as important to her as her family, and she took action very quickly. Mrs. Gray soon began producing a magazine, the *Flower Journal*, sending it to anyone who was interested. Next she organized the Begonia Club of Round Robin Letters. Bessie Buxton was the club's secretary, yet there is no record that they ever met each other.

Mrs. Gray's work became known when she issued 'Nelly Bly' in 1923.[9] She then made a signal contribution when she crossed *Begonia aconitifolia* A.DC. with *B. coccinea* 'Lucerna' in 1926, leading to the Angel Wing Group of hybrids. *B. coccinea* 'Lucerna' was a "chance hybrid" found in a garden in Lucerne in 1892. *B. aconitifolia,* one of the cane-like begonias, had been introduced from Brazil in 1892.

She created new hybrids in her Pacific Beach nursery but only sold plants by mail order. *B.* 'Nightingale' was one of her varieties, introduced

Eva Kenworthy Gray and Rudolf Ziesenhenne, two leaders of begonia breeding in Southern California.
Reproduced by permission of Michael Ludwig/ABS

before 1938. This was a cultivar of the tall cane-like begonia and had ruffled edges. *B.* 'Medora' is her best-known variety.

It is said that she was an imposing and stately lady who inspired respect and affection. When her lath house became too overcrowded to hold any more plants, a group of lads in her neighborhood spontaneously built her another one.

Theodosia Burr Shepherd

Theodosia Burr Hall (1845–1906) was the daughter of William Hall, later chief justice of Iowa. Her mother died when Theodosia was very young. Her father made every effort to overcome that loss and kept her close to him as much as possible. Judge Hall taught his daughter all the correct names of the flowers and plants they saw as he made his circuits on horseback, but when he remarried, his new wife was the classic unpleasant stepmother. In spite of the great and enduring affection between father and daughter, Theodosia married William Shepherd very impulsively to get away from an uncongenial household.

The Shepherds went to Ventura from the Midwest in 1876 while the town was still in its formative stages. To call it "primitive" is perhaps a little insulting, but there was not much there yet. William was taken on as editor of the local newspaper. He was a worthy man, well educated but somewhat lacking in social skills and initiative.

The story of how his wife started her career with swapping in a lady's magazine is now quite well known. Her arrangements of dried flowers were so beguiling to the other readers that she began to grow more and more flowers to meet the demand. Eventually her few acres became a large commercial nursery with a catalogue rich in petunias, begonias, and succulents.

Mrs. Shepherd enjoyed crossing the petunias but was often too busy. She taught one of her neighbors how to do it. In the following season, Mrs. Gould presented Mrs. Shepherd with twenty plants, each quite different from the other but all in the Grandiflora Series. The leading nurseryman of the day, Peter Henderson of New York, lauded her work and named the flowers "The Giants of California." Some of the descendants of this line, the Theodosia, continued to be grown until the 1950s. Henderson's encouragement led Mrs. Shepherd to persist and found the packaged flower seed industry in California.

Mrs. Shepherd also worked on begonias. Harry Butterfield's useful booklet on the begonia included an impeccable historical background.[10] He attributed two cane-like varieties to Mrs. Shepherd: *Begonia* 'Catalina' (*B. odorata* × *B. fuchsioides*) before 1905, and *B.* 'Marjorie Daw' (*B. coccinea* × *B. glaucophylla*) in the 1880s. Mrs. Shepherd also introduced *B.* 'Silver Cloud', a rex variety.

Mrs. Shepherd died in 1906, but her son-in-law and former manager, Willard H. Francis, and his wife, Myrtle Shepherd Francis, as well as her sister, Margaret Oakes, continued the retail nursery until 1916. Mrs. Francis carried on her mother's hybridizing.

Rudolf Ziesenhenne

Rudolf Ziesenhenne (1911–2005), the dean of Southern California begonia growers, was affectionately known as "Mr. Begonia."[11] He was born in Chicago and moved to Long Beach as a child in 1923. His family had come from Germany in 1883. While the trail is not completely clear, Rudolf Ziesenhenne's son, Skee, has found some early clues to his father's immense attachment to the begonia.

He did not learn it at home. The family had no particular interest in gardening. His father was a butcher. While still in high school, the young Rudolf was deeply involved with photography. Later he built his own dark-room. Once he devoted himself to the begonia, he bought relevant books on microfilm from all over the world and printed the pages he wanted using his enlarger.

Rudolf's sister, Edna, was interested in plants and attended Herbert Dyckman's lectures on how to grow vegetables at the Adult Education depart-ment of the Long Beach City schools. This was valuable knowledge in the Depression. By then Ziesenhenne had decided to concentrate on begonias, and Edna mentioned this to Dyckman. In 1933 their mother's aunt gave him two begonias as a gift.

During the Great Depression, there were very few jobs to be had. His father-in-law helped him with some property for a nursery. Rudolf also worked as a jobbing gardener for a time. In 1934 he opened his begonia nurs-ery in Santa Barbara. The California Begonia Society was still very new, and Ziesenhenne had not heard of it yet.

Ironies abound. Dyckman visited the nursery and allowed Rudolf Zie-senhenne to attend three of his meetings but would not let him join the soci-ety. It was only after the society became national that Ziesenhenne was allowed to join. He was number 127.

During World War II, Rudolf Ziesenhenne worked at the Port Hueneme naval base in Ventura County. Once discharged from the navy, he returned to his nursery and closed it only in 2004.

Rudolf Ziesenhenne was in charge of the American Begonia Society's research division in 1942. He handled nomenclature from 1940 to 1942 and again from 1953 to 1978. This was a very appropriate role for him, as he be-longed to both the American Society of Taxonomists and the International Association of Plant Taxonomists. Nomenclature was crucial. He was re-sponsible for assigning botanically correct names to new forms. He did this work solely based on his own experience and observations. Unlike botanists in large institutions, he did not have the benefit of an herbarium behind him. For example, the species he named *Begonia macdougalli* turned out to be identical to *B. thiemie* many years later.

Ziesenhenne drew each plant and its parts very accurately and also photographed them. His descriptions were crisp, and he taught himself Latin to comply with academic requirements. It was a mark of honor when he named a new species after someone. Eva Kenworthy Gray was honored by *Begonia* 'Kenworthyae'. To celebrate the birth of his son he issued 'Freddie' (*B. manicata* var. *aureomaculata* × *B. barkeri*). This cultivar is considered to be one of his finest. He introduced eighty-eight hybrids in all.

Established figures were somewhat threatened by Ziesenhenne's achievements, although everyone who knew him says he was the kindest and mildest of men, without an ounce of self-importance. Frank Reinelt was one of his closest friends.

In addition to his prolific hybridizing, Ziesenhenne collaborated with Thomas MacDougall, an amateur plant collector and naturalist from New York. MacDougall worked as a landscape architect but over the winters visited Chiapas and Oaxaca in Mexico looking for new begonias and echeverias. In all he brought back 326 specimens, though some were duplicates. He wrote about some of his collecting trips in *The Begonian*. It was a very tough job.

At first MacDougall gave the new specimens to the taxonomy department at the New York Botanical Garden for identification and classification, the descriptive and naming tasks. This was a very slow process, and he grew impatient. He suggested to Ziesenhenne that the latter be his taxonomist. They collaborated for more than thirty years until MacDougall's death in 1976. Together they released the names of dozens of new species.

By now it can be seen that Ziesenhenne made seminal contributions to the world of begonias, but there was still another way in which he transformed the field. In 1969 he issued *A Suggested Guide to Classification of Begonias for Show Purposes.*[12] Judging the entries at begonia shows was a very hit-or-miss affair until he brought clarity and logic to the process. He recommended that each plant start out with 100 points. Judges would then deduct points for various flaws until they reached a final number as the endpoint.

This made a huge difference. All the branches were then operating in the same way. An award given in Boston or San Diego had the same meaning.

Antonelli Brothers

Three of the four Antonelli brothers—John, Patrick, and Peter—opened their own begonia garden in Santa Cruz. As young men, they had worked for

Vetterle and Reinelt. Before that, they had been truck farmers. Patrick died in 2001. Antonelli's premises burned down in 2005. A year or two later, they moved their business to Watsonville. The present owner, David Bobbitt, is the son of Linda and Dennis Bobbitt and the grandson of Peter Antonelli. As was true of Vetterle and Reinelt, their begonia garden was a destination as well as a business.

This was not the first time that a California nursery was so beautiful that the public visited it solely for the purpose of enjoyment, treating it as if it were a park. Back in 1851, the citizens of Sacramento took their Sunday afternoon walks in the grounds of A. P. Smith's nursery near the river. In the early part of the twentieth century, Dr. Franceschi's "acclimatizing" gardens in Santa Barbara were used in the same way, as was E. O. Orpet's nursery.

The Antonellis had a "Chapel of Flowers" hung with myriad baskets of begonias and furnished with picnic tables and benches. The value of such publicity was incalculable. They competed with Vetterle and Reinelt and its "Cathedral of Begonias" more or less benignly and again at the annual Capitola Festival of Begonias in the fall, a festival they had set in motion.

Brown Bulb Ranch

The Browns grew begonias on a gigantic scale in Capitola for many years. Worth A. Brown wrote a very useful primer on their care in 1948.[13] This firm saw the possibilities in the mass market and grew many millions of plants each year, distributing them to chain stores across the country. They were the first nursery to supply begonias to Woolworth's and later to Sears.[14] In 1972, the firm planted 1,000,000 begonia tubers in its Capitola fields and 5,000,000 in its Marina fields.

This business began in 1911, just before the First World War. James Brown had done well selling cars and buggies in the Midwest. He decided to move to Capitola and started growing berries on several acres. Strawberry wilt disease made this too uncertain. Shortly afterward, he bought a herd of dairy cows to obtain manure without a lot of weed seeds in it. The cows gave so much milk that he created a chain of ice cream stores, but his principal interest remained horticulture and the growing of bulbs. Bulbs eventually took over entirely. James died in 1932 at the age of forty-nine. His sons, Alan and Worth A. Brown, expanded the company and concentrated all their efforts on the bulbs.

In the next generation, their sons took over from them. Capitola declared itself the "Begonia Capital of the World," starting with the annual Capitola Begonia Festival in 1954.

At present, the Browns still grow begonia bulbs, but not in Capitola. They have other growing grounds in different parts of California and in Baja California, Mexico. Family members manage the firm and develop new hybrids.

Henry A. Hyde

Henry Hyde (1871–1949) moved to California from Maine in 1898. He established a most successful nursery in Watsonville right on the main street. Hyde was one of the earliest nurserymen to realize that he would profit from supplying all the necessities for the home gardener, not just seeds and plants. If you visited the Hyde nursery, you could get a landscape architect to advise you on how to lay out the garden, or you could find all the tools and sundries to carry out this design. A stonemason was available, and rockwork could be undertaken.

Begonias were important from the start. Hyde eventually sold almost all types of the new tuberous begonia hybrids: giant single, frilled, crested, and fimbriata; double; rosebud; marmorata; and the hanging *Begonia lloydii* (hort). As a sign of his seriousness, Hyde took on a well-known Belgian plant breeder, Monsieur Dossche, in the early 1930s.

Another line of business was strawberries. It is not by chance that the bulk of California's strawberries are grown in Watsonville. Hyde with Robert Driscoll and a few other men created the industry.

The Hyde nursery prospered until 1959, when it was closed down. Hyde had three sons, one of whom died quite young, leaving small children behind. One of the surviving brothers is still in the strawberry business. He is a wholesaler of several varieties of plants specially bred by the University of California to flourish in the Watsonville conditions.

The strawberry seedlings are propagated and raised near Shasta in Northern California before being sold to farmers and grown down south. This cycle has been shown to give the maximum yields. The very low temperatures in the mountainous region destroy the dormant forms of pests, leaving clean, healthy plants.

Demise of the Begonia as an Engine
of California's Horticulture

This story can be told very quickly. It is all part of the inexorable laws of economics. If the same, or a seemingly equivalent, item can be produced for less money, it will drive out the more expensive one. The once glamorous and expensive orchid previously followed the same trajectory. A modestly priced version becomes available at mass outlets, allowing many more people to enjoy the plants, that is, democracy at its best.

Turning formerly rare plants into commodities and using industrial systems to propagate and sell them has this consequence. It is the old story of "be careful what you wish for, you may just get it."

～⊶～

Political Footnote

Just when one thought that everything possible had been done with the begonia, along comes *Begonia* 'Kimjongilia', bred by the Japanese master Motoderu Kamo in 1988 as a birthday present for Kim Jong Il's father, Kim Il Song. They may not have enough to eat in Pyongyang, but there was a monster exhibition of 30,000 begonias to commemorate the former Dear Leader.

DAHLIA

Almost everyone agrees that news of this resplendent flower first reached Europe in the late 1500s, maybe 1580 or 1585.[1] It was found and illustrated by Francisco Hernandez, Philip II of Spain's physician. The king sent Hernandez to Mexico in 1570 to prospect among its natural riches and report back to him. After Hernandez left Spain, the king seemed to neglect his emissary, maybe because Hernandez was rumored to be a crypto-Jew and his enemies circled around his back.

Whatever the reason, long after Hernandez reported back to the king that he had completed his task and asked to go home, he was left to stew in the tropical heat of Mexico for five more years. When he did get back, his papers were shoved away in a corner and neglected.[2] Thirty years after his death, part of his work was published. The final blow was that all his originals were lost in the great fire of the Escorial in 1671.

What follows is open to question. Many original documents have been lost, and a great deal of what has been offered as fact may simply be wishful thinking and now even mythical. Hernandez described three Aztec plants that were unequivocally dahlias by their native names: *acocotli, cocoxochitl,* and *acocoxochitl.* The words in Nahuatl correspond to "water pipe," "hollow-stem flower," and "water-pipe flower," respectively. Aztec men were known to use one type of hollow-stemmed plant as a pipe.

Martin Kral explains that much of this is open to misunderstanding.[3] The images in Hernandez's texts were muddled up by later editors, and scholars in Mexico City do not think that they represent the dahlia at all. Aztec gardeners seemed to have modified these plants. Hernandez's pictures show that some flowers were partially double. The tubers are nutritious, and native people used them as food and in ceremonial rituals. The flowers were almost an epiphenomenon.

Almost a century later, the Italian scholar Vitalis Mascardi published a work in 1651 in which he showed a double-flowered dahlia, but not until the end of the eighteenth century did dahlias come into their own. After two hundred years of dry pictures, living seed reached Madrid. The director of the botanical garden in Mexico City, Vincente Cervantes, sent seed to Abbé Cavanilles, director of the Royal Gardens in Madrid, in 1789. Everyone was excited by the tall plants with brilliantly colored flowers.

Cavanilles named the new flower for Andreas Dahl, a former pupil of Linnaeus. Dahl was a Swedish botanist who lived and worked in Berlin. Cavanilles and Dahl never met. At least two types of dahlia were in that original shipment: *Dahlia pinnata* Cav. and *D. coccinea* Cav. A lot was going on in Europe at the time, but there were still people with enough leisure and enthusiasm to welcome many other new plants from the New World.

The French botanist André Thouin in Paris was one of the scientists who received dahlia tubers very early. Thouin (1747–1824) was a gardener and a student of Bernard de Jussieu. Following his father, Thouin was director of the Jardin des Plantes in Paris. In 1802 a Dr. Thibaud traveled to Madrid and returned with a gift from Cavanilles. He carried dahlia seed or tubers for

Thouin. Thouin planted them in pots in the greenhouse. When some plants were left outside over the winter by mistake, they died. Thouin realized that they had come from a very hot country.

The last vestiges of the French Revolution were still in effect. Thouin had a mandate to spread the importance of gardening far and wide in the country, to improve the diet of the poor and benefit other classes with handsome flowers. Dahlias lent themselves to this project.

The French sent dahlia seed to England. Dahlias were first said to flower in London in 1798. *Curtis's Botanical Magazine* for 1804 showed a picture of a living dahlia, *Dahlia coccinea*, "at Mrs Fraser's of Sloane-Square, who has the credit of introducing this ornamental plant among us from France."[4]

There is a lovely story about Empress Josephine and her jealous possessiveness over dahlias at that time. She was said to be very happy and excited about being the sole dahlia grower in France. When she found out that someone had bribed her gardener to give him some tubers, she flew into a rage and commanded the gardener to tear out all the plants and burn them. If she could not be the sole grower, she did not want anything more to do with them. Alas, like so many other lovely stories, this one has no basis in fact.

There was some connection between the empress and the dahlia. Alexander von Humboldt (1769–1859) sent dahlia seed from Mexico, both to Paris and to Berlin, in 1804. These seeds were of a different species, unlike the ones already known to the French. He had collected them from a coastal mountain at an elevation of 4,000 feet. These are believed to have been dwarf species, previously collected in the Mexican Sierra del Ajusca in 1750, *Dahlia dissecta, D. tenuis,* and *D. pubescens.* Humboldt commented that they were only "5 or 6 thumbs high."[5]

When Humboldt returned to Europe, he settled in Paris for many years, causing Napoleon Bonaparte to be very jealous. Humboldt cut a much greater figure than Napoleon in every respect. His traveling companion Aimé Bonpland (1773–1858), a French surgeon and botanist, had no personal resources, and Humboldt arranged for him to become Josephine's superintendent of gardens. It is said that "Bonpland" was a corrupt version of his nickname, "Bonne plante." His actual family name was Goujaud.

This appointment cut across the position of Count Lelieur de Ville-sur-Arce, who was breeding dahlias at Malmaison. Josephine unceremoniously let the count go, and he stalked off to St. Cloud, another royal estate, in high dudgeon. He took the dahlia seedlings away with him and continued to breed new ones very successfully. He released a fully double flower in 1817. Lelieur also bred roses and has in general been both underestimated and forgotten.[6]

Bonpland left no record of developing any dahlias. He seems to have been a rather restless and disorganized man. Once Josephine was dead, he returned to South America and held a good position for a short time at a botanical garden, but he soon wandered off into the wild to collect plants. There he was captured by the dictator of Paraguay, Dr. José Francia, and held prisoner for more than nine years. Not even the prestige of Humboldt could get him released. In his final years, he lived in great simplicity and poverty in a remote part of Uruguay.

The very distinguished botanist Augustin-Pyrame de Candolle (1778–1841) worked with dahlias at the same time. He introduced a great range of colors in his series of dahlias. Originally from Geneva, he was the director of the botanic gardens at Montpellier, an old university town. He and his son, Alphonse (1806–1893), with grandson Casimir, formed the preeminent botanical dynasty in Europe during the nineteenth century.

In the botanical garden at Louvain, Belgium, M. Donckelaar, whom we have met in connection with camellia and hydrangea, was also profoundly interested in dahlias. He bred many double varieties.

From these beginnings, it took only a few years for dahlias to exhibit almost all the colors now available. The explanation for the explosion in color was the crossing of *Dahlia pinnata* of the ivory-magenta group with *D. crocea* (syn. *D. coronata*) of the cream-yellow-scarlet group. This gave rise to relatively fertile octoploids. *D. coccinea* was the ancestor of the later single-petaled flowers.

A century later, William Lawrence at the John Innes Horticultural Institution in Norfolk studied the inheritance of color in dahlias in the 1920s and 1930s and provided the above explanation. This work was useful in developing better classification systems.

The rapid spread of the dahlia coincided with the period in which the Horticultural Society of London, later the Royal Horticultural Society, was formed and getting established. The society soon employed the German gardener Karl Theodor Hartweg (1812–1871) to collect plants for them in the New World. Hartweg brought back many unknown species but no new dahlias.

Following his successful career in London, Hartweg was appointed the grand duke's chief gardener in Baden. He bred a completely double flower in 1810, and in 1811 a pure white dahlia was released. Gardeners on the Continent and in England worked feverishly to introduce all sorts of new dahlias.

Johann Wolfgang von Goethe (1749–1832) settled in Weimar in 1776 and paid a great deal of attention to his garden. He cannot be said to have actually done much in the way of gardening as we think of it, but he encouraged nurserymen to explore new plants. Goethe talked to many horticulturists and spent time with the Sckell family, who took care of Duke Carl August's gardens. He visited the botanical garden at Jena and saw the dahlia plantings there. He chose many of the cultivars for his own estate. In Weimar he also patronized the nurseryman Dreyssig, and he found that the hybrid dahlias validated his theory of the metamorphosis of natural beings.

GERMANY

Botanists now counted over fifty varieties of dahlia, both single and double flowered.[7] Because Europe was in turmoil and travel was very difficult, the great German botanist Carl Willdenow did not know that the flowers had already been named and gave the species a new one in 1804. He decided to honor Johann Georgi, a Russian naturalist. The flowers were called "Georgina" in Germany until quite recently. The Ernst Benary catalogue for 2005–7 lists the flowers as dahlia but adds the name "Georgine" as well.

The period from 1810 to 1850 involved even more frenzied activity in dahlia breeding. To cope with the confusion, Willdenow recommended that all dahlias growing in Europe at the time be called *Dahlia variabilis* Desf.

Christoph Friedrich Otto

Willdenow's gardener Christoph Friedrich Otto was fascinated by the new dahlias as they arrived in Berlin at the beginning of the nineteenth century. Working closely with his director, Otto started to cross them. His work was important for other centers of dahlia culture. Otto sent seed to London when the English plantings failed. He also shared his seeds with the botanical gardens in Jena and Leipzig, as well as Karlsruhe and Erfurt. Hartweg in Karlsruhe may have received his dahlia seed from Otto.

Probably using Otto's seed, the gardener at the Leipzig court bred more than one hundred varieties and pretty soon turned to selling them. The tubers were valuable.

When Willdenow died in 1812, Otto became director for a few years. He took a very broad view of his responsibilities. As soon as new and beautiful plants were available, he believed they should be shared with the public, though whether he sold them or gave them away is not clear. (Thirty years later at the botanic garden in Melbourne, Australia, the German émigré Ferdinand von Mueller gave new trees and shrubs away, seeing that as his duty. He was rewarded by the undying hatred of the nurserymen, who felt that he was undercutting them unfairly.) During that very early period, much more was going on in Germany than in other countries. There were centers of dahlia breeding in Potsdam, Altenburg, Cassel, and Köstritz.

Christian Deegen

The foundation of dahlia growing in Köstritz, a small city in Thuringia, began with one Christian Deegen's infatuation. Deegen (1797–1888) started his career as a minor bureaucrat, but when he won a lottery in 1820, he gave up his desk and his quill and bought property to start his own nursery. As a youth, he had pursued his hobby of collecting and drying plants. Carl Sckell gave him some dahlia tubers to encourage him, thereby igniting the passion.

By 1826 Deegen was ready to issue a catalogue containing more than twenty fully double varieties of his own raising. He was one of the earliest breeders to realize that the weak stem was a disadvantage and breed new cultivars for a sturdier stem. His last introduction was an orange ball type, 'Kaiser Wilhelm'.

Johann Sieckmann followed Deegen in Köstritz. He was the head gardener at a large estate nearby but, like Deegen, followed his inclination and opened his own business. One of Sieckmann's handsomest cultivars was the deep red 'Alexander von Humboldt', released in 1836.

Wilhelm Pfitzer

One of the most prolific dahlia raisers in nineteenth-century Germany was Wilhelm Pfitzer (1821–1905), who started his nursery in 1844 on land near

Wilhelm Pfitzer Senior. A relief of Wilhelm Pfitzer's head was cut on this bronze medallion. *Reproduced by permission of Klaus Pfitzer*

Stuttgart given to him by his prosperous father, a harness maker. Pfitzer was attracted to penstemons, dahlias, and gladioli very early. He opened his nursery in Fellbach in 1844.

Pfitzer built a reputation with these flowers, but the dahlia was his tour de force. In the hands of Pfitzer's children and grandchildren, the firm was very successful for more than a century, but by the 1980s it had shrunk materially. The familiar combination of competition from warmer countries and the accumulated stresses of the war led to the Pfitzer nursery closing in the 1980s. Two world wars and the huge upheaval in post–World War II Germany were a large part of the problem, but the shift of the floral industry to warmer climates with their cheaper wages was the finishing touch.

Pfitzer was born in the village of Fellbach and loved nature as a child. This led to him being apprenticed to a nurseryman in nearby Stuttgart. Pfitzer soon built his own nursery and laid the basis of its stellar reputation. His son and grandsons carried it on until after World War II.

Pfitzer's great-grandson Klaus Pfitzer has his own small business, primarily raising dahlias. He has very generously allowed me to see a number of his family's records including a set of catalogues from 1866 to 1875, plus the one for 1911. Even almost thirty-five years later, in 1911, dahlias were still the leading item. The sheer volume of dahlias offered for sale is staggering.

There were five dahlia species in general use during that period: the original *Dahlia pinnata* and *D. coccinea* and Humboldt's three discoveries, most likely dwarf. Year after year, the dahlia alone took up four or even five pages of fairly small print in Pfitzer's catalogues. Several hundred varieties resulted from breeding just the above species, even before *Dahlia juarezii* and later the "cactus" types were introduced.

Pfitzer used different classifications as his work progressed. At first he divided the flowers into classes I and II. In 1870 he added a dwarf category, initially retailing flowers bred by Gebruder Mardner (that is, the Brothers Mardner) of Mainz.

It is interesting to follow the fate of newly introduced cultivars over time. One assumes that most nurserymen used common sense in making a living. Persisting with merchandise that does not sell is self-destructive. A nursery will carry certain items to please its more discriminating customers, but this can only be a marginal activity in a large general business. Another assumption is that the cultivars listed were actually available, so that if a customer ordered six dozen 'Dorothée', for example, they could be supplied. There were enough changes in the catalogue from year to year to recognize that the printers reset them. The pages were not slavishly carried from one year to another, something I have noted when working with older catalogues. When all type was set by hand, printing was very expensive, so it was tempting not to make changes unless absolutely necessary.

In an analysis of one hundred years of Burpee catalogues, it was found that some marigold cultivars persisted for more than seventy years in spite of the usually very fickle attitudes of the public. By contrast, the half-life of a new cultivar was less than five years and often only two years.

When the Pfitzer output is examined, a similar pattern emerges among the new cultivars. In 1866, more than 350 new cultivars were listed, divided into classes I and II. In the next three years, more than half of these disappeared. Initially it seemed that Pfitzer used a single code number for a cultivar no matter when or where it appeared, but the system was not applied consistently.

By 1875, Pfitzer had renamed his classes under four new subsections. The dwarfs (*zwerg*) occupied the first section, and the old class II now appeared in the fourth section. The numbering system eventually went up to 1,291, but this included many repeats of formerly differently numbered kinds. Specialists believe that Pfitzer released 223 new cultivars. Any new cultivar coming out after about 1895 was the work of his son or maybe his grandson.

In the 1911 catalogue, the only dahlias listed were derived from the cactus type imported into Europe at the end of the nineteenth century. Almost all the others have gone. No one wanted them any more.

ENGLAND

Some of the English breeders were able to amass very considerable fortunes. The Industrial Revolution was moving very fast, and there was a lot of new money being made. As a man succeeded in business, he wanted to show off. One very good way was to build or buy a big house with a conservatory and extensive grounds. Shrewd nurserymen played on that vanity with ever-showier flowers. Dahlias were the ideal vehicles. To buy complete control of a fine new variety such as 'Yellow Defiance', a purchaser might pay as much as two hundred pounds, a great deal of money in the 1840s.[8]

John Keynes

The brilliant economist John Maynard Keynes's grandfather, John Keynes (1805–1878), was a renowned dahlia breeder in Salisbury, Wiltshire, ending up as mayor of the city.[9] When the business was sold after his death, there was enough money to provide his son, John Neville Keynes, with a very handsome annuity of £800 per annum. That was a lot of money in those days. John Keynes's first wife had died, leaving him with one daughter. John Neville was the son of his second marriage, to Anne Neville.

John Maynard Keynes may have been the apostle of the Great Depression, but he grew up in comfort and even affluence. When he looked carefully at the sources of his family's money, he believed that his grandfather had not only been a successful nurseryman but also may have speculated cleverly in land. The rapid expansion of the railways increased the value of land in their path. John Keynes also expanded into banking later in life. He was said to have had complete control of his affairs until the end, taking care of the firm's books himself at all times.

Grandfather Keynes introduced dozens of cultivars. His own father owned a brush factory in Salisbury, but the son never cared for that work and went off on his own into horticulture. Keynes dahlias started to appear in 1833 and went on until almost the end of the century, long past the date of Keynes's death. The firm must have employed a professional hybridizer. His contemporaries commented that Keynes's nursery contained only fashionable and popular plants that sold very well. He chose very shrewdly and did not waste time or space on other types of plant.

Samuel Widnall

In Grantchester, a village near Cambridge, immortalized by Rupert Brooke, Samuel Widnall also bred dahlias. He too introduced dahlia cultivars by the dozen. Widnall had one son who seems to have been rather spoiled, Page Widnall. Unlike John Maynard Keynes, growing up in a family in which hard work was expected no matter how much money you had, Page spent his life in charming leisurely pursuits. He bought the old vicarage in Grantchester, which Brooke had written about in his poems, and then proceeded to do nothing for forty years.

James Levick

James Levick had a nursery in Pinstone Street in Sheffield. He bred many dahlias and was said to be the first person to produce one with two colors in its petals, *Dahlia* 'Levick's Incomparable'. This cultivar won twelve prizes. His *D.* 'Beauty of Sheffield', introduced in 1834, is shown here. In that era Sheffield, like Birmingham, was a very large and wealthy manufacturing city but still had no representation in Parliament. Levick was working at the time the 1832 reform bill was passed, finally remedying this injustice.

Dahlia Shows

The Horticultural Society encouraged dahlia growing. In 1846, the society published the first known register of dahlias, a fourteen-page pamphlet. The register listed more than seven hundred varieties and even had a few lithographs.[10] Small amateur dahlia societies sprang up, largely made up of workingmen and lower-level civil servants. Each group held its own show,

LEVICK'S BEAUTY OF SHEFFIELD.

T. Gray Del   J & J. Parkin Sc

James Levick's 'Beauty of Sheffield', 1834, the first dahlia cultivar with
bicolored petals.
Reproduced by permission of Harry Rissetto

often at a local pub, but for a long time dahlias (like so many other exciting new imported plants) were largely the province of the wealthy. The first show devoted solely to dahlias was held in Edinburgh in 1818 by the Caledonian Horticultural Society. The Veitch nurseries also held dahlia shows in the 1830s.

Turner Family

In 1858, John Keynes and a colleague, Charles Turner of the Royal Nurseries in Slough, organized the First Grand National Dahlia Show at St. James Hall in London. Charles Turner (1818–1885) was an extremely energetic man who worked with several different types of flower during his life. He introduced dozens of new dahlias, but perhaps his true love was the carnation. In 1851 he founded the National Carnation and Picotee Society and put on the first show at his own premises. Slough holds him dear for the introduction of *Dianthus* 'Mrs Sinkins'. Mr. Sinkins was in charge of the Slough workhouse in the 1860s. The flower is a double white and very fragrant, but somehow Mr. Bumble doesn't seem very far away.

Turner clearly had a serious reputation, because Charles Darwin wrote to him in 1863 with a question about the spacing of newly crossed hollyhocks.[11] Darwin had seen bees pollinating these flowers and was concerned that unless the experimental hollyhocks were separated widely enough, this ruined any attempt to breed a new pure hybrid. Turner's reply has not been found, but Darwin incorporated it into his book about the variations among plants and animals.

The Turner family is remembered because of another seminal introduction. The rose 'Turner's Crimson Rambler' came from Japan in about 1890. In 1892, Charles's son, Arthur Turner, entered it in a show and put it out for sale. It is a thornless rose with a deep reddish-purple color and very handsome inflorescence. Its genes entered nearly all the ramblers and purple roses that came after. The most famous of its descendants is *Rosa* 'Dorothy Perkins', Jackson & Perkins's blockbuster, bred for them by Alvin Miller.

More Dahlia Shows

Ted Collins, until recently secretary of the National Dahlia Society, believes that the success of the Great Exhibition at the Crystal Palace could have been the incentive for so many new shows. The National Dahlia Society was not formed that year, as some people believe, but in 1882. The plans were drawn up in 1881. This was at about the same time another Grand National Dahlia Show was proposed.

CHANGING INTERESTS

Hundreds of varieties had come to be known, but even as this was happening, the public's interest waned, both in England and on the Continent. All the flowers had the same shape, and it began to be boring. The flower heads tended to be rather stiff and uniform. "Footballs on sticks" is a rather unkind designation that has also been derisively applied to some exuberant cultivars of marigold.

Dwarf "Pompon" dahlias had been found and piqued interest in France, though not so much in England. They did little to restore enthusiasm. At first the varieties were called "Lilliputians," but the flower head's resemblance to the pompon on the French sailor's cap held the public's fancy better. J. Sieckmann of Köstritz bred a pompon variety in 1851. By 1863 the name was a fait accompli. Keynes and another Salisbury nurseryman, J. T. West, liked them and bred quite a few.

French breeders were not interested in the tight confines of the English show system and preferred to breed a broader range of flowers. Besides the pompon, they bred dahlias with collarettes, orchid-like flowers, peony-like flowers, and anemone-like flowers.

Andrieu, of Vilmorin-Andrieux, tried his hand at breeding dahlias, as did young James Veitch at the Chelsea branch of the family firm. Another French rose fancier, Henri Cayeux, also bred dahlias briefly. The dwarf *Dahlia* 'Lucifer', with black foliage, was bred in France by Rivoire Père et Fils in Lyon. The first modern collarette is said to have been bred by N. Gerbereaux of Nancy and released in 1898. He called it *D.* 'Gloire de Nancy', taking a leaf from the Lemoine book. By 1903 Peter Henderson was selling the tubers in New York.

The appearance of *Dahlia juarezii* (hort) in 1872 signaled a change in direction. *D. juarezii* (hort) reached the Netherlands from Mexico, though many years later its actual source turned out to be Guatemala. The petals were elegantly curved. It was the forerunner of the cactus dahlia. Now the breeders had new material, and they set to work with a will.

Almost all sources give the impression that *Dahlia juarezii* entered the garden repertoire in much the same as the cattleya orchid did. This is the outline of the myth. Menheer J. T. Van den Berg, a Dutch nurseryman, received a shipment of mixed plants from Mexico in very poor condition. One tuber was so depleted that it could send up only a single shoot, but that was enough. The tall stem supported a deep-red, ravishingly elegant flower, and he seized upon it skillfully. Anyone less careful might simply have thrown the shriveled tuber away.

In the case of the cattleya orchid, William Cattley saved some seemingly dead orchid plants that had been used as packing material for other plants from South America. This was simply due to his general frugality and hatred of waste. William Swainson had sent the precious plants to him from Brazil in 1818. The superlative *Cattleya* genus emerged as a result of Mr. Cattley's care.

Martin Kral, skeptical debunker of dahlia myths, consigns the story about *Dahlia juarezii* to the scrap heap too. Far from being a brand new species, *D. juarezii* was probably an early Mexican cultivar from a French nursery.[12] Menheer Van den Berg was apparently being somewhat disingenuous. That does not negate the fact that the flower was handsome and set off new avenues of hybridization.

At first, breeders thought this flower was sterile, but the introduction of the bright red *Dahlia* 'Etoile de Diable', the first *juarezii* cultivar, and a host of other cultivars quickly disposed of that notion. Kral also comments on the work of J. T. West in England, who bred the cactus derivative *D.* 'Beauty of Brentwood' from a single viable seed he found.

There are now many thousands of cultivars, maybe up to ten thousand. The half-life of a cultivar in commerce is quite short, and most cultivars disappear quickly. Yet the late Thomas Brown in Petaluma was able to find more than three thousand varieties originating before 1900.[13]

Serious dahlia societies sprang up and eventually began to bring order to the chaotic world of dahlia cultivars. There was a period of schism in the National Dahlia Society for a time, but by 1913 it was in its recognizable modern form. The officers had squabbled over which type of dahlia to include. It is delightful to note that one of the last pre–World War I cultivars was *Dahlia* 'Sherlock Holmes'.

The outbreak of World War I destroyed much of the dahlia world, as it did so much else. Men were drafted, horses were requisitioned, land had to be devoted to growing food, and no one had the time or inclination for frivolous pursuits. No shows were held until 1919.

Two varieties with unusual names appeared in the late 1920s. Joseph Cheal and his brother in Crawley, Sussex, introduced a peony-flowered cultivar called *Dahlia* 'Mrs W. R. Dykes'. Elsie Katherine Dykes was the widow of the famous expert on irises, William Rickatson Dykes, and a noted flower painter in her own right.

Dahlia 'Bishop of Llandaff' appeared in 1929, bred by W. Treseder. This name set off some controversy, not least because Llandaff was a Dissenting congregation and there were no bishops in that sect. There were moves to change its name, but the rules insist that the name first given is the sole correct one.

In the United States, the American Dahlia Society set up trial grounds in conjunction with the Connecticut State College at Storrs in 1917. Simply growing as many varieties of dahlia as could be found would help in classifying them. This was the same strategy that the peony society adopted. Today's dahlia world continues to be exciting and vibrant, thanks to the work of the early devotees.

HEMEROCALLIS (THE DAYLILY)

Hemerocallis is the formal name of the daylily. Rather than the usual Latin used in plant nomenclature, it is based on the Greek for "one day" (*hemero*) and "beauty" (*kalis*). It is a tough and hardy genus with trumpet-shaped flowers that bloom and decline within a twelve-hour period. That is why Linnaeus gave it the name: "beauty for a day." All the species are to be found in Asia. One species, *Hemerocallis fulva*, probably came to North America in the seventeenth or eighteenth century.

Records show that it reached Europe early, certainly by the mid-eighteenth century, and maybe sooner.[1] By the time someone took it to America, they probably had no notion that it was not native to Great Britain. Conditions in North America were so suitable that it escaped from gardens and naturalized itself. In some states, *Hemerocallis fulva* is now regarded as a noxious weed.

Part of the reason for its success is that the leaves grow fairly tall and thus obtain sunlight easily. They are coated with a waxy material that makes them almost impervious to toxins of various types. They can reproduce powerfully without external assistance. Many are triploid and sterile, but even a small piece of embedded root can generate a new plant. Botanists believe that *Hemerocallis fulva* is an ancient complex hybrid, accounting for this behavior. One other daylily—*H. lilioasphodelus*, the yellow daylily—has done more or less the same thing. Daylilies differ from true lilies in the fact that the latter have corms, flowering stalks, and flowers that last longer than one day.

LAYING THE FOUNDATIONS

Lemoine Bechtold

In a delightful nod to a great plant breeder, Lemoine Bechtold's mother named her son "Lemoine" to celebrate the life and work of Victor Lemoine.[2] She and her husband were both avid gardeners, and they hoped that their son would also follow suit. Her hopes were requited. Mr. Bechtold (1896–1963) spent all his spare time (apart from his work in the Denver music business) breeding daylilies. He was fascinated by spiral-petaled daylilies and in 1922 set out to breed a whole new series of them.

Lemoine Bechtold is only one of a set of devoted specialists who developed the handsome plants we grow today. The American Daylily Society issued several landmark publications, and in one of them they describe briefly the life and work of two Englishmen, George Yeld and Amos Perry, who laid the foundations of modern hemerocallis breeding from which many other efforts have been derived.[3]

George Yeld

George Yeld (1845–1938) lived and worked in Yorkshire. He was a schoolmaster whose avocation was horticulture. He could have been the inspiration for James Hilton's *Goodbye Mr. Chips,* teaching for more than fifty years and taking a kindly interest in all the boys. After he retired, he moved to London. Visitors remarked on his energy and vigor well into his nineties.

Yeld bred the first modern hybrid daylily, *Hemerocallis* 'Apricot'. Yeld left thirty-seven new cultivars, starting with *H. fulva, H. flava*, and other species such as *H. mittendorfii* and *H. dumortieri* as parents. 'Apricot' was a cross between *H. mittendorfii* and *H. lilioasphodelus*. Yeld introduced it in 1893. It was a milestone because of the low fertility of the species.[4]

Amos Perry

Amos Perry (1871–1953) was an English nurseryman who also bred daylilies. The two men, Perry and Yeld, were friends. Perry registered many more cultivars than Yeld and went on to join the new American Hemerocallis Society in the United States. He needed new flowers every year to improve sales at the nursery he started, the Hardy Plant Farm in Enfield. Eventually he released more than 270 cultivars of hemerocallis, but almost none of them are still in commerce. Perry was a sophisticated grower and bred valuable hybrids in many other species.

His nursery still exists and shows prize-winning plants in season. When Perry died, he was very sincerely mourned, especially by the iris fanciers. Perry's Siberian irises were held in the highest esteem.

Two other imports, *Hemerocallis aurantiaca major* from Japan and *H. fulva rosea* from China, led to a great burst of activity in daylily breeding. Perry was overjoyed when Arlow B. Stout sent him a specimen of *H. fulva rosea* from New York as a gift (see below).

Daylilies were not a common interest on the Continent, but two men, Charles Sprenger in Germany and Willie Mueller in Italy, made useful contributions. In addition, there were the Sass brothers. All three of them were born in Germany. They emigrated to the United States and set up their nursery in Nebraska. Hans Peter Sass (1868–1949) bred the prize-winning *Hemerocallis* 'Revolute' and *H.* 'Hesperus'. He had been trained as a botanist before leaving Germany.

THE UNITED STATES

In the United States, several figures are revered for their pioneering work in breeding new cultivars and forming the American Hemerocallis Society. There

Hemerocallis 'Revolute', a cultivar released by the Sass brothers (registered by Hans P. Sass).

Reproduced by permission of Dr. Linda Sue Barnes

Hemerocallis 'Dauntless', a cultivar released by Dr. Arlow B. Stout.
Reproduced by permission of Dr. Linda Sue Barnes

was great interest in the plant in the Midwest, and a society started there very early. It was the precursor of the national society.

Arlow Burdette Stout (1876–1957) is perhaps the best-known American breeder of daylilies in the early to mid-twentieth century. He was the director of laboratories at the New York Botanical Garden for more than thirty years. As a child, he had noticed that tiger lilies and daylilies in his mother's garden did not set seed and produce capsules. He devised experiments to elucidate the reproductive system of *Hemerocallis fulva*. His findings enabled him to release more than one hundred excellent hybrids, and he found an acceptable way to capitalize on them. Stout's work led to the great expansion of form and color that characterize the modern daylily.

Hemerocallis 'Prima Donna', a cultivar released by Ophelia Taylor.
Reproduced by permission of Dr. Linda Sue Barnes

Dr. Arlow B. Stout is shown here in his daylily field. Note the hoods on the experimental flowers protecting them from extraneous pollen.

Reproduced by permission of New York Botanical Garden

The New York Botanical Garden did not wish to go into business growing and selling flowers. Stout made arrangements with the Bertrand Farr nursery in Pennsylvania to promote his cultivars. Farr was a kindly man with vision. He gave Stout a large space to raise his plants, even though many of them were not suitable for sale. The proceeds from the daylilies that did sell went to the science fund at the New York Botanical Garden.

Always a rather introverted man, Stout withdrew even further into himself after the death of his only son at the age of nine. His daughter, Elizabeth, kept all her father's papers and memorabilia after he died.

Dr. Stout is considered to be the dean of hemerocallis studies and is commemorated in the annual Stout Award for the best new cultivar of the year. A Canadian botanist working in China, Albert Steward, sent dozens of new wild species to Dr. Stout from the University of Nanking, further increasing the range of material for his breeding work.

Jim Folsom, director of the Huntington Botanical Gardens, is profoundly interested in the daylily. He and his wife analyzed about twenty years of

Stout winners and found that almost half of them had at least one previous Stout winner as a parent.[5] He also noticed that if a breeder had already won one Stout medal, he or she was more likely to win another. In addition, he found that certain forms and colors were favored over others in the selection of winners.

W. Quinn Buck was a major breeder of diploid hemerocallis in Southern California. After his death, his collection went to the Huntington Botanical Gardens. This acquisition stimulated Dr. Folsom to organize a historical display with representative cultivars from other California breeders. Quinn Buck worked before the modern trend toward tetraploid forms and is one of the figures whose work with the earlier diploid forms reached a peak in that epoch. Since the end of that era, almost everyone breeds tetraploid forms now.

At first, the polyploidy was achieved by treating plants with colchicine. Dr. Robert Griesbach, chair of biological sciences at De Paul University, is best known for pioneering this method in hemerocallis. Like so many other impassioned plant breeders, he had learned a great deal about plants from his father, in their family's garden. His graduate advisor at the University of Chicago, Dr. Voth, was a pupil of Ezra Kraus, another legendary breeder of daylilies. One of Griesbach's most important early contributions was establishing the deciduous daylily's temperature and light requirements.

Dr. Griesbach taught biology and cytogenetics. Using colchicine was part of his standard practices. It is hardly surprising that he would turn to it for his avocation. The biggest questions surrounding colchicine were dosage and the method of administration. Most treated plants died off quickly, leaving very few to be used for breeding. The surviving plants had problems with stability and fertility.

There are advantages and disadvantages to the shift to tetraploids. Some of the striking vigor and pest resistance of the species plant have been lost because of it. The result is more susceptibility to diseases that previously caused only minor damage to the plants.

There are many other American growers who contributed to the development of today's daylily. Brother Charles Reckamp, Ralph Wheeler, Ophelia Taylor, Elizabeth ("Miss Betty") Nesmith, and Ezra Kraus are still remembered. Each one made a change that someone else could build upon.

Brother Charles developed his *Hemerocallis* Heavenly and Angel Series at his monastery's Mission Gardens in Techny, Illinois. When the monastery closed the nursery, Roy Klehm, of Song Sparrow Nursery in Avalon, Wisconsin, came to Brother Charles's rescue. Mr. Klehm is a master of peonies but is also devoted to Brother Charles's delicately colored and perfectly ruffled hybrids. Mr. Klehm's father had been a good friend of Brother Charles. The earliest ruffled daylilies were quite attractive but a bit untidy and clumsy. Brother Charles waited to release a ruffled daylily until he was certain it met the vision in his head. Song Sparrow Nursery still sells Reckamp cultivars.

Ralph Wheeler, of Winter Park, Florida, won the Stout Silver Medal in 1956. Edna Spalding in Iowa, Louisiana, used Mrs. Nesmith's insights to carry her own work forward. W. B. MacMillan in Abbeville, Louisiana, then advanced Mrs. Spalding's work. His output was small, but he had very unusual ideas. For one thing, he was able to reduce the time the plant took to flower to about half. The scapes were low, the leaves were evergreen, and the flowers were full, flat, and often ruffled.

Violet, purple, and deep-red colors emerged as a result of such stepwise changes. David Hall, a practicing lawyer in Wilmette, Illinois, bred daylilies in pink and red, which marked a turning point. Hall sold the rights to the Gilbert H. Wild nursery in Sarcoxie, Missouri. Every spring, Mr. Hall traveled to Sarcoxie to work on his crosses. In 1969, Hall won the Stout Medal for *Hemerocallis* 'May Hall', a pink blend flower.

Newer forms with more-varied colors and resistance to climate and disease are being sought every day. Daylilies mass very well and are excellent for highways and roadside beds. Once they are established, their maintenance can be kept to a minimum.

LILY

Lilies have a wonderfully sculptural quality. The flowers are set off by enormous petals with baroque curvature and incredible color schemes. Some are trumpet shaped. Even the stamens are color coded in many cases. It is hard to be indifferent to these beauties. The old saw about not "gilding the lily" is easy to understand. Who could make these perfect flowers any better than they are?

There are about eighty species of lilies around the world, with the largest number found in temperate zones. China abounds in them, as does Japan. North America has a respectable number but nowhere nearly as many as there

Lilium henryi, showing recurved petals.
Reproduced by permission of Janos Agoston

are in Asia. Many of the American species are concentrated in the western states. According to taxonomists, the speciation of the lily is still fluid.

THE LILY REACHES WESTERN EUROPE

Many notable species arose in Eastern Europe and the western parts of Asia. These were the first lilies to arrive in Western Europe more than a thousand years ago. The best known were *Lilium candidum,* the "Madonna lily," and *L. chalcedonicum,* or "the Red Martagon of Constantinople."

Lilium candidum traveled circuitously from the Balkans to southern Europe. It was then transported over the Alps to northern Europe and thence to England. The Venerable Bede, abbot of a monastery in Jarrow, Northumberland, in the seventh century, was the one who showed theological sleight of hand in transforming a heathen symbol into a Christian one. This lily now symbolizes the purity of the Madonna. Bede wrote the first history of England in 630 CE.

The "Red Martagon" or "Turks Cap" lily, *Lilium martagon,* reached England from the Near East early in the seventeenth century. John Parkinson noted it in his book *Paradiso in Sole,* published in 1629. It was an instant success with its rich color and phenomenally shaped petals. *L. chalcedonicum* followed it fairly soon from Turkey or Hungary, though it is also found in Iran. It too is mentioned in Parkinson's book.

Once the New World opened up, lilies from the eastern regions of America reached Europe first. *Lilium canadense* enchanted gardeners in England and France in the seventeenth century. There was also *L. superbum* from the Atlantic region.

Even more extraordinary lilies were imported after collecting flowers in China and Japan became possible. *Lilium lancifolium,* the Asian Tiger Lily, grew in European gardens by the early nineteenth century. About fifty years later, *L. auratum* and *L. speciosum,* handsome Oriental lilies, came on the scene. After that, the great trumpet lilies of the Himalayas were found, culminating in the magnificent *L. regale.*

The species lilies were so arresting that intentional crossing was not done very early. Bulb dealers dug up wild lilies and sold them at a profit, but there were a few attempts at hybridizing. Jan de Graaff's great-grandfather, Cornelis de Graaf, bred a lily hybrid in 1790 (see below). Unlike many other plants, *Lilium* saw the great bulk of crossbreeding take place in the twentieth century.

Many enthusiasts started to write books about lilies in the nineteenth century. The first serious monograph was by D. Spae, in 1847: *Memoire sur les éspèces du genre Lis.* In 1862, The arrival of *Lilium auratum* in Europe caused enormous excitement. With more species in circulation, there was more material for another Frenchman, Duchartre, to write a text on lilies: *Observations sur le genre Lis,* in 1870.

In 1880, Henry John Elwes (1846–1922), an amateur English naturalist and botanist, issued a monograph on the lily that has never been equaled for its scope and beauty.[1] Elwes was heir to a large estate and served in the Scots Guards for five years as befitted his rank in society, but he was not by nature a mindless warrior. He then traveled widely throughout India and the Himalayas, both on his own and as a member of an expedition, studying and learning about wildlife. One of his visits to the Himalayas led to his interest in lilies. Here was a man with a great many privileges who used them very positively. Elwes published *Trees of Great Britain and Ireland* with Augustine Henry, professor of forestry at Trinity College Dublin and one of the greatest plant collectors of all time.

Elwes grew dozens of species of lilies at his estate in Gloucestershire, but although he was looked upon as an expert, he was concerned that he would not get everything precisely right. He consulted many professionals both for the text and for the illustrations. All the pictures were hand colored by well-known artists.

The monograph on the lily appeared in seven parts during Elwes's lifetime. After his death, one of his relatives paid for more parts to be issued, and two final supplements came out in 1960 and 1962, almost a century later. In the first parts, some of the pictures were life-size.

The next major milestone was the appearance of *Lilium regale*, sent by Ernest H. Wilson from China in 1905. If it was possible for there to be more excitement, this flower caused it. Ernest Wilson considered that to be his most triumphant prize, even though he broke his leg coming back and had to limp ever afterward. He narrowly missed having the leg amputated, so the limp was actually a good outcome. Wilson issued his study *Lilies of East Asia* in 1925.[2]

Lilium longiflorum, now known as the "Easter Lily," is sold in the thousands every year. The 'Tom Thumb' version is grown in pots, suitable for a living room table or sideboard.

EARLY COLLECTORS AND HYBRIDIZERS

Carl Purdy

There used to be great stands of wild lilies in California. Carl Purdy (1861–1945), working from his home in Ukiah, was an indefatigable collector, digging up thousands of bulbs a year. In that era, there was very little concern about nature renewing itself. Nature always had taken care of itself and was expected to continue to do so for the foreseeable future. Purdy sent Native Americans out to collect for him, expanding his reach.

Purdy shrugged off any suggestion that his collecting helped to bring about the dwindling of the stands and eventual loss of the wild lilies.[3] He thought the encroachment of cities and towns was to blame, by eliminating the habitats. This is quite probably the principal cause of the loss, but he helped to push it along. *Lilium occidentale,* the Western Lily, is now on the federal endangered species list and the object of some serious recovery plans in Oregon and Northern California. Just when things seemed to be at their bleakest, two new stands of the wild lily were found near Crescent City in the 1990s.

Wilson also dug bulbs in the thousands, destroying whole hillsides in China. The tragicomic irony was that on at least one occasion the bulbs almost all perished en route back to England, rotting in their clay cases.[4]

Purdy was a man of simplicity and integrity. He did not dig everything up to prevent anyone else from following him and getting bulbs. Whatever he did was to meet the requirements of his business. Wilson was also probably very honest, but it was not unknown for master collectors working for acquisitive nurseries to do just that, try to spike the competition. The most extreme miscreants were the orchid seekers in Central and South America. At one point in the mid-1950s they almost completely destroyed the cattleya stands, to satisfy the rage for cattleya corsages and make sure no one else could have them.

Purdy was also an expert hybridizer. He encouraged Luther Burbank when the latter started with a native lily, *Lilium pardalinum,* crossing and recrossing them to set up a good race for parents. Burbank then used pollen from some of the new Asian lilies to obtain stronger and more vivid cultivars. Purdy used *L. humboldtii* for his own crosses, and the resulting cultivars formed the basis of the Bellingham Hybrids.[5] The latter came about because Dr. Griffiths, the USDA hybridist from Bellingham, Washington, visited Purdy and received a packet of the new seeds as a gift. Dr. Griffiths issued half a dozen new crosses, such as *L.* 'Kulshan', 'Star of Oregon', 'Douglas Ingram', and 'Shuksan'. The latter is still a favorite and in commerce today. Other parents for these hybrids are known to be *L. parryi, L. humboldtii* var. *magnificum, L. humboldtii* (type) and possibly *L. columbianum.*

Carl Purdy knew Luther Burbank and admired him but also acted as his conscience. When Burbank made unsubstantiated claims about the success of the *Lilium pardalinum* hybrids, Purdy set the record straight by pointing out that only some of them were useful.

As a general principle, lily hybrids can be unstable. Many early hybrids did not last more than a year or two. The genus has a strong tendency to reproduce parthogenetically, even when supposedly pollinated. Simply because pollen was applied does not mean that the seeds are actually hybrids. Some breeders have devised elaborate techniques to circumvent this tendency.

Isabella Preston

In the section about lilac in an earlier chapter, we came across Isabella Preston, the Englishwoman who moved to Ottawa and worked at the Central Farm as a hybridizer. Miss Preston was equally known for her work on the lily—possibly more so. She was a cofounder of the North American Lily Society (NALS).[6]

After Miss Preston finished her studies at the Ontario Agricultural College, Professor W. J. Crow put her in charge of potted lilies in the greenhouse. This responsibility stimulated her to make many crosses, and she began her career in this way. Miss Preston observed that many lilies are self-sterile, possibly because they are in fact ancient hybrids and not pure species.

In 1916, she released hybrids based on crossing *Lilium sargentiae* × *L. regale*. One of the descendants, *L.* 'George C. Creelman', went on to be very successful. This plant contributed its genes to many modern hybrids. For her Ottawa Hybrids, Miss Robertson crossed *Lilium davidii* with *L. willmottiae*, leading to very good results. The plants were six feet tall with dozens of flowers on each stem. *L. willmottiae* had been found in central China by Augustine Henry and reached England in 1888. It was named for the now-legendary Miss Ellen Willmott, born into great wealth, who basically bankrupted herself because of her passion for exotic garden plants while forgetting the cost of their upkeep. A camellia hybrid, *Camellia* 'Warleyensis', was also named for her. She lived in the village of Great Warley, Essex.

Isabella Preston's later work led to two excellent series, Stenographers Names and Fighter Aircraft. These were based on the crossing of *Lilium davidii* var. *willmottiae* and *L. dauricum*. The hybrids in the first series were named for women who worked in the office at the Central Farm: *L.* 'Brenda Watts', 'Edna Keane', 'Grace Marshall', 'Lilian Cummings', 'Lyla McCann', 'Marie Condie', and 'Phyllis Cox'. Of these, two, 'Brenda Watts' and 'Lyla McCann', are still in commerce, or were in the late 1990s. Edward McRae saw them growing in Vancouver. Later breeders based much of their work on these hybrids.

Miss Preston then open pollinated these plants and obtained a second series of equally arresting plants: tall and strong with bright red and orange coloration. With the Second World War in full swing at the time, she chose the names of the heroic British fighter planes: *Lilium* 'Hurricane', 'Spitfire', and 'Corsair', for example. The Scots-Canadian plant breeder Frank Skinner also took up lilies. He dogged Miss Preston's footsteps in lilac and probably could not resist offering his lily output too.

IMPROVING LILIES

This stupendous output was all very well, but at this point it is necessary to touch base with reality. Amateur gardeners with modest back gardens did not adopt all lilies equally. In fact, there were long periods of time in which lilies were more or less shunned. One could say that while many liked the "idea" of lilies, the actual plants were cumbersome, unwieldy, and quite often hard to grow. An unpredictable and temperamental eight-foot beanpole of a plant affects the scale of today's smaller spaces, no matter how handsome the efflorescence. Breeders faced the challenge of altering the plant's scale and removing its weaknesses, particularly susceptibility to disease.

Professional growers were equipped to deal with all the problems of monocultures and willing to take the trouble for a very lucrative market: cut flowers. Weddings and funerals were only part of it. Any mixed "Dutch" bouquet at a supermarket today has at least one lily stem, often a 'Stargazer', based on the original Asian species.

In the second half of the twentieth century, several skilled hybridizers took up the challenges, eventually allowing the ordinary citizen the pleasure of growing lilies. Hardiness, size/habit, and resistance to disease were the prime issues. Most lilies came from warmer zones than much of upper North America. As in the case of the Griffiths roses, the best experiment was completely laissez-faire: plant the bulbs in the far reaches of North Dakota or northern Minnesota and just see what happens.

Cecil Patterson did this in Saskatchewan and watched the carnage winter by winter. At the end of a few years, he had a handful of tough survivors allowing him to move forward. These were the result of crossing *Lilium davidii* var. *willmottiae* with *L. cernuum*, source of a beautiful pink color. Whole series of successful plants came from two of his best hybrids: *L.* 'Edith Cecilia' and 'Lemon Queen'. The lilies were upright in habit, and their descendants had a range of pale colors.

In another situation, the same end occurred for different reasons. A breeder at the Oregon Bulb Farm set out his field of crosses in the 1960s without any idea that a severe virus was lurking in the strain. Lily symptomless virus (LSV) is the commonest pest, and as its name implies, it cannot be diagnosed before the plant gets too weak and succumbs to any other trouble in the field. If a plant is infested with aphids, the virus is a possibility. Only two of his new Mid Century hybrids managed to survive. The disappointment was profound, but the lesson was powerful. One of the two survivors was *Lilium* 'Holland', now perhaps the most widely grown lily as a flower for cutting.

Jan de Graaff

The Oregon Bulb Farm was a very important part of the development of modern lily breeding. Jan de Graaff (1903–1989) was from the Netherlands. As a young man, he studied horticulture in England. He was a direct descendant of the De Graafs of Leiden, prominent bulb dealers since the end of the eighteenth century. The spelling of the family name varies.

Jan had been a diplomat and pursued other careers but was always fascinated by plants and in 1935 decided to concentrate on growing bulbs on a quiet farm in Oregon. That was the only quiet thing about him. De Graaff knew how to promote and market his goods. He also knew how to pick superb staff and let them do what they did best. Several of the stellar figures in the lily world worked for him, among them Judith McRae Freeman, Edward McRae, Harold Comber, and Earl Hornback.

Harold Comber (1897–1969), one of H. J. Elwes's gardeners and trained at the Royal Botanic Gardens in Edinburgh, had spent two years collecting in South America. Once back in England, he worked for W. A. Constables, the large retail nursery. By the time he left, he was the manager. Comber was a careful and methodical man, exceedingly useful because of his administrative ability. Comber prepared a horticultural classification of lilies in the late

1940s, with six divisions: martagon, American, candidum, Oriental, Asiatic, and trumpet. In 1964, the Royal Horticultural Society produced a more definitive classification with nine categories. That system is now bursting at the seams and newer ones are being considered.

At first de Graaff worked with Dutch daffodils and irises, but by the 1950s he had shifted entirely to lilies. He understood the threat of chronic virus infestation in lilies and set out to create resistant plants. De Graaff imported every type of lily available and spent more than twenty years sorting through their characteristics.

In 1960 he released *Lilium* 'Enchantment' in the Netherlands. It was to be one of the most important hybrids.[7] Anything with the genes of *L. davidii* seemed able to resist the virus. That is why Isabella Preston's varieties were so useful. The umbrella term "Mid Century Hybrids" was coined to cover the vast mass of crosses coming from the Oregon Bulb Farm. They are now subsumed in the Asiatic group.

De Graaff sold his farm in 1968 and moved to Manhattan, where he pursued a very different type of life. He had written a very useful book with F. F. Rockwell and Esther Grayson.

Judith Freeman read this book when she was very young and was heavily influenced by it. She went on to study genetics at the University of Oregon and began breeding lilies at the Oregon Bulb Farm in Gresham. Mrs. Freeman edited the NALS yearbooks from 1974 to 1981. For some years now, she has run her own lily nursery in Vancouver with the help of her daughter.

Samuel L. Emsweller

Samuel L. Emsweller (1898–1966) was a very distinguished and effective director of the USDA National Arboretum with a particular interest in plant breeding and genetics. The 1937 yearbook of the USDA was devoted to plant breeding.[8] Most of the articles discussed agricultural crops but Emsweller and several of his colleagues prepared a hundred-page essay on ornamental plants. It laid out what was known until then about the history of many commercially important flower crops and how their breeding could be improved by even a small amount of attention to genetics. Imagine how much disappointment and wasted time could be avoided if the grower knew beforehand that the two flowers he hoped to cross could never mate.

Emsweller enjoyed breeding lilies, and for two separate years, 1963 and 1966, he edited the yearbook of the North American Lily Society. His coauthor of *Improvement of Flowers by Breeding,* F. D. Mulford, was another powerful figure in his day.

In the recent past, scientists have perfected embryo rescue and other laboratory methods of obtaining striking new crosses.

MARIGOLD

Before you tip your aristocratic noses in the air, stop a minute and think about this beautiful flower. See what Gertrude Jekyll, the supreme arbiter of garden taste, wrote about it in 1916: "[A] valuable annual should not be neglected because it is so common and easy to grow and because it was so much overdone in monotonous lines in the old bedding days. Many good plants have of late suffered from a kind of mistaken prejudice on this account [but] it should be remembered that if the plant was misused it was not the fault of the plant but that of the general acceptance of a poor sort of gardening."[1]

You will say that that's all very well but she did not have to contend with some of the current hybrids, which may be a bit over the top. We shall take a look as we go along.

Why do people react with such disdain? Is it because the more ambitious a gardener becomes, the more he or she wants to grow complex, challenging plants? Simply planting a seed and watching a sturdy plant grow and blossom is too easy.

With ambition comes subtlety. Muted tones and shades of gray-green replace the loud, blaring colors we adored as children. Marigolds, together with Zonal pelargoniums, shout municipality, regimentation, and, we have to say it, vulgarity.

That clinches it for aspiring social-climbing gardeners whose dreams of admission to the ranks of the elect are second only to their aspirations for their children's futures. You won't get there by growing marigolds. The garden writers ("hortographers") and arbiters of horticultural taste have made this decision.

This is all a terrible pity, for there is nothing more joyous and life-enhancing than golden, tawny, bronze, or orange marigolds in full bloom, day after day and week after week. The people who do not read elegant garden books buy the plants in their millions and grow them year after year. We use the term *vulgar* while metaphorically holding our noses, to mean in poor taste, and beloved of the benighted masses who don't know any better. In the case of marigolds, *vulgar* is actually appropriate; it means "pertaining to the people."

The largest users of vivid annuals such as marigolds are city parks. The employees of parks and recreation departments know that civic pride requires organized displays of reproducible flowers in clear, bright colors making very forthright statements. They also must be sure the flowers perform as well as possible for the amount of time, money, and effort devoted to their preparation. Sturdy hybrids answer this purpose.

With that in mind, the general public is right behind them. Statistics help to set the scene. The USDA conducts its Floricultural Census every ten years. They monitor twenty-four of the best-selling annuals in numbers of flats and pots sold as well as the aggregate amount of money generated. The following figures were derived from the 1998 USDA tables.[2]

The largest number of plants grown in flats and pots combined was *Pelargonium*, with 132,000,000. The smallest number of the plants on the list was *Nicotiana*, with an aggregate of 715,000. The marigold, *Tagetes*, came in seventh on the list, with a total of 12,510,000 in all. Impatiens, both New Guinea and *I. walleriana* Hook.f. cultivars, pansies and violas, begonias, and petunias were second, third, fourth, fifth, and sixth, respectively. This impressive showing for marigolds does not take into account the millions of plants grown by ordinary people from seed (growing marigolds from seeds is extremely easy to do). There is no reason to believe that ratios of these figures will change substantially in the next census.

Very little is written about the flower in garden literature. Do a quick search either at a library or on the Internet, and you will find almost no monographs or other works devoted to the species or cultivars of *Tagetes*. One can only find information about them in compendia devoted to annuals in general.[3] The herbal literature offers some discussion, but you suddenly realize that they are referring to *Calendula*, the pot marigold, and not *Tagetes*.

Many of the modern marigold's manifest virtues were instilled into them in California over the past eighty years. Much of this was due to the enthusiasm and drive of one man, David Burpee.

HISTORY

Discovery

Tagetes species are endemic to the Americas, primarily Mexico and Central America , no matter what their common names of "French Marigold" and "African Marigold" may indicate. An additional species is found in Africa, but it is not the plant commonly known as the African Marigold. Some authorities believe that this plant may be a naturalized weed. In all, there are about forty species of *Tagetes*. Two species are the basis of almost all the modern garden varieties.

Tagetes erecta, called the African Marigold because the first European herbalists thought it originated in Africa, is tall and bushy with a rather uncompromising habit. For many years, the flower was called "the rose of the Indies." Returning Spanish and Portuguese sailors, colonists, and missionaries probably took the seeds from Mexico back to Spain with them in the decade after Columbus first found the New World. Some seeds may have been planted in monastery gardens. The native peoples used various marigolds for medicinal purposes. That, combined with the cheerful color, was probably why the Iberians took the seeds back with them. *Tagetes* species were also recorded in Portugal and North Africa very early, but very little is known about how they migrated.

One could speculate that migration took place because travel between Spain and Portugal was frequent. There was probably also considerable movement back and forth across the Straits of Gibraltar and other passages between Iberia and the northern coast of Africa. It is hardly surprising that an attractive and useful plant would end up in new lands.

This all seems to have occurred before Hernan Cortés conquered the Aztec stronghold of Tenochtitlán, now named Mexico City, in 1522. Two years later, the Franciscans sent Father Valencia and the "twelve apostles" to build a church and schools. Father Bernardino de Sahagún sailed for Mexico in 1529 to teach in those schools.

European visitors to North Africa thought the wildflowers they saw were native to those lands. The leading herbalists of the epoch cemented this view by including the exotic new flowers in their work throughout the sixteenth century.

A field of mixed *Tagetes* cultivars growing in India. *Photographer Dr. R. K. Roy. Reproduced by permission, Dr. R. K. Roy.*

In his *Herbal* of 1542, Leonhard Fuchs described a flower he called *Indian-ische negelen* and thought it was an *Artemisia* because of its smell. This could have been *T. patula,* but it could also have been an error. *Negel* is Dutch for a clove.[4] Classification and taxonomy were still in their very early fluid stages.

In 1550, Hieronymus (Jerome) Bock described a flower that was clearly *T. erecta* under the name of *Garyophillis indica.* Bock said that the flowers reached Germany in the time of the Emperor Charles V, who also happened to be Charles I of Spain.

Charles V sent his armies into North Africa to fight the Turks in 1535. Historians believe that those troops took flower seeds with them, but when English and other explorers traveled to Tunis that year, the flower was already well established. It had evidently escaped from cultivation some time before and become naturalized. Charles V's army was not the instrument for spreading *Tagetes* seed to North Africa.

Mattias de L'Obel published a drawing and description of *T. erecta* in his book *Plantarum, seu, Stirpium Historia* in 1576. He was the one who first used the term *Flos africanus,* in another book, this one published in 1581. He thought it came from North Africa and commented that the flowers grew spontaneously on the banks of the Tagus River.

By the end of the sixteenth century, marigolds were being intentionally cultivated in Iberian gardens. In their natural form, they are not good "team players" for the modern garden, but they do have very bright colors and are very vigorous. The leaves contain terpenes, which cause the characteristic chemical or medicinal odor. That odor may have been one reason native people used the plants for medicinal purposes. Europeans had the impression that such an odor could be effective medicinally but do not enjoy it in their gardens.

Tagetes patula, named the "French Marigold" because people thought it originated in France, is smaller and much more graceful. Not much is known about how it got to France. The seeds were sent to the royal garden in Paris quite soon after the plant was found, under the impression that it came from China. William Robinson, the uncompromising author of *The English Flower Garden,* actually recommended the French Marigold for borders in the late 1880s.[5] *T. patula* also comes in many colors, some in warm bronze and reddish tints. These colors plus its diminutive structure have made it indispensable to plant breeders and home gardeners.

Another species, *Tagetes tenuifolia,* the Signet Marigold, is sometimes found in modern gardens because of its delicate lacy foliage and small size. A recent cultivar is *T.* 'Cottage Red'. *T. lucida,* the Sweet Marigold, was grown for many years as a species plant but was not part of modern commercial breeding. It is sold by nurseries specializing in culinary herbs.

The definitive sources documenting the flowers' origin came later. Spanish missionaries and other observers described the plants and animals they found in the New World meticulously, and there are two principal Spanish records and one indigenous Mexican text in which *Tagetes* species can be found.

While botanists claim these works as the earliest descriptions of plants in the New World, medical historians also claim them as the first textbooks of medicine in the Western Hemisphere. The books hold enormous importance in both disciplines.

Fray Bernardino de Sahagún (ca. 1499–1590), the first European person to chronicle a so-called savage society respectfully, prepared a monumental treatise in twelve volumes about every aspect of Aztec society.[6] The work was ready by about 1569. He was truly a "proto-anthropologist." Fray Bernardino questioned the elders and important people in the community and made a note of what they told him, including their medical system and use of plants.

He also witnessed Aztec ceremonies and rites firsthand, many barbarous and cruel. The church was horrified by the pagan cults and did everything it could to expunge all traces of the Aztec religion. If it were not for Sahagún, very little would have come down to us about Aztec customs.

His work is astounding in many respects. One of them is that he wrote it in the Nahuatl language. Sahagún learned this language as soon as he arrived in Mexico City and developed a phonetic system enabling him to write in it. Another important aspect of his work is that he illustrated it with numerous pictures, many of them in color, clearly outlining what took place.

Only many years later did he create a bilingual version of his book with Nahuatl in one column and Spanish in the other. As a teaching friar, he instructed promising young Aztec men in how to read and write in their own language, as well as teaching them Latin, Spanish, and the word of the Lord.

The Franciscan order sent Fray Bernardino to Mexico as a teacher in 1529. He died there at the age of ninety in 1590. Examining the facsimile of the Nahuatl version, one is overcome with admiration and awe for a man who five hundred years ago could arrive in a strange and terrifying country, settle down to learn the language, cope with the myriad difficulties and privations of such an existence, and yet produce a masterpiece of enormous distinction.

In the volume devoted to medicine and herbals, Sahagún mentioned a plant with yellow flowers that he called *cempo-alxochitl* (also spelled *sempo-alxochitl* in modern Mexico). *Xochitl* means ornamental flower in Nahuatl.

He described both single and double forms and thought they had a nice smell. They were grown intentionally, but he also noticed plants coming up as volunteers. He included black and white drawings of the flowers. There is little doubt that this was *Tagetes erecta*. The only problem in the identification is that he said the plant had a nice smell. Very few people think that *T. erecta* has a nice smell.

Fray Bernardino also mentioned the Nahuatl term *yhautli* and associated it with a flower that was possibly a marigold but not *cempo-alxochitl*. A distinguished Mexican scholar, Patrizia Granziera, has explained that some plants could themselves be a god to the Aztecs. That was the case with maize, their staple food. Other plants were associated with a specific god and its sphere of influence.[7] *Cempo-alxochitl* was associated with Cihualcoatl-Quilaztli, the serpent goddess, in her role as protector of mothers in childbirth and also with festivals for the dead.

Dr. Granziera's observations support the idea that the Aztec people domesticated the marigold long before the Europeans arrived, far back into antiquity. This was also Lawrence Kaplan's view. The Aztecs thought it had magical, religious, and medicinal value. An extract of one of the marigolds, *yhautli*, was used for urinary and gastrointestinal complaints, including the hiccups.

Its supposed power to avert lightning strikes and keep someone safe while crossing a river indicates the Aztec belief in its magical properties. The drug was also known as *yyhautlili* or *ihautli*. The variations in spelling stem from the phonetic representation of the Nahuatl words. It has been said that *yhautli* is Nahuatl for *Tagetes lucida*, but the identification with that particular species is not completely clear.

Professor Granziera comments that *Tagetes lucida* represented Tlaloc, the god of rain, because it grows in swampy regions. It is used for its hallucinogenic effects. The modern name is pericon. She states that this is *yhautli*.

Before Fray Bernardino's work was completed, two of his former Aztec students prepared what is now known as the *De la Cruz–Badianus Aztec Herbal* of 1552. Martin de la Cruz had been a pupil at Sahagún's school and had gone on to become a traditional Aztec healer and physician. He wrote a small textbook of Aztec medicine in Nahuatl, and it was translated into Latin by his friend and colleague Juan Badianus, a Latin teacher at the school.

The friar had not had medical training in Spain and did not know the Latin or Spanish names of most plants. It was one of the few things he could not teach the Aztecs. His pupils used the native names, and so did he. This is very important when considering priority.

De la Cruz painted pictures of the flowers and plants he used at the top of each page, and Badianus squeezed the Latin words into the rest of the space. The book is tiny, about six inches tall, but done with extreme care. The two young men dedicated it to the son of the viceroy, don Francisco de Mendoza. The viceroy himself died before he could see it. Eventually it ended up in the Vatican Library, where it was found by an American scholar in 1928. Its discovery created a minor sensation.

In the 1930s, two other American scholars, William Gates and Emily Emmart, worked on this book.[8] Dr. Emmart was a botanist; Gates was not.

In her book, three references are made to *yhautli*, and there are paintings at the top of those pages. Two of the plates are considered to be *Tagetes*, but the Nahuatl words used by the author of the Badianus Manuscript and Sahagún are not the same. In the Badianus Manuscript, the picture is labeled "Mexixquitl."

None of the very stylized little paintings closely matches any marigold previously seen, nor does the text refer to *cempo-alxochitl*, but according to Dr. Emmart, *yhautli* represents *Tagetes lucida*.

In a footnote, Dr. Emmart indicated that this interpretation was based on work by Eric Thompson, author of *Mexico before Cortez*,[9] but I was not able to find any reference to this in his book. Thompson was a noted archaeologist at the Field Museum in Chicago. He used the term *yhautl* to describe a sacrificial victim awaiting his fate. Another distinguished pre-Columbian archaeologist of that period, George Vaillant, commented in his book about early Mexico that *yhautli* powder was blown onto the victim's face to dull his senses before he was thrown on the burning pyre.[10]

In the litany of conditions for which *yhautli* (possibly *Tagetes lucida*) was prescribed, it was not said to have anesthetic properties; if anything, it served as a stimulant. The case for the Badianus Manuscript having true priority in the story of *Tagetes* remains far from clear.

The slightly later work by Dr. Francisco Hernandez, Philip III's "protomedico" for New Spain, confirms Sahagún's observations about *cempo-alxochitl*.[11] Hernandez completed his work in 1577, but the book was not published until 1651. Hernandez (1514–1587) notes that the Spanish called this flower the "dianthus of the Indies"—not a bad description. Unlike Sahagún, Hernandez did not stay in one place. Dr. Hernandez spent much of his time in the botanical garden of Huastepec but also visited the royal garden of Tezcozinco.

The authors of the first European herbals such as Bock, Fuchs, and L'Obel worked from the actual flowers and the accounts of travelers who had seen them in Spain, Portugal, France, and Africa. None of the above Spanish texts would have been available to them. Fuchs was the first person to call it *Tagetes*, in the mid-sixteenth century. He arrived at this name by some complicated philological argument.

Because of this history, Lawrence Kaplan, an ethnobotanist at Roosevelt University in Chicago, suggested that the commonly accepted derivation of the name from Tages, an Etruscan god, may not actually be the case.[12]

Regardless of the etymology, Linnaeus continued its use when he came to name the flower formally. It is perhaps interesting that Kaplan, a very thoughtful scholar, did not mention the Badianus Manuscript in his references.

There are references to the Badianus Manuscript in the late 1960s by another ethnobotanist, Robert Neher.[13] This seems to be one of the first references to the Badianus Manuscript suggesting the *Tagetes* connection. Neher quoted the Gates translation with its black and white images. Neher used the Nahuatl term *yyhautli* (referring to *T. lucida*) and *quauh-yyhautli* for a woody form of the plant in describing its actions. Since then, various other publications have referred to the Badianus Manuscript.

The Renaissance herbalists used various different names, but their woodcuts are quite accurate. They called *Tagetes patula* "T. indica." They really did not know where it came from, but India seemed like a good possibility. An alternative explanation of the word "Indica" comes from the editor of the *Besler Florilegium*, Gérard Aymonin.[14] He notes that in the late sixteenth and early seventeenth centuries, the term "Indica" could mean "from the Indies" (that is, the West Indies, the Caribbean Islands).

Later travelers in Mexico noted that the flowers of other species of marigold had several uses apart from being very attractive to look at. One of the most striking uses is for celebrating the Day of the Dead on All Souls Day in Guatemala and Mexico. Another name for the marigold is therefore Flor de Muerto. Both fresh and dried flower heads are used for cemeteries and graves. This practice goes back into antiquity. An Aztec rite has been grafted onto Christian observance. Dr. Granziera has shown that individual flowers not only symbolized the gods but were in themselves gods on occasion.

Decoctions of the flower heads were used as a tea. These decoctions are still drunk today. They are very stimulating and diuretic, rather like the drink from *Camellia sinensis* we simply call "tea." The plants were exceedingly common in rural areas. People collected the stems, formed them into bales, dried them, and used them as fuel.

India

Marigolds are so entwined with religious life in India that it is hard to imagine they were only imported about 350 years ago. The flowers are braided into garlands and swags for weddings and decorate temples for many cere-

"Elephants" for a festival in India made entirely of marigold blossoms.
Reproduced by permission of Professor Jules Janick

monies. No other flower is as popular in India. In addition, the flowers are
used as a dye, for medicinal purposes, and as a flavoring.

Sir George Watt, an Indian civil servant and former superintendent of
the industrial section of the Indian Museum, suggested in his *Dictionary of
Economic Plants from India* (1893) that their primary appearance in western
India coincided with the activities of the Portuguese colonists in Goa.[15] They
in turn are said to have received the seeds from their colleagues in Central
and South America. Watt was a thoughtful and competent civil servant, and
it is worth trying to unravel whether his assumptions were correct.

Possible Origins in Portugal and Spain

It could be useful to see whether there is any substance to these statements
or any contemporary supporting evidence. First let us examine the role of
Portugal in South America. Portuguese activity in South America was primarily confined to Brazil. The pope had allotted it to them in the 1494 Treaty

of Tordesillas. One of their first enterprises in the newly conquered country was to found sugarcane plantations and sugar mills.

The Spanish colonists and explorers were very interested in new plants in their territories, mainly for medicinal purposes. Because a good deal of money could be made by importing valuable raw materials, the Spanish crown set up the Casa de Contratación in Seville in 1503, something the Portuguese had done in the preceding century: the "Casa da India."

The Casa de Contratación was a central trading house and procurement agency with iron control over anything that entered or left Spain, including new plants. It was also the customs and excise arm of the state.

In theory, everything had to be registered with the Casa de Contratación and could only be imported or exported through the official port of Cádiz, some sixty miles away from Seville. In fact, many merchants quite openly flouted its control, landing their goods at other, smaller ports along the Spanish coast.[16] Once there, the new merchandise slipped into commerce quietly and easily.

American plants were being grown in Seville very early. Columbus's younger son, Hernando (Fernando), was proud of his "American" garden in 1503, but precisely what he grew there is not known. Perhaps the most notable exotic garden in Seville belonged to the physician Nicholas Monardes (ca. 1493–1578).

Monardes was a well-regarded physician with a comfortable practice and good connections. He never traveled to the New World, but in 1569 he published *Dos libros,* a compendium of information about the new drug plants from the Indies and New Spain.[17] Much of it consists of fantastical stories that he never attempted to verify, but it does represent a point of departure for the new epoch. English readers know it as *Joyfull Newes out of the New Founde Worlde,* John Frampton's translation in 1577.[18]

Monardes grew quite a few of the plants in his own garden and used them on his patients. He found tobacco (*Nicotiana*) to be very effective in many complaints. Nothing in his book sounds much like a marigold, and we shall never know whether he had *Tagetes* in his garden.

The closest I could find was what Frampton called the "floures of the blood." Monardes said he received the seeds from Peru. "The hearbe cometh to bee of the height of twoo paumes, little more or less, the bowes doeth caste out very straight with certaine round leaves, very greene and thin, in the hiest of the bowes there doeth growe a flower beyng yellow, very high in couller, and only he beareth five leaves, and in the middle of every leafe there is figured a droppe of blood, so redde and firmly kindled in couller, that it can not bee more. This flower hath at the foote of it a stalke very long, which commeth out a good space from the flower: it is a flower very beautifull, which doeth adornate the gardens, and it groweth very well of the seed or of the Plante: and beyng tasted it hath the same savour and taste the Mastuesso hath, it is notable hotte."[19]

Even this is highly unlike any marigold we have seen, but he described a tall plant with a bright yellow flower and red center, as well as a tangy taste. Its "round" leaves and origin in Peru give one pause, but in other respects it is a fair fit. Monardes did not believe that this plant had significant medicinal properties.

Once in Spanish commerce, it was not long before many of the new plants from South America became available in Portugal, chiefly Lisbon. When the great French botanist Carolus Clusius traveled in Spain in the early 1560s, he saw the plants and found Monardes's book. He also found Garcia da Orta's book in Lisbon.

In his usual indefatigable way, he translated both of them into Latin and had those versions published in Antwerp: Garcia da Orta's in 1567 and Monardes's in 1574. This was a valuable way of disseminating the information. He did not translate Garcia da Orta's in toto but used tightly edited excerpts. This kept the book short and easy to assimilate.

Portuguese Colonization of India

The Portuguese were in India before anyone else. Prince Henry the Navigator (1394–1460) saw huge possibilities on the horizon and encouraged his citizens to build sturdy caravels and explore. They traveled farther east and south than any other European nation at the time.

One of their principal goals was to take over the lucrative spice trade from the Arabs. They knew that much of what the Arabs traded came from India. By continually extending their knowledge of the west coast of Africa, they paved the way for sailing around the Cape of Good Hope and on to India. To cope with the expected influx of new goods, the Portuguese created the Casa da India in the late 1400s.

Between 1415 and 1487, the Portuguese were setting up "acclimatizing" gardens long before the Dutch started to do that.[20] This was to accommodate a rather complex but not highly organized transfer of plants to and from Africa, the Caribbean, and later Brazil. Indian and Arab merchants had exchanged plants in the region for many years before the Portuguese began their commerce. The latter simply added new plants from South America to the established routes.

They then adapted the system for their own purposes. One result was the introduction of several economically useful plants into Europe. The exchange of plants continued after the Portuguese took over Goa. Citrus was one of the most important.

In 1498 Vasco da Gama, a Portuguese nobleman, was the first European to reach the coast of India by sea. Even so, he might not have reached Malabar if he had not hijacked an Arab fisherman and his boat. He was followed in 1510 by Afonso Albuquerque, a bellicose fellow who attacked Goa and destroyed its defenses.

Once a colony was established, missionaries were among the first to go there. The Franciscans sent their first cadre in 1518. They started the construction of the first Christian church in Goa, the cathedral of Saint Francis. It is still standing today.

Goa was also a great haven for tormented Portuguese Jews who either refused to convert to Christianity and had to flee the Inquisition or did convert but were still regarded with immense suspicion. Some of these people were scholars and physicians. It is possible that they carried the seeds of *Tagetes* with them to use the plant for medicinal purposes.

The most famous of these émigrés was Garcia da Orta. His book *Colloquios dos simples e drogas da India* was the first to describe medicinal plants from the tropics.[21] It also happened to be only the third book ever printed in India.

The Jesuit Francis Xavier (1506–1552) traveled to Goa in 1541 and was annoyed by the presence of so many Jews, as well as by the behavior of "rice Christians," Hindus who had converted after being bribed with food. Xavier was a colleague and student of Ignatius Loyola and one of the seven priests who initiated the Society of Jesus.

Xavier converted the local Hindu population very actively, but their adherence was only skin-deep. They sullenly acquiesced in his proselytizing because of draconian penalties if they did not. Under his guidance, the Portuguese conquerors destroyed almost all the Hindu temples and made it very difficult to practice the religion.

In 1546 he wrote to King Joao III and asked him to send representatives of the Inquisition to restore the purity of Christianity in Goa. Two secular canonists, Aleixo Dias Falco and Francisco Marques, arrived in 1560 a few years after Francis Xavier's death. The Inquisition they instituted was very brutal and considered to be one of the worst examples of its kind in the Iberian world.[22]

Francis Xavier forbade the Hindus to do almost everything they enjoyed. Among the "crimes" was the use of turmeric, basil, marigolds, and incense. Francis Xavier turned these renegades over to the Inquisition too. The value of this story is in showing how early marigolds penetrated Hindu society.

In spite of all this tangential and tantalizing information, the questions of how and when the marigold reached India remain unanswered. The plant had no obvious commercial or medical value, so no one paid any attention to its movements.

The Marigold in India

Marigolds appear in classical Indian paintings. Princes and rajahs spent much of their time in their gardens and liked to be painted there. In one series of such paintings from the mid-eighteenth century, the Ragamalas, marigolds area clearly seen in the flower border at the base of the picture.[23]

At present, *Tagetes erecta* and its cultivars are grown in considerable numbers throughout India. Dr. R. K. Roy, a horticulturist at the Indian Botanical Research Institute in Lucknow, prepared a useful booklet for growers in 2000.[24] The name of the flower varies by province and local language. *Genda* (or variants on this term) is one of the commonest names, probably derived from the Sanskrit roots *sandu* or *ganduga*.

When Dr. Roy prepared his book, the commonest cultivars of *Tagetes erecta* in Indian commerce were 'Atlantis' and 'Discovery' from Bodger and Son; 'Crackerjack' and 'Vanilla' from Burpee; and 'Galore', 'Gold Coin', 'Jubilee', and 'Papaya Crush' from John Mondry, all from California.

Two Indian cultivars listed were *Tagetes* 'Pusa Basanti Gainda' and 'Pusa Narangi Gainda', both bred by Dr. S. P. S. Raghava at the Indian Agricultural

Research Institute in New Delhi. *T.* 'Pusa Basanti Gainda' is a cross between 'Crackerjack' and 'Golden Jubilee'. 'Pusa Narangi Gainda' comes from 'Golden Yellow' and 'Sun Giant'.

Fewer varieties of *Tagetes patula* were grown: 'Disco', 'Hero', 'Honeycomb', and 'Safari' from David Lemon; and 'Red Brocade' from Burpee. These are all U.S. cultivars. There is one Indian cultivar of *T. patula,* 'Pusa Arpita'. It emerged from a heterozygous population and was bred by Dr. Kanwar Pal Singh of the Indian Agricultural Research Institute in New Delhi.

In the recent past, several Indian horticulturists have also been working on cultivars more suited to the Indian climate.[25]

USES OF THE MARIGOLD

A modern use for the marigold is in poultry keeping. The standard commercial poultry feed is low in xanthines (yellow pigments), even though it is otherwise adequate and nutritious. The problem is that on this diet the chickens look pallid and their egg yolks are pale. The public believes that chickens with creamy yellow skin are more appetizing, while rich yellow egg yolks give the impression that they have better nutritional value. The poultry firms tried to make up for this deficiency in different ways, but nothing worked very well until someone thought of using the marigold.

Marigold petals are rich in these pigments. Adding marigold petals and extract to the chicken feed just might do the trick. The owners of Ralston Purina approached David Burpee in the 1960s and asked him to help them. He began trials of his orange cultivars, *Tagetes* 'Indian Chief', 'Superchief', 'Guinea Gold', and 'Orange Hawaii'. These were quite successful, but he persisted in seeking further improvements. The firm developed even better plants for this purpose: *T.* 'Orangeade', 'Deep Orangeade', and more recently, 'Scarletade'.

These highly pigmented series were grown on a gigantic scale in Mexico and Peru, but India and China currently grow the largest crops to supply this market.[26] In a rather odd way, David Burpee was back to where his father had started by selling chicken feed.

Reacting to anecdotal reports that marigolds protected tomato plants from nematode worms, Burpee introduced a cultivar, *Tagetes* 'Nema-Gone', in 1997. The evidence for its efficacy is not strong, but many home gardeners still plant marigold seeds in their vegetable beds anyway.

DISSEMINATION

Three species of *Tagetes* crop up sporadically in nineteenth-century English and American nursery catalogues. Alice Formiga, a former intern at the Special Collections department of the Oregon State University library, prepared an online exhibit of a sample of the university's nursery catalogue holdings.[27] Even in this fairly limited sample, three well-known English nurseries are seen to have offered *Tagetes* species as early as 1830.

The flowers were introduced into the United States at different times.[28] The first notice of *Tagetes erecta* was in 1760. Townley of Boston offered "Africans." Spurrier's nursery listed *T. patula*, French Marigolds, in 1793. By 1858, Joseph Breck in Boston referred to these as "well known tender annuals, one of the old fashioned flowers; deservedly popular from the brilliancy and variegation of its flowers."[29] It is amusing to see them listed as "old fashioned" in 1858. "Striped dwarfs" were available in the United States by 1800. *Tagetes tenuifolia* was first introduced in 1797 and could be purchased in Boston in 1867.

The very successful nineteenth-century nurseryman James Vick of Rochester was rather halfhearted about marigolds. He mentioned a few in his book but gave them no prominence.[30] He too thought they came from Africa.

BREEDING MARIGOLDS

Lyman White (1906–1996) wrote a short book about flower breeding based on his wide experience and reading.[31] White was a very well respected plantsman from the small town of Cambridge, New York, near the Vermont border. Among other things, he was a lifelong judge for the All-America Selections trials. His knowledge and understanding of horticulture were encyclopedic.

After a stint at some California seed companies, White moved to Cambridge and worked for the Asgrow Seed Company. He opened his own business, the Cambridge Pacific Seed Packet Company, in retirement. He devoted

A SURPRISING OMISSION

THE GREAT Exhibition of 1851 was a showcase for exotic plants. Hundreds of palms and ferns were supplied
to the Crystal Palace by the leading nurseries of the day. All
the plants were inside the building. Joseph Paxton's giant
greenhouse was constructed in London's Hyde Park solely
for the purposes of the exhibition, and no exterior planting
was allowed.

The following year, the palace was rebuilt in a less-
populated part of London, Sydenham. Here there was room
for a park. Paxton ordered many thousands of bedding plants
for the extensive grounds surrounding the building.[28]

I had assumed that marigolds would supply the bright
yellows and oranges needed for colorful patterns. Contrary
to my suppositions, Paxton used yellow calceolarias, not
marigolds. One can look in vain for any mention of marigolds in the *Gardeners Chronicle* just before, during, or just
after these events.

Maybe the rise of carpet bedding later in the 1880s and
1890s encouraged the use of marigolds to supply reliable yellow, orange, and gold tints to create the patterns. This can be
deduced from Miss Jekyll's comments.

a short chapter in his book to the marigold. White was the first person to adorn seed packets with photographs rather than paintings.

White recorded how improvements in marigolds slowly rumbled along in fits and starts. At the start of his career, there were only a few "African" varieties, mainly the fistulosa type (with many single flowers) and the carnation-flowered type (with fewer petals). In 1933, the English seed company Watkins and Simpson won the Gold Medal at the All-America Selections for *Tagetes* 'Guinea Gold'. Livingston Seed Company won the Gold Medal in 1935 for 'Yellow Supreme'.

Tagetes patula moved forward in two major leaps. At the end of the 1920s, the German firm of Mauser brought out *T.* 'Farbenklang' (literally 'Color Peal', as of a bell), sold in England as 'Harmony'. At first it was dismissed as just another French Marigold, but it bloomed reliably even when the weather was not so good. Glenn Goldsmith commented that *T. patula* flowered late in damp climates. It was a minute powerhouse.

Tagetes 'Farbenklang' genes were used for many crosses over the years. Peter Henderson of New York's 1941 catalogue listed eighteen kinds of marigolds, three of them the 'Harmony' type. A few years later, Darrell Decker in Chula Vista, California, released *Tagetes* 'Sparky', another watershed hybrid. Its flowers were larger than those of 'Harmony'. This cultivar came into flower a bit later, but it was also very reliable. Several of its descendants, such as Decker's 'King Tut', Bodger's 'Brocades', and three or four others, built on its strengths.

The mid-1930s saw a large increase in the number of hybrid *Tagetes* available, both *T. erecta* and *T. patula*. David Burpee had started his breeding program in parallel with the others then in existence. The new plants came on line at that time. An analysis of more than one hundred years of Burpee catalogues indicates that the firm offered between ten and twelve cultivars for sale annually between 1887 and 1931, but then the numbers began to climb almost exponentially.[32]

They rose to forty in 1936 and for the next forty years hovered between forty and fifty, quite often reaching fifty-five, sixty, or in 1980, eighty cultivars. Almost all of these were bred by the Burpee staff, though they did offer some attractive plants from other seed houses.

Flower breeders were always looking for improvements in the flower's hardiness, length of season, uniformity of height and blossom size, and disease resistance. *Tagetes* can be susceptible to spider mites and a few other pests. Once the switch to F1 hybrids was almost complete, the cost of producing the seeds or young plants in bulk became an important factor.

Recounting the story of the improvements in marigold breeding really rehearses the way in which previously unreliable and inefficient methods of open pollination and much hand work with hit-or-miss methods have given way to highly predictable systems for breeding new cultivars in all ornamental plants. Some of this was spurred by the increasing cost of land and labor.

Converting horticulture to reliable factory-like methods was also hastened by the enactment of plant patenting laws. This made it worthwhile to install expensive new systems. Any seed company doing this could expect to reap the benefit over many years and not see the competition cleaning up.

Perhaps the most striking innovation was the capacity to produce F1 hybrid seed on a mass, commercial scale. This started in the 1950s. The arrival of reliable F1 seeds coincided with the rise in sales of small seedlings rather than seed alone. The public reacted very favorably to this labor-saving development. Even a careless weekend gardener with two black thumbs could have something quite attractive growing very quickly in his backyard. The F1 seeds were important to this endeavor, as their good germination rate and vigor led to reduced wastage. Reducing overhead and increasing the yield was always an important requirement.

MARIGOLDS REACH CALIFORNIA

Marigolds first reached California in 1873. One important person, the influential Dean Edward J. Wickson at the College of Agriculture of the young University of California, made his views known very quickly. He did not like their smell. He was from upstate New York and may have met them there. Sweet peas and asters were at the peak of their glamour at the end of the nineteenth century and the beginning of the twentieth. The combination of World War I, disease, and a natural decline in vigor led to these flowers losing popularity.

David Burpee recognized that a new flower was needed to take their place in the public's imagination. The marigold seemed like a good choice. He had inherited his father's seed company in 1915 and within a few years began to put money into breeding marigolds. Burpee was an instinctive promoter of the first order, always understanding how to build on the public's needs and desires.

Perhaps the best way to follow the progress of the marigold is by taking a look at the various series of cultivars created by different breeders. As with any other plant, the breeders were seeking to overcome disadvantages in the species plants and manipulate naturally occurring advantages. *Tagetes erecta* was too tall and overbearing. Some of the larger ones need staking. *T. patula* was a bit wimpy but had a wide range of colors and tints. Once breeders made a really powerful advance, they worked on deriving more cultivars using the same methods and thus creating a series to give the public greater choice.

Although the marigold is tough and can survive, it is still a semitropical plant, and that may be one reason it did so well in California. There were many successful efforts to improve the flower in England and on the Continent, but nothing on the scale later reached in California.

For example, Robert Godard at the French company Clause et Cie created the Zenith Series of marigolds. Some workers in this field thought the Zenith Series came from Ron Schlemmer at Harris-Moran in Rochester, New York. The confusion could arise from the fact that Clause and Harris-Moran were both bought by the Vilmorin group in 2002. The two companies were under the same umbrella.

In England, David Haswell worked on the triploid "Afro-French" hybrid. *Tagetes erecta* is a diploid ($2n = 24$). *T. patula* is a tetraploid ($2n = 48$). A cross between these two species leads to a triploid version.

Haswell's tasks were primarily to test field performance. He examined the behavior of dozens of imported varieties to see which ones did best in the English climate. He was pitting field performance with a long season and good ground coverage against fast turnaround, good sales, and augmented bench populations needed by the propagators. These qualities were not always found in the same cultivars.

The triploid hybrids were a great success, with a longer flowering season and an increased number of blossoms per stem. Some of these hybrids flowered until mid-December, very late for the cool English autumn and early winter. This type's flowers were brilliantly colored, another advantage. They had the added benefit from the nurseryman's point of view of being sterile.

Ferry Morse dismissed it as a "stinky weed," yet by the sheer force of his personality Burpee turned it into a national favorite.

One of Burpee's former colleagues and employees, Gerald Burke, has written an interesting article about David Burpee's personality and behavior in business.[35] He was a hard driver and completely in control at all levels. No one could influence his decisions unless he was ready to make that particular concession. David Burpee was rigid in some ways and unpredictable in others, and that made his workers anxious. Even as you thought you were doing what he wanted, he could catch you on the wrong foot.

His wife's influence softened this harsh tone in his private life. Lois Burpee was a sensible and effective woman whose missionary father had taken the family to live in the then Palestine. She was exposed to different ways of life and foods at an early age and became quite flexible in her attitudes. One of her contributions to the firm's success with vegetable seeds was the publication of *Lois Burpee's Gardener's Companion and Cookbook*. Her son Jonathan recalls her very affectionately.

The Burpees supported missions in China very generously. As will be seen below, this actually helped him in business. One of their beneficiaries, the Reverend Carter D. Holton, sent him seeds of an odorless marigold.

One way to build interest in a new flower was to issue a very difficult challenge to the public; the other was to start a society of enthusiasts to boost the plant. Burpee did both. The society was useful but ran out of steam after a while. The challenge was to find a completely white marigold without even the faintest trace of yellow. This competition was announced in 1954 and offered a prize of ten thousand dollars. That is a substantial sum of money now and was worth even more fifty years ago.

For many years, no one was able to breed a truly snow-white marigold. Hopeful contestants offered ivory- and cream-colored varieties, but nothing that met the criteria for pure white. In 1975 a widow in Iowa, Alice Vonk, surprised everyone by producing the first pure white flower and received the grand prize. She took it all in stride. According to her, she had just dabbled in her garden to pass the time.

Another of David Burpee's brilliant promotional campaigns was to have the marigold declared the American national flower. He roped in well-known powerful politicians like Senator Everett Dirksen, but the plan never succeeded. The rose was chosen instead. This is mildly ironic.

There are indeed native roses in the United States, but the ones grown most of the time are hybrids from China. At least the marigold is endemic to the Western Hemisphere. During the course of this debate, the public naturally bought a great many of Burpee's marigold seeds.

Before World War II, Burpee had bred many new cultivars by selecting from open-pollinated flowers. In 1937 they released the 'Crown of Gold' and in 1939 the 'Red and Gold' marigold. *Tagetes* 'Crown of Gold' won a gold medal at the All-America Selections show that year. Three of Burpee's introductions changed marigold history: *T.* 'Crown of Gold' (see below); 'Red and Gold', the first interspecific hybrid; and Nuggets, the first triploid series, in 1966.

As F1 hybrid breeding became feasible, Burpee introduced the Climax Series in the late 1950s. These were tall African cultivars with fully double flowers. They were followed by the Gold Coin type. It is said that Burpee called the series "Climax" because it was the end of a very long period of experimentation.

In the roughly seventy years of the All-America Selections trials, there have been forty-eight awards for marigolds and three gold medals. Burpee won seventeen of the forty-eight awards.[36]

Because some of their customers had complained about the strong smell of marigolds, Burpee decided to breed a flower without any smell. Although they accomplished that by using a sport from China, the resulting seeds, *Tagetes* 'Crown of Gold', did not sell. This was a classic example of the fickleness of the public: when it got what it said it would like, it no longer wanted it. The firm managed to recoup its losses by offering both odorous and odorless versions of the flowers. This work was done at Fordhook in Pennsylvania.

Through the years, Burpee has introduced dozens of marigold cultivars. I have analyzed the number and types of marigolds listed in Burpee catalogues from 1887 to 1997. Only a very small number of catalogues was missing. Some of the highlights of this analysis show that there were more than 330 varieties and cultivars. The longest-lasting one was *Tagetes* 'Orange Ball', from 1892 to 1962, seventy-one years. It was not uncommon for some cultivars to last for fifty to sixty years.

For many years, Burpee offered between forty and fifty cultivars annually, with a peak of eighty-two kinds in 1980. More than 30 percent of new cultivars lasted only one season. Another 12 percent lasted two seasons, and 4.5 percent lasted three seasons. A total of 59.5 percent lasted only up to five years.[37]

At present, Burpee features twenty-three varieties of marigolds for sale. More than half of them are old stalwarts that have been in commerce for more than twenty years. One of these, *Tagetes* 'Sunset Giants', was released in 1941, more than seventy years ago. The others have been introduced since 1997. The new 'Cottage Red' is a cultivar of *T. tenuifolia*.

David Denholm

The Denholm story is different and somewhat more recent. The Scottish David Denholm was very well trained in England. He won the Joseph Banks Medal in London. After emigrating to California, he worked for Morse and Bodger before starting his own company with two other men: Harry Buckman, a noted figure in Lompoc, and Ted Holden, in 1939. The firm put a lot of effort into the marigold and won seven awards at the All-America Selections.[38]

According to Glenn Goldsmith, Denholm was a master of visual selection in a large field of open-pollinated blooms. Several of the flower-breeding experts mentioned in this section worked for Denholm at one time or another.

Goldsmith Family

Glenn Goldsmith was a university-trained horticulturist who started out by working for a small California nursery soon after graduating.[39] His doctoral thesis at the University of California at Los Angeles was on the French Marigold. One of his first responsibilities was to supervise the gang of men sent into the fields to "rogue" hybrid marigolds. (Roguing is the removal of any plant that does not conform to the standard required.) Goldsmith was also responsible for teaching some of Denholm's employees the techniques of flower breeding. After eight years at Denholm, he became director of research for the PanAmerican Seed Company. Once he gained experience, he decided to go into business for himself and founded his own seed house in Gilroy, California, in 1962. It has always been a wholesale firm.

His sons went into the business with him as they grew up, and they took over when he retired. The firm has recently been sold to the Syngenta Corporation, but Joel Goldsmith remains in charge. The firm grows many of its seedlings in Guatemala. Glenn Goldsmith was a very enlightened employer and offered stability and employment in a country where both are in very short supply. Like Claude Hope in Costa Rica, he improved the lives of his workers with access to health care and other benefits.

The Goldsmiths have introduced many excellent hybrid plants, and marigolds are no exception. They were the first to breed some of the new tall, half tall, and dwarf marigolds. The Inca Series (released in 1982) remains very popular, with short sturdy stems and large, uniform flowers at the top.

Their series of Petites, *Tagetes* 'French Petite', 'French Janie', and 'French Aurora', resulted from a search for a more freely blooming, earlier, and longer-lasting flower. As noted above, the Harmony variety was important, supplying gold and orange hues as well as red /yellow tints. The actual parents of that series are not known. One of the enduring successes of the Goldsmith series is *T.* 'French Janie', named for Mrs. Goldsmith.

The dwarf *Tagetes patula* 'Lemon Drop' was another successful discovery. It was found in a field of open-pollinated flowers and was very prolific. A repeat flush of bloom from it in the same season was an important characteristic. Goldsmith took seed from the best plants. He started with one hundred rows of seeds, and when he found the one he liked best, he sowed this seed in pots.

Tagetes 'Spun Gold' appeared as an African sport. They found one miniature in a field of flowers close to three feet tall. Starting in 1962, Goldsmith crossed *T.* 'Spun Gold' with a double-flowered mixture, *T.* 'Crackerjack', and eventually came up with *T.* 'Aztec Orange'. This took many generations of breeding, selecting for dwarf determinate growth and large double flowers with crested centers. They received a patent in 1975. *T.* 'Aztec Gold' and 'Aztec Yellow' were developed at the same time. *T.* 'Spun Gold' won its own prize at the AAS trials.

Some idea of the size and scope of Goldsmith's plant breeding program can be gained from the fact that the firm employed seven plant breeders at one time.

Individuals Working in California

Denis Flaschenriem

Denis Flaschenriem works for PanAmerican Seed Company. He has developed many important cultivars of zinnia and marigold, among them *Tagetes* 'American Taishan'.

Mathilde Holtrop

Dr. Mathilde Holtrop, now retired, worked for Goldsmith Seeds for twenty-eight years. She was involved in numerous aspects of the firm's plant breeding work and required several assistants to carry out all her projects.

Mathilde Holtrop was born in Indonesia to Dutch parents. The family moved back to the Netherlands just before World War II, but soon after the war was over they emigrated to Canada. Mathilde then moved to San Diego and has remained in California ever since. She took her doctorate in plant genetics at the University of California at Davis. Shortly after that, she started to work for Glenn Goldsmith. Glenn was beginning to breed *Tagetes* very seriously.

One of her first tasks was to develop a short-stemmed, fully double *Tagetes erecta* cultivar with a large head. This became the Inca Series. It was very successful, but Glenn wanted an even richer double flower. Dr. Holtrop crossed the Inca seed parent with an F2 derivative of Bodger's *T.* 'First Lady'. This led to *T.* 'Inca II'.

She also bred a chrysanthemum-flowered marigold, 'Merrimum', and anemone-flowered *Tagetes patula* marigolds, the Aurora Series. One of her colleagues, Carolyn James, had left many lines of experimental *T. patula* varieties before moving to Guatemala. Dr. Holtrop bred the best of these and came up with *T.* 'Janie Gold', an award-winning flower.

Much of her work in the 1980s was devoted to perfecting Inca seed for machine plugs, the system whereby individual seed containers were each planted with one seed in an industrial setting. This led to a huge expansion in wholesale plant sales while keeping labor costs down. Dr. Holtrop has also bred prize-winning cultivars of pelargonium, petunia, and pansy.[40]

David Lemon

David Lemon has bred numerous exceptional cultivars of all the most useful annual plants and gives no sign of ceasing at any time. One of the germs of this work was his telling me that Christopher Lloyd addressed him as "Marigold Man" at their only meeting. David is indeed "Marigold Man." It can be considered a badge of honor, but he could just as easily be hailed as "Pelargonium Man" or "Sweet Pea Man."

David was born in Dublin and began his horticultural training at the Dublin Botanical Garden. Subsequently he went to England for an honors diploma at the Royal Horticultural Society's Wisley Garden. For a time he worked at a seed company in London, Watkins and Simpson, and enjoyed being involved in this type of business. In 1964 he moved to the United States. Once in Lompoc he worked for Burpee, Denholm, Ball, and Bodger at different times, eventually breeding pelargoniums for Oglevee and its successor, Ecke.

There is little point in even trying to count the number of awards and prizes his flowers have garnered. Many of David Lemon's awards were at the European trials, Fleuroselect. He has prepared some useful papers on the lobelia, pelargonium, and verbena for the USDA Agricultural Research Service/Germplasm Resources Information Network (ARS/GRIN).

He devoted himself to the French Marigold for many years. The following are David Lemon's cultivars: *Tagetes* 'Showboat Yellow' (triploid), 'French Honeycomb', 'French Boy', 'French Gate', 'French Bonanza', 'French Hero', 'French Little Hero', 'French Safari', and 'French Disco'. None of these is an F1 hybrid. The apetalous form of *T. patula* is not needed for this work.

John Mondry

John Mondry (1917–1994) worked both for Bodger and for Burpee, actually going back to Burpee after retiring from Bodger. He was born in Pennsylvania but lived in California for many years. He was known as an expert plant breeder and worked on the zinnia as well as the marigold. His flowers frequently received awards at the All-America Selections trials. In 1986 the University of Michigan awarded him an honorary doctorate for his contributions to horticulture.

Mondry was a very impressive man. His father worked in the coal mines but educated himself at night school to become a manager. All the children were expected to make something of themselves. After John Mondry retired, he enrolled in a creative writing course and prepared a brief autobiography for his family. His children very kindly made it available to me.

Money, or rather, its lack, had a profound effect on John Mondry's career, but in the end he overcame this seeming constraint. When he left high school, he began to do manual labor to earn a living, but a few months later a junior college was opened near his home. Mondry enrolled and remained there for three years. At first he signed on for pre-med and combined school with work in the mines. He was then obliged to switch to biology and chemistry to become a teacher, as he could not afford to study medicine.

The professor of botany and genetics recognized his gifts and found him a scholarship to pursue graduate work. Next he came to the attention of the Burpee firm. They gave him a fellowship and employed him to breed vegetables between 1943 and 1945, until he had to enter the U.S. Navy.

Burpee took him back but consigned him to more and more deskwork. Miserable and bored, he accepted an offer from Bodger Seeds and took his family to California to direct research on annual flowers.

The large-scale production and marketing of F1 hybrids in both vegetables and flowers led to very profound changes in horticultural practice. Flowers have to be stripped of their stamens to avoid self-fertilization and make sure that the chosen external pollen is the sole fertilizing agent. The process is made easier when a naturally apetalous, male-sterile, version of the flower is available.

That happened in both the zinnia and the marigold. One of the managers at Burpee, Al Condit, noticed two large stands of male-sterile marigolds on the company's land. Mondry took full advantage of this finding, developing *Tagetes* 'American Climax' (tall), 'American Gold Coin' (tall), 'American Jubilee' (half tall), 'American Galore', 'American Space Age', and 'American Crush'.

Part of his great skill lay in carrying the male-sterile line over the years, making sure it did not revert to the standard form. This presents many practical difficulties. The male sterile factor is carried in the cytoplasm, and there has to be careful back breeding.[41]

Elwood S. Pickering

Elwood S. Pickering (1919–2004) worked for Burpee as a plant breeder until he retired. *Tagetes* 'American First Lady', 'Triploid Nugget', and ' Triploid Seven Stars' were the most significant of his introductions. 'American First Lady' is an attractive semidwarf type. He also played a major role in the development of the odorless marigold.

Blair Winner

Blair Winner works at PanAmerican Seed. He introduced the Bonanza and Durango Series.

Darrell Decker

The late Darrell Decker was an independent flower breeder in Chula Vista, California. He first introduced *Tagetes* 'Sparky', a valuable *T. patula* hybrid, and later 'Dolly', a dwarf African type. Decker subsequently developed *T.* 'King Tut' from 'Sparky'.

Yoshiro Arimitsu

Yoshiro Arimitsu worked for Bodger and bred the American Discovery and American Voyager Series. Arimitsu prepared some useful papers on zinnias and other annuals for ARS/GRIN.

⌒⌒⌒

MANY other men and women have contributed to the development of marigolds in California.[42] Lyndon Drewlow and Ron Schlemmer are still very active. Besides all the people listed above, old-timers talk about Jeannette Lowe, Al Condit, and a few others.

NARCISSUS

Narcissus is the Latin name for daffodil, and the two words are used more or less interchangeably. William Wordsworth immortalized the daffodil in England. Even nonliterary types know about his "host of golden daffodils" while he "wandered lonely as a cloud." Most English people consider the yellow trumpet form to be a daffodil and refer to the flat white forms as "narcissi."

Not every daffodil is golden. Many are white or in tones of white, and some have orange centers or an orange ring around a white cup, giving the breeder many choices and pathways to follow. The cups vary widely in depth, forming the basis for most systems of classification now in use.

E. A. Bowles, a true scholar and devotee of all bulbous plants, delved into the various names by which this plant is known.[1] *Daffodil* is said to be a corruption of the word *asphodel*. Early modern poets celebrated the asphodel. It was a flower known in antiquity but precisely what it actually was is not clear.

When it came to the Latin name, *Narcissus*, Bowles suggests that the bulb, not the Greek myth about the nymph Echo and the self-obsessed youth ("narcissistic") Narcissus, lay behind the name. The bulbs had long been used to encourage sleep, or *narcosis.*

There are arguments about the number of genera and species. The best estimate is about twenty species. Scholars and growers adhere either to A. Fernandes's mid-twentieth-century system or to the *Flora Europaea* one.[2] Fernandes has divided the genera into many species. *Flora Europaea* has fewer separate species but makes up for it in subspecies. Most species are found in the countries of the Mediterranean rim, with only a few in northern Europe. *Narcissus pseudonarcissus* is native to England. Almost all the other daffodils have come from Spain, Portugal, or North Africa.

MOVEMENT OF NARCISSUS WITHIN EUROPE

The great Leiden botanist Clusius grew narcissus and made them better known by the late 1570s. Small bulbs were among his greatest passions. John Gerard mentioned narcissi in his *Herball or Generall Historie of Plantes.* John Parkinson considered daffodils to be special and devoted many pages to them in *Paradisus in Sole.* He said he received them from Breton sailors at Bristol.

In 1753 Linnaeus named the six species he was given. Bulbs were easy to transport, and this helped to disseminate them widely. The bulbs were used for food and medicinal purposes, but the beauty of the flowers was an early lure. Even before 1600, there were two forms of double-flowered narcissus in circulation.

Once daffodils reached Ireland, they took hold with amazing ease. The mild damp climate suited them very well. Some even escaped from gardens and naturalized in ditches. Several of the best breeders of narcissus have come from Northern Ireland (see later discussion). Lionel Richardson (1890–1961) and his wife, Helen (1903–1978), were originally from that province, even though they later worked in County Wexford, Eire. Guy Wilson (1885–1962) was another Ulsterman who bred remarkable narcissus.

Precisely why the daffodil should have become a national emblem for Wales, another part of the United Kingdom, is not known. The leek preceded it in that capacity by about five hundred years. The Welsh names for leek and daffodil include the same word: *cenhinen* = leek, *cenhinen pedr* = daffodil. In country places, daffodils are called "daffydowndillies." *Taffy* is a slang term for a Welshman, and one possibility is that maybe the syllabic similarities played a role. *Taffy* is a corruption of *Daffyd* (David), and the flower sounds very much like it.

Besides Wordsworth and his useful promotion, several names remain fresh in narcissus history. Peter Barr may be the prime one, but Mrs. R. O. Backhouse comes a close second. She was the daughter-in-law of William Backhouse, another almost-legendary breeder.

Dean Herbert led the way in this, as in so many other endeavors. He believed that it would be good to work on the daffodil, even though he was a little cavalier about some of the classification and descriptions of species.[3] He himself made widely divergent crosses. Herbert wanted to create an orange trumpet flower, using chiefly *Narcissus hispanicus* and *N. poeticus*. The latter contributed the orange coloration.

INFLUENTIAL INDIVIDUALS

English and Scots Breeders and Collectors

Peter Barr

Peter Barr (1826–1909) was already a successful nurseryman when he got his start in narcissus from a devotee of Dean Herbert. Edward Leeds, a wealthy stockbroker, decided to collect and breed narcissus possibly after reading Dean Herbert's work. As he grew older, illness made it impossible to continue. Peter Barr bought his collection of twenty-four thousand plants in 1874. Barr consolidated his lead by buying another leading collection, that of William Backhouse in Wolsingham, Durham.

With this magnificent base, Barr asked J. G. Baker, the head of the herbarium at the Royal Botanic Gardens at Kew, to create some sort of order among the 360 kinds of narcissus he now controlled. Baker had impressed him by his writing in F. W. Burbidge's book on narcissus.[4] Burbidge (1847–1905) was the curator of the Trinity College Dublin botanical garden. Barr built on all these contributions and issued his own catalogue of narcissus in 1884.

Whether he was influenced by William Morris's revival of early English style at the time or whether he simply wished to shock his audience into attention, Barr entitled his book *Ye Narcissus or Daffodyl Flowere with a Compleat Liste of all the Species and Varieties known to Englyshe Amateurs Containing Hys Historie and Culture &c.* and listed the publisher in mock antique style, "And to be solde by Barre and Sonne, over in King Street (No. 12 and 13) in the Parish of Saint Paul, in ye Covent Garden (nigh to ye Strande), Westminster." Peter Barr haled from Scotland.

His "liste" was very thorough, and the catalogue almost amounted to a monograph. This wonderful book cost one shilling, a sum now about equal to an American quarter but serious money back in the 1890s. Barr also worked hard at the Royal Horticultural Society, serving on committees and setting up conferences on narcissus.

He made another lasting contribution to the field. Peter Barr traveled widely through Spain and Portugal, often in great discomfort, using mule or donkey trains, searching for the originals of the species then found in the British Isles.

Trumpet daffodils are the epitome of the flower for gardeners. Most breeders have used *Narcissus hispanicus* (now known as *N. pseudonarcissus* L. ssp. *major* (Curtis) Baker) , *N. obvallaris, N. moschatus,* and *N. bicolor* as breeding material. In 1887 the Dutch breeder S. de Graaff released *N.* 'Mme de Graaff', and in 1889, 'King Alfred' was introduced. These hybrids formed the basis for much future work until the present. The parents of 'King Alfred' are not known. 'Mme de Graaff', a white trumpet, came from crossing *N. albescens* with 'Empress' pollen. William Backhouse had bred 'Empress'.

Percival Dacres Williams

Narcissus hispanicus grew very well in Cornwall. Percival Dacres Williams continued to breed daffodils even though his cousin J. C. Williams had decided to work with other plants. P. D. Williams dominated the British shows and breeding trials in the 1920s and 1930s, but toward the end of the latter decade the Scottish Brodie of Brodie challenged him very seriously. The Reverend George Herbert Engleheart, with whom the Williams cousins had started out breeding narcissus, died in 1936 at the age of eighty-five, one year after Percival Williams died.

P. D. Williams worked for more than forty years. His legacy is obvious. Almost half of all commercial daffodils grown in the United Kingdom were Williams cultivars, at least until 1990. The arena in which many of these challenges played out with very genteel ferocity was the Engleheart Cup. Winning this cup established the breeder's reputation for life.

William Backhouse

William Backhouse (1807–1869) began breeding narcissus in 1856. *Narcissus* 'Empress' and 'Emperor' were his best-known cultivars. Although he did not keep records, he believed that *N.* 'Empress' came from crossing *N. bicolor* with a form of *N. pseudonarcissus*. Backhouse came from a notable family in the Society of Friends. One branch founded the Backhouse bank.

William's brother, James, bought George Telford's nursery in York, renaming it the Backhouse nursery, in 1815. The temperamental plant explorer George Caley, a man who tried even Sir Joseph Banks's exceptional patience, worked briefly for Telford's. Even though James Backhouse went on to become a missionary, the nursery continued under that name. George Russell of lupin fame was one of their employees later in the century. The Backhouse men were shrewd in business but also, like so many other Friends, enlightened about social issues.

Sarah Backhouse

Sarah Elizabeth Backhouse, née Dodgson (1857–1921), worked closely with her husband, Robert Ormston Backhouse, at their Hereford property. Both bred narcissus, but Mrs. Backhouse is remembered because she bred the first pink daffodil. It came out in 1923, two years after her death. Robert Ormston Backhouse was William Backhouse's youngest son and lived on until 1940. Other breeders helped him to continue his wife's work. Some of the Dutch nurseries bought her lines.

In narcissus-speak, orange is known as "red" or "pink." Mrs. Backhouse created at least two striking flowers with bright red centers, but Michael Jefferson-Brown, a contemporary expert, believes that her name is indelibly connected to *Narcissus* 'Mrs R.O. Backhouse', a trumpet type of flower whose crown starts out as yellow but fades into a definitely pink color as the season wears on.[5]

Lionel Richardson introduced another of Mrs. Backhouse's crosses, *Narcissus* 'Hades', in 1925. This had a bright red corona and is the ancestor of almost all modern red-and-white narcissi in commerce.

Ian Brodie

Ian Brodie (1868–1943), the "Brodie of Brodie," in traditional Scottish parlance, was the head of an old clan more given to warlike pursuits in previous centuries than to flower breeding. The drive and focus of a clan chief served him in good stead for the almost forty years in which he crossed narcissus. Guy Wilson and Lionel Richardson, both celebrated narcissus breeders, sold his bulbs through their catalogues, long after his death. They also used his cultivars for crossing some of their own flowers.

John S. B. Lea

Between 1975 and 1984, one man won the Engleheart Cup every year: John S. B. Lea.[6] His winning streak started in 1971. That was the first time in forty years that an Englishman had defeated the Richardsons from Northern Ireland. Lea was known for his skill with form and clarity of color. Ramsay considers that *Narcissus* 'Dailmanach' may be Lea's most effective legacy. Dozens of cultivars have been bred from this pink-cupped daffodil.

Breeders in Northern Ireland

In Northern Ireland, Guy Wilson and the Richardsons led the way, and Brian Duncan is one of their heirs. Wilson was obsessed by the flower even as a child but lived to see huge improvement in the shape and constitution of his favorite plant because of his work. He enjoyed working with *Narcissus hispanicus* and *N. obvallaris* but also paid attention to varieties of different colors. Duncan is a powerhouse in today's narcissus circles, with a wide range of accomplishments.

Dutch Breeders

Dutch bulbs are world famous. De Graaff was only one of many skillful breeders who extended the range of the narcissus. The Krelage family introduced important cultivars before the First World War. The house of Warnaar's *Narcissus* 'Golden Trumpet', released in 1927, remained successful for fifty years.

Breeders in the United States

Breeding narcissus began later in the United States than in northern Europe, but the gap was rapidly narrowed. There are legions of devoted breeders who fuel the work of the American Daffodil Society. Two men are very well known.

Dr. Thomas D. Throckmorton, a practicing surgeon in Des Moines, Iowa, was most interested in flowers that changed color after opening. Dr. Throckmorton died in 2000. The Royal Horticultural Society uses his system of color coding for international classification purposes.

Grant Mitsch (1907–1989) began breeding daffodils in Oregon in 1934. He covered a very wide range of types, not just a narrow selection. Michael Jefferson-Brown notes that the first of his flowers to become internationally known were his lemons. Anyone in the United States reading this might assume he means that they were "lemons," an American synonym for failures, but Jefferson-Brown is only referring to the color!

Throckmorton made very good use of some of Mitsch's cultivars. Other breeders also benefited from his work. John Pearson made them the basis of his reverse bicolors. Mitsch's daughter and son-in-law have continued his business and introduce elegant new cultivars themselves.

Breeders in New Zealand

When the first British settlers arrived in New Zealand, they found a breathtaking flora; nevertheless, they chose to grow familiar flowers they knew very well from home. They planted daffodil bulbs in many of the new towns, and the bulbs naturalized very successfully. Christchurch in particular is noted for its daffodils.

The emigrants not only took the bulbs with them, they also took their keen competitive spirit and desire to improve their favorite flowers too. Very active daffodil societies hold shows at least once a year. This has been going for more than eighty years. In 1926 the National Daffodil Society of New Zealand was formed. The fact that such a society was even contemplated indicates how vigorously daffodil breeding was thriving already.

John Hunter, the society's historian, recorded the fact that the first New Zealand nurseryman to list daffodils in his catalogue was Henry Budden (1842–1902).[7] Budden had been trained as a gardener in England before moving to New Zealand. In 1877 he opened his own nursery. By 1895 his grounds were full of daffodils. The following year he was able to exhibit two hundred varieties at a flower show.

Another pioneer was Ben Hart. Originally from Tasmania, he had won prizes for his daffodils before migrating to New Zealand in the 1850s. By 1880 he had resumed his breeding of daffodils. Hart did everything on a very large scale, growing thousands of seedlings. He created "Daffodil Day" as a national event across the whole of the country. Hart's whole family, including his son and granddaughter, grew narcissus very enthusiastically.

The North and South Islands of New Zealand hold separate and possibly competing shows. Of the about 14,500 known narcissus cultivars in the America Daffodil Society's Data Bank, starting in the 1890s, about 5,400 are from Great Britain, 3,260 from Australia, 2,000 from New Zealand and 1,900 from the United States. Contrary to the public's perception, the Netherlands comes in last, with about 1,400 forms. The great skill of the Dutch lies in propagating and growing the bulbs successfully.

A great many narcissus breeders are amateurs. If some of their releases are very successful, they either sell them through an established company or start their own business. Some never sell any of them.

James O'More

James O'More (1911–1996) was a much-loved narcissus breeder who worked as a postman in Wellington. During his lifetime, he named over one hundred

Narcissus 'Sentinel', a large-cupped pink cultivar descended from *N.* 'Mrs Backhouse' (seed parent: 'Precedent'; pollen parent: 'Carla'—bred by Grant Misch). *Reproduced by permission of John Scheepers Flower Bulbs (photographer, Jo-Anne van der Berg-Ohm)*

varieties. His protégés formed a supportive coterie around him as he grew old and frail. They had all benefited from his generosity of spirit and felt they wanted to ease his difficulties the best they could. Even when he was confined to a hospital bed, they decorated the wall with his latest blue ribbons.

As a final act of homage, the group lobbied the Royal Horticultural Society to award him the Peter Barr Cup. They succeeded, and the cup was awarded to him in 1991, a few years before he died. O'More refused to sell his bulbs but gave them freely to those he felt would carry on the work in the right way. One of his colleagues, Peter Ramsay, had the feeling that there had been some unspoken test which he had passed without knowing he had been under scrutiny.[8]

Like all other great flower breeders, O'More was ruthless in his selection. He was looking for particular characteristics, and if a new plant did not meet his requirements he threw it out. He kept careful records in small field notebooks. One code was "D" for dump. Over the thirty-four years in which O'More actively bred new plants, he evaluated 2,398 crosses.

The records show that he used pedigree parents for his experiments. Many came from the Irish growers, Lionel Richardson and Guy Wilson. Each cross was meticulously recorded, and he could trace a pedigree back generation by generation. His successes were thus due not to chance but to a rational and carefully thought-out program.

O'More's most memorable varieties included *Narcissus* 'Sea Dream', 'White Glen', 'Red Era', and 'Red Ember'. Among white-and-pinks, his 'Pink Era' remains high on the list. Ramsay comments that O'More used Australian cultivars as the parents for these flowers. Australian breeders led the narcissus world in breeding pink flowers from about 1940 to about 1980.

Impact of New Zealand Narcissus

The great ferment in narcissus breeding in the Southern Hemisphere has only very gradually permeated the Northern Hemisphere, in spite of the quite startling numbers above. Everything starts with the shows. If a plant is not successful at a show, its future is in doubt. In some cases, the flowers may not be accepted at a show or may be considered ineligible for some reason or other.

The philosophy of displaying the flower stems used to differ between the two poles, but the style in New Zealand has moved toward the British one.

In spite of these obstacles, at least three New Zealand cultivars have had a worldwide impact. One flower, *Narcissus* 'Trena', a cyclamineus hybrid, has received many awards at international shows. Mavis Verry bred it in the 1950s. A sport of the double tazetta hybrid *N.* 'Grand Monarque' named 'Erlicheer' is grown all around the world as a commercial cut flower. The miniature triandrus hybrid *N.* 'Hawera' also wins prizes at many shows, not only in New Zealand. It was bred by Dr. Thompson in the 1930s.

Recent evaluations of the direction in which narcissus is heading suggest that high priority will be given to the miniature forms.

ORCHID

The orchid family is vast, and there are many terrestrial species. For this reason, I shall only attempt to cover the exotic, tropical orchids and their breeders here. The maintenance of wild populations depends on effective pollination for the flower to set seed. Insects, including hymenoptera, are often the primary pollinators in the wild. Some orchids are so precisely adapted to their niches that human beings have great difficulty in mirroring this function.

One of the best-known cases is that of the Madagascar orchid, *Angraecum sesquipedale*, with its immensely long nectar tube of about eleven inches. In 1862, Charles Darwin prophesied that a moth with a proboscis of the same length would have to pollinate the flower. He added that should the moth disappear the orchid would become extinct.[1] People rolled on the floor laughing at his foolishness, but in 1903 scientists found this moth, *Xanthopan morganii praedicta*. In 2006, a very persistent biologist, Professor Phil De Vries, a University of Wisconsin biologist formerly of the Center for Biodiversity Studies at the Milwaukee Public Museum and currently at the University of New Orleans, left sensitive videorecorders running all night in the jungle and photographed *Xanthopan* actually feeding on the *Angraecum* flower, just as Darwin had imagined.[2]

CREATING NEW HYBRIDS
INTENTIONALLY

Given these extreme complexities in natural pollination, when John Dominy set out to hybridize *Calanthe,* he employed great care and dexterity. This was the first time anyone succeeded in creating an orchid hybrid deliberately, though there were some prior attempts. The Reverend William Herbert, dean of Manchester, wrote about his experience with orchids in 1847. Herbert , as we have seen in earlier chapters, was a distinguished figure in Victorian horticulture who knew a lot about roses and many other plants as well as orchids. He pollinated *Orchis* with *Ophrys* and obtained viable seed capsules. Two similar reports were published in the *Gardeners' Chronicle* in 1849, but all this was still very preliminary.

Orchid seed is as fine as dust and contains no internal nutrients for its growth. The roots of wild orchids are always infested with a mycorrhizal fungus of the genus *Rhizoctonia,* which makes up this deficit. Early growers did not know about the fungus or its role. It was discovered in 1904 by a French botanist, Noel Bernard.[3]

One reason collectors did the equivalent of clear-cutting when gathering wild orchids was that there was no reliable method for reproducing the plants in the nursery. Without this fungus, the seed cannot germinate or grow. Even in 1885, a thoughtful English collector, Mr. B. S. Williams, was shocked by the wanton destruction of the orchids in their habitat. Ultimately the authorities in the countries of origin forbade anyone from exporting living orchid plants without explicit permission.

Presumably the specimens that Dominy worked on came from the wild and still had enough of the fungus attached to their roots to supply the deficit. After a few years, the soil in the pots had a plentiful supply of the fungus. Some astute observers developed proprietary methods on their own, usually based on using the remains of the parent plants, without understanding the basis of their success. They were the equivalent of brewers and bakers until the twentieth century, keeping a piece of dough, the "levain," from one brewing or baking to another.

This was why Lewis Knudson's later research and discoveries were so extremely important. By supplying sugar in the growing medium, he unleashed the ability to reproduce orchids on an unprecedented scale (see below).

ENGLAND

John Dominy

John Dominy (1816–1891) did his work quietly in the Exeter nursery of the Veitch firm. After his apprenticeship, Dominy started to work for the prosperous nursery of Lucombe and Pince in Exeter, founded by William Lucombe in 1720. Dominy stayed there only a few months. Robert T. Pince, the founder's grandson, was skilled at hybridizing, but Dominy probably never had time to observe him at work. With one brief interlude as head gardener for J. P. Magor in Redruth, Dominy spent his entire working life in the service of the Veitches.

A local surgeon in Exeter, John Harris, was very interested in botany and the structure of orchids. The male and female organs of most tropical orchids are fused into a single column. This anatomy had defeated would-be hybridizers for a long time until Harris unraveled it. He helped Dominy understand the sexual parts of an orchid flower and how to work with them.

Harris urged Dominy to make some crosses. Veitch's obsessional secrecy is easier to understand in this context. This work gave him an immense advantage commercially, and naturally he did not want to share it with anyone. Keeping Dominy out of sight in Devonshire made a lot of sense.

Dominy crossed *Calanthe furcata* with *C. masuca*. The first flowers bloomed in 1856. John Lindley, secretary of the Horticultural Society of London and the leading expert on orchids in the world, was invited to Exeter to see them and uttered his famous remark, "You will drive the botanists mad!"

Dominy followed this success with the first intentional intergeneric orchid hybrid to flower, *Ludisia [Haemaria] discolor* × *Dossinia marmorata*. It was originally registered as *Dossinimaria dominyi*. When the name of *Haemaria discolor* was changed to *Ludisia discolor* in the 1970s, the hybrid's name was changed to *Dossisia dominyi*. The cross was probably registered in 1861. That is the year it appeared in Sander's list of orchid hybrids. The foliage is striking in itself, quite apart from the beauty of the flower.

The actual crossings required great patience and optimism. Many capsules turned out to be empty, and even when a seedling was coaxed to appear, there was the question of how to grow them properly. Dominy's even temperament was important to his success. Some intergeneric crosses failed.

Orchid hybrid *Dossisia dominyi*, a modern re-creation of John Dominy's first successful intergeneric hybrid to flower at the Veitch nursery, circa 1861.
Reproduced by permission of Leon Glicenstein

While frustrating to Dominy, this was useful information for the scientists about the affinity between the various genera.

It would take more than the new hybrid to affect Lindley's robust mental health, but the phenomenon did get him thinking about orchid species and the possibility that plants which had been called species might really be spontaneous ancient hybrids from many generations back.

Lindley's discomfiture was only temporary, for in 1859 he named the plant *Calanthe* × *Dominyi* to honor Dominy. To cap this achievement, Dominy released his cattleya hybrids in 1859. Lindley named them *Cattleya hybrida*. Dominy recognized his debt of gratitude to Harris and named a subsequent hybrid of paphiopedilum *P. harrisianum*.

John Seden

A few other men crossed various orchids, but the next major figure on the scene was Dominy's successor at Veitch's, John Seden (1840–1921). For almost twenty years, Veitch's kept the lead in orchid breeding. In the course of the numerous crosses Seden made, some cultivars emerged identical to the ones Lindley was questioning. Lindley requested Seden to cross *Phalaenopsis amabilis* with *Phalaenopsis rosea*.[4] The resulting hybrid was indistinguishable from a wild form, previously known as a variant of *P. amabilis*. Lindley was on the right track. Heinrich G. Reichenbach, the leading European expert on orchids, weighed into the discussion in 1869. He considered that it would be beneficial to science if the origins of all putative early hybrids could be identified. Darwin's *The Origin of Species* was out now, and it stimulated more research and questions. It had appeared in 1859.

Seden also crossed *Phalaenopsis amabilis* with *Phalaenopsis violacea* in 1886. Only one plant resulted. It was sold to Erastus Corning of Albany, New York. Corning chose to name it *P.* 'Harriettae' for one of his daughters. The flower won a First Class Certificate at the Royal Horticultural Society show in 1887.

Seden came from Essex and also began his work as a gardener very young. In those days, poor boys had very little chance of an education and did not have the luxury of dithering about. Working families could not afford to keep children after the age of about eleven or twelve, in most cases. Gardening was very hard physical work but not dangerous to life or limb.

At first Seden worked in the Chelsea branch of Veitch's but in 1861, Veitch sent him to Exeter to learn from Dominy. He had caught glimpses of fabulous orchids as a child and was a very apt pupil. When he returned to Chelsea, he was put in charge of the entire subtropical department. The first of his hybrids to flower was *Paphiopedilum sedenii,* in 1873. After that, his crosses took on the heroic cast of the classic Victorian mode. He bred more than 150 *Paphiopedilum,* 140 laeliocattleyas, and countless others. Orchids were not his only interest. Seden worked with nepenthe, gloxinia, and begonia and later in his life turned his skill to improving fruit. The grand total of all his crosses was 497.

The Royal Horticultural Society took note of what he did and awarded him the Victoria Medal of Honour in 1897, very soon after the award was set up. Merle Reinikka comments that Seden retired to Worthing, a pleasant seaside resort, in 1905. He died in 1921. One wonders what he did with himself for that last sixteen years after his incredible productivity at work. Presumably he just put it all behind him and spent his time playing lawn bowls. The town is indelibly printed on the public's mind by Oscar Wilde's play *The Importance of Being Earnest.* The great naturalist James Bateman, author of spectacular books about orchids, also lived in Worthing at the end of his life but had died in 1897. Numerous efforts to track down any information about Seden in Worthing were unsuccessful.

Veitch's success attracted a lot of imitators. Specialized orchid nurseries sprang up in England. Among the best known were Sander in St. Albans and Stuart Low in Hackney.

Henry Sander

Henry Frederick Konrad Sander (1847–1920) was born in Germany but settled in England at the age of sixteen.[5] It was clear that with his enormous energy and initiative he would succeed very rapidly. Marrying the daughter of a wealthy man gave him the financial backing that fueled his rise. As the business peaked, he spread himself too thin, with places in St. Albans, Bruges, and then Mamaroneck, New York, fifteen miles from New York City. He had to retrench but made many brilliant contributions to the field.

Sander was the official orchid grower to Queen Victoria. He sat on important committees at the Royal Horticultural Society. Like Veitch, Sander employed his own collectors in the wild. He was able to pry Benedict Roezl away from the Van Houttes and employed him until Roezl died in 1884. There was a time when Sander had more than twenty men collecting for him.

He too won the Victoria Medal of Honour at the Royal Horticultural Society in 1889. Sander introduced *Vanda sanderiana, Aerides, Dendrobium*s, *Cymbidium*s, and *Cattleya*s. He came to be known as the "Orchid King." In one of his frequently astonishing moves, he imported more than one million seedlings of *Phalaenopsis schroederianum*.

Sander's business fell prey to the disastrous changes in upper-class life due to the First World War. The formerly exceedingly rich were no longer so rich, and orchids went into a decline. World War II completed the process. The firm hung on until the 1950s but then had to be dissolved. His grandson David became a physician and grew orchids only as a hobby.

Low Family

The Lows were stalwarts in the exotic plant business in East London. Their grandfather Hugh Low opened his nursery in 1822. He had found exquisite orchids in the Malay Peninsula. The firm lasted until 1970. Hugh Low's great-granddaughter W. Eileen Low died in 1971. She was over ninety and a noted breeder whose favorite flower was the *Cattleya*. Miss Low was perhaps best known for her *Cattleya*s of the "splash petalled" variety. In 1951 she named a *Paphiopedilum* for Winston Churchill. That was the year he became prime minister again after his ignominious rout in the 1945 elections at the end of World War II. This hybrid became the parent of many future *Paphio-pedilum*s because of its vigor and fertility.

Joseph Charlesworth

Joseph Charlesworth started a very successful nursery in Sussex in 1887. He trained George Baldwin, a young Yorkshireman who later worked at Sander's nursery in Mamaroneck and then opened his own firm there.

H. G. Alexander

A very prominent amateur who depended heavily on the skills of his professional hybridizer H. G. Alexander was Sir George Holford of Westonbirt. Alexander (1875–1972) worked for Sir George for twenty-seven years, from

1899 to 1926. Holford was one of the wealthiest men in England and was a favorite at the English court, both of Edward VII and of George V. Late in life he married Susannah Wilson Menzies, mother of the all-powerful British spymaster in World War II, "C" (Sir Stewart Menzies). On Sir Stewart's watch, the dreadful duo of Burgess and McLean defected to Moscow in 1951 after holding very high positions in MI6.

Alexander's name never appeared on any of the Holford hybrids at the orchid shows, but Sir George was actually a generous man and left most of his collection to his breeder. This enabled the latter to set up in a very lucrative business. He continued working for another twenty-seven years. Alexander left a very large number of significant cultivars in several species, such as cattleyas, cypripediums, and cymbidiums. Ernest Hetherington considered *Cymbidium* Alexanderi 'Westonbirt', *Sophrolaeliocattleya* Falcon 'Westonbirt', and *Laeliocattleya* Lustre 'Westonbirt' to be landmark cultivars. Many of them were used as parents for the next generations of new forms.

FRANCE

Orchid hybridizing started in France in the early 1880s. Edward A. White notes that M. Bergmann issued the first hybrid in 1881.[6] In 1882, the firm of Louis Van Houtte in Belgium produced a hybrid *Cypripedium*, but it was not created by Van Houtte himself. He had died in 1876.

UNITED STATES

As in England, orchid breeding also burgeoned in the United States. Several firms resulted from private collectors moving into the commercial sphere. Orchid nurseries appeared across the country, from the East Coast to the West Coast. E. S. Rand had a famous collection as early as 1873, though he did not sell any of his plants. Mr. and Mrs. Sherman Adams were very noted collectors and breeders. Mrs. Adams did the crossings. Another married couple, Judge and Mrs. W. A. Way, split the work in the same way as the Adamses.

The firm of Lager and Hurrell was preeminent between the wars. They took over Sander's somewhat ill-fated premises in New York and moved the business to New Jersey. John E. Lager was a Swede who immigrated to the United States in 1888 after training at the Royal Botanic Gardens at Kew and later at the Jardin des plantes in Paris. For a time he collected orchids in the wild for Henry Sander, but when Sander's business foundered Lager proposed he receive the Summit, New Jersey, branch as compensation. Henry W. Hurrell immigrated from England a few years later. He had been growing orchids since 1872. Hurrell's skill lay in business and finance, extremely important for the new business.

Armacost and Royston led the way in Los Angeles. Under the guidance of the Bracey brothers, they introduced orchids in many more colors than before. Benjamin O. Bracey was a perfectionist, trained in England. One of his mentors was H. G. Alexander at Westonbirt. In 1934, Ernest Hetherington began to work for Armacost and Royston as a young lad. He is now a patriarch of the orchid hybridists. Bracey's legacy contains the very well-known and popular cultivars *Laeliocattleya* 'Bonanza', 'Albery Heinecke', and 'S. J. Bracey'.

A few years before, Dr. Lewis Knudson was teasing out the chemical milieu of the growing orchid seed and identifying how it could be done in the laboratory. He perfected his methods in the 1920s, and although he was a bench scientist at Cornell University, Armacost and Royston enticed him to Southern California to teach the Bracey brothers how to do it. Armacost and Royston became the first company to grow cattleyas en masse in the United States, using Knudson's Solution A and Solution B.[7] They were commercial pioneers.

The solutions allowed them to propagate the seedlings in hitherto unimaginable numbers. Knudson always carried a small flask of his solutions in his pocket filled with young embryos. If anyone wanted to know about his work, he would pull the flask out of his pocket and demonstrate. Knudson built on Noel Bernard's work. Bernard had shown that orchid seed would germinate in a solution of sugar.

In his article, Ernest Hetherington pays tribute to seven men he considers the leaders of the orchid world in the twentieth century.[8] They were not all breeders, but without their work little of the modern development of orchids would have occurred so expeditiously. He lists H. G. Alexander, H. F. K. Sander, Dr. Georges Morel (the creator of tissue culture methods), Lewis Knudson, Benjamin O. Bracey, Dr. Gustave A. Mehlquist (a geneticist from Connecticut), and Gordon Winston Dillon (artist and editor).

World War II was a major watershed in the history of orchid breeding, as it was in so many other spheres, large and small. Until the early 1940s, most of the important action in orchid growing was in Europe, but once there was no fuel to heat greenhouses, no men to work in them, and governments required the nurserymen to grow food for victory, the whole structure of the orchid business collapsed. The lucky ones were able to sell their stock to the Americans. Others just closed up shop. From that time on, the United States had the lead and never looked back until the Taiwanese challenge.

At first, the orchid nurseries relied on new cattleyas, constantly coming in from the wild, to make the lucrative corsages. When Dr. Mehlquist perfected his tissue culture methods in the early 1950s, they could breed millions of plants for themselves and no longer needed to decimate tropical slopes.

For many years, Southern California was at the center of new orchid work, but in the past thirty years, the cost of doing business there has increased and the principal action is now in Asia, particularly Taiwan. There were also excellent orchid breeders in many other parts of the United States, in spite of the dominance of Southern California.

In North Carolina, the Duke estate became a force in orchid breeding. Robert Beene bred *Phalaenopsis* 'Doris', the source of perhaps 95 percent of all succeeding white phalaenopsis.[9] The McLellan brothers had nurseries in Northern California: Rod in South San Francisco and E. W. in Mount Eden. E. W. McLellan had large greenhouses in Colmar and Watsonville. Rod sold his business to the Taiwanese.

The firm of Odoms was in Fort Pierce, Florida. Jerry Lee Fischer ran Orchids Limited in Plymouth, Minnesota. Orchids Orlando was founded by Governor R. H. Gore, a wealthy Florida businessman who became governor of Puerto Rico. The residents of Puerto Rico were very unhappy with the appointment of a Kentucky farmboy as their governor, and his tenure lasted only six months. Oak Hill Gardens was in Dundee, Illinois. Oliver Lines bred orchids in Signal Mountain, Tennessee.

William Rhodehamel founded the specialty nursery Hoosier Orchids in Indianapolis, appointing Leon Glicenstein as manager. Rhodehamel is a member of the prominent Ames family. Oakes Ames was a renowned orchid specialist at Harvard. Edwin Hausermann's company grew orchids in Chicago successfully for seventy years. The Fennells of Homestead, Florida, are on to the third generation in their orchid business.

Hetherington maintained excellent records of every firm with which he dealt and was able to recall individual foibles and odd behavior many years later.[10] There were men like Dr. Herman Sweet, who wrote a book about the genus *Phalaenopsis* in 1981, and his colleague Dr. Jack Fowley, a general practitioner in the area who was devoted to orchid breeding. Sweet and Fowley would argue for hours over the content of this book.

The Vasquez family, Amado and his son George, focused on phalaenopsis at their nursery Zuma Canyon Orchids in Malibu, California. They are still in business in 2014. After World War II, the largest firm of orchid breeders was the wholesale house of Thomas Young. They specialized in corsages and other cut flowers.

Ernest Hetherington kept track of growers in Australia, New Zealand, Brazil, France, and Germany. Vacheron et Lecoufle is perhaps the oldest extant orchid breeding firm in France. Henri Vacheron started the firm in 1886. In 1913, he added Maurice-Etienne Lecoufle, his son-in-law. His grandchildren Michel Vacheron and Maurice Lecoufle took the results of Georges Morel's experiments with cloning in the 1950s and moved orchid growing another step forward.[11]

Armacost and Royston traded with Vacheron et Lecoufle, even as the French company split into several segments. Orquidário Catarinense in Brazil was founded by Roberto Seidel in 1906 and inherited by his son, Alvim Seidel, in his turn. Roberto's great-grandson, Donato Seidel, runs it today with his own son, Donato Jr. A few years ago, the company's name was changed to Alvim Seidel Orquidário Catarinense.

Alvim Seidel died in 2007 after a lifetime spent in making sure that massive deforestation of the Brazilian jungle did not spell the loss of Brazilian orchids. He traveled throughout the country collecting wild orchids and bromeliads. The dynasty was founded by Wenzel Seidel, who had emigrated from Germany to Brazil.

He may have come from the Seidel family of Dresden, but his great-grandson Donato Seidel is not aware of any connection. Donato told me that Wenzel was a crystal polisher who left Hamburg in 1876 at the age of thirty-five. He had grown up in Reichenberg, formerly Sudetenland and now Liberec, the Czech Republic. All the succeeding generations were born in Brazil. By an apparent coincidence, there is another Alvin Seidel, a nurseryman in Victoria, Australia. That family came from Saxony.[12]

The Wichmann firm of Hannover, Germany, was important in German orchid affairs. They are still in business and creating new cultivars. In all, Ernest Hetherington had records on about one hundred firms.

He wrote tirelessly about the people who made the orchid world what it is today in the *Orchid Digest,* which he edited for many years. Besides the men and women noted above, he listed others who have really been forgotten. They include Fred Stewart, San Gabriel, California; Bob Scully Sr. and the Merkel Brothers, Florida; Ferguson Beall, Washington state; Samuel Mosher, Dos Pueblos, California; Rapee Sagarik, Thailand; Helen Adams, Massachusetts; and G. C. K. Dunsterville, Venezuela.

The founder of Rivermont Orchids in Tennessee, Clint McDade, is another one of Hetherington's silent heroes. McDade introduced *Cattleya* 'Bow Bells' in the 1940s. Its derivative 'Bob Betts' set new standards of quality. Don Wimber worked very quietly but effectively to bring order into the orchid family. He worked for Dos Pueblos in Goleta and bred *Cymbidium* Jungfrau 'Dos Pueblos'.

The ascent of the *Cymbidium* took place in California. The climate there, with evening and nighttime drops in temperature, is ideal for the genus. After the war, there was a great demand for this handsome and versatile orchid, but very few plants were available. Stewart Orchids of San Gabriel began to meet the demand, as did Emma Menninger of Arcadia, California. Stewart and Menninger began the miniature line. Mrs. Menninger used the term *miniature* for the first time in relation to *Cymbidium.*

Hetherington lists several men from Hawaii, particularly Dr. Yoneo Sagawa and Dr. Haruyuki Kamemoto, who developed the state into an orchid powerhouse. W. Goodale Moir also worked in Hawaii, producing innumerable crosses of all sorts that were quite outside the conventional wisdom.

The number of hybrids introduced every season soon threatened to overwhelm buyers and sellers alike. The *Gardeners' Chronicle* undertook to add each new hybrid to a list as it appeared. Other books and lists came out, but the most prominent and long-lasting one was started by Frederick K. Sander in 1901 as *The Orchid Guide. Sander's Complete List of Orchid Hybrids* is the modern descendant of his initial efforts.[13] The Royal Horticultural Society took over from Sander's firm as the International Registrar of Orchid Hybrids in 1960.

Modern orchid breeding is now done on factory lines with regimented vials of clonal segments growing in aseptic conditions. Very little is left to chance, so that the high overhead can be offset by maximum yield. Once a new cultivar is bred from seed, its terminal cells are replicated faithfully time after time after time.

PELARGONIUM

Pelargoniums are part of the Geraniaceae, the geranium family. When pelargoniums were first imported into England, they were considered to be in the genus *Geranium*.[1] The name stuck for centuries. There are six horticultural groups of pelargoniums: Angel, Ivy-leaved, Regal or Martha Washington, Scented-leaved, Unique, and Zonal. Another term for the Regal Group is *Pelargonium × hortorum* Bailey, and the Zonal Group is also known as *Pelargonium × domesticum* Bailey. People still call the gorgeous pillar-box red flowers of the zonal pelargoniums "geraniums," and they probably always will, in spite of the "nomenclature police."

The zonals are split into subgroups, according to the shape of the blossom: cactus-flowered, double- and semidouble-flowered, fancy-leaved, formosum hybrids, rosebud, single-flowered, and stellar. These variations reflect the composition of this loose, horticulturally determined group. *Pelargonium zonale* is not the only species in its makeup, and thus the skillful breeder can draw upon a backlog of useful genes depending on what he or she wishes to create.

HISTORY

According to Harry Butterfield, *Pelargonium inquinans, P. hybridum,* and *P. frutetorum* are in its ancestry.[2] *P. inquinans* imparts the scarlet hue to the modern zonals. There is even less certainty about the ancestry of the regals, but *P. cucullatum* (formerly *P. angulosum*) and *P. grandiflorum* are part of it. Another source of the bright red is *P. fulgidum,* an otherwise uninteresting plant in itself.

Butterfield also lists the dates some other species arrived in Europe. Up to 1724, *Pelargonium odoratissimum, P. vitifolium, P. inquinans, P. zonale,* and *P. peltatum* all trickled in. In 1774, *P. cordatum, P. crispum, P. quercifolium,* and *P. radula* were introduced. *P. denticulatum* and *P. echinatum* came in 1789. *P. capitatum,* a fragrant species, came in 1790. First Linnaeus and then L'Héritier named almost all these species. Linnaeus's son named *P. quercifolium.*

Pelargoniums came from the Cape of Good Hope in the Dutch colony in South Africa, and the first place they reached in Europe was Leiden in the Netherlands. The Dutch East India Company's physician of that epoch, Dr. Paul Hermann, had collected plants in Africa and the Far East before becoming the director of the Leiden Botanic Garden in 1679. He held that post until his death in 1695.

Hermann was very farseeing. He had heated greenhouses built to care for the many exotic and tender species arriving, and he expanded the collection to about three thousand species. In 1689 Hermann wrote *Paradisi Batavi Prodromus.*[3] The book mentions the initial pelargonium, now called *P. grossularioides,* found on Table Mountain. At that time, the Italian botanist Ferrari called the flowers "Donna Bella," though scholars in northern Europe did not know that.

Hermann was gifted and versatile and drew the plants himself. His widow had these drawings engraved for a posthumous publication. William Sherard edited it, and they dedicated the book to Bishop Compton. Sir Hans Sloane recommended the book in England. Eventually Sir Joseph Banks bought the original drawings, and they are now in the British Museum, Natural History Division—just one more instance of Sir Joseph's amazing range of interests.

In 1632, John Tradescant the Elder grew a small inconspicuous plant, *Pelargonium triste,* in his garden at Lambeth. He had bought it from M. René Morin in Paris some years before and understood that the flower came from India. Morin and his brother were nurserymen. It is an oddity in the pelargonium world with its dull coloring, a subterranean habit, and nocturnal perfume; it is grown purely for its historical role. No one is certain about how this plant reached Paris so early in the seventeenth century, but to reach India in those days, one had to round the Cape. *P. triste* could have been collected there.

The showier flowers reached England around 1690. With the death of James II in 1688, the year of the English Revolution, his niece Mary, with her husband, William of Orange, took over the throne jointly. They brought the Dutch interest in gardens with them, and William appointed his chief counsellor, Hans (Willem) William Bentinck (1649–1709), to be the superintendent of gardens.

Bentinck was, of course, far too grand to do anything so menial himself, but he subcontracted the tasks to the royal gardener George London, later owner of the Brompton Nursery. Pelargoniums were flowing in from Leiden, and George London distributed them as he went around the countryside seeing to large aristocratic estates and gardens. Bentinck was ennobled as the Earl of Portland, and his son became the duke. In the next generation, one of the Portland girls married a Cavendish, and behold, one has the Cavendish-Bentincks, later dukes of Devonshire.

Bentinck was not a particularly likeable person. He refused to learn English and would speak only French. The English nobility were very suspicious of him and his motives, believing that he was a spy.

At the time, *Geranium (or Pelargonium) cucullatum* was listed at Kew. The Dutch botanist and nurseryman Jan Monickx' catalogue listed *P. zonale*. He published a renowned atlas between 1689 and 1690. Caspar Commelin (1668–1731) was another Dutch botanist. He was the nephew of Jan Commelin, the curator of the Hortus Botanicus in Amsterdam. Caspar recorded eight species of pelargonium. *P. peltatum* and *P. lobatum* were the most important. Caspar Commelin completed some of the books left by his late uncle. Jan Commelin followed John Ray's system of classification.

Dr. John Dillenius, curator of James Sherard's garden at Eltham, grew *P. zonale* in 1732 and listed it in his *Hortus Elthamensis*. Within forty years, the numbers of available species increased. Philip Miller had seven in the first edition of his dictionary. By 1768 there were forty-eight. The first pelargonium seeds reached America in 1760. They were sent to John Bartram.

In 1787, the French botanist Charles L'Héritier de Brutelle (1746–1800) proposed splitting the pelargoniums from the geraniums. He worked for some years in London using Sir Joseph Banks's library and benefiting from his goodwill. Other experts, such as Carl Thunberg and H. C. Andrews, did not agree with his suggestion. L'Héritier was murdered in 1800 but probably not because of his radical taxonomic views. Andrews was not a professional botanist but published so many botanical works that he became expert himself.

During this period, Francis Masson discovered more than fifty species of pelargonium at the Cape of Good Hope and sent them back to Sir Joseph Banks. Now English gardeners had their own sources and did not have to depend on the Dutch so much. In spite of that, very few of these species were exploited for hybridization. It is worthwhile noting, as Liberty Hyde Bailey pointed out, that the pelargonium craze of the early 1800s encompassed only greenhouse and show plants, not bedding ones.[4]

ENGLISH BREEDERS

Robert Sweet

Until the days of Robert Sweet, all hybrids were the result of spontaneous crossing between the various species. Sweet (1783–1835) was among the very first to pollinate pelargoniums deliberately. He was a Devonshire man, trained in propagation by David Stewart and polished by working for John Julius Angerstein at Blackheath. From there he became foreman at James Colvill's successful nursery in London. Sweet wrote *Geraniaceae* between 1820 and 1830, ending up with five volumes.[5]

The magisterial horticultural scholar John C. Loudon described Sweet's work as hybridization "by manipulation." Sweet exploited Colvill's unrivaled collection of pelargoniums. All of these were the single-blossomed type. There were no double blossoms yet. As Sweet developed his hybrids, he gave them Latin names and listed them in his book.

Unfortunately, he made some powerful enemies and one of them, probably William Aiton ("Old Jock"), the chief at Kew, got his own back in a very nasty way. Someone hid identifiable stolen flowers in Sweet's workshop at Colvill's. As a result, Sweet was dragged to the Old Bailey for a criminal trial.[6]

He was lucky that several highly placed and important people spoke for him. He was acquitted and not sentenced to transportation, but the effect on his life and reputation was never erased. He died in poverty, like so many other pioneers in this field, barely over fifty years old.

Richard Hoare

Sweet had another resource for his work, Richard Colt Hoare's collection. Hoare (1758–1838) owned Stourhead, the great estate in Wiltshire. He was principally interested in the ancient British tombs all over his estate but also collected pelargoniums en masse and had his own classification system.

According to Hoare there were five classes, outlined in his monograph on the subject. He wanted to breed new varieties and indicated his thinking by his ideas on classification. He preferred to use *Pelargonium fulgidum* for its color rather than *P. inquinans,* even though he was fully aware of inquinans' color.

Hoare found one particularly useful seedling from his fulgidum crosses and called it *Pelargonium ignescens.* It had scarlet and black in its petals and was used as a parent for many more hybrids. There were large numbers of named offspring and maybe as many unnamed ones too. This was the period in which breeders recognized that the pelargonium could survive in the open and began working on bedding types.

Wilkinson notes that *Pelargonium* 'General Tom Thumb' was considered to be the best bedding plant in its day.[7] By 1844, *P.* 'Golden Chain' was one of the earliest variegated-leaved forms used in bedding. All this set the scene for the Victorian delight in "carpet bedding," something that was not feasible without the right kind of flowers to plant.

FRENCH BREEDERS

In 1860, Henri Lecoq noticed a double-blossomed sport in his garden in Clermont-Ferrand. He was astute enough to recognize its potential and planted the new forms. A year later, Louis Van Houtte in Ghent obtained one of these varieties, as did other nurserymen, and more double flowers emerged.

Victor Lemoine

In 1863, Victor Lemoine led the way in transforming the pelargonium into a brilliant and proud bedding plant of arresting hues. He used some of the new pollen on a pink zonal, *Pelargonium* 'Beauté de Suresnes', and created *P.* 'Gloire de Nancy'. One Lemoine hybrid that remains in commerce is *P.* 'Paul Crampel', a rich red flower.

Jean Sisley

Another French breeder, Jean Sisley, created the first double white pelargonium in 1872. He crossed a single white with a double red, and the white was

The pelargonium hybrid *Pelargonium* 'Marquis de Montmort', bred before 1901 by the French nurseryman Paul Bruant.
Reproduced by permission of Donn Reiners

dominant. By 1874, these new flowers were on sale in California, one more example of how up-to-date the California nurserymen were. James Hutchison in Oakland offered them at one dollar each. The great New York houses, such as James Vick of Rochester, also obtained these varieties very early.

USES OF THE PELARGONIUM

Among gardening snobs (see James Bartholomew's hilarious *Yew and Non-Yew: Gardening for Horticultural Climbers* for the relevant social background), the zonal pelargonium is absolutely verboten.[8] To a certain set, it has become a gardening cliché, a trite municipal decoration that only the great unwashed could possibly enjoy.

Unfortunately for these self-appointed guardians of the public taste, many millions of zonal pelargoniums are sold each year. In the USDA horticultural census of 2000, 3,987,000 flats of seedlings were sold nationwide.[9] They provide a cheerful accompaniment to civic activities and are the pride of many a small suburban garden. The bright scarlet blossom typifies the pomp and circumstance of military dress uniforms, appropriate for band concerts in parks and plazas. Zonal pelargoniums also decorate window boxes very effectively, enlivening the dull tones of masonry and concrete. There is a reason things become a cliché.

In cold climates, zonal pelargoniums behave as annuals and die back unless they are protected in a greenhouse, but in warmer places they are perennial, indicating their natural habitat in the western section of the Cape of Good Hope, South Africa. Some species are exceptionally well adapted to the harsh condition of the Cape's desert areas, growing on very inhospitable looking dry scree.

The large number of species and the relative ease with which someone of even modest means can breed pelargonium, unlike trees and large shrubs, has meant that there are dozens, maybe hundreds, of enthusiastic amateur breeders, each of whom has made a contribution to the improvement and dissemination of the genus. Anyone going into this field nowadays needs to select a variety and stick with it rather than cast around all over the place.

IMPROVING THE PELARGONIUM

Peter Grieve

Gorer credits Peter Grieve (1812–1895), gardener first to the Earl of Lanesborough and later to Edward Richard Bengon at Culford Hall in Bury St. Edmunds, with creating the series known as "Tricolors."[10] Grieve introduced varieties with ornamental and variegated leaves to great effect. He knew that plants with completely white flowers had been around since about 1860. He published a book on this subject, *A History of Variegated Ornamental Zonal Pelargoniums,* in 1868. The book became a classic and was reissued by the British Geranium and Pelargonium Society in 1977.

Even in the 1860s, the parentage of many pelargonium hybrids was murky. Grieve first used white-margined and gold-margined varieties in 1855. He recorded the parents of some of his varieties but not all of them. Probably this was to keep ahead of the competition.

Fʀᴇɴᴄʜ, German, English, American, Australian, and South African breeders have all made important contributions and continue to do so in the present. In Germany, Gerhard Fischer started his business in 1959, near Koblenz. He focused on disease resistance and in about fifteen years released *Pelargonium* 'Grand Prix', 'Tango', 'Rio', and 'Schöne Helena'. Ingeborg Schumann did much of Fischer's hybridizing.

The American firm Oglevee solved the problem of growing pelargonium on a commercial scale free of disease. David Lemon worked with Oglevee until the business was sold to Ecke, of poinsettia fame.

Wilhelm Elsner

Wilhelm Elsner (b. 1921) worked on zonals in Dresden during the period of East German isolation. His plants became better known once Germany was reunified. These cultivars were easier to produce commercially and bloomed their heads off for long periods of time. Both Oglevee and Lemon defied the political difficulties and made sure Elsner's cultivars were known in the West.

The original subtitle of this book was "the work of forgotten flower breeders." The Elsners have not been forgotten, but they were in an inaccessible place for many years and their work was difficult to assess in the English-speaking world. Thus, outside the very narrow field of pelargonium professionals and fanciers, most of the public have not heard of Elsner.

The firm was founded in 1889 in Dresden by the current Wilhelm Elsner's grandfather. By 1923 they had decided to concentrate on pelargoniums, although they still grew anthuriums and chrysanthemums in large quantities. They issued their first catalogue in 1926. In 1964 they trademarked the acronym "PAC" to reflect their activities.

From the start, the company was forward thinking. They built greenhouses and a laboratory very early. Over the next decades, they added several more state-of-the-art laboratories. Heat treatment to prevent *Xanthomonas* was one technique they incorporated; meristem culture was another. The meristem is the actively growing tip of the plant. Very small sections of this structure can form many new plants asexually.

Wilhelm Elsner has continued to produce exceptional hybrids of pelargonium.

Reproduced by permission of Andrea Ludwig, Wilhelm Elsner's daughter

An announcement in an Elsner catalogue, 1990. Wilhelm Elsner reestablished his old family business after the reunification of Germany.

Reproduced by permission of Andrea Ludwig, Wilhelm Elsner's daughter

Pelargonium cultivars growing in the Elsner PAC greenhouses.
Reproduced by permission of Andrea Ludwig, Wilhelm Elsner's daughter

The Communist government of East Germany confiscated the Elsners' business in 1972, keeping Wilhelm on as manager. This is similar to the history of the Haages in Erfurt. Elsner's PAC was folded into a giant state enterprise, or *kombinat*. The government kept all his staff on, but he could no longer make any important decisions himself, and of course the government also took at least of half of his earnings. Elsner's integrity kept him working at maximum intensity, and the firm was rewarded with various honors within the Eastern bloc's closed system.

In 1990, after the reunification of Germany, the business was restored to them. When communism failed and he received his business back again in 1990, Elsner inserted an advertisement into *Der Deutsche Gartenbau,* celebrating the fact that the firm was once again private. Today Elsner has licenses and contracts all over the world and is a dominant player internationally.

Elsner has written an autobiography and has given many talks about his work and the influence of his father.[11] He tells of his father having to fight in the First World War and that he had to do the same thing in the Second World War. The younger Wilhelm was sent to Greece in one campaign and then to North Africa in 1943. There he was taken prisoner and ended up in a camp in Oklahoma until the war ended. In his typically thorough manner, he includes a floor plan of the prisoner-of-war camp in Tonkawa, Oklahoma, in his book.

During the dark years of the Communist regime, he occupied himself with breeding experiments on old and rare cultivars. Some of them had been bred by Ted Both in Australia using *Pelargonium staphysagrioides* Sweet and *P.* × *hortorum* L.H. Bailey. Elsner crossed these with many diploid PAC F1 hybrid zonals.

He wanted to develop robust varieties for vegetative reproduction that would be commercially valuable but not affect the existing market for zonals. After numerous vicissitudes, these bore fruit once he had control again. Zonals with "faces" and the PAC Fireworks Series are some of the results.

More recently, he has suggested additional goals. It might be nice to have popular ornamental varieties with scented leaves. Creating plants with yellow or blue flowers are constant grails. Clifford Blackman in Geelong, Australia, has gone further than anyone else in creating a yellow pelargonium.[12] Another crucial breakthrough would be inbred bacterial resistance. Elsner had very clear ideas of what he wanted to accomplish, truly "visions of loveliness."

Ernest Walters

Ernest Walters (1911–1990) is a different story. He worked in the English Midlands, an industrial relations officer in engineering by day, a pelargonium enthusiast by night. He was the quintessential amateur. His daughter told me he had wide-ranging intellectual interests and wrote poetry on occasion.

Walters was devoted to the regal type and made several unusual crosses, using *Pelargonium crispum* and *P. quercifolium,* among others. It all started in 1949 when Walters bought a couple of neglected and bedraggled little pelargoniums at a local nursery, a *P.* 'Carisbrooke' and a 'Prince William'. Very much like George Russell with the vase of sad-looking lupins in his employer's kitchen, this signaled the beginning of his life's work.

Walters had clear aims: to extend the flowering season, to create more-vigorous growth, and to introduce a tough race of plants able to withstand incompetent or inexperienced handling. The inflorescence also needed improvement. Walters added some well-known hybrids as a basis for his new varieties: *Pelargonium* 'Lady Mary Fox' (with a crimson flower) and *P.* 'Mrs J. Douglas' (maroon). These flower very late in the year, in the fall and winter.

After thirty years of work, Walters introduced three main groups of hybrids: Tudor Regals, Royal Regals, and Romany Regals. His personal generic term for them was "domino flowers." Some of them flowered perpetually, and others would flower for seven or eight months of the year. The strong stem held the bloom firmly above the leaves. They had a very wide range of color and form the basis of many modern widely grown varieties.

Walters believed that the ability to flower so continuously was related to day length. His accomplishment was to have bred day-neutral varieties. This was an advantage for the trade. Pelargoniums of this type could be sold at any time of the year and were not limited to the spring. All of them were much shorter and more compact than previous varieties, another advantage. The dissemination of these plants owed a lot to Bob Oglevee, who bought the intellectual property rights and moved the operation to the United States. It was too late for Walters. He had died before this happened.

Walters was also interested in creating pelargoniums with a scented leaf and a large, round domino-shaped blossom. This was set up by a three-way cross of *Pelargonium* × *domesticum* × *P. crispum* × *P. quercifolium*. Before the heyday of double-blossomed pelargoniums, English florists in the early nineteenth century had sought to breed an almost completely circular-faced flower, with overlapping petals, not unlike a pansy. It seems a rather repugnant idea now.

Continental breeders had different ideas, preferring the flower to have two lips and keep the petals distinct. It is very gratifying to revive the name of a truly outstanding flower breeder. Very few people have heard of Walters in spite of his sterling contributions to the development of the Regal line.

※

WOMEN play a large role in the pelargonium world. Hazel Key in England runs the Fibrex Nursery and has devoted her career to the pelargonium. Faye Brawner in the United States remains active. She has bred many zonal cultivars, including Stellar varieties. Wilhelm Elsner's daughter Andrea Ludwig now manages her father's business in Dresden with her sister.

PEONY

Like so many other flowers considered in this book, most of the dazzling ornamental peonies came from the Far East. There is only one species endemic to North America, *Paeonia brownii.* Many other temperate species are known, with *P. officinalis* native to southern Europe and a few species native to the Caucasus region, but most of the commonly grown ornamental forms are descended from *P. albiflora* Pall. (syn. *P. lactiflora* Pall.), the Chinese peony. Despite its name, meaning a "white flower," varieties of *P. albiflora* now come in numerous colors.

The European form, *Paeonia officinalis,* has been known and appreciated for centuries. The name *peony* stems from the Greek deity Paeon, a student of the god Aesculapius (or Asclepius), healer and physician. Paeon used a plant he received from Apollo's mother, Leto, to cure Hercules of a bad wound. His success made Aesculapius very jealous. Pluto saved Paeon from Aesculapius's wrath by changing him into this very plant, now to be known as *Paeonia.*

Peonies are very long lived once established and have very few requirements. One of those is a cold enough winter for chilling to occur. They do not do very well in warmer climates, where the winters are too mild for them.

HISTORY

In China and Japan, peonies have been cherished and cultivated for hundreds of years. Robert Fortune sent forty varieties of tree peony, or "moutan," from China to England in 1846. They created a minor sensation. *Paeonia suffruticosa* Andrews, the moutan, was said to be more popular than the herbaceous peony in China, but both are recorded very far back in history. Fortune also saw specimens of the plant in the wild and noted the skillful way in which the Shanghai gardeners took care of their plants.

In 1908, J. Eliot Coit wrote an article in the Cornell University College of Agriculture's *Bulletin* about the ancient history of the peony.[1] He quoted from known sinologists and described how the "moutan" was called the "King of Flowers" because its beauty lit up a garden and *Paeonia albiflora* held second place, as the "King's Minister." Coit referred to ancient Chinese authorities, Hung King, 536 CE, and Soo King, 656 CE.

Peony 'Festiva Maxima'. Auguste Miellez created this cultivar in 1851.
Reproduced by permission of www.songsparrow.com (photographer, Roy Klehm)

Richard Gorer, a very careful scholar, found even earlier references to "moutan," or the tree peony.[2] The poet Hsieh Kang-Lo talked of it in 265 CE. Gorer also quoted from a treatise by Ouyang Hsiu written in the eleventh century. This text contains references to more than ninety varieties known to be in cultivation. It clearly describes budding techniques.

The Chinese sage Gow Yang Sew prepared a genealogical register of the moutan, recording the characteristics of the plants as they grew from seed, starting in 724 CE. This was also the period in which the plants were exported to Japan. The name there became "botan." Scholarly work of this order languished until Joseph Needham undertook his landmark studies of the Chinese literature in the mid-twentieth century.

No doubt Liberty Hyde Bailey was the inspiration for Coit. Just a few years before, Emile Vasilievich Bretschneider was doing much the same sort of research in Beijing's old Russian Embassy.[3] He found ancient Chinese documents and work by Russian sinologists, but his principal contribution was to record the extraordinary discoveries of European botanists in the China he inhabited. Bretschneider listed every peony found there.

Paeonia officinalis was also widely distributed across China, especially the northern sector. Both herbaceous and tree peonies were exported to Japan in the eighth century CE. Philipp von Siebold sent peonies from Japan after his short sojourns there. Chinese peonies were taken to France by the middle of the nineteenth century, and many breeders, particularly amateurs, seized upon them eagerly. This work laid the foundations of the plant's later popularity.

Development of the European peony began early in England. Even in late medieval times, peonies were considered to be part of an aristocratic garden. Their culinary and medicinal properties were still important at the time. European peonies make their appearance in Gerard's and Parkinson's herbals. Philip Miller grew them at the Chelsea Physic Garden.

The Chinese peony arrived in England in time for the profound movement toward floral "improvement" in the early and mid-nineteenth century. Bretschneider indicates that there were numerous references to the "moutan" in the English botanical literature at the turn of the nineteenth century. Sir Joseph Banks had given a specimen to Kew in 1787. The secretary of the Horticultural Society of London, later the Royal Horticultural Society, Joseph Sabine, reported on seven double herbaceous peonies in 1816, including *Paeonia edulis.*

John Potts sent a very fine specimen of *Paeonia albiflora* in 1822. It was named after him, *P. pottsii.* John Reeves was the British East India Company's resident superintendent of their tea business in Canton and a passionate gardener. He too was honored with a "reevesii" type.[4] These names reflect horticultural usage, not botanical terminology. All the numerous variations reported were selections of naturally occurring traits rather than true, intentional hybridization.

An important event in the history of the peony was Andre Donckelaar's rescuing one of Philipp von Siebold's specimens from the docks at Antwerp during a brief period of war. Donckelaar (1788–1858) was the director of the Botanical Garden in Brussels. In 1838, he introduced *Paeonia* 'Festiva'.

Mrs. Harding notes that Loddiges advertised the first large collection of named varieties in 1845.[5] Another nurseryman, Salter, offered more varieties and sold them amazingly quickly. John Salter was an English nurseryman who decided that land was cheaper and weather conditions better in France and opened a nursery in Versailles. Salter began with a strong interest in pansies and peonies. His final days were devoted to the chrysanthemum. It was to grow these plants more effectively that he moved to France.

Salter started with *Paeonia grandiflora nivea plena,* developed by Nicolas Lémon in France in 1824, and *P. lutea plenissima,* developed by the talented amateur Monsieur Buyck in Belgium in 1842.[6] There was a great deal of reciprocal trade between English and Continental nurserymen and seedsmen across the Channel at the time.

The names of two prominent English nurserymen, James Kelway of Somersetshire and Peter Barr in London, are associated with the rise of the peony's popularity, but the French growers had set that process in motion. Receiving a first-class certificate at the Royal Horticultural Society's show in 1885 for the first time was a sign that the peony had arrived in the United Kingdom. The Kelway Nursery still exists.

Intentional crossing of peony species began almost simultaneously in England and France. Selection had produced many elegant varieties with differing petal structure and color. Very few now remember Monsieur Lémon in Paris, but his *Paeonia* 'Edulis Superba', introduced in 1824, is still on the market today.

FRANCE

Lémon Family

Nicolas Lémon (1787–1837) grew peonies from seed very early. Starting in 1818, Lémon did something very unusual for his time.[7] He saved pollen from *Paeonia chinensis* for more than two weeks until his *P. albiflora* came into flower. He then pollinated the *P. albiflora* with the saved pollen.

He had to wait eight years for the first seedlings to flower. In 1826 that first peony yielded precisely two seed capsules. The flowers from one of them bloomed white, the other pink. The white one became known as *Paeonia* 'Edulis Superba'.

James Boyd credits Lémon with growing fifteen varieties between 1824 and 1830. Lémon gave them specific names, but they were not truly separate species. In light of the above information about the first cultivars, the dates should probably be amended to read 1826 and 1830. The names of the species have changed since his time. Lémon thought he was using two species, *Paeonia chinensis* and *P. albiflora*, but today these are both considered to be forms of *P. lactiflora*.

Nicolas Lémon was orphaned at the age of five and was brought up by his uncle, a gardener at the Castle de la Malgrange near Nancy. At thirteen, he went to work as a gardener for General Gouvion-St. Cyr. He opened his own business in Belleville near the Porte St. Denis in Paris in 1815 and remained there for twenty years, until he had serious personal and financial reverses. Lémon worked successfully with iris, pelargonium, phlox, and other plants during this period. One of his triumphs was the cultivation of the pineapple, *Ananas comosus* L. Merr. (It was known as *Ananassa sativa* in his day).

When Nicolas Lémon died, his son Jean-Nicolas was only seventeen years old. The boy managed to continue the business with the help of one of his late father's close friends, Henri Jacques. Jacques was a very distinguished horticulturist and had extensive collections of his own. For a long time, almost nothing was known about this son beyond his name. In the 1990s, Clarence Mahan worked with a French genealogist and found that Jean-Nicolas Lémon (1817–1895) had a most successful career himself. One reason for the confusion was that the public tended to conflate the son and the father into one person.

Jean-Nicolas Lémon continued to breed new peonies, but he had the clever idea of giving each new variety an accessible name in French, rather than the more forbidding Latinate version. It was a lot easier to buy a peony named 'Gabrielle' or 'Marguerite' than *Paeonia* 'Edulis Superba'. Jean-Nicolas made another excellent move. He married Modeste Guérin's daughter.

Modeste Guérin

Modeste Guérin worked for more than thirty years, from 1835 to 1866, improving the peony. Even before a reliable yellow species, *Paeonia wittmanniana*, appeared, three of Guérin's varieties had a distinct yellow tinge: *P. grandiflora* 'Lutescens', 'Reine de France', and 'Triomphe de Paris'. He also introduced a deep-red peony based on *P. pottsii*.

Lemoine Family

More than a dozen able French breeders contributed to the development of the peony, but in this, as in so many other plants, some of the most effective progress was made by the Lemoine family. Striking introductions at the turn of the twentieth century came from Emile Lemoine, Victor Lemoine's son: *Paeonia* 'La Fiancée', 'Madame Emile Lemoine', 'Sarah Bernhardt', and many others.

EUROPEAN CONTRIBUTIONS

Some idea of the relative involvement of French and other breeders during the nineteenth century can be seen in the accompanying table. The Dutch nursery Felix & Dijkhuis, known principally for azaleas, also offered a vast array of peonies, about two hundred varieties in all. Each item lists the breeder and the date and a brief description of the cultivar's color and habit. This makes the catalogue extremely useful for at least some superficial comparisons.

The table is only a digest of the peonies in one catalogue and thus cannot be said to be fully representative, but it is suggestive. Breeders operated over certain epochs and, as in the case of Jacques Calot, often sold their businesses to another generation of breeders. Felix Crousse (1840–1925), for example, bought the Calot nursery. Auguste Dessert learned about peonies from his grandfather, Etienne Méchin (1815–1895). When his grandfather died, Dessert took over the business in Chenonceaux. Subsequent owners, the Doriat family, moved the business to Lapalisse, near Vichy. In 1896, Dessert showed three new tree peonies at the Société Nationale d'Horticulture de France to wide acclaim: *Paeonia* 'Souvenir d'Etienne Méchin', 'Paul Transon', and 'Edouard André'.

Another French family enterprise based on the peony has continued to the present day. Fleury Jean-Baptiste Gabriel Ruitton (1813–1893) was the first nurseryman to offer herbaceous peonies, in Caluire, near Lyon. Benoît Rivière (1865–1913) married Fleury's daughter and, working with his wife's brother, François, developed the nursery extensively. He introduced tree peonies very successfully. In the end he took over the business, and it became known as Rivière's. They offered 360 varieties of herbaceous peony and 240 types of tree peony in 1908.

Benoît Rivière died at the age of forty-eight, when his son, Antoine, was only eleven years old. Madame (Ruitton) Rivière kept things going until her son was old enough to take over, and now the grandson, Michel, manages the nursery for the family. His son, Jean-Luc, is in charge of research and breeding. The firm no longer sells any other type of plant.

In addition to the very busy breeders noted in the table, there was a handful of people who were represented by only a few cultivars. Very little can be deduced from this. John Richardson of Massachusetts was an enthusiastic amateur working on a very small scale, and it is quite surprising to see any of his introductions in a European catalogue. H. A. Terry in Iowa had a larger operation.

There was also a modest number of cultivars without attribution or dates. The analysis tends to corroborate Mrs. Harding's opinions.

Table 1.

The number of cultivars of peonies introduced by active breeders in Europe, 1820–1910

Name	Dates of activity	No. of cultivars	Notes
Jacques Calot	1856–1885	33	
Modeste Guérin	1840–1863	32	
Félix Crousse	1879–1897	27	
Auguste Dessert	1888–1911	22	Worked with Etienne Méchin part of the time
Victor Lemoine	1894–1911	7	Probably incomplete; Emile Lemoine also bred these flowers
Auguste Miellez	1850–1858	?	Victor Lemoine studied with Miellez
Nicolas Lémon	1824–1853	5	

Source: Felix & Dijkhuis, Boskoop, the Netherlands, 1923 catalogue

AMERICA

The European peony was first recorded to have reached America in 1806, but it may have come earlier. Bernard M'Mahon and the Bartrams noted it in the various lists they compiled. The highly modified forms began arriving very actively after about 1850. Within a few years, the numbers outstripped any attempt to organize the varieties reliably.

The American Peony Society was formed in 1903 to sort things out and bring order to the chaos that prevailed. Names were applied at random and ceased to mean anything. Straightening this out was important not only scientifically but also to restore confidence in the breeders and nurserymen. There was rampant dishonesty, with the purchaser believing he was getting something valuable only to find that was not the case.

One of the first steps the new society took was to request Auguste Dessert to supply them with a list of all peonies known to have been bred by French and Belgian horticulturists. It was a very serious task, and he acquitted himself well. In *Herbaceous Chinese Peonies.* he documented 549 varieties.[8] Dessert addressed this list to Mr. C. W. Ward, President of the American Peony Society, September 3, 1903. (Ward was a horticultural polymath. For many years, he managed the Cottage Gardens Nursery in Queens, New York, and he was an expert on the carnation.)

The society established an early link with the horticulture department at the Cornell Experiment Station to study all the available types of peony. Acting jointly, the experimental station and the new society planted as many varieties of peony as they could.

Alice Harding mentions many of the "peony pioneers" in the United States who were active during her lifetime, from the end of the nineteenth century to the early years of the twentieth century. H. A. Terry of Iowa started out by buying peonies from William Prince of the Linnaean Gardens in Long Island, New York, in the 1860s and growing the thousands of seedlings that resulted. Prince advertised forty varieties of peony as early as 1829.

Terry's process of selection was draconian. He said that not more than five in a thousand were any use at all. He persevered and ultimately sold his collection for what was then a large sum of money, $2,500.

Two gardeners in Massachusetts, John Richardson and George Hollis, also enriched the supply of elegant plants. Neither of these men operated on Terry's scale, but their small space did not preclude them from refining the forms.

The well-known nurserymen Ellwanger and Barry in Rochester, New York, worked with the peony very effectively. Denise Adams lists the many significant varieties and hybrids the firm introduced: *Paeonia* 'Albert Crousse',

'Felix Crousse', 'Baroness Schroder', and 'Monsieur Jules Elie' are among the ones still in circulation.[9] Ellwanger and Barry's nursery was very important not only in Rochester but also in the development of California horticulture.

In 1928, the American Peony Society produced its *Manual,* a powerful compilation of everything to do with the peony, including useful biographical sketches of its earlier luminaries. James Boyd edited the initial volume. A supplement was edited and compiled by A. P. Saunders, in 1933.

Saunders also contributed a valuable bibliography to the 1928 edition, based on such sources as *Index Kewensis* and not just standard horticultural texts. He showed remarkable erudition and open-mindedness in listing these references. His timeline for specialized articles about the peony began in 1806. Saunders considered Alfred Rehder's recent *Manual of Cultivated Trees and Shrubs* to be a sound source for information on the shrubby species.[10]

SWEET PEA

The modern sweet pea story began in Sicily in the late 1690s. The monastery gardener at Misilmeri, Francisco Cupani, sent a specimen of sweet peas to Caspar Commelin, a botanist in the Netherlands, and possibly to Roger Uvedale in England. That original plant was small with dark blue and purple hooded flowers and was intensely fragrant. Both the recipients recorded the gift, and in London a specimen was passed along to Leonard Plukenet, Queen Mary's physician.

Philip Miller also grew it at the Chelsea Physic Garden. Thirty years later, he commented in his *Dictionary* that another kind had become available, a "pale red" one. Little is known about this archaic phase, whether the new varieties were English sports or had also come from Sicily. It is doubtful whether anyone had been breeding them intentionally.

The cultivated sweet pea, *Lathyrus odoratus* L., is native to the Mediterranean region. This could be part of the reason it has been so successful in California with its Mediterranean climate. Whether the specimen sent to London was wild or cultivated is not known, but it was new to Cupani. In 1737, 'Painted Lady' was offered for sale by Mason's, a seedsman in Fleet

Street. It was pink and white and very fragrant. Could this have been Miller's "pale red"?

The modern word *pink* used to describe the familiar color arose because the ruffled, deckle-edged ("pinked") flowers of carnations were so frequently pink in color and of course long known as "pinks." The original meaning lies in the anatomy of the petals.

BREEDING SWEET PEAS

After about 150 years of obscurity in which the two known varieties of sweet pea in England expanded slowly to four and later five, there was a sudden burst of glory in the late 1870s. It was fueled by the award of a first-class certificate for *Lathyrus* 'Invincible Scarlet' at a Royal Horticultural Society show in 1865 (see discussion in chapter 3).

At about the same time as James Carter, Thomas Laxton, who had established a fine reputation for breeding apples and edible peas, started to work on sweet peas. His cultivars *Lathyrus* 'Etna', 'Madame Carnot', and 'Princess May' were all extremely successful. People sat up and took notice.

Almost all the plants grown during the years that followed were varieties and cultivars of *Lathryus odoratus* L. This rather modest plant is an unlikely candidate for fantasy and furor, but that is what happened for about forty years, between about 1880 and 1920. After that, a large number of the flowers were still grown for sale but the market had shifted.

Excellent work still goes on in breeding new types of sweet pea, constantly making them easier to cultivate, better for small gardens, resistant to disease, and with more and more attractive blossoms. They are no longer as dominant in horticulture as they used to be, but there is always the search for a pure yellow flower, a haunting goal like the blue rose.

Some nurseries now make a feature of stocking the older varieties, from during or just after the First World War. In the English-speaking countries, sweet pea societies proliferated, always a stimulus to improvement. The mania was diffused very widely through society. At one English wedding, for example, the bride and her seven attendants all carried bouquets of sweet peas. The bride's bouquet was pure white, the bridesmaids' pale pink.

Almost everything that can be thought of has been done to the sweet pea. The plant has been dwarfed; it has been made taller. The flowers have been enlarged, the tendrils have been removed by genetic manipulation, and a leafless variety has been bred. Many more blossoms are carried on each stem. The hood has gone. The plant's period of bloom has been extended, responding to the wide range of climate within the United States, and it now can tolerate greater extremes of heat and cold that were never possible before.

There is always a search for more wild species to improve the genetic profile, and crosses between the usual *Lathyrus odoratus* and unusual species such as *L. nervosus* have been attempted without success. Specialists such as Keith Hammett prospect around the Mediterranean for more wild species to improve the germplasm. In the 1970s, he found the key wild plant in Sicily that is now known as the 'Original' or 'Cupani's Original'.[1] Once the process started, it has never ceased.

The outpouring of enthusiasm for sweet peas takes me back to a question I cannot answer. What was happening in the mind of the person who initiated the craze?

Henry Eckford

Not many people can transform the world in which they live, but Henry Eckford was one of them. He changed the concept of what a sweet pea should be and how it should look. Henry Eckford (1823–1905) took up breeding sweet peas in 1870 after a successful career breeding pelargonium, verbena, and dahlia for the Earl of Radnor. Eckford was a professional Scottish gardener from Midlothian. Perhaps he saw the wave of enthusiasm as a way to improve his career, but any abstract love of beauty had to be tempered by the necessity of earning a living.

Another employer, a Dr. Sankey, lured him away from the earl and wanted Eckford to breed new flowers for him, too. Sankey's estate was in Shropshire. Soon after moving south, Eckford's wife died, leaving him a widower with seven young children. Fortunately he was able to remarry and later opened his own nursery in the small Shropshire town of Wem in 1888.

In 1883 he won a first-class certificate at the Royal Horticultural Society's show for a new sweet pea, *Lathyrus* 'Bronze Prince'. His work further

Henry Eckford created the Grandiflora Series of sweet peas.

Courtesy of Lompoc/RHS

transformed the flower. By the time he retired, he had developed 153 culti-vars, of which 26 remained in commerce by 1917 (assuming that the Morse list is exhaustive). The type he developed was known as "Grandiflora." The flowers were larger than previously, with a huge range of color. The hood had been reduced and the stems were longer.

The showier Spencer type was a sport from one of Eckford's cultivars, *Lathyrus* 'Prima Donna'. Although it lacked fragrance, the sport was so ex-quisite in form with wavy and frilly petals that it superseded the Grandiflora type very quickly. Curiously, almost the identical sport appeared in several gardens simultaneously. Silas Cole's work and the magical name of the Spencer family ensured that his introduction in 1901 received the lion's share of attention. Cole was the Earl Spencer's head gardener, and the flower arose in his sweet pea border at Althorp, later Princess Diana's resting place.

Grandifloras went on being successful, but the Spencers rapidly gained ground, and eventually almost no new Grandifloras were bred. In the recent past, that imbalance has begun to be redressed.

Miss Hemus

The reader might enjoy a short diversion into the life and fate of a relatively minor figure in this story but one not without interest. She emerged in solitary splendor from among all the great panjandrums of sweet peas in the early years of the twentieth century: Miss Hemus, of Upton-upon-Severn in Worcestershire.

Her name appeared time after time in the useful list prepared by Lester Morse in 1917.[2] She bred champion flowers very seriously. At least one of her cultivars, *Lathyrus* 'Evelyn Hemus', won prizes and remained in the gardener's repertoire for many years. She was not a lady dilettante but still, all the credits said was "Miss Hemus." The sole additional piece of information about her was the name of the town in which she lived, Upton-upon-Severn in Worcestershire, in the list of subscribers to the National Sweet Pea Society, in the 1908 annual.

～✧～

HENRY ECKFORD was the dominant figure in the early stages. Then dozens of others took it up: Bolton, Burpee, Dobbie, Ferry, Sutton, Unwin, and many more. Some are still household names today in the seed business.

Using Lester Morse's 1917 list as a data source, here are a few numbers just to get a perspective.[3] This is the total number of cultivars each of them released until that date—good, bad, or indifferent.

Bolton	77
Burpee	42
Dobbie	48
Eckford	252
Ferry	4
Hemus	136
Morse *(with others)*	67
Sutton	19
Unwin	49

If one takes a look at the survival of their work, quite a different view appears. Of Ferry's four cultivars at the time, one was *Lathyrus* 'Blanche Ferry', the progenitor of almost every major cultivar for years afterward. The

Hilda Hemus Ashworth was the "Miss Hemus" of the early National Sweet Pea Society competitions. *Reproduced by permission of Jean Ashworth Waterworth, Mrs. Ashworth's daughter, Napier, New Zealand*

Ferry company eventually produced more cultivars in combination with other breeders, but novelty for its own sake had no ultimate staying power.

So many cultivars were created that seemed to be completely alike that the National Sweet Pea Society had to lay down a rule preventing an entrant from showing almost identical cultivars in any one event. If a breeder entered *Lathyrus* 'Evelyn Hemus', he could not enter 'Charles Breadmore', for there was no true difference between them. Unfortunately, almost all of the Hemus cultivars vanished within a few years. The Lester Morse catalogue indicates how soon a cultivar became obsolete.

In 2007, the keeper of the English National Sweet Pea collection, Roger Parsons, received some seeds from a source in Canada, said to be the Hemus *Lathyrus* 'Prince of Orange'. Mr. Parsons planted the seeds, which had originated with Hem Zaden, a Dutch seed company.[4] Subsequent research showed

Evelyn Hemus Fyfe was Hilda Hemus's sister and active in their sweet pea business.
Reproduced by permission of Wendy Betteridge, Mrs. Fyfe's granddaughter

that in 1928 Ferry Morse introduced a variety also named 'Prince of Orange'. The flowers from the Hem Zaden seeds resemble pictures of the Ferry Morse cultivar. It is hoped that one day a picture of the Hemus 'Prince of Orange' will emerge for comparison.

This cultivar also had a possible duplicate. Miss Hemus issued this variety, 'Prince of Orange', but at about the same time Robert Holmes, another important sweet pea breeder, issued *Lathyrus* 'Mrs Thomas Stevenson' in 1910, identical in appearance.

As a snapper up of unconsidered trifles, the author was determined to find out more about a woman who could do all this, to see if possible what drove her and why she spent her time in this way. At first, the task was not promising. Miss Evelyn Hemus had made it to Google with a single entry, so in today's currency she existed, but merely as the sister-in-law of a much better known man, Sir Rowland Biffen (1874–1949).[5]

The trail ran extremely cold until Simon Wilkinson, a retired headmaster who lives in Upton-upon-Severn, took on the challenge. He has found living descendants of the Hemus family. Additional descendants live in New Zealand and have recently become known to the author.[6] Finally Miss Hemus has a human face, but the facts indicate that behind the decorous façade, there were tumultuous doings within the family.

It turns out that there were four Hemus daughters: Mary (who married in 1899), Hilda, Evelyn, and Lucy. There were two sons, Charles and Guy. In the etiquette of the time, the epithet "Miss Hemus" meant the eldest unmarried daughter.

The first surprise was that although most sweet pea fanciers believe Evelyn Hemus was the breeder, it was in fact her elder sister Hilda. Hilda Hemus was an energetic and capable woman who ran a successful seed company, earning both money and prestige. Her firm issued several yearly catalogues. Not many women were doing anything like that in 1909. At the height of her business, she employed twenty men.

Samuel Ryder, the owner of Ryder's Seeds, one of the largest seed houses in England at the time if not the largest, bought all the seeds she produced on her twenty-nine acres in Upton for several years. He paid her £1,200 per annum, a respectable sum of money. Ryder's Seed Company then sold the seeds at a penny a packet. One of Ryder's inspirations was to sell the seeds by mail, as well as at unconventional outlets, like the early Woolworth's stores. Both Miss Hemus and Ryder were satisfied with this arrangement. Ryder also owned another successful firm, the Heath and Heather Seed Company, largely concerned with culinary herbs.

Ryder took up golf to improve his health in 1909, when he was fifty. Always an enthusiast, he had the idea of developing a golf tournament with a valuable cup. In 1927, the Ryder Cup competitions began, between golfers from England and America. It was said that he made much of his money from the sweet pea seeds supplied by Hilda Hemus.

He was active with the National Sweet Pea Society for a time and was very committed to civic life. Ryder became mayor of St. Albans in 1906. An unanswered question is why Ryder chose to work with Hilda Hemus, rather than the larger, well-established firms of sweet pea breeders run by men. Maybe both felt they were outsiders. Perhaps he was attracted to her. She was a beautiful woman.

Although Miss Hemus employed men to do the heavy work, her sisters evidently also helped out in the fields on occasion. Her next sister, Evelyn, believed that she should have received more recognition for her assistance than she did.

When there were medals to be won or royal hands to be shaken, Hilda not unnaturally got all the credit. Feelings of outrage and injustice were transmitted down to the next generations in Evelyn's family, and there was very little contact between the sisters or their children. Over the years, Hilda did stay in close touch with her sister Mary. Her daughter Jean has some of the letters. Mary sent clothes for her niece Jean after Hilda married Robert Ashworth and the family emigrated to Australia. Hilda did not correspond with Evelyn.

To understand the situation, we need to step back a little. The father, Edmund Hemus (1844–1910), was a prosperous ironmonger in Tewkesbury. He moved to Upton-upon-Severn in 1891 with his large family and leased Holdfast Hall Farm. Edmund Hemus had grown up on a farm. He was said to be a cousin of Herbert Spencer, the prominent Victorian political philosopher who supported the rights of women. That could be true. The Hemus girls were very well educated for their time.

After his death, the farm stayed in the family for a while. Edmund's sons took on the lease. The property, 260 acres in all, belonged to the wealthy Dowdeswell family. A 13-acre field named "Paradise" was used to grow sweet peas. This explains why the names of so many of the Hemus cultivars are prefaced by the term "Paradise."

Mary, Hilda, and Evelyn all married men who were to become, or were already, successful. Mary (b. 1872) married Rowland Biffen, later Sir Rowland, in 1899. The Biffens were of modest origin, but Rowland was a gifted scholar and rose rapidly in academic circles. He held a chair in biology at Cambridge, where he and his wife lived for the rest of their lives.

Biffen enjoyed working with the Hemus family in the summertime and at first wanted to marry Hilda. She refused him because she said she was too busy. Not daunted by this rejection, he turned instead to her sister Mary.

Hilda (b. 1874) married Robert Ashworth, a former army officer, in 1911. He had done very well financially supplying uniforms to cavalry regiments. Once she was married, she hoped that her sisters might marry, too.

Hilda Hemus Ashworth's daughter in New Zealand, Mrs. Jean Waterworth, informed one of the author's colleagues that her mother had helped

Evelyn to find a husband by paying for her to spend some time in India.[7] The strategy worked. Evelyn met her future husband on the outward passage to India and married Jack Fyfe, a shipping executive of Scottish descent, in December 1911, in India.

The other siblings were not involved with the sweet pea business. One of Evelyn's descendants believes that the fact that Mary became Lady Biffen caused some gnashing of teeth. Being knighted by the queen was a considerable mark of esteem. Sir Rowland's wife automatically beecame Lady Biffen. This same grandson mentioned that Jack Fyfe was offered a knighthood for his work in India but rejected it because of the financial burden. Granny Fyfe, the children's name for her, might well have become Lady Fyfe if Jack had not been so prudent. Jack Fyfe died in 1950, and Evelyn Fyfe (née Hemus) died in 1961.

The grandson remembers his Granny Fyfe muttering darkly that "Hilda got all the credit while I [meaning Evelyn] did all the work." Granny Fyfe never talked about Lady Biffen, and the children hardly ever saw their aunts. Many years later, there are indications that Hilda corresponded with Mary but not with Evelyn.

Miss Hemus's hybrids began to appear in 1903. The *Field Notes* show that she issued *Lathyrus* 'Severn Queen' that year. In 1906, she brought out another new cultivar, *L.* 'Ivorine'. Eight new cultivars appeared in 1907, three of them with "Paradise" in their name. 1908 and 1909 were relatively quiet years, but in 1910 and 1911 her activity exploded. There were 31 cultivars in 1910, at least half with "Paradise" in their name, and 47 in 1911, the majority carrying the term "Paradise." Several more appeared in 1912, 1913, and 1914, but then it all ceased abruptly.

It is interesting to look at what took place in light of the family circumstances. Mary's marriage to Rowland Biffen (1874–1949) probably started or intensified an interest in flower breeding among the sisters. (Rowland Biffen's experimental wheat, his primary academic interest, was grown at Holdfast Hall Farm.) The first modern international conference at which Mendel's work was "rediscovered" and made widely known took place in 1900. Mary herself won a gold medal at the Royal Horticultural Society in 1907 for "Mendelian sweet pea cultures."

One cultivar credited to Biffen-Hemus, *Lathyrus* 'Zero', came out in 1911. Biffen also was credited with a cultivar introduced in 1906 by Unwin, *L.* 'Zoe'.

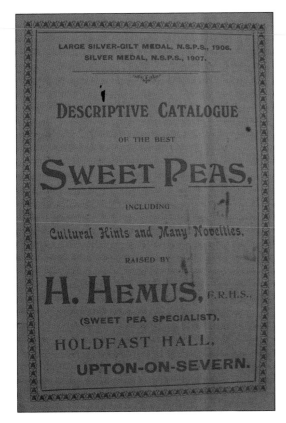

The cover of a catalogue for the Hemus sweet pea nursery.
Reproduced by permission of Keith Hammett, photographer

Their father, Edmund Hemus, died in September 1910 after an extended illness. The children's mother, Harriete, had died in 1907. This left the three unmarried daughters to nurse their father. It is possible that Hilda was negligent in her filial duty and expected Evelyn and Ethel to take care of their father while she pursued her work on the sweet pea. This could have been a source of the later ill feeling.

Hilda Hemus married Robert Ashworth in April 1911. The household would have been extremely busy and somewhat disrupted by these two events. At the same time, Evelyn was preparing for her wedding in India. Once Hilda was married, all sorts of new responsibilities would have been expected of her.

This lends a little weight to the idea that the creator of the extraordinary numbers of new hybrids in those two years might have been one of the other sisters, Evelyn or Ethel Lucy. Mary was living in Cambridge, a long way from Upton.

Roger Parsons, a present-day expert in sweet pea lore, was asked what he thought. He confirmed that "Evelyn Hemus" was the name he had always heard. This is echoed in at least one article in an old *Sweet Pea Annual*.[8] Mr. Parsons is aware of the fallacy of conflating the name of the cultivar with the name of an actual person, though. Regardless of the common belief, the catalogues make it abundantly clear that the firm belonged to Miss H. Hemus, that is, Hilda.

When one consults the April 19, 1911, *Longdon, Bushley, Queenhill and Holdfast Almanac,* one finds the following item: "Miss Hilda Hemus who has won such great fame throughout England for her sweet peas was married on this day at Queenhill Church to Captain Ashworth who served in the Commissariat Department of the Army and has seen much service in India. They have bought from Mr. Dowdeswell the land which forms the Sweet Pea Farm and which has been known from time immemorial as Paradise—a fit name for a garden of such beauty. They have built a house upon it, with the requisite outbuildings, which we hope will be their home for many years to come."

Apart from the fact that the reporter could have used some help with his grammar, it does explain why the next few years' cultivars were all called "Paradise." During the second half of World War I, growing flowers commercially was discouraged. All farms and other holdings with open fields had to produce wheat, followed by fruit and vegetables. The government issued strict rules in 1916 about the production of food. German vessels patrolled the Atlantic and sank many merchant ships carrying food for the Allies.

In 1915, one hundred new cultivars of sweet pea were introduced across the board. In 1916, this was reduced to fifty-eight. By 1917, only four new cultivars were introduced. In any event, the Hemus nursery workers and horses were conscripted, and Hilda could not have grown any flowers even if it had been permitted. Late in the war, she raised a lot of eyebrows by requisitioning German prisoners of war as farm laborers. They turned out to be good workers.

There is no doubt that Hilda had the reputation. The irony is that in spite of the reporter's pious hopes, the Ashworths emigrated to New Zealand in the 1920s. Robert Ashworth had spent much of his adult life in warm climates and found living in Worcestershire very uncomfortable. He insisted that their family move to New Zealand in 1922. Her family indicates that Hilda was not keen to go there but had very little choice. Once she left Upton, production at Holdfast Hall ceased, and Ryder was very disappointed.

Hilda developed rheumatoid arthritis and eventually gave up growing sweet peas. She tried for a time, but Christchurch's excessively hot summers made it too difficult. Her daughter Jean recalls helping her mother as a child in Upton, before they emigrated, putting little cotton bags over the newly pollinated buds to prevent casual pollination by the wind or insects.

After returning to England with her son for a short time when her husband died, Hilda went back to live in Christchurch and died in New Zealand in 1954, aged eighty.

The cultivar *Lathyrus* 'Evelyn Hemus' won an award of merit at one of the Royal Horticultural Society shows in 1908. In 1909, the *Times* reported that Mr. E. G. Mocatta won the National Sweet Pea Society's Henry Eckford Memorial Cup with twelve bunches of sweet peas, including *L.* 'Evelyn Hemus'; this was an indication of how well-known the cultivar was. Mr. Mocatta was a leading amateur gardener.

Hilda Hemus joined the National Sweet Pea Society in 1907 at the half-guinea level. Between 1911 and 1914, her name was removed and that of Captain Ashworth substituted. Once he rejoined his regiment for the war, neither name appeared. Hilda's daughter told horticulturist Keith Hammett that her mother despised the society and held it in very low esteem. That could have reflected the fact that the "old boys' club" froze her out.

Although Hilda entered Royal Horticultural Society and National Sweet Pea Society competitions in London, she preferred to show her flowers in northern cities like Harrogate. It is tempting to believe that this success may have made them think about going into business. The Hemus family did not own the Paradise field before Hilda's marriage. Planting the flowers on a much larger scale and the building of Holdfast House along with offices and storerooms suggests a commercial approach. Captain Ashworth must have played an important role in this decision.

The Birmingham nurseryman Robert Sydenham was also said to be helpful to the sisters. Sydenham was known for his daffodils, and his principal interest was in bulbs. He did not breed his own plants but sold other people's varieties. At one point, he was president of the National Sweet Pea Society. In spite of his friendship with the Hemus family, a recent review of Robert

Sydenham's catalogues in the collection at the Massachusetts Horticultural Society shows that he carried *L.* 'Evelyn Hemus' only for a time. He listed many other cultivars.

It is possible that there was a falling-out later. At one point, he wrote, "Next to the late Mr. Henry Eckford I am inclined to think the Sweet Pea world owes as much to Mr. Biffen, of Cambridge, as to anyone in England. It is through his careful and scientific researches that so much has been done in hybridising, the results of which I am inclined to think are distributed by Miss Hemus."[9]

Sydenham seems to have been reducing Miss Hemus to an epiphenomenon, suggesting that she was not the dominant plant breeder herself but merely Rowland Biffen's handmaiden. From other evidence available, this unkind and mean-spirited attempt to diminish her accomplishments is completely erroneous. Hilda Hemus was interviewed more than once by newspapers and ladies' magazines and described in great detail exactly what she did and how it worked.

SWEET PEAS IN THE UNITED STATES

Within a few years, there was a large demand for sweet peas from the United States. Very soon after opening his own business, Eckford started to supply James Breck in Boston with seed in 1886. Another American enthusiast, the Reverend W. T. Hutchins, drove the demand by his excitement. Here is another minor figure who offers considerable interest.

Reverend W. T. Hutchins

Part of how the fever spread to the United States was due to tireless promotion by an obscure Massachusetts clergyman, the Reverend William T. Hutchins (1849–1917). In reading the literature of the period, Reverend Hutchins keeps popping up all over the place. A booster and camp follower, he traveled to meet the luminaries of the field, and he frequently wrote about the flower. Hutchins intrigued me, and I set out to learn whatever I could about him.

Lathyrus 'The Senator', a sweet pea cultivar bred by the Reverend William T. Hutchins. From Hutchins, *All About Sweet Peas* (1892).
Courtesy of P. E. M. Rowland, Owl's Acre Sweet Peas. Reproduced by permission of the Albert R. Mann Library, Cornell University.

Reverend William T. Hutchins wrote the first book solely devoted to the sweet pea in the United States, *All About Sweet Peas,* published in 1892. *From the* Springfield Republican, *July 27, 1895. Courtesy of the Lyman and Merrie Wood Museum of Springfield History, Springfield, Massachusetts.*

The first known book devoted to sweet peas in the United States was Hutchins's *All About Sweet Peas: An Art Monograph,* published in 1892 by the Burpee Seed Company. In 1897, he brought out *Sweet Peas Up-to-Date,* also published by Burpee. The firm sent out fifty thousand copies of the first book. It is uncertain whether he received any payment for these books.

The books were a promotion for the seed company rather than a pure scholarly exercise and were illustrated by black and white line drawings.

The sweet peas developed by Burpee are prominently mentioned. One of the news items in the Springfield, Massachusetts, press of the time notes that he went to England on behalf of the Burpee company in 1895, to meet Henry Eckford.

Hutchins continued to promote Burpee, stating that "our American novelties are not only equal to Mr. Eckford's best work but have the advantage of stronger, well-acclimated seed, and of being offered in more liberal packets and for one-fourth the price of the imported sealed packets." He waxed almost lyrical about Burpee's introduction of the first dwarf cultivar, *Lathyrus*

'Cupid' in 1893. This was a sport of *L.* 'Emily Henderson' and originally found by C. C. Morse. At almost the same time, Ernst Benary in Germany also found a dwarf sport. At first he called it *L.* 'Tom Thumb', but later he switched to 'Cupid' too.

Hutchins experimented with sweet peas himself. He produced *Lathyrus* 'Daybreak' and some other useful cultivars. Liberty Hyde Bailey, the dean of horticulture at Cornell, commented that Hutchins had explained how modern sweet peas had evolved, in a graphic form. A large quantity of the seed used in the trials at Cornell in 1896 came from Hutchins.

William T. Hutchins was born in Massachusetts in January 1849. He died at his own hand on February 1, 1917.

Hutchins's father, James, was a cabinetmaker who had worked in various communities. At the outbreak of the Civil War, the family was in Illinois. One of Hutchins's brothers also became a minister. His oldest sister, Adelaide, married Henry Sykes, a prosperous Connecticut farmer.

William may not have known what he wanted to do with his life until quite late. In 1870 the census listed him as a "labourer" on the Sykes farm, but in 1876 he graduated from Yale University and was ordained later the same year.

All the surviving anecdotes indicate a man with a very engaging personality, full of enthusiasm. He had a beautiful garden in Indian Orchard, Massachusetts, which he opened to the public when the flowers were at their peak. As soon as he found sweet peas, he was enchanted for life.

In 1950, Charles H. Curtis wrote, "Fifty years ago a parson from Indiana [*sic*] Orchard, Massachusetts, stood on the platform in the Lecture Hall of the Crystal Palace. He was the Rev. W. T. Hutchins, an enthusiastic grower of Sweet Peas, who had a voice as sweet and pervasive as the fragrance of his subject. I can hear him now."[10] Hutchins had been invited to attend the sweet pea bicentenary celebrations on July 20 and 21, 1900, at the Crystal Palace in Sydenham.

Curtis recorded more of what Hutchins had said: "[T]he Sweet Pea has migrated, and now America not only desires to pay her debt with interest to Great Britain, but would be glad to put a liberal row of Sweet Peas into every garden on the face of the earth." Hutchins ended by proclaiming that the flower has a "fragrance like the Universal Gospel, yes a sweet prophesy of welcome everywhere that has been abundantly fulfilled."

In spite of these strengths, Hutchins wrote to his friend Nelson Adams in 1909, "I feel impatient to have the years speed on, that I may go to a more congenial world" and continued in even more despairing tones. One can only imagine how he felt during the dark days of the First World War. America did not formally enter the war until 1917, but the public was very much aware of it.

He and his wife, Charlotte (née Hills), who was a little older than he was, had two children. After the Hutchinses were married in 1876, they lived in Ohio with Charlotte's parents. The elder child, William H., was born in 1878. He also went to Yale. This young man was probably too old to serve in the First World War. There is no further reference to the second child beyond the fact of its birth.

As Hutchins grew older, he left the stable world of Indian Orchard and its congregation. In 1903 he went to Northampton, Massachusetts, in some pastoral capacity. He also served a term as "cor sec" (presumably corresponding secretary) at the Springfield Ethical Union.

Doctrinal differences lay behind his moves. The Springfield press has several articles about the serious problem that arose when he announced he no longer believed in miracles or in the divinity of Jesus. The Congregational authorities sent a deputation to his house (in the charming words of the day, they "waited on him") to call upon him to retire from this ministry. His new views were not compatible with the church's teachings. Because he was so amiable, everything was done in the most conciliatory manner possible.

At one point, he was known to have been a Unitarian minister. He drifted out to California and in 1910 was living in a rooming house in Santa Rosa. While there, Hutchins went to see Luther Burbank. He was very much alone. His final home was in Francestown, New Hampshire.

One topic that is not mentioned is his financial circumstances. None of the positions he held were very lucrative, but a shortage of money does not seem to have been a problem. William was able to educate his son at Yale and possibly support the latter as he tried to become an artist. He could have inherited money from his father, or Burpee may have paid him an honorarium.

Hutchins introduced the work of Henry Eckford to the United States. He was the go-between for Eckford and James Breck, the Boston nurseryman. As word of Eckford's improved varieties reached the United States, American nurserymen wanted to stock them. Communications may not have been instantaneous in the 1890s, but they were certainly swift enough and efficient.

Hutchins visited California more than once, to see the growing fields and report back. He was very fond of Morse and Burpee, commenting in his reminiscences, which appeared posthumously, "that two such men as Lester Morse and W. Atlee Burpee should have plighted their troth to this lovely flower will always be a veritable romance in its history."[11] In another section he referred to them both as "beautiful men."

He traced the source of his excitement about the flower to the really fine sweet peas grown by the former mayor of Newton Highland in Massachusetts, J. F. C. Hyde, in 1881. The Massachusetts Horticultural Society had been giving prizes for sweet peas a long time before others followed suit. Hutchins was invited to give a special lecture to the society in the early 1890s. He also entered one hundred vases of flowers in their show.

As a conscientious clergyman, he decided to use the sweet peas to raise money for his church missionary society, starting in 1890. He sold sweet pea seeds and donated the proceeds to the mission fund.

The Reverend Hutchins's death must have been very distressing for his family. He shot himself while visiting one of his sisters in New Haven. He chose to die in an undertaking establishment and left the family a note. About twelve years before, he had had what was called in those days a "nervous breakdown," an acute episode of depression. In early 1917, he was convinced that the condition had recurred and that he was losing his mind. His wife had died of chronic renal failure in 1903.

We shall not see his like again. Customs and behavior have changed. His odd combination of naiveté and astuteness, the idealistic streak that let him down at some point, all tend to be wrung out of us as we grow up nowadays.

Early Varieties

Independent breeding in the United States, both by selection and by deliberate crossing, began very early. By 1910, the firm of Morse and Co. had four hundred acres of sweet peas under cultivation. Peter Henderson in New York also bred new varieties. *Lathyrus* 'Emily Henderson' gave him a long period of prosperity. The American work was on such a high plane that their introductions soon started to win prizes at the Royal Horticultural Society's shows. Burpee's first dwarf variety, 'Cupid' won an Award of Merit in 1893.

At first the work was mainly on the East Coast. The well-known *Lathyrus* 'Blanche Ferry' was introduced in 1889. D. M. Ferry bought the rights to a very special sweet pea from a countrywoman in upstate New York. She had saved the seed of her *L.* 'Old Painted Lady' plants every year, sowing it in the same rocky plot for twenty-five years. Her soil was shallow and without any natural enrichment. The plants became tougher, shorter, and very resistant to disease over this period.

Ferry gave the variety the name by which it is now known. The quarry-man's wife had been using an old variety that predated the modern breeding programs. That could be the reason its descendants in California did so well. It still had considerable vigor.

The descendants were legion. It was very quickly found that some culti-vars of *Lathyrus* 'Blanche Ferry' would blossom earlier in the season, indicat-ing that they were a little more resistant to cold and shorter days. Ferry ran out of names for them. Starting with *L.* 'Early Blanche Ferry', he gradually used up the serial superlatives he needed. Many experts believe that after a while the lots of the new "early" cultivars were only slightly different, with-out any real distinction between them.

This is a not-unheard-of situation in the plant-breeding world. Each business wants the public to believe that it alone has all the varieties anyone could need and so will pursue a breeding program fated to produce redun-dancies in the market. A well-run and completely impartial plant society like the National Sweet Pea Society in the United Kingdom, chartered in 1901, can be very important and helpful in sorting out this situation. In collabora-tion with the Royal Horticultural Society and other groups, it ran trials and graded the new cultivars for various qualities.

Development of Major Nurseries

One of the major legacies of the California gold rush was a flourishing horti-cultural industry. The California soil was extremely fertile if it received enough water. Franciscan missionaries had grown bumper crops at the end of the eighteenth century. When thousands of men descended on the fledgling state in 1849 and afterward, seeking gold, feeding them was a huge task. Wheat, which had been king, declined by about 1880 because it could no longer compete with extremely cheap new sources in Canada and the Ukraine, for example, but orchards and row crops continued to expand and prosper. Flowers too had a place in this expansion.

Early San Francisco had many nurseries and places to buy seed. The plants were grown on-site for sale and not just trucked in from somewhere else. Each business might have quite extensive property, an unheard-of luxury today, given the value of land in a modern city. When the newly rich miners and mining suppliers from the gold rush built their ostentatious houses to show the world how much money they had, they always incorporated large gardens in the plans. That in turn fostered the growth of the nursery trade.

Charlie Abraham's Western Nursery covered several acres in Cow Hollow. William Walker, an Alabama lawyer who came to San Francisco for the gold rush, opened his famous nursery on Folsom Street, between Third and Fourth Streets. His property is now, most aptly, the site of the Society of California Pioneers. Several major nurseries from the East Coast established a presence in the city.

John Saul's United States Nursery represented Ellwanger and Barry from Rochester, New York, a premier firm in the "Flower City." The smart set ordered their plants from Ellwanger and Barry just as we might buy our clothes from Paris rather than the chain stores. It had more cachet.

By the mid-1870s there were more than 150 nurseries in the state of California, drawn by the rapidly expanding market. After two fairly bad business recessions in the 1870s and 1890s, things picked up again.

In Ventura, Theodosia Burr Shepherd developed the California flower seed industry, starting in 1874. She began in a very small way, swapping through a ladies' magazine, but after a few years, she expanded her property and grew flowers for their seeds. She sold them by type in separate little envelopes. As she became more certain of her work, she started to cross many petunias to grow sturdy and elegant new varieties.

One of the nation's leading nurserymen, Peter Henderson of New York, commended her work and prophesied a great future for flower seeds in California. In 2000, California, Michigan, and Florida led the country in horticultural production, so his prediction was prescient.

In the mid-nineteenth century, Detroit was a center of horticulture. As will be seen below, a modest seed store in Detroit became significant for the Bay area. R. W. Wilson from Rochester, New York, moved to Santa Clara for his health. He had always been a seed grower, so it was not surprising he would grow 'Prizehead' lettuce on his farm in 1874. This was said to be the first commercial crop grown for seed on the Pacific coast. Wilson sold the

Sweet peas for sale in the Peter Henderson catalogue, circa 1940. Peter Henderson of New York had one of the best-known seed houses in the United States for many years and was a leading authority on commercial horticulture.

entire crop of seed to D. M. Ferry. Wilson's health unfortunately got worse, and in 1877 he sold his business to Charles Copeland ("C. C.") Morse and Mr. A. L. Kellogg, a Methodist minister. By this time, the farm was more than a hundred acres. Other crops were added to the lettuce.

C. C. Morse and Co.

C. C. Morse died very abruptly in 1900 at the age of fifty-eight. His assistant came in one afternoon and found him slumped over his desk. He could not be resuscitated. His son, Lester, took over the company. Lester had expanded the crops and developed new types of carrot, onion, and lettuce, as well as various flowers. As a way of expanding still further, Lester bought E. J. Bowen's seed business in 1905. Bowen's brother was C. C. Bowen, who had also been a pioneer of seed growing in California and one of Ferry's associates. Bowen's offices were in San Francisco near the waterfront.

In this way, the first stage of a major new company began. The firm of C. C. Morse had been incorporated in 1884 after Morse had bought out Kellogg. By itself his name is probably not familiar to most people, even those interested in gardening. As part of Ferry Morse, purveyors of seeds in little paper packets, it is indeed well known.

Every spring one can rely on row upon row of colorful packets appearing in garden centers, hardware stores, and many other outlets. Huge crimson radishes, enticing ears of golden corn, and elegant string beans beckon to us. Marigolds and zinnias compete with snapdragons and four o'clocks for our attention.

For us it is a question of choosing between all the pretty packages: Burpee, Ferry Morse, and other well-known names. Most of the seed companies are now part of much larger businesses due to consolidation of the industry in the past fifteen or twenty years, but in their day they led the market. Ferry Morse is currently owned by Groupe Limagrain, a large French farming cooperative.

Although both Ferry and Morse had each started a business at the end of the nineteenth century, the familiar company was not put together until 1930 when C. C. Morse and Co. decided to merge with the D. M. Ferry Co. of Detroit. Neither of the founders was still alive by then, but the Ferry firm was growing much of its seed in California, and it made good sense. Ferry had excellent distribution facilities and had been in close touch with the Morse people for many years.

The combined firm rapidly became the largest seed company in the world. Safe new ways of canning fruit and vegetables created an even greater demand for seed. The outbreaks of botulism in the previous decade had finally led to serious reform.

D. M. Ferry and Co.

Dexter Mason Ferry was born in Lowville, near Binghamton, upstate New York, in 1833. He died in California in 1907. In the twenty-first century, Lowville is very small town, with only about three thousand inhabitants. In

Frank Cuthbertson in the fields of the Ferry Company's sweet peas in Lompoc, California. *Courtesy of the California Historical Society*

the nineteenth century, it was probably beyond the back of beyond. Ferry grew up on a farm and gained a lot of experience with crops.

He was just a little too young for the gold rush but went to Detroit in 1853. Detroit was a center of horticultural activity at the time. His aim was to save enough money to go to college. He began to work for Milo Gardner at the American Seed Store. By saving his money carefully, he entered into partnership with Mr. Gardner and later with Eber Church, to open Gardner, Ferry and Church in 1856. After his partners retired, he continued the retail store as D. M. Ferry and Co., incorporated in 1879.

Ferry introduced several key changes in the seed business. He had a very keen sense of how to make his business succeed. His main insight was that since no one could tell by looking at a seed whether it would germinate successfully, the principal weapon of the merchant was in an unassailable reputation for honesty and integrity.

Acting on that, he threw out any seed remaining at the end of a season. Only fresh new seed was sold. In this way, he more or less guaranteed adequate germination, which was absolutely essential for farmers and gardeners. He was among the first to put seeds of each variety into small separate envelopes, labeled and even illustrated later, something only the Shakers were doing at the time. Perhaps he had seen the Shaker methods during his boyhood in upstate New York.

He also had the idea of displaying the packets on a "commission rack" in the seed dealer's showroom. In addition, he made sure that the seeds he sent out would do well in the part of the country where they were to be grown, further ensuring success. All these arrangements are now routine, and we do not give them a second thought, but they were real innovations when he started in the 1860s. Ferry created the modern seed business.

The catalogues reflected his imaginative philosophy. He inserted classical quotations or wrote small homilies on the benefits of growing vegetables. Chromolithographs illustrated the pages from a very early date. In some of them, the field workers are seen to be women, though men are the supervisors.

Ferry believed that "ladies" would benefit from gardening and exhorted them to "cultivate flowers as an invigorating and inspiring outdoor occupation. Many are pining from monotony and depression, who might bury their cares by planting a few seeds." (This view is echoed in the immortal words of "Doc" in John Steinbeck's *Cannery Row*. Doc said that someone should invent a machine in which hypochondriacal wealthy women would be obliged to go through the movements of a using a washtub, wringing out the laundry and then ironing it. This would restore them to health very fast.)

Ferry bought vegetable and flower seed from growers in the Detroit area, using a number of suppliers. He developed many valuable crops, such as the lettuce noted above, and was able to lay down strict criteria and specifications.

Morse Family

Charles Copeland Morse was born in Thomaston, Maine, in 1842. His father died when he was very small, leaving a young widow with four children and no source of income. To help his mother make ends meet, his grandparents in Warren took care of him until he grew up.

Morse rapidly saw that it was extremely hard to earn a living by farming in Maine. When he was about eighteen, he went to sea and reached California in 1862. He liked California and stayed on doing a variety of jobs such as painting houses. In an informal biography of his father, Lester Morse notes that Charles Morse was very prudent and spent as little money as possible on everyday expenses in order to build some capital.

With each job, he managed to save a bit more. First he bought the painting business, and later, when he was ready, he had a chance to buy into Wilson's farm. It was a good business to have. Charles Morse was a perceptive businessman, not particularly a plant person.

Morse married Maria Josephine Victoria Langford and lived most of his life in Santa Clara County. Their house in Santa Clara is now an architectural landmark. In 1974, it was restored and is currently used as offices by a firm of lawyers.

Morse and his wife had five children. His son Lester L. Morse (1871–1953) became a noted expert on horticulture, known for his breeding of sweet peas. The crossings of the flowers were supervised by Frank Cuthbertson, a Scottish gardener, and later Cuthbertson's son, William. Cuthbertson also wrote the descriptions and notes in Morse's *Field Notes on Sweet Peas.* The younger Morse commented that sweet peas were the newest vogue at the time the firm decided to add flowers to their wares in about 1884.

Lester Morse was eventually succeeded by his own son, Charles Pierce Morse. The latter died in 1970 at the age of sixty-three. By then the company had moved its garden seed headquarters to Fulton, Kentucky.

The 1906 earthquake and fire completely demolished Morse's first premises. For a time they worked out of the old Santa Clara office, but they quickly moved to a large temporary building in San Francisco. In 1907 they found permanent space in Front Street. This was achieved by the acquisition of the Cox Seed and Plant Company, a well-known jobbing firm and successful in the commission packet business. C. C. Morse's son Lester managed the flower growing, and later his own son Charles took this over from him.

This combination put Morse in the retail commission seed business and in turn led to the need for more acreage. By 1910, the Morse company had concentrated its seed growing in San Juan Bautista. A few years later, the company bought the Sacramento River Ranch and later property in Salinas. It was not long before Morse had one thousand acres in production.

In 1915, the Morse company won the grand prize for gardens at the Pan Pacific Exposition. A few years later, the nursery department was separated and sold to the Vallance Nursery. The brothers John and James Vallance had previously managed this department for Morse. Divesting themselves of this division allowed C. C. Morse and Co. to focus on seeds.

The Role of Sweet Peas

Almost immediately after Eckford began winning his prizes, a nurseryman in Boston, James Breck, imported Eckford seed and began selling it in this country. Eckford seed was also featured in an early catalogue of the Cox Company before the merger with Morse. By 1915, Morse was offering about 70 varieties of sweet pea, many bred in-house. The *Field Notes* include more than 1,600 varieties by 1917. World War I was taking its toll on European breeders, as so many men were sent into the trenches and killed at an alarming rate. That did not happen with such ferocity in the United States, expanding the opportunities for American breeders.

Morse had become involved with sweet peas in the 1880s. A close study of the 1917 *Field Notes* indicates that sometimes he worked alone in the early 1890s but that he also joined with W. A. Burpee, a future giant of the seed business, in introducing new cultivars. In 1921, Ferry bought the commission packet division from Morse.

Responding to the wishes of the public and even anticipating them is one hallmark of a successful business. Both Ferry and Morse were distinguished by this characteristic. If it had not been sweet peas, it would have been something else.

Modern sophisticated San Francisco no longer seems to be a place where seed merchants could be some of the most prominent firms in town, but remembering what things were like a hundred years ago is valuable. Very few people remember that San Francisco was once a ship-building town and that over the years four million tons of coal from the nearby Diamond mines in Antioch were consumed to make the steel for the ships.

Several old-fashioned sweet peas believed to have come from England were actually developed in the United States in that period. English gardening was at the height of its prestige, and nurserymen liked to cash in on anything that would give them a marketing edge. They might not have actually claimed that their introductions came from England, but if the public chose to believe it, they made no strenuous efforts to disabuse them.

Sweet Peas in California

The year 2007 was a centennial of sorts; exactly one hundred years before, in 1907, sweet peas were first grown in California on an agricultural scale. A visitor asked a local bean farmer in Lompoc, Robert Rennie, to grow the flowers. Rennie planted half an acre in sweet peas on his ranch, which is now part of the center of the town. Precisely who the visitor was is not known. C. C. Morse had died in 1900, but it might have been one of his employees.

Within two years, W. Atlee Burpee of Philadelphia had set up shop in Lompoc. Sweet peas were one of his principal crops. Some of the seed he used had been developed by the Reverend Lewis Routzahn in the late 1880s, working at the ranch of his father-in-law, T. H. McClure.

The situation of the peninsula, its rich soil, and its climate were ideal for growing the flowers. Wind and fog from the Pacific cooled the worst of the heat.

Anyone who drove through the valleys of central California before about 1980 remembers field upon field of glorious color at the peak of the sweet pea season. The long colorful rows were even visible from the air. The fields were active for almost a century but now have run their course. Fashions changed. The public switched from buying packets of seed to buying starter plants, and the cost of growing flowers of any type in California became too high. All of the flowers grown, particularly sweet peas, were very labor intensive. In addition, the value of the land increased as development pushed through.

It became much cheaper to send seed down to Central or South America to be grown. By the mid-1980s, the valley had changed. Burpees left, and eventually that business was bought by George Ball of BallFloraPlant Company. Sweet peas no longer lord it in Lompoc, but at one time many tons of seed were gathered there.

We tend to think solely of Lompoc as the sweet pea "capital," but the flowers were also cultivated on a large scale in other California agricultural valleys. D. M. Ferry from Detroit had a ranch in Salinas, Monterey County. C. C. Morse worked in San Francisco but grew his seed in Santa Clara. After 1930 the firm of Ferry Morse Seeds, which resulted from their merger, occupied land near San Juan Bautista in San Benito County.

In California, the names of Ferry, Morse, and Burpee are the most prominent, but at one time many gardeners also knew of the Zvolanek family and the brothers William and Frank Cuthbertson, who did the crosses for Morse and Denholm Seeds.

Only ten years after the California epoch started, Lester Morse published his *Field Notes on Sweet Peas* in 1917, in San Francisco. The body of this booklet was a catalogue of all the varieties and cultivars, English, American, and other nationalities, in existence before that date. It is a mine of information. The actual collecting and organizing of the facts in the booklet were done by Frank Cuthbertson.

The Move to California

English breeders quickly realized that it made sense for them to send the seed developed from new lines to California to be "bulked up." W. J. Unwin of Histon near Cambridge was one of the first to do so. He complained about the cost, because he paid everything for himself, but knew it was the best way to do things. The more predictable climate and larger scale in California was one of the main reasons, but this activity further confused the national origin of the hybrids.

In the five years leading up to the outbreak of war, more British sweet pea firms set up permanent operations in central California, begging the question of whether the new introductions were American or not. The dominant players in Lompoc were Bodgers and Denholms, both from the United Kingdom. It was not only that the principals were from Britain but also that they employed many other British horticulturists to do the crossing.

William and Frank Cuthbertson were Scottish. One of their protégés, David Lemon, is from Ireland. Among his many achievements, David has made distinct contributions to the sweet pea, working on the ones without tendrils, the Snoopea Series.

The Cuthbertsons had introduced a series, or possibly even a race, of sweet peas with distinctive characteristics, which are still collectively known as "Cuthbertsons." While they have some advantages in dealing with heat, their range of color and form is somewhat restricted, and they have not remained very popular.

STABILITY OF THE SEED

One of the chief difficulties that confronted all breeders of sweet peas was the uncertain behavior of the subsequent generations. The exquisite *Lathyrus* 'Spencer' suffered seriously from this. The seed did not breed true. The new cultivar might reproduce itself fairly well in a small garden plot, but when it was bred on a large scale, there was considerable reversion to the parental forms. These were the "rogues."

Before the breeders became aware of this, they had sold seed to the public too soon and then had to refund disappointed customers. The initial Unwin cultivars rapidly became very successful because they did not have this problem. W. J. Unwin was a grocer who dabbled in sweet peas on the side. With *Lathyrus* 'Gladys Unwin', he abandoned grocery and opened a new business.

Unwin's variety was one of the other sports that appeared almost simultaneously with Silas Cole's Spencer type, but it bred true from the beginning. According to the late Roy Genders, 'Gladys Unwin' propelled the sweet pea into national prominence.[12] That may not strictly be true when one considers what had been happening in the previous decade, but it certainly took things to a new level. One large wholesale house bought every single Unwin seed the year he released *Lathyrus* 'Gladys Unwin' to the trade, 1904. The reason for the stability of Unwin's *L.* 'Gladys Unwin' is unclear.

Curiously, Unwin's business story is paralleled by that of W. A. Burpee, a Pennsylvania poultry merchant who needed seed to feed the poultry and later switched to horticulture for the same reason. The seeds were more successful than the initial business.

In the ten years from 1906 to 1916, Unwin bred eighty-three cultivars, of which forty-three remained in cultivation, a better ratio than Eckford's. One of the striking findings that emerged from a close reading of the Morse list was how many cultivars were completely transient, disappearing almost as fast as they were introduced. Failure to breed true was one of the principal reasons, but poor habit, weak growth when challenged on a large scale, susceptibility to the dreaded disease "streak," and a lack of anything truly unique about the cultivar were also very important. Streak was due to a virus but has now become less common.

To attack the problem of new hybrids having little true merit or differentiation between them, the National Sweet Pea Society started a list of cultivars that resembled each other so closely that an exhibitor could no longer show both types in the same vase. That rule, made in 1905, helped to bring about more-sensible breeding.

The huge fields in California allowed growers to spot rogues promptly and take steps to weed them out. Roguing was costly, as it had to be done by hand, but it was essential for the integrity of the industry. Not the least of the merits of *Lathyrus* 'Blanche Ferry' was the stability of its descendants' seed, requiring a minimum of roguing. W. J. Unwin sent his foreman, Mr. G. H. Burt, to California in 1910 to supervise the development of seed of each variety in the reliable climate. It was a very good investment for his firm. The yield from several varieties that had done poorly in the English summer improved markedly. Transferring the relatively lightweight seed back to England was not an expensive business.

NEW CULTIVARS

An analysis of the list that constitutes the bulk of Lester Morse's *Field Notes on Sweet Peas* gives a very good idea of where things stood at the height of the First World War. All plant breeding has a huge tail. Hybrids released in any particular year may have been seven, ten, or more years in the making. Counting plants introduced in 1914 does not really describe the activity of 1914 itself. By 1915, gardeners were beginning to disappear in England, called up for the war effort. This was even more true by 1916.

Morse lists 104 new cultivars appearing in 1915, but this dropped to 36 in 1916. As before, the majority were still British, the standard names well represented. This seemingly conventional snapshot has to be set against another set of statistics, which Morse had confined to an appendix.

The breeding of the early varieties had been going along in parallel. In 1916, Anton Zvolanek in California released 80 new cultivars, Burpee offered 14, and various other breeders issued a total of 101 more.

Anton Zvolanek

Anton Zvolanek (1862–1958) was a nurseryman from Bohemia who emigrated to New Jersey in 1888. He was born in the remote village of Krucemburk but possibly attended the horticultural school at Brno. That seems to be have been where he learned the technique of flower breeding, because he was already a skilled hybridist when he came to the United States. One almost feels Mendel's aura over his head.

It took him more than five thousand crosses between his own winter-flowering variety and the new Spencer type in his greenhouses at Bound Brook, New Jersey, to come up with the plant that he believed would succeed. He decided to have it "bulked up" in Lompoc. By 1910, he had moved his entire operation to Lompoc.

In 1906 William Scott, author of the *Florists' Manual,* wrote this:

> Finally we discovered we had been attempting something that could not be done. And not until we procured the Zvolanek strain of seed did it appear that our trouble was the attempt to *flower* in the dark of winter such beautiful varieties as Blanche Ferry, Emily Henderson and other varieties so grand in June and July. They slumbered till the bright suns of March and April. Here is what the Zvolanek type will do. Sown where they were to flower about August 18, they were in bloom by Thanksgiving and by December 10 we were picking a full crop.[13]

Zvolanek's son, William, served in the First World War. When he returned, he joined his father and kept the firm going until 1975, when it was sold to Bodgers. William Zvolanek maintained his father's high standards. In 1947, he released a new multiflowered cultivar, *Lathyrus* 'Early Zvolanek', with a good strong stem and up to five or six flowers on each one.

Eleven years later, William issued four new semidwarf multiflowered cultivars. All these, and many other Zvolanek cultivars, were widespread throughout the sweet pea industry, yet both father and son ran the business on a very modest scale, supplying tiny orders by hand. Someone commented that a pound of seed was a large order for them.

EPITAPH

It is sad to have to write an epitaph of sorts, but the events noted above have taken place in many other sections of the horticultural world. The rows of greenhouses in the Bay area of California have gone. Fuel costs too much, and labor is also now prohibitive. The roses they held are now almost all grown in Central America. Orchid growing was once spread widely across many countries and continents and thrived in California, but the Taiwan Sugar Company aced them all. No one can produce fine plants as cheaply as they can.

Moving sweet peas to California was a step toward turning horticulture into an industry. In a way, no one should complain about the process being pursued to a logical conclusion, but that does not make it any more acceptable to those who earned their living by it or those who cherish the older ways.

APPENDIX

Benary Hybrids

THE Benary dwarf petunias 'Erfurter Zwerg' and 'Weisse Flocke' were very well known. As Ernst Sr. grew older, his sons and their descendants took over. The loss of the company records and memorabilia prevents us from learning whether the later crosses were made in conformance with Mendel's findings. The firm's connection with the Augustinian monastery suggests they might have been quite aware of the findings as soon as they became known.

Between 1843 and 1951 more than five hundred cultivars of ornamental plants were bred from genera such as *Abutilon, Ageratum, Alonsoa, Angelonia, Anthirrhinum, Aquilegia, Arabis, Armeria, Calistephus, Begonia, Bellis, Browallia, Calceolaria, Calendula, Campanula, Celosia, Centaurea, Cheiranthus, Chrysanthemum, Cineraria, Clintonia, Coleus, Collinsia, Coreopsis, Cuphea, Cyclamus, Cynoglossum, Delphinium, Dianthus, Echium, Erigeron, Exacum, Gaillardia, Gloxinia, Sinningia, Godetia, Heuchera, Iberis, Impatiens, Lathyrus, Leucanthemum, Linaria, Lobelia, Lupinus, Lychnis, Mimulus, Myosotis, Papaver, Penstemon, Petunia, Phacelia, Phlox, Primula, Pyrethrum, Rudbeckia, Saintpaulia, Salvia, Saponaria, Scabiosa, Schizanthus, Sedum, Silena, Statice, Tagetes, Tropaeolum, Verbena, Viola, Zinnia,* etc.

This is essentially the whole palette of ornamental herbaceous plants in commerce at the time and even today. Benary did not work with shrubs (www.desicca.de Dr Rolf Schlegel).

ACKNOWLEDGMENTS

THE author is grateful to the following people for their kindness and generosity in helping her with her research:

Axel Borg, state oenological librarian, Shields Library, University of California at Davis

Dr. Brent Elliott, Lindley Librarian, Royal Horticultural Society, London

Elizabeth Gilbert, Lindley Library, Royal Horticultural Society, London

Jane Glasby, librarian, San Francisco Botanical Garden at Strybing Arboretum; currently librarian, San Francisco Public Library

Dr. Keith Hammett, VMH, scholar and plantsman, Auckland, New Zealand

Maureen Horn, librarian, Massachusetts Horticultural Society

Professor Jules Janick, James Troop Distinguished Professor in Horticulture, Department of Horticulture and Landscape Architecture, Purdue University

Norma Kobzina, science librarian, Valley Biosciences Library, University of California at Berkeley (deceased)

David Lemon, plant breeder, formerly of Oglevee-Ecke Ranch, Lompoc, California

Darryl Morrison, head of Special Collections, Shields Library, University of California at Davis

Dr. James Nau, archivist, BallFloraSeed

Barbara Pitschel, head librarian, Helen Crocker Russell Library, San Francisco Botanical Garden, Strybing Arboretum (deceased)

Charles Quest-Ritson, scholar and rosarian, Amfreville, France, and Salisbury, England

John Skarstad, Special Collections, Shields Library, University of California at Davis, retired

Freek Vrugtman, International Lilac Registrar, Hamilton, Ontario, Canada

George Waters, editor emeritus, *Pacific Horticulture*

Chapter 3: Flower Breeders in Europe

Ernst Benary

Rudolf Benary, Ernst Benary's great-great-grandson, now deceased

Klaudia Benary Redlefsen, president, Ernst Benary Samenzucht

Delphinium

David Bassett, delphinium breeder, United Kingdom

Sweet Pea

John Coulter, local history librarian, Lewisham, London
Alice Formiga, Oregon State University, Special Collections, Corvallis, Oregon

Haage & Schmidt

Ulrich Haage, descendant of Friedrich Haage

Louis Van Houtte

Ingrid Verdegem, scholar and historian, Ghent, Belgium
Luc D'Haeze, scholar and historian, Ghent, Belgium
René De Herdt, director, Museum of Industrial Archaeology and Textiles, Ghent, Belgium

Chapter 4: Flower Breeders in the United States

Frank Reinelt

The author is very grateful to Frank Reinelt's children, Aphra Reinelt Katzev and Frank Reinelt Jr., for the story of their father's life
Reverend Jan Dus, the Czech Republic, genealogist, for information about the Brno Pomological Institute and A. Zvolanek

Chapter 5: Plants by Genus

Azaleas and Rhododendrons in Continental Europe

Harold Greer, rhododendron breeder and expert, Eugene, Oregon
Holger Hachmann, German rhododendron breeder
Birgit Hobbie, German rhododendron breeder
Tijs Huisman, floral photographer, the Netherlands
Sonja Nelson, editor emerita, *American Rhododendron Society Bulletin*
Ingrid Verdegem, scholar and rosarian, Belgium

Azaleas and Rhododendrons in Asia

Hideo Suzuki, Japan
Professor Taisaku Komeie, Kyoto University, obtained and translated Tomoo Wada's note about his late father, Koichiro.

Camellia

Luc D'Haeze, scholar and author, Ghent, Belgium
Rene De Herdt, director, Museum of Industrial Archaeology and Textiles, Ghent, Belgium
Lawrence Currie, California Academy of Sciences
Becky Morin, California Academy of Sciences
Dr. Hubert Linthe, Germany
Sue VerHoef, Kenan Research Library, Atlanta, Georgia
Donnchadh MacCarthaigh, professor of horticulture, Germany

Hydrangea

Mihaela Romoscanu, librarian, Bibliotheque Centrale, Agroscope Changins-Wädenswil

Lilac

Freek Vrugtman, International Lilac Registrar
David Galbraith, Royal Botanical Gardens, Hamilton, Ontario

Magnolia

Mark Flanagan, director, Windsor Great Park
Charles Williams, Caerhays Castle

Rose

Annette Bloch, rosarian, Luxembourg
Jane Borg, board member, Pajaro Valley Historical Society
Peter Evans, Wayne County historian, Wayne County, New York
William Grant, rosarian, Aptos, California
Jiangye He, University of California at Berkeley, Asian Studies Library
Victoria Hollowell, Missouri Botanical Garden
Steve Jones, president, American Rose Society
Brian Lym, Hunter College, New York
Jinshuang Ma, scholar and botanist, Shanghai
Rebecca Johnson Melvin, University of Delaware Special Collections Library
Jane Milem, Office of the County Historian, Wayne County, New York
Roger Phillips, rosarian, England
Charles Quest-Ritson, rosarian, England
Elizabeth Scholz, Hunter College, New York
Josef Thomas, president, Czech Rose Club
Iris Verdegem, rosarian, Belgium
Claude Vion, rosarian, Luxembourg

J. Craig Wallace, Northern Ireland Rose Society
Ya-li Zhang, Shanghai Botanical Garden
ZuoShuang Zhang, chairman, Chinese Rose Society

Chapter 6: Herbaceous Plants

Begonia

Axel Borg, state oenological librarian, University of California at Davis
Jane Borg, board member, Pajaro Valley Historical Society
Elizabeth ("Bess") Christensen, plant historian (deceased)
Amy Dunning, historian, Santa Cruz
Reverend Jan Dus, genealogical researcher, the Czech Republic
Jack Golding (deceased), begonia expert and taxonomist
Maureen Horn, librarian, Massachusetts Horticultural Society
Rosalind L. Hunnewell, library volunteer, Massachusetts Horticultural Society
"Hal" Hyde, grandson of H. A. Hyde
Aphra Reinelt Katzev, Frank Reinelt's daughter
Michael Ludwig, curator of KOLZ, a private begonia archive, San Diego
Sherrel Miller, Everett Vetterle's granddaughter
Jim Nau, archivist and historian, Ball Seed Company
Carol Notaras, begonia expert, American Begonia Society
Frank Perry, Capitola
Barbara Pitschel, librarian, Helen Crocker Russell Library, San Francisco Botanical
    Garden at Strybing Arboretum (deceased)
Frank Reinelt Jr., Frank Reinelt's son
Bob Rivers, Capitola
John Skarstad, Archivist, University of California at Davis
Andy Snow, Golden State Farms, Watsonville
Judy Steen, Capitola
Carolyn Swift, Capitola Museum
Berrnie Wiener, American Begonia Society, Pennsylvania chapter
Patricia Williams, Everett Vetterle's granddaughter
Rudolf ("Skee") Ziesenhenne, Rudolf Ziesenhenne's son

Dahlia

Thomas Brown, garden historian, Petaluma, California (deceased)
Keith Hammett, VMH, dahlia breeder, Auckland, New Zealand
Martin Kral, plant historian, Seattle, Washington
Tom Collins, former general secretary, National Dahlia Society
Harry Rissetto, American Dahlia Society, Washington DC
Mac Boyer, American Dahlia Society

Hemerocallis (the Daylily)

Dr. Linda Barnes, Hemerocallis collector
Nick Chase, Hemerocallis devotee
Ken Cobb, archivist, American Hemerocallis Society
Sydney Eddison, author and expert
Mary Collier Fisher, president-elect, American Hemerocallis Society
James Folsom, director, Huntington Botanical Gardens, San Marino, California
Marie Long, New York Botanical Garden Library
Marjorie Sturman, British Hosta and Hemerocallis Society

Lily

Judith McRae Freeman, lily breeder, Vancouver

Marigold

Lance Bentley, Bentley Seeds, Cambridge, New York
Bill Borchard, PanAmerican Seeds, Santa Paula, California
Gerald Burke, plantsman and garden writer
Elizabeth ("Bess") Christensen, horticultural historian, Lompoc, California
  (deceased)
David Combe, reference librarian, Ventura Public Library
Simon Crawford, horticultural consultant, South Warwickshire, England
Florike Egmond, historian, Rome
Denis Flaschenriem, plant breeder, PanAmerican Seed
Glenn Goldsmith, founder of Goldsmith Seeds, Hawaii
Ken Gottry, historian, Cambridge, New York
David Haswell, plant breeder, Leicester, England
Dr. Mathilde Holtrop, retired flower breeder, Placerville, California
Nona Koiovula, National Garden Bureau
Peter Lapinskas, horticulturist, Coventry, England
Budd LaRue, PanAmerican Seeds
David Lemon, plant breeder, Lompoc, California
Myra Manfrina, widow of Walt Manfrina, Lompoc
Dr. Maria Amelia Martins-Loucao, director, Jardim Botanico, Lisbon, Portugal
Bliss White McIntosh, daughter of Lyman White, Cambridge, New York
Mark Mondry, son of John Mondry
Dr. Jim Nau, historian, Ball Seed Company
Dr. Lisa Renken, director, Lompoc Museum, Lompoc
Dr. R. K. Roy, horticulturist, National Botanical Research Institute, Lucknow,
  India
Dr. Janakiram Tolety, head, Division of Floriculture and Landscaping, Indian Ag-
  ricultural Research Institute, New Delhi

Dr. Ruth Varela, University of Santiago de Compostela
Judy Wayno, reference librarian, Arthur Mann Library, Cornell University, Ithaca, New York

Narcissus

Peter Ramsay, narcissus breeder, New Zealand
John Hunter, narcissus breeder, New Zealand
Keith Hammett, plant scientist and dahlia breeder, New Zealand

Orchid

Ernest Hetherington, orchid hybridizer
Leon Glicenstein, orchid hybridizer
Donato Seidel, orchid grower, Brazil

Pelargonium

Rudolf Benary, Ernst Benary Seed Company
Mary Bodill, Ernest Walters's daughter
Sandra Connerley, pelargonium breeder, northern California
David Lemon, pelargonium breeder, central California
Tony Hutchinson, pelargonium breeder, Warwickshire, England
Andrea Ludwig, Wilhelm Elsner's daughter, Dresden

Peony

Jane Glasby, formerly librarian, San Francisco Botanical Garden at Strybing Arboretum
Kathy Crosby, librarian, Brooklyn Botanical Garden, Brooklyn, New York
Celine Arsenault, librarian, Montreal Botanical Garden, Montreal, Quebec, Canada
Roy Klehm, nurseryman and scholar, Avalon, Wisconsin

Sweet Pea

Wendy Betteridge, Evelyn Hemus Fyfe's granddaughter, New Zealand
Tony Fitch, Evelyn Hemus Fyfe's grandson, United Kingdom
Mrs. Mary Griffiths, Guy Hemus's daughter, United Kingdom
Keith Hammett, VMH, scholar, plant collector, and breeder, New Zealand
Robin Hawkins, Evelyn Hemus Fyfe's grandson-in-law, United Kingdom
Doreen Hopwood, genealogist, City of Birmingham Library, United Kingdom
Maureen Horn, librarian, Massachusetts Horticultural Society
Roger Parsons, National Collection of *Lathyrus odoratus*, United Kingdom
Dan Pawson, Jean (Ashworth) Waterworth's friend, New Zealand
Jackie Surtees, Web master, www.upton.uk.net

Robert Ryland, archivist, City of Birmingham Library, United Kingdom
Jean Waterworth, Hilda Hemus Ashworth's daughter (deceased)
Simon Wilkinson, historian, Upton-upon-Severn, United Kingdom

Sweet Peas in the United States—Hutchins

Keith Hammett, scholar and plantsman, Auckland, New Zealand
Roger Parsons, sweet pea expert in England
Maggie Humberston, librarian, the Connecticut Valley Historical Museums, Springfield, Massachusetts
Stephen Ross, archivist, Yale University, New Haven, Connecticut

Sweet Peas in the United States—Ferry Morse Company

Mike Tate, current director of sales for Ferry Morse
Maurice Smith, president, Harris Moran Seed Company, Davis, California
Dan Stephens, communications director, Harris Moran Seed Company, Davis, California
Malgosia Myc, Bentley Historical Library of the University of Michigan
Tanya Hollis, the California Historical Society
Wendy Welker, the California Historical Society
The staff of the San Francisco Public Library History Room
Mrs. Janet Brian, the San Benito Historical Society, Hollister, California

Sweet Peas in the United States—California

Reverend Jan Dus, genealogist, the Czech Republic
Mrs. Elizabeth ("Bess") Christensen (now deceased), Lompoc, California
Keith Hammett, VMH, scholar and plantsman, Auckland, New Zealand
David Lemon, plant breeder, formerly of Oglevee-Ecke Ranch, Lompoc, California

NOTES

Introduction

1. For more-specific information about the molecular and genetic science underlying the new methods, see George Acquaah, *Principles of Plant Genetics and Breeding* (Malden, MA: Blackwell Publishing, 2007).

2. Joachim Camerarius, *Hortus medicus et philosophicus* (Frankfurt am Main, 1588); Nehemiah Grew, *The Anatomy of Plants* (London: printed for the author by W. Rawlins, 1682); John Ray, *The History of Plants,* 3 vols. (London: typography Maria Clark, published by Henry Faithorne, 1686–1704).

3. Quoted in Sydney Eddison, *A Passion for Daylilies* (New York: Harper Collins, 1992).

4. Katharine White, *Onward and Upward in the Garden* (New York: Farrar, Strauss and Giroux, 1979).

5. Clarence Mahan, *Classic Irises and the Men and Women Who Created Them* (Malabar, FL: Krieger Publishing, 2006).

6. Anna Pavord, *The Tulip* (London: Bloomsbury Publishing, 2004).

Chapter 1: The Compression of History

1. H. R. Fletcher, *The Story of the Royal Horticultural Society, 1804–1968* (London: Oxford University Press for the Royal Horticultural Society, 1969).

2. Anonymous, *Selection of Physiological and Horticultural Papers Published in the Transactions of the Royal and Horticultural Societies by the Late Thomas Andrew Knight, to Which Is Prefixed a Sketch of His Life* (London: Longman, Orme, Brown, Green, 1841).

3. R. A. Fisher, "Has Mendel's Work Been Rediscovered?" *Annals of Science* 1 (1936): 115–37.

4. William Bateson, *Mendel's Principles of Heredity, a Defense* (London: Cambridge University Press, 1902).

5. James Logan, "Some Experiments Concerning the Impregnation of the Seeds of Plants," *Philosophical Transactions of the Royal Society of London* 39 (1736): 192–95.

6. Wilhelm Focke, *Die Plantzen-Mischlinge: Ein Betrag zur Biologie der Gewachse* (Berlin: Gebrüder Borntraeger, 1881).

7. Dutch Academy of Sciences prize contest, established 1830.

8. See Fletcher, *Story of the Royal Horticultural Society.*

9. Ibid.

10. Anonymous, *Selection of Physiological and Horticultural Papers.*

11. Charles Darwin, *The Correspondence of Charles Darwin,* ed. Frederick Burkhardt and Sydney Smith (Cambridge: Cambridge University Press, 1985).

12. Charles Darwin, *On the Origin of Species* (London: John Murray, 1859).

13. James Watson and Francis Crick, "A Structure for Deoxyribose Nucleic Acid," *Nature* 171 (1953): 737–38.

14. George Acquaah, *Principles of Plant Genetics and Breeding* (Malden, MA: Blackwell Publishing, 2007).

15. Simon Mawer, *Gregor Mendel: Planting the Seeds of Genetics* (New York: Abrams, in association with the Field Museum, 2006); Acquaah, *Principles of Plant Genetics.*

16. Roger J. Wood and Viteslav Orel, *Genetic Prehistory in Selective Breeding: A Prelude to Mendel* (New York: Oxford University Press, 2001).

17. Roger J. Wood and Viteslav Orel, "Scientific Breeding in Central Europe during the Early Nineteenth Century: Background to Mendel's Later Work," *Journal of the History of Biology* 38 (2005): 239–72.

18. Gregor Mendel, "Versuche über Pflanzenhybriden" (Experiments on Plant Hybridization), in *Verhandlungen des naturforschenden Vereines in Brünn,* vol. 4 (Brno: Vereines, 1866): 3–47.

19. Robert Olby and Peter Gantry, "Eleven References to Mendel before 1900," *Annals of Science* 24 (March 1968): 7–20.

20. Jim Endersby, *A Guinea Pig's History of Biology* (Cambridge, MA: Harvard University Press, 2009).

21. R. A. Fisher, "Has Mendel's Work Been Rediscovered?" *Annals of Science* 1 (1936): 115–37.

22. Margot Benary, Benary family history.

23. Focke, *Die Plantzen-Mischlinge.*

24. Bateson, *Mendel's Principles of Heredity.*

25. Darwin, *Correspondence.*

26. C. Stanier, archivist, Stamford Museum, Stamford, Lincolnshire, personal communication.

27. See Fletcher, *Story of the Royal Horticultural Society;* Thomas Laxton, "Notes on Some Changes and Variations in the Offspring of Cross-Fertilized Peas," *Journal of the Royal Horticultural Society,* n.s., 3 (1872): 10–13.

28. Laxton, "Notes on Some Changes."

29. William Laxton, "The Cross-Breeding and Hybridisation of Hardy Fruits," in *Report of the Third International Conference, 1906, on Genetics* (London: Royal Horticultural Society, 1907), 468–73.

30. Joseph Needham, *Botany,* part 1 of *Biology and Biological Technology,* Science and Civilisation in China, vol. 6 (Cambridge: Cambridge University Press, 1986).

Chapter 2: The Onrush of New Plants

1. Sue Shepard, *Seeds of Fortune: A Gardening Dynasty* (London: Bloomsbury Publishing, 2003).

2. Emil V. Bretschneider, *History of European Botanical Discoveries in China* (1898; reissued London: Ganesha Publishing, 1991).

3. René De Herdt, *Floralies gantoises et floriculture en Belgique,* translated from Flemish into French by Jean-Pierre Colson (Namur, Belgium: Erasme, 1994).

4. Peter Collinson and Alan W. Armstrong, *Forget Not Mee and My Garden: Correspondence of Peter Collinson* (Philadelphia, PA: American Philosophical Society, 2001).

5. For a recent book giving credit where credit was due, see Toby Musgrave, *The Head Gardeners* (London: Aurum Press, 2007).

6. Howard Higson, "The History and Legacy of the China Rose," Quarryhill Botanical Garden website (2008), available at www.quarryhillbg.org.

Chapter 3: Flower Breeders in Europe

1. Margot Benary, Benary family history.

2. Ibid.

3. Brian Langdon, *Begonias: Care and Cultivation* (London: Cassell, 1989).

4. Helen Dillon, 2004, http://homepage.eircom.net/~ranunculaceae/plants/plant_of_the_month/2004_07_Delphinium.html.

5. David Bassett, *Delphiniums* (Portland, OR: Timber Press, 2007).

6. John E. M. Thirkell, "The Contemporary Delphinium—Its Development and Its Future," *Delphiniums: Yearbook of the Delphinium Society* 47 (1978): 81–114; Thomas Fischer, "Delphiniums," *Horticulture* 197, no. 5 (2000): 42–45.

7. Judith M. Taylor, Keith Hammett, and Simon Wilkinson, "Setting the Record Straight: The Trouble with James Carter in 1865," *National Sweet Pea Society Annual* (2009): 71–72.

8. François Hirtz, "Victor Lemoine: Un grand nom de l'horticulture mondiale," thesis for doctor of pharmacy, Faculty of Pharmaceutical and Biological Sciences, University of Nancy, Nancy, France, 1993.

9. J. Beaujean, "Le voyage de Liege: De A. P. De Candolle, 2 Juin–2 Octobre, 1810," *Lejeunia,* n.s., 184 (2008): 17–18. De Candolle kept a meticulous diary. In 2003 it was rediscovered and printed in its entirety for the first time, as *Mémoires et souvenirs d'Augustin Pyramus de Candolle, 1778–1841,* ed. Jean-Daniel Candaux (Geneva: Georg, 2003).

10. Louis Van Houtte, *Flore des Serres et des Jardins de l'Europe* (Greenhouse and garden flowers in Europe) (Ghent, Belgium: published by the author, 1845–83); François Joyaux, *La Rose: Une passion française* (Paris: Editions Complexe, 2001).

11. Susan Chamberlin, "The Life of Dr. Francesco Franceschi and His Park," *Pacific Horticulture* 63, nos. 3–4 (2002): 4–12.

12. Thomas Brown, *Syringa before 1900* (Petaluma, CA: published by the author, 2004).

13. Sue Shepard, *Seeds of Fortune* (London: Bloomsbury Publishing, 2003).

14. Liam Wilkinson, information specialist, City of York Libraries, personal communication.

15. Pat Edwards, *The Russell Lupin Story* (Guildford, Surrey: National Council for the Conservation of Plants and Gardens, ca. 2003).

16. William Robinson, *The English Flower Garden and Home Grounds* (London: John Murray, 1903).

17. Available at City of York, www.york.gov.uk.

18. Le Texnier [François Le Tesnier], *Louis van Houtte, Notices sur les jardiniers célèbres et les amateurs de jardins* (Paris: Librarie Horticole, 1911). Translations by Judith M. Taylor.

19. H. Trivier, *Remarkable Men in Belgian Horticulture* (Ghent, Belgium: Syndicale Kamer van de Belgische Tuinbouw, 1985).

20. Ray Desmond, "Victorian Gardening Magazines," *Garden History Journal* 5, no. 3 (1977): 47–64.

21. *Centenaire de la naissance de Louis van Houtte: Notes biographiques et souvenirs,* program for fêtes jubilaires 1910 (Ghent, Belgium: Commission Organisatrice des Fêtes, 1910).

22. Merle A. Reinikka, *A History of the Orchid* (Portland, OR: Timber Press, 1972; reissued 1995).

23. H. Harold Hume, *Camellias* (New York: Macmillan, 1951).

Chapter 4: Flower Breeders in the United States

1. Charles Darwin, *The Variations of Animals and Plants under Domestication* (New York: Orange, Judd, 1868).

2. Robert D. Berka, "Burbank's Hybrid West Coast Lilies," *Pacific Horticulture* 72, no. 3 (2011), http://www.pacifichorticulture.org/articles/burbanks-hybrid-west-coast-lilies/.

3. Jane S. Smith, *The Garden of Invention: Luther Burbank and the Business of Breeding Plants* (New York: Penguin, 2009).

4. Neal O. Anderson and Richard T. Olsen, "A Vast Array of Beauty: The Accomplishments of the Father of American Ornamental Plant Breeding, Luther Burbank," paper presented at the American Society for Horticultural Science Annual Conference, Desert Springs, CA, July 2013.

5. Louella Dirksen with Norma Lee Browning, *The Honorable Mr. Marigold: My Life with Everett Dirksen* (Garden City, NY: Doubleday and Company, 1972).

6. Judith M. Taylor, "The Marigold in California," *Pacific Horticulture* 71, no. 4 (2010).

7. Eliza Farnham, *California In Doors and Out; or, How We Farm, Mine, and Live Generally in the Golden State* (1856; facsimile, Nieuwkoop, the Netherlands: B. De Graaf, 1972).

8. Patrick Barry, *Treatise on the Fruit Garden* (Rochester, NY: Barry and Ellwanger, 1851; new ed., 1872).

9. Ricardo Arias Martinez, *The Master of Seeds: Life and Work of Claude Hope* (Cartago, Costa Rica: published by the author, 1992).

10. Christopher Grey Wilson, *Impatiens of Africa* (Rotterdam: A. A. Balkema, 1980).

11. Ray Morgan, *Impatiens* (Portland, OR: Timber Press, 1980).

12. Robert J. Griesbach, "Petunia: *Petunia* × *hybrida*," in Neil O. Anderson, *Flower Breeding and Genetics* (Dordrecht: Springer, 2006), 301–4.

13. Christopher Brickell and Judith Zuk, eds., *The American Horticultural Society A–Z Encyclopedia of Garden Plants* (New York: DK Publishing, 1997).

14. The URL for the institute's website is www.skolarjhrad.cz.

15. Frank Reinelt, "Delphiniums in the United States," *Journal of the California Horticultural Society* 8, no. 4 (1947): 140–47.

16. Brian Langdon, *Begonias: Care and Cultivation of Tuberous Varieties* (London: Cassell, 1989).

17. "Report of the Proceedings . . . ," *Journal of the Royal Horticultural Society* (1963): 142–58.

18. C. Burr, "Frank Reinelt," *Pacific Horticulture* 41, no. 2 (1980): 48.

Chapter 5: Shrubs

Azalea and Rhododendron

1. Mea Allen, *The Tradescants* (London: Michael Joseph, 1964).

2. Hermann Sleumer, *An Account of Rhododendron in Malesia* (Groningen, the Netherlands: P. Noordhoff, 1966).

3. J. G. Millais, *Rhododendrons First Series: The Prospectus* and *Rhododendrons Second Series* (London: Longmans, Green, 1917 and 1924).

4. Waterers Nursery, "Waterers Heritage," available at www.waterersnursery .co.uk.

5. C. E. Lucas Phillips and Peter N. Barber, *The Rothschild Rhododendrons: A Record of the Gardens at Exbury* (London: Cassell, 1972; reissued 1979).

6. E. H. M. Cox, *Plant Hunting in China* (London: Scientific Book Guild, 1945).

7. Peter Cox, "Euan Hillhouse Methven Cox, 1893–1977," *Journal American Rhododendron Society* 31, no. 4 (1977): 233–35.

8. Peter Cox, *Cox's Guide to Choosing Rhododendrons* (Portland, OR: Timber Press, 1990).

9. Kenneth Cox, ed., with contributions by Kenneth Storm Jr. and Ian Baker, *Frank Kingdon Ward's Riddle of the Tsangpo Gorges: Retracing the Epic Journey of 1924–1925 in South East Tibet* (Woodbridge, Suffolk: Antique Collectors' Club, 2001).

10. Richard W. Bosley, "Bosley Dexter Rhododendrons," *Journal American Rhododendron Society* 25, no. 3 (1971): 175–78.

11. Heman A. Howard, "Dexter Rhododendrons: Their Past, Present and Future," *Journal American Rhododendron Society* 26, no. 2 (1971): 70–73.

12. Donald W. Hyatt, "Joe Gable's Rhododendrons—A Legacy" (1971), www.tjhsst.edu/~dhyatt/azaleas/new/gable.html.

13. Homer Salley, "The Delp Hybrids: Part 1, A Passion for Rhododendron Hybridizing," *Journal American Rhododendron Society* 49, no. 1 (1995): 23–25.

14. Philip A. Livingston and Franklin H. West, *Hybrids and Hybridizers: Rhododendron and Azalea for Eastern North America* (Newtown Square, PA: Harrowood Books, 1978).

15. Walter Schmalscheidt, *Rhododendron-Züchtung in Deutschland* (Westerstede, Germany: Cramer-Druck, 1980).

16. Herbert Heckenbleikner, "Some Rhododendron Gardens in Germany, Switzerland and Holland," *Quarterly Bulletin of the American Rhododendron Society* 26, no. 4 (1972): 260–63.

17. Schmalscheidt, *Rhododendron-Züchtung in Deutschland;* Heckenbleikner, "Some Rhododendron Gardens"; Friedrich W. Dürre, "The Breeding of Hardy Rhododendrons," trans. Herbert Heckenbleikner, *Quarterly Bulletin of the American Rhododendron Society* 26, no. 3 (1980): 146–51.

18. Itoh Ihei, *The Brocade Pillow: Azaleas of Old Japan* [1692], trans. and ed. John Creech (Boston, MA: Weatherhill, 1984).

19. Koichiro Wada, "*Rhododendron yakushimanum,*" *Quarterly Bulletin of the American Rhododendron Society* 35, no. 2 (1981): 74–75.

20. Michael Haworth-Booth, *Effective Flowering Shrubs* (New York: St. Martin's Press, 1965).

21. Tomoo Wada, "Wada Koichiro no denki (A Biography of Koichiro Wada)," *Rhododendron* 11 (1982): 62–63.

22. Frank Doleshy, "Koichiro Wada," *Quarterly Bulletin of the American Rhododendron Society* 35, no. 2 (1981): 77.

23. Hideo Suzuki, 2008, personal communication.

Camellia

1. Luc D'Haeze, personal communication.

2. Robert Fortune, *A Journey to the Tea Countries of China* (London: Mildmay, 1857; reissued 1987).

3. Stirling Macoboy, *Illustrated Encyclopedia of Camellias* (Portland, OR: Timber Press, 1998).

4. Alice Coats, *Garden Shrubs and Their Histories* (New York: Dutton, 1964).

5. Peter Longhurst and T. J. Savige, *The Camellia* (Sydney: Bay Books, 1982).

6. Mustafa Haikal, *Das Geheimenis der Kamelie* (Dresden: Sandstein, 2008).

7. Alvin Seidel, *The Seidels: A Victorian and Saxonian Saga* (Toorak, Victoria: published by the author, 1994).

8. Alexandre Dumas, *fils, La Dame aux Caméllias* (Paris, 1848).

9. Abbé Lorenzo Berlèse, *Monographie du genre Camellia* (Paris, 1840).

10. Abbé Lorenzo Berlèse, *Iconographie du genre Camellia,* 3 vols. (Paris, 1841–43).

11. H. Harold Hume, *Camellias: Kinds and Culture* (New York: Macmillan, 1951).

12. Stirling Macoboy, *A Colour Dictionary of the Camellia* (Portland, OR: Timber Press, 1982).

13. Ambroise Verschaffelt, *Nouvelle iconographie des camellias,* 13 vols. (Ghent, Belgium: published by the author, 1848–60).

14. Ambroise Verschaffelt, *New Iconography of the Camellias, 1848–1860,* trans. E. A. McIlhenny (Avery Island, LA: privately printed, 1945).

15. Michael Reynolds, "A History of Fruitland Nurseries, Augusta, Georgia and the Berckmans Family in America," *Magnolia: Bulletin of the Southern Garden History Society* 18 (Winter 2002–3): 1–13.

16. Roland M. Harper, "Development of Agriculture in Upper Georgia from 1850 to 1920," *Georgia Historical Quarterly* 6, no. 2 (1922): 3–27; Harper, "Development of Agriculture in Lower Georgia from 1850 to 1920," *Georgia Historical Quarterly* 6, no. 2 (1922): 97–121.

17. Alhambra is where John Muir settled after his epoch-making treks in the Sierra. He married Dr. Theodore Strentzel's daughter and managed the doctor's orchards.

18. William Hertrich, *Camellias in the Huntington Gardens,* 3 vols. (San Marino, CA: Huntington Botanical Gardens, 1954).

Hydrangea

1. Michael Dirr, *Hydrangeas for American Gardens* (Portland, OR: Timber Press, 2004).

2. Corinne Mallet, *Hydrangeas: Species and Cultivars* (Varengeville-sur-mer, France: published by the author, 1992).

3. C. J. Van Gelderen and D. M. Van Gelderen, *Encyclopedia of Hydrangeas* (Portland, OR: Timber Press, 2004).

4. Fritz Meier, *Tellerhortensien-Zuchtungen* (Wädenswil, Switzerland: Eidgenössische Forschungsanstalt für Obst-, Wein- und Gartenbau, 1990).

5. Michael Haworth-Booth, *The Hydrangeas* (London: Constable, 1984).

Lilac

1. Alice Harding, *Lilacs in My Garden: A Practical Handbook for Amateurs* (New York: Macmillan, 1933).

2. Father John L. Fiala, revised and updated by Freek Vrugtman, *Lilacs: A Gardener's Encyclopedia* (Portland, OR: Timber Press, 2008).

3. Leonid Kolesnikov, *Lilac* (Moscow: Foreign Languages Publishing House, 1955).

4. Edwinna von Baeyer, "The Horticultural Odyssey of Isabella Preston," *Canadian Horticultural History* 1, no. 3 (1987): 125–75.

5. Frank Skinner, *Horticultural Horizons: Plant Breeding and Introduction at Dropmore, Manitoba* (Winnipeg: Manitoba Department of Agriculture and Conservation, 1966).

6. Fiala, *Lilacs.*

7. Susan Delano McKelvey, *Lilac: A Monograph* (New York: Macmillan, 1928).

Magnolia

1. Dorothy J. Callaway, *The World of Magnolias* (Portland, OR: Timber Press, 1994).

2. James A. Gardiner, *Magnolias: A Gardener's Guide* (Portland, OR: Timber Press, 2000).

3. Suzanne Treseder, *A Passion for Plants: The Treseders of Truro* (Bodmin, Cornwall: Alison Hodge, 2004).

4. Valentine S. Paton and Jean M. Paton, *Magnolias in Cornish Gardens* (Fowey, Cornwall: Alexander Associates, 2001).

5. J. G. Millais, *Magnolias* (London: Longmans Green, 1927).

6. Treseder, *Passion for Plants.*

Rose

1. For more on roses, see Peter Beales, *Classic Roses* (New York: Holt, Rinehart, 1985); Charles Quest-Ritson, *Climbing Roses of the World* (Portland, OR: Timber Press, 2003); and Jack Harkness, *Makers of Heavenly Roses* (London: Souvenir Press, 1985).

2. Gu Cuizhi and K. R. Robertson, "*Rosa* L.," in *Flora of China,* vol. 9, *Connaraceae-Rosaceae,* ed. C. Y. Wu, P. H. Raven, and D. Y. Hong, 339 (Beijing: Science Press; St. Louis: Missouri Botanical Garden Press, 2003).

3. John Lindley, *Rosarum Monographia; or, A Botanical History of Roses* (London: James Ridgway, 1820), www.biodiversitylibrary.org/item/101095#page/5/mode/1up.

4. François Joyaux, *La Rose: Une passion française; Histoire de la rose en France, 1778–1914* (Paris: Editions Complexe, 2001).

5. Roger Phillips and Martyn Rix, *The Quest for the Rose* (New York: Random House, 1993).

6. Graham Stuart Thomas, *The Graham Stuart Thomas Rose Book* (Portland, OR: Timber Press, 1955; reissued 1994).

7. Brent C. Dickerson, *The Old Rose Adventurer* (Portland, OR: Timber Press, 1999).

8. Claude-Antonin Thory, *Monographie; ou, Histoire naturelle du genre groseillier, contenant la description, l'histoire, la culture et les usages de toutes les groseilles connues . . .* (Paris: P. Dufart, 1829).

9. Claude-Antonin Thory, *Prodrome de la monographie des espèces et variétés connues du genre rosier, divisées selon leur ordre naturel, avec la synonymie, les noms vulgaires, un tableau synoptique . . .* (Paris: P. Dufart, 1820).

10. To see Thory's chart, go to www.biodiversitylibrary.org/item/52912#page /44/mode/1up.

11. J. H. Nicolas, *A Rose Odyssey* (Garden City, NY: Doubleday Doran, 1937).

12. Joyaux, *La Rose.*

13. Philipp Franz von Siebold and Joseph Gerhard Zuccarini, *Flora Japonicae familiae naturales adjectis generum et specierum exemplis selectis* (1845), 128.

14. In medical history, a Jean Descemet (1732–1810) was the discoverer of the important posterior corneal layer still known as "Descemet's membrane." Whether the two men were related is not known.

15. Dickerson, *Old Rose Adventurer.*

16. Henry B. Ellwanger, *The Rose: A Treatise* (New York: Dodd, Mead, 1882; reissued 1914).

17. Quest-Ritson, *Climbing Roses of the World.*

18. Charles Quest-Ritson, personal communication.

19. Thomas, *Graham Stuart Thomas Rose Book.*

20. Odile Masquelier has written a useful brief essay about this grower: "François Lacharme's Noisette Roses" (n.d.), available at www.venturarose.org.

21. Harkness, *Makers of Heavenly Roses.*

22. Quest-Ritson, *Climbing Roses of the World.*

23. Ingrid Verdegem, personal communication.

24. Quest-Ritson, *Climbing Roses of the World.*

25. National Rose Society 1890 obituary of Henry Bennett.

26. Betty Massingham, *Turn on the Fountains: The Life of Dean Hole* (London: Victor Gollancz, 1974).

27. Quest-Ritson, *Climbing Roses.*

28. William Paul, *The Rose Garden* (London: Kent and Co., 1848).

29. Quest-Ritson, *Climbing Roses.*

30. Harkness, *Makers of Heavenly Roses.*

31. Ellwanger, *The Rose: A Treatise.*

32. William Grant, personal communication.

33. William A. Grant, "Padre of the Roses," in *Old Garden Roses and Beyond* (2003), www.paulbardenroses.com/padre.html.

34. Herbert C. Swim, *Roses: From Dream to Reality* (Ontario, CA: Stumpf Publishing, 1988).

35. Judith M. Taylor, *The Olive in California: History of an Immigrant Tree* (Berkeley, CA: Ten Speed Press, 2000).

36. Francis E. Lester, "Roses of the Forty-Niners," *American Rose Annual 1932* (Harrisburg, PA: American Rose Society, 1932), 100–101.

37. Rebecca Johnson Melvin, University of Delaware Special Collections Library, personal communication.

38. Nicolas, *Rose Odyssey.*

39. Robert W. Wells, *Papa Floribunda: A Biography of Eugene Boerner* (Milwaukee, WI: BBG Publishers, 1989).

40. Harkness, *Makers of Heavenly Roses.*

41. William Grant, personal communication.

42. Erich Unmuth, "Rudolf Geschwind," *Rosa Mundi* 21, no. 1 (Autumn 2006): 7.

43. Quest-Ritson, *Climbing Roses of the World.*

44. Annette Bloch, personal communication.

45. Harkness, *Makers of Heavenly Roses.*

46. Peter Valder, *The Garden Plants of China* (Portland, OR: Timber Press, 1999).

47. At that stage in Chinese history, these roses were not yet known as Banksia.

48. Xu Zhou, *Luoyang hua mu ji* Series: *Shuo fu*, vol. 14, 1927.

49. Valder, *Garden Plants of China,* 218–19.

50. Hazel LeRougetel, *A Heritage of Roses* (Owings Mills, MD: Stemmer, 1988).

51. Mikinori Ogisu, "Some Thoughts on the History of China Roses," *New Plantsman* 3, no. 3 (1996): 1152–57.

52. Zhang ZuoShuang, *Rose of China* (Beijing: China Forestry Publishing House, 2006).

Chapter 6: Herbaceous Plants

Begonia

1. USDA, ARS, National Genetic Resources Program, *Germplasm Resources Information Network—(GRIN)* [online database], National Germplasm Resources Laboratory, Beltsville, MD, www.ars-grin.gov/cgi-bin/npgs/html/queries.pl.

2. Mark C. Tebbitt, *Begonias: Cultivation, Identification and Natural History* (Portland, OR: Timber Press, 2005).

3. Simon Varey, Rafael Chabran, and Dora Weiner, *Searching for the Secrets of Nature: The Life and Works of Dr. Francisco Hernandez* (Stanford: Stanford University Press, 2000).

4. Tebbitt, *Begonias.*

5. Judith M. Taylor, *Tangible Memories: Californians and Their Gardens, 1800–1950* (Philadelphia, PA: Xlibris Press, 2003).

6. Helen K. Krauss, *Begonias for American Homes and Gardens* (New York: Macmillan, 1947).

7. Charles Chevalier, *Les Begonias,* trans. Alva G. Graham (Pasadena, CA: American Begonia Society, 1938; reissued 1973).

8. Eva Kenworthy Gray, *Begonias* (Pacific Beach, CA: published by the author, 1931).

9. Worth A. Brown, *Tuberous Begonias: A Complete Guide for Amateur and Specialist* (New York: M. C. Barrow, 1948).

10. H. M. Butterfield, *Growing Begonias in California,* University of California Agricultural Extension Bulletin 162 (Berkeley: University of California Press, 1960).

11. Janet Brown, "Honoring Mr. Begonia," *The Begonian* 65, no. 5 (1998): 176–80.

12. Rudolf Ziesenhenne, *A Suggested Guide to the Classification of Begonia for Show Purposes* (Pasadena, CA: American Begonia Society, 1969).

13. Brown, *Tuberous Begonias.*

14. For younger readers, F. W. Woolworth and Company, or Woolworth's, was the first national chain of very modestly priced department stores, making it possible for people without much money to buy attractive and useful merchandise.

Dahlia

1. Simon Varey, Rafael Chabran, and Dora Weiner, *Searching for the Secrets of Nature: The Life and Work of Dr. Francisco Hernandez* (Stanford: Stanford University Press, 2000).

2. Samuel L. Emsweller, P. Brierley, D. V. Lumsden, and F. D. Mulford, "Improvement of Flowers by Breeding," in *United States Department of Agriculture Yearbook,* 890–998 (Washington, DC: USDA, 1937).

3. Martin Kral, "Dahlia Myths," in *Dahlias of Today* (2001 to 2008), yearbook of the Puget Sound Dahlia Society, Seattle, WA.

4. Harold R. Fletcher, *The Story of the Royal Horticultural Society, 1804–1968* (London: Oxford University Press for the Royal Horticultural Society, 1969).

5. Emsweller et al., "Improvement of Flowers by Breeding."

6. Kral, "Dahlia Myths."

7. Gerald Weland, "The Alpha and Omega of Dahlia," *Bulletin of the American Dahlia Society* 83, no. 2 (1996): 58–70; 83, no. 3 (1996): 69–79; 84, no. 1 (1997): 75–87; 84, no. 2 (1997): 42–60; and 84, no. 3 (1997): 52–64.

8. Ted Collins, lecture to the Midlands Dahlia Society, Kenilworth, UK, 2008.

9. Robert J. Skidelsky, *John Maynard Keynes,* vol. 1 (New York: Viking, 2001).

10. Collins, 2008 lecture to the Midlands Dahlia Society.

11. Frederick Burkhardt, Duncan Porter, Sheila Ann Dean, Jonathan R. Topham, and Sarah Wilmot, eds., *The Correspondence of Charles Darwin,* vol. 11 (Cambridge University Press, 1985), 291.

12. Kral, "Dahlia Myths."

13. Thomas Brown, personal communication.

Hemerocallis (the Daylily)

1. Emile V. Bretshneider, *European Botanical Discoveries in China* (1898; reissued London: Ganesha, 2002).

2. Frances Gatlin, *Daylilies: A Fifty Year Affair* (Edgerton, MO: American Hemerocallis Society, 1995).

3. Frances L. Gatlin, with James R. Brennan, eds., *The New Daylily Handbook* (Edgerton, MO: American Hemerocallis Society, 2002).

4. Harold R. Fletcher, *The History of the Royal Horticultural Society, 1804–1968* (London: Oxford University Press for the Royal Horticultural Society, 1969).

5. James and Debra Folsom, "Stout Winners," *Hemerocallis Register (Region 7)* 21, no. 2 (1992): 18–20.

Lily

1. Henry John Elwes, *Monograph of the Genus Lilium* (London: Taylor and Francis, 1880).

2. Ernest H. Wilson, *Lilies of Eastern Asia* (London: Dulau, 1925).

3. *North American Lily Society Yearbook 2004* et seq. (Geneva, NY: North American Lily Society).

4. Ernest H. Wilson, *Aristocrats of the Garden* (Garden City, NY: Doubleday Page, 1917).

5. David Brown, "Bellingham Hybrids," *North American Lily Society Quarterly Bulletin* 38, no. 3 (1984): 10–11.

6. Edward A. McRae, *Lilies: A Guide for Growers and Collectors* (Portland, OR: Timber Press, 1998).

7. F. F. Rockwood, Esther C. Grayson, and Jan de Graaf, *The Complete Book of Lilies* (Garden City, NY: Doubleday, 1961).

8. Samuel L. Emsweller, P. Brierly, D. V. Lumsden, and F. L. Mulford, *United States Department of Agriculture Yearbook 1937,* 890–998 (Washington, DC: USDA, 1937).

Marigold

1. Gertrude Jekyll, *Annuals and Biennials: The Best Annual and Biennial Plants and Their Use in the Garden* (London: Country Life; New York, Scribner, 1916).

2. *United States Department of Agriculture Floricultural Census 1998* (Washington, DC: USDA, 1998).

3. Christopher Lloyd and Graham Rice, *Garden Flowers from Seed* (London: Viking Press, 1991).

4. This information comes from a distinguished Dutch horticulturist, Florike Egmond.

5. William Robinson, *The English Flower Garden* (New York: Amaryllis Press, 1984).

6. Father Bernardino de Sahagún, *Historia general de los cosas de Nueva España* (Mexico City: Museo Nacional de Arqueológica, Historia y Etnográfica, 1926).

7. Patrizia Granziera, "Concept of the Garden in Pre-Hispanic Mexico," *Garden History* 29, no. 2 (Winter 2001): 185–213.

8. Emily Walcott Emmart, ed. and trans., *The Badianus Manuscript (Codex Barberini Latin 240)*, *Vatican Library* (Baltimore, MD: Johns Hopkins University Press, 1940); William Gates, *The de la Cruz–Badiano Aztec Herbal of 1552* (Baltimore, MD: Mayan Society, 1939).

9. Eric Thompson, *Mexico before Cortez: An Account of the Daily Life, Religion, and Ritual of the Aztecs and Kindred People* (New York: Charles Scribner, 1933).

10. George Vaillant, *Aztecs of Mexico* (Garden City, NY: Doubleday Books, 1947).

11. Simon Varey, Rafael Chabron, and Dora B. Weiner, eds., *The Life and Works of Dr. Francisco Hernandez* (Stanford: Stanford University Press, 2000).

12. Lawrence Kaplan, "Historical and Ethnobotanical Aspects of Domestication in Tagetes," *Economic Botany* 14 (1960): 200–202.

13. Robert Trostle Neher, "The Ethnobotany of Tagetes," *Economic Botany* 22, no. 4 (1969): 317–25.

14. Gérard Aymonin, ed., *The Besler Florilegium: Plants of the Four Seasons* (New York: Harry N. Abrams, 1989).

15. Sir George Watt, *A Dictionary of the Economic Products of India*, vol. 4, part 3 (London: John Murray, 1893).

16. J. E. Hernandez Bermejo and J. Leon, eds., *Neglected Crops: 1492 from a Different Perspective*, published in collaboration with the Botanical Garden of Córdoba (Spain) as part of the Etnobotánica 92 Programme, Andalusia, 1992 (Rome: Food and Agriculture Organization of the United Nations, 1994).

17. Nicholas Monardes, *Dos libros: El uno que trata de todas las cosas que traen de nuestras Indias Occidentales* (Seville: Hernando Diaz, 1569).

18. John Frampton, *Joyfull Newes out of the Newe Founde Worlde* (1577; reissued London: W. Norton, 1925).

19. Ibid.

20. Richard Grove, "Indigenous Knowledge and the Significance of Southwest India for Portuguese and Dutch Constructions of Tropical Nature," *Modern Asian Studies* 30, no. 1 (1996): 121–43.

21. Garcia da Orta, *Colloquios dos simples e drogas da India* [Colloquies on the Simples and Drugs of India] (Goa: Johannes de Endem, 1563).

22. Arun Sinha, *Goa, India: A Critical Portrait of Post-colonial Goa* (New Delhi: Bibliophile South Asia in association with Promilla, 2002).

23. Dr. T. Janakiram, personal communication.

24. R. K. Roy and A. N. Sharga, *Marigold* (Lucknow: India Economic Botany Information Service, National Botanical Research Institute, 2000).

25. For more information about the work in India, see Judith Taylor, "Visions of Loveliness Supplement," www.horthistoria.com, under "Articles."

26. Daniel Meyer, *All The Best and Nothing Else: The Story of Ball Horticultural Company* (West Chicago, IL: Ball Horticultural Company, 2005).

27. Alice Formiga, "A Short History of the Seed and Nursery Catalogue in Europe and the U.S." (2009), http://scarc.library.oregonstate.edu/omeka/exhibits/show/seed.

28. Brent Elliott, *Victorian Gardens* (Portland, OR: Timber Press, 1986).

29. Denise Wiles Adams, *Restoring American Gardens: An Encyclopedia of Heirloom Ornamental Plants, 1640–1940* (Portland, OR: Timber Press, 2004).

30. James Vick, *Vick's Flower and Vegetable Garden* (Rochester, NY: James Vick's Sons, 1876).

31. Lyman White, *Heirlooms and Genetics* (Cambridge, NY: published by the author, 1988).

32. For a list of these flowers, see Judith Taylor, "The Marigold in California: A Supplement," www.horthistoria.com, under "Articles" section.

33. Ibid.

34. Ibid.

35. Gerald Burke, "I Knew David Burpee," *Heirloom Gardener* 2, no. 1 (2004): 33–35.

36. Taylor, "Marigold in California."

37. Ibid.

38. Ibid.

39. Glenn Goldsmith, personal communication.

40. For a more complete list of Dr. Holtrop's cultivars, see Judith Taylor, "The Marigold in California: A Supplement," www.horthistoria.com, under "Articles" section.

41. Jules Janick, *Horticultural Science*, 4th ed. (San Francisco, CA: W. H. Freeman, 1986).

42. Bess Gedney Christensen, *Acres of Loveliness: The Flower Seed Industry of the Lompoc Valley* (Lompoc, CA: Lompoc Botanic and Horticultural Society, 2006).

Narcissus

1. E. A. Bowles, *A Handbook of Narcissus* (London: Martin Hopkinson, 1934).

2. A. Fernandes, *Keys to the Identification of Native and Naturalized Taxa of*

the Genus Narcissus *L.,* Daffodil Tulip Year Book 54 (1968); T. G. Tutin, V. H. Heywood, N. A. Burges, D. M. Moore, D. H. Valentine, and S. M. Walters, eds., *Flora Europaea,* vol. 5 (Cambridge: Cambridge University Press, 1980).

3. Michael Jefferson-Brown, *The Narcissus* (Portland, OR: Timber Press, 1991).

4. F. W. Burbidge, *The Narcissus: Its History and Culture* (London: L. Reeve and Co., 1875).

5. Jefferson-Brown, *The Narcissus.*

6. Peter Ramsay, "John S. B. Lea," in *New Zealand Daffodil Annual 2009* (National Daffodil Society of New Zealand, 2009).

7. John Hunter, "History of the National Daffodil Society of New Zealand," in *New Zealand Daffodil Annual 2001* (National Daffodil Society of New Zealand, 2001), 5–25.

8. Reg Cull, John Hunter, Max Hamilton, and Peter Ramsay, "A Daffodil Giant," in *New Zealand Daffodil Annual 2009* (National Daffodil Society of New Zealand, 2009).

Orchid

1. Charles Darwin, *On the Various Contrivances by Which British and Foreign Orchids Are Fertilised by Insects* (London: Longmans Green, 1862).

2. Phil De Vries, "Bug Alert," *Nature* television series (New York: Public Broadcasting Service).

3. Jan Sapp, *Evolution by Association: A History of Symbiosis* (Oxford: Oxford University Press, 1994).

4. Merle A. Reinikka, *A History of the Orchid* (Portland, OR: Timber Press, 1972; reissued 1994).

5. Arthur Swinson, *Frederick Sander: The Orchid King: The Record of a Passion* (London: Hodder and Stoughton, 1970).

6. Edward A. White, *American Orchid Culture* (New York: A. T. De La Mare, 1948).

7. Ernest Hetherington, "The Twentieth Century: The Golden Century of Orchid History," *Orchid Digest* 63, no. 3 (1999): 116–23.

8. Ibid. Ernest Hetherington turned ninety in 2010. Not only did he have a distinguished career as an orchid breeder, beginning in 1934, but his stewardship of as much material as he could collect will be of inestimable benefit to future historians.

9. Lewis C. Vaughn, "The First *Phalaenopsis* Hybrid," *Bulletin of the American Orchid Society* 42, no. 1 (1973): 13–15.

10. Ernest Hetherington, personal communication.

11. Henri Vacheron's grandson Maurice Lecoufle celebrated his hundredth birthday in October 2013.

12. Alwin C. Seidel, *The Seidel Saga: Saxonian and Victorian* (Toorak, Victoria: published by the author, 1994).

13. Frederick Sander, *Sander's Complete List of Orchid Hybrids* (St. Albans, Hertfordshire: Sander and Sons, 1915).

Pelargonium

1. Richard Gorer, *The Development of Garden Flowers* (London: Eyre and Spottiswoode, 1970).

2. Harry M. Butterfield, "History of Pelargoniums," *Journal of the California Horticultural Society* 2, no. 3 (1941): 173–76.

3. Paul Hermann, *Paradisi Batavi Prodromus sive plantarum exoticarum in Batavorum Hortis observatorum* (Leiden, 1689).

4. Liberty Hyde Bailey, *The Standard Encyclopedia of Horticulture* (New York: Macmillan, 1916).

5. Robert Sweet, *Geraniaceae: The Natural Order of Gerania, Illustrated by Coloured Figures and Descriptions . . .*, vols. 1–5 (London, 1820–30).

6. The Old Bailey is the folk name for the Central Criminal Court in London.

7. Anne Wilkinson, *The Passion for Pelargoniums* (Stroud, Gloucestershire: Sutton Publishers, 2007).

8. James Bartholomew, *Yew and Non-yew: Gardening for Horticultural Climbers* (London: Arrow Books, 1988).

9. Judith M. Taylor, *The Global Migrations of Ornamental Plants: How the World Got into Your Garden* (St Louis: Missouri Botanical Garden Press, 2009).

10. Gorer, *Development of Garden Flowers.*

11. Wilhelm Elsner, *Lebenserinnerungen* (Dresden: published by the author, 2005).

12. Sandra Connerley, personal communication.

Peony

1. Alice Harding, *The Peony,* introduced and updated by Roy Klehm (Portland, OR: Timber Press, 1993).

2. Richard Gorer, *The Development of Garden Flowers* (London: Eyre and Spottiswoode, 1970).

3. Emile Vasilievich Bretschneider, *History of European Botanical Discoveries in China* (1891; reissued London: Ganesha Publishing, 2002).

4. Judith M. Taylor, *The Global Migrations of Ornamental Plants: How the World Got into Your Garden* (St. Louis: Missouri Botanical Garden Press, 2009).

5. Harding, *The Peony.*

6. The nomenclature is obsolete.

7. James Boyd, ed., *Peonies: The Manual of the American Peony Society* (American Peony Society, 1928).

8. The full title was *Herbaceous Chinese Peonies: A List of Authentic Varieties According to the Catalogues of Modeste Guerin, 186; Verdier, 186; Méchin, 1860–1880; Calot, 1862–1873; Crousse, 1875–1900; Lemoine, 1898–1902; Dessert, 1880–1902.*

9. Denise Wiles Adams, *Restoring American Gardens: An Encyclopedia of Heirloom Ornamental Plants, 1640–1940* (Portland, OR: Timber Press, 2004).

10. Alfred Rehder, *Manual of Cultivated Trees and Shrubs* (Jamaica Plain, MA: Arnold Arboretum, 1927).

Sweet Pea

1. K. R. W. Hammett, B. G. Murray, Kenneth R. Markham, and I. C. Hallett, "Interspecific Hybridization between *Lathyrus odoratus* and *L. belinensis*," *International Journal of Plant Sciences* 155, no. 6 (1994): 763–71.

2. Lester Morse, *Field Notes on Sweet Peas* (San Francisco, CA: Ferry Morse, 1917). The historical research into the life of Miss Hemus was done by Simon Wilkinson of Upton-upon-Severn in Worcestershire. Additional information has come to light through the efforts of Keith Hammett in New Zealand. A very prominent horticulturist, Dr. Hammett was approached quite unexpectedly by Mr. Dan Pawson, a total stranger who was a friend of Jean Waterworth's, Hilda Hemus Ashworth's daughter. Mr. Pawson was anxious to ensure that the Hemus legacy was preserved. Mrs. Waterworth was in her early nineties at the time and died about a year later.

3. Morse, *Field Notes on Sweet Peas.*

4. Roger Parsons, personal communication.

5. Judith M. Taylor and Simon Wilkinson, "Miss Hemus: Sweet Pea Breeder in Worcestershire," *National Sweet Pea Society Annual 2008* (Didcot, Oxfordshire: NSPS, 2008), 75–79.

6. A. J. Fitch, personal communication.

7. Jean Waterworth, personal communication.

8. Charles Curtis, *1950 National Sweet Pea Society Annual* (Didcot, Oxfordshire, NSPS, 1950).

9. Robert Sydenham, *All About Sweet Peas,* 5th ed. (Birmingham, UK: published by the author, 1910), 6.

10. Curtis, *1950 National Sweet Pea Society Annual.*

11. William T. Hutchins, "Some Reminiscences," *Sweet Pea Annual, 1918,* 12–14. Reproduced from the *American Sweet Pea Bulletin.*

12. Roy Genders, *Sweet Peas for Exhibitor and Market Grower* (London: John Gifford, 1957).

13. William Scott, *The Florists' Manual,* 2nd ed. (Chicago: Florists' Publishing Company, 1906).

RECOMMENDED READINGS

Barnes, A. T. *The Dahlia Grower's Treasury.* London: W. H. and L. Collingridge, 1954.

Bennett, Jennifer. *Lilacs for the Garden.* Buffalo, NY: Firefly Books, 2002.

Brown, Jane. *Tales of the Rose Tree: Ravishing Rhododendrons and Their Travels around the World.* New York: David Godine, 2006.

Christensen, Bess Gedney. *Acres of Loveliness.* Lompoc, CA: Lompoc Valley Botanical and Horticultural Society, 2006.

Clark, David. *Pelargoniums.* Portland, OR: Timber Press, 1988.

Davidian, H. H. *The Rhododendron Species.* Vol. 4, *Azaleas.* Portland, OR: Timber Press, 1995.

Desmond, Ray. *A Dictionary of British and Irish Botanists and Horticulturists.* 2nd ed. London: Royal Horticultural Society, 1994.

Durrant, Tom. *The Camellia Story.* London: Heinemann, 1982.

Eddison, Sydney. *A Passion for Daylilies.* New York: Harper Collins, 1992.

Ewan, Joseph, ed. *A Short History of Botany in the United States.* New York: Hafner Publishing, 1969.

Fletcher, Harold R. *The Story of the Royal Horticultural Society, 1804–1968.* London: Oxford University Press for the Royal Horticultural Society, 1969.

Fotsch, Karl Albert. *Die Begonien.* Stuttgart: Eugen Ulmer, 1933. Translated by Hans Schmok, 1939.

Gorer, Richard. *The Flower Garden in England.* London: B. T. Batsford, 1975.

Haegeman, J. *Tuberous Begonias: Origin and Development.* Vaduz, Lichtenstein: J. Cramer, 1979.

Hambidge, Colin. *The Unwin's Book of Sweet Peas.* Cambridge, UK: Silent Books, 1996.

Hammett, Keith. *The World of Dahlias.* Wellington, NZ: Reed, 1954.

Horton, Catherine. *Potted History.* London: Francis Lincoln, 2008.

Jones, Bernard. *Complete Guide to Sweet Peas.* London: Garden Book Club, 1965.

Kraft, Ken. *Garden To Order: The Story of Mr Burpee's Seeds and How They Grow.* Garden City, NY: Doubleday Books, 1963.

Leach, David G. *Rhododendrons of the World.* New York: Scribner, 1961.

McGeorge, Pamela. *Lilies.* Toronto: Firefly Books, 2004.

Munson, R. W., Jr. *Hemerocallis, the Daylily.* Portland, OR: Timber Press, 1989.

Pim, Sheila. *A Hive of Suspects.* (Detective story based on the fact that honey made from rhododendron blossom is toxic.) Boulder, CO: Rue Morgue Press, 1952. Reissued 2001.

Preston, Isabella. *Lilies for Every Garden.* New York: Orange, Judd, 1947.

Rice, Graham. *The Sweet Pea Book.* Portland, OR: Timber Press, 2003.

The Sweet Pea Annual. National Sweet Pea Society, vols. 3–18, 1906–20.

Thompson, Mildred L., and Edward J. Thompson. *Begonias: The Complete Reference Guide.* New York: New York Times Books, 1981.

Unwin, C. W. J. *Sweet Peas: Their History, Development and Culture.* Cambridge: Heffer, 1986. First issued 1952.

Webb, W. J. *The Pelargonium Family: The Species of Pelargonium, Monsonia and Sarcocaulon.* London: Croon Helm, 1984.

White, Katharine S. *Onward and Upward in the Garden.* New York: Farrar, Straus and Giroux, 1979.

Zirkle, Conrad. "Plant Genetics and Cytology." In *A Short History of Botany in the United States,* edited by Joseph Ewan, 58–66. New York: Hafner Publishing, 1969.

Internet Sources

www.offpollen.typepad.com/pollenatrix

www.herbs2000.com/flowers/s_history

www.sweetpeas.org.uk

www.lathyrus.com/history

www.fragrantgarden/com/sweetpea

INDEX

Page numbers in **BOLD** refer to illustrations.

1/15